Eschatology a

Volume 176

This book focuses on the Gospel of Mary in the context of a broader analysis of early Christian dialogue gospels – a popular literary genre used to present Jesus as conversing with select disciples and answering a series of questions on life, death and the cosmos at the conclusion of his earthly career. Jesus' teachings in these texts can vary greatly, from affirming the resurrection of the flesh to denying it completely. This book highlights the diversity of perspective within this genre, bringing together New Testament, 'gnostic' and (proto-)orthodox texts. Yet each text is based on the premise that it contains new or clarified teaching from the risen or glorified Lord, often in the form of a final revelation concerned with the disciples' eschatological salvation. This book offers a fresh and in-depth analysis of the Gospel of Mary in the context of the dialogue gospel genre, concentrating on the narrative frame, the eschatological teachings and the relationship between the two.

SARAH PARKHOUSE is a research fellow at the Australian Catholic University. She is co-editor of *Connecting Gospels* (2018) and is interested in bringing New Testament texts into conversation with other early Christian literature.

SOCIETY FOR NEW TESTAMENT STUDIES
MONOGRAPH SERIES

General Editor: Edward Adams, Kings College, London

176 ESCHATOLOGY AND THE SAVIOUR

Recent titles in the series:

157. The Eschatology of 1 Peter
KELLY D. LIEBENGOOD

158. The Hermeneutics of Christological Psalmody in Paul
MATTHEW SCOTT

159. Corinthian Wisdom, Stoic Philosophy, and the Ancient Economy
TIMOTHY A. BROOKINS

160. Faith and the Faithfulness of Jesus in Hebrews
MATTHEW C. EASTER

161. Covenant Renewal and the Consecration of the Gentiles in Romans
SARAH WHITTLE

162. The Role of Jewish Feasts in John's Gospel
GERRY WHEATON

163. Paul's Political Strategy in 1 Corinthians 1–4
BRADLEY J. BITNER

164. The Pauline Church and the Corinthian Ekklēsia
RICHARD LAST

165. Jesus and the Temple
SIMON J. JOSEPH

166. The Death of Jesus in Matthew
CATHERINE SIDER HAMILTON

167. Ecclesiology and Theosis in the Gospel of John
ANDREW J. BYERS

168. The Book of Revelation and Early Jewish Textual Culture
GARRICK ALLEN

169. The Origin of Divine Christology
ANDREW TER ERN LOKE

170. Romans 7 and Christian Identity
WILL N. TIMMINS

171. Inventing Hebrews
MICHAEL WADE MARTIN, JASON A. WHITLARK

172. Jesus' Death and Heavenly Offering in Hebrews
R. B. JAMIESON

173. The Role of Emotion in 1 Peter
KATHERINE M. HOCKEY

174. Jesus Christ as the Son of David in the Gospel of Mark
MAX BOTNER

175. Narrative and Drama in the Book of Revelation
LOURDES GARCIA URENA, DONALD MURPHY

Eschatology and the Saviour

The Gospel of Mary among Early Christian Dialogue Gospels

Volume 176

SARAH PARKHOUSE

Australian Catholic University, Melbourne

CAMBRIDGE
UNIVERSITY PRESS

CAMBRIDGE
UNIVERSITY PRESS

University Printing House, Cambridge CB2 8BS, United Kingdom

One Liberty Plaza, 20th Floor, New York, NY 10006, USA

477 Williamstown Road, Port Melbourne, VIC 3207, Australia

314-321, 3rd Floor, Plot 3, Splendor Forum, Jasola District Centre, New Delhi - 110025, India

79 Anson Road, #06-04/06, Singapore 079906

Cambridge University Press is part of the University of Cambridge.

It furthers the University's mission by disseminating knowledge in the pursuit of education, learning and research at the highest international levels of excellence.

www.cambridge.org
Information on this title: www.cambridge.org/9781108712866
DOI: 10.1017/9781108689953

First published 2019
First paperback edition 2020

A catalogue record for this publication is available from the British Library

Library of Congress Cataloging in Publication data
Names: Parkhouse, Sarah, author.
Title: Eschatology and the Saviour : the Gospel of Mary among early Christian dialogue gospels / Sarah Parkhouse, Australian Catholic University, Melbourne.
Description: New York: Cambridge University Press, 2019. |
Series: Society for New Testament studies monograph series; Volume 176 |
Includes bibliographical references.
Identifiers: LCCN 2019019725 | ISBN 9781108498937 (hardback) |
ISBN 9781108712866 (pbk.)
Subjects: LCSH: Gospel of Mary – Criticism, interpretation, etc. |
Mary Magdalene, Saint.
Classification: LCC BT1392.G652 P37 2019 | DDC 229/.8–dc23
LC record available at https://lccn.loc.gov/2019019725

ISBN 978-1-108-49893-7 Hardback
ISBN 978-1-108-71286-6 Paperback

CONTENTS

ACKNOWLEDGEMENTS

This book is a revised version of my PhD thesis, which was funded as part of the Arts and Humanities Research Council project 'The Fourfold Gospel and Its Rivals'. I firstly must thank the project's principal investigator and my doctoral supervisor, Francis Watson, for his enthusiasm for non-canonical gospel literature, never-ending suggestions and meticulous reading alongside many, many cups of tea – and a fair few pub trips.

Secondly, I'd like to thank Karen King and Hugo Lundhaug for being generous hosts during short research stays at Harvard and Oslo. There is no one better equipped than Karen to talk with about the Gospel of Mary, and Hugo transformed my approach to Nag Hammadi literature. Thirdly, I'd like to thank Joan Taylor and Carol Downer at King's College London for reading the Gospel of Mary in their respective Greek and Coptic reading groups at the earliest stages of the project. I also express my gratitude to John Barclay and Mark Goodacre, my doctoral examiners, for their engagement and perceptive questions. In an act of great kindness, Ismo Dunderberg read the entire book, offered incisive comments and saved me from numerous embarrassing mistakes. And a big thank you to Madison Pierce for diligently proofreading the manuscript and pointing out that I am 'parentheses happy'. Without all of these people (and many more), this would have been an inferior project. I'd also like to thank Eddie Adams and the team at Cambridge University Press for accepting this book for publication and patiently guiding me through to the final stages, and my colleagues at the Australian Catholic University for their encouragement.

My greatest gratitude goes to those who have no idea or interest in what this book is about – my family. My parents, Joan and Steve, for supporting me in all sorts of ways throughout my life. Don't worry, I don't expect you to read beyond this page. Sean, who has championed my every whim and makes daily life that much better; and our daughters Florence and Elowen, both born since this project began, for keeping me constantly and happily unfocused. And my grandad Eddie, for always asking.

ABBREVIATIONS

Ancient Sources

1 Apol.	Justin, *First Apology*
ad Autol.	Theophilus, *Ad Autolycum*
Adv. Haer.	Irenaeus, *Adversus Haereses*
c. Cels.	Origen, *Contra Celsum*
Dial.	Justin, *Dialogue with Trypho*
Ep. Flora	Ptolemy, *Epistle to Flora*
Exc. Theod.	Clement of Alexandria, *Excerpta ex Theodoto*
Ep. Trall.	Ignatius, *Epistle to the Trallians*
Her.	Philo, *Heir of the Divine Goods*
Hist. Eccl.	Eusebius, *Historia Ecclesiastica*
Or. Graec.	Tatian, *Oratio ad Graecos*
Phaed.	Plato, *Phaedo*
Phaedr.	Plato, *Phaedrus*
POxy.GM	Papyrus Oxyrhynchus 3525 (the Gospel of Mary)
PRyl.GM	Papyrus Rylands 463 (the Gospel of Mary)
Strom.	Clement of Alexandria, *Stromata*
Tim.	Plato, *Timaeus*
Vit. Phil.	Diogenes Laertius, *Vitae Philosophorum*

Modern Sources

AGJU	Arbeiten zur Geschichte des antiken Judentums und des Urchristentums
AB	Anchor Bible
ABRL	Anchor Bible Reference Library
BCNH:E	Bibliothèque copte de Nag Hammadi: Études
BCNH:T	Bibliothèque copte de Nag Hammadi: Textes
BECNT	Baker Exegetical Commentary on the New Testament

BZNW	Beihefte zur Zeitschrift für die neutestamentliche Wissenschaft
CBQ	*Catholic Biblical Quarterly*
CSCO	Corpus scriptorum christianorum orientalium
CGL	Coptic Gnostic Library
HTR	*Harvard Theological Review*
HTS	Harvard Theological Studies
ICC	International Critical Commentary
JBL	*Journal of Biblical Literature*
JECS	*Journal of Early Christian Studies*
JEH	*Journal of Ecclesiastical History*
JSNT	*Journal for the Study of the New Testament*
JSNTSup	*Journal for the Study of the New Testament*, Supplement Series
JTS	*Journal of Theological Studies*
LNTS	Library of New Testament Studies
NIGTC	New International Greek Testament Commentary
NHMS	Nag Hammadi and Manichean Studies (formerly NHS)
NHS	Nag Hammadi Studies
NovT	*Novum Testamentum*
NovTSup	Novum Testamentum, Supplements
NTS	*New Testament Studies*
SBL	Society of Biblical Literature
SBLDS	Society of Biblical Literature Dissertation Series
SBR	Studies of the Bible and Its Reception
SEPT	Septuagint Commentary Series
SNTSMS	Studiorum Novi Testamenti Societas Monograph Series
STAC	Studien und Texte zu Antike und Christentum
TENT	Texts and Editions for New Testament Study
TU	Texte und Untersuchungen
VC	*Vigiliae Christianae*
VCSup	Supplements to Vigiliae Christianae
WUNT	Wissenschaftliche Untersuchungen zum Neuen Testament
ZNW	*Zeitschrift für die neutestamentliche Wissenschaft*

INTRODUCTION

The earliest Christians penned stories that narrate Jesus conversing with one or more of his disciples either immediately before his passion or after his resurrection. A number of these texts survive today. In these 'dialogue gospels', Jesus answers the disciples' questions, which are typically centred around the three following issues: how they are to deal with life in his absence, where he intends to go when he leaves them and how they might follow him there. The Gospel of Mary is one example of a dialogue gospel. In this fragmentary text, Jesus answers questions put to him by individual disciples, and in a 'farewell discourse' immediately before his departure, he issues his final instructions that consist of finding the Son of Man within and preaching the gospel of the kingdom. The male disciples cannot cope with his departure; they weep in fear that they will be persecuted if they fulfil his command to preach to the nations. At this point Mary comes to the fore, comforts them and explains how their souls can reach eschatological salvation. Her story does not allay their fears; Peter and Andrew refuse to believe Mary, and Levi must step in to remind them all of Jesus' last instructions.

The form of Jesus answering questions from his disciples finds its companions across a range of texts, from the Johannine Farewell Discourse (13.31–17.1) to the Epistula Apostolorum to the Pistis Sophia. Thirteen texts have been selected to construct the 'dialogue gospels' genre, each converging at two main points: (1) Jesus as revealer on the eve of his departure and (2) dialogue with one or more disciples. All but one of our texts have been brought to light by a series of manuscript discoveries.[1] The dialogue gospels share the

[1] The texts in view are as follows, in order of their years of discovery and publication: *Pistis Sophia* (PistSoph), 1772/1848; the *Apocalypse of Peter* (ApocPet), Greek 1886–87/1892, Ethiopic publ. 1910; the *Epistula Apostolorum* (EpAp), Coptic c. 1895/1919, Ethiopic publ. 1912; the *Gospel of Mary* (GMary: Berlin Gnostic Codex = BG 8502,1), 1896/1955; the *Apocryphon of John* (ApJohn: BG 8502,2 [+ Nag Hammadi Codices = NHC 2,1, 3,1, 4,1]), 1896/1955; the *Sophia* (or *Wisdom) of Jesus Christ*

same goal as the canonical gospels, which is to bring their readers/hearers to a fuller understanding of their salvation, which is through Jesus. Where the canonical gospels primarily narrate the life and death of Jesus, dialogue gospels narrate his final revelations as the risen or glorified Christ. In one sense, the preference for Jesus as *risen* Saviour comes closer to Paul than to the Synoptics, but the dialogue format and the narrative context place them straight into the 'gospel' category.[2]

These 'dialogue gospels' may be grouped together to construct a genre, but they hardly form a homogeneous group, varying considerably in setting, characters, length and treatment of their subject matter. They may be set before the risen Jesus ascends (Book of Thomas) or before he is crucified (Gospel of Judas). The revelation may be directed to one privileged disciple (Apocryphon of John), or two (Apocryphon of James), or to a larger group of twelve apostles and seven women (Sophia of Jesus Christ). The text may confirm the authority of the Twelve, with Peter as leader (Epistle of Peter to Philip), or profess that salvation will only come through a future generation (Apocryphon of James). It may be concise, with only a few queries from the disciples (Johannine Farewell Discourse), or it may be so long that Jesus himself gets annoyed with the disciples' relentless and repetitive requests for knowledge (Epistula Apostolorum). What they have in common is Jesus as revealer, answering the questions of the disciple(s) who are concerned that they lack the knowledge they need. Dialogue gospels also vary in content and theological persuasion. They may narrate a tour of the heavenly realms and their corresponding initiation-mysteries (Pistis

(SophJesChr: BG 8502,3 [+ NHC 3,4]), 1896/1955; the *First Apocalypse of James* (1ApocJas: NHC 5,3 [+ Codex Tchacos = CT 2]), 1945/1979 the *Apocryphon of James* (ApJas: NHC 1,2), 1945/1985; the *Book of Thomas* (BookThom: NHC 2,7), 1945/1989; the *Dialogue of the Saviour* (DialSav: NHC 3,5), 1945/1984; the *Epistle of Peter to Philip* (EpPetPhil: NHC 8,2 [= CT 1), 1945/1991; the *Gospel of Judas* (GJudas: CT 3), publ. 2006. Also included here within the dialogue gospel genre is the Johannine Farewell Discourse. Except where specified above, the twelve non-canonical texts are extant only in Coptic, although Greek fragments have been found of the Gospel of Mary (POxy 3525, PRyl 463) and the Sophia of Jesus Christ (POxy 1081), as well as a Latin fragment of the Epistula Apostolorum preserved in a palimpsest (Cod. Vind. 16). The selection of these texts will be justified in Chapter 1.

[2] I here follow Tuckett and Gregory in what they deem a 'looser' definition of the term 'gospel' as referring to 'a text which purports to give information about the life and teaching of Jesus', Andrew Gregory and Christopher Tuckett, 'Series Preface', in *Gospel of Mary*, ed. Christopher Tuckett (Oxford: Oxford University Press, 2007), vi. On this definition, a text may be a 'gospel' (or gospel-like) even if its ancient or modern readers view it as an apocalypse, apocryphon, epistle or gospel.

Sophia) or a tour of the regions of hell where different sins receive their corresponding punishments (Apocalypse of Peter). Their agenda may be to promote asceticism due to the corrupt nature of the material world (Book of Thomas) or to confirm the corporeality of the resurrected body (Epistula Apostolorum). They may profess that the material realm is the work of an ignorant demiurge (Apocryphon of John), or they may acknowledge the highest Father as the creator (Dialogue of the Saviour).

The dialogue gospels reflect the complex and diverse literary landscape of emerging Christianity. Traditionally, texts found at Nag Hammadi were labelled 'gnostic', stemming from the non-Christian religion of 'gnosticism', and thought to be at best superficially christianized, while the firmly Christian Epistula Apostolorum was seen as borrowing the dialogue gospel genre to combat those heretical 'gnostics' who created it.[3] However, the concept of 'gnosticism' has changed. Almost all scholars who engage with non-canonical early Christian texts accept that the labels of 'gnostic' and 'gnosticism' need nuancing (whether or not they think that they should be used). The deconstruction of the term and so-called religion of 'gnosticism', led by Williams and King over twenty years ago, has prevailed in most quarters, which has resulted in a backlash against those who hold dear the rigorous bifurcation of orthodoxy and gnosticism.[4] It is now more common to talk of trajectories of early Christianities, of which 'gnosticism' represents just one.[5] Yet there is still a sense that 'gnosticism' is something different to Christianity proper, something that can be separated from it and pinned down as its own thing. And, consequently, the 'gnostic' dialogue gospels will be assumed to share basically the same 'gnostic' ideology, to be at

[3] For an example, a binary opposition between two competing religions is implied in the title of Birger A. Pearson's book, *Gnosticism and Christianity in Roman and Coptic Egypt* (New York: T&T Clark International, 2004). For Pearson, 'Christianity' is not the same as 'Gnosticism'. According to Klauck, the Epistula Apostolorum 'has a special place among the dialogue gospels: its author has borrowed its genre from his gnostic opponents and turned it into a useful weapon against them', Hans-Josef Klauck, *The Apocryphal Gospels: An Introduction*, trans. Brian McNeil (London: T&T Clark, 2003), 159.

[4] Michael A. Williams, *Rethinking 'Gnosticism': An Argument for Dismantling a Dubious Category* (Princeton, NJ: Princeton University Press, 1996); Karen L. King, *What Is Gnosticism?* (Cambridge, MA: Harvard University Press, 2005). More recently David Brakke, *The Gnostics: Myth, Ritual, and Diversity in Early Christianity* (Cambridge, MA: Harvard University Press, 2010).

[5] This concept has been heavily influenced by James M. Robinson and Helmut Koester, *Trajectories through Early Christianity* (Philadelphia: Fortress Press, 1971).

odds with their 'proto-orthodox' counterparts, and to depict a Jesus who is fundamentally different to the Jesus of the New Testament.

We do not see in the dialogue gospels any such ideology. Those once called 'gnostic' share as much in common with their 'orthodox' neighbours as with each other, with many points of both similarity and difference. The genre itself is thoroughly diverse, and it is this diversity that makes the texts good conversation partners. This work, by putting dialogue gospels into conversation with each other and with New Testament texts, will continue to blur any sort of remaining bifurcation between the 'ortho-' and 'heterodox'. To make the case, I shall develop an 'open' view of genre – one that recognizes both the fluidity of generic categories and the role of the modern scholar in constructing a genre that suits his or her own concerns. Such a view can bring together a variety of texts for comparative analysis, whether they are within the same genre or a literary neighbour. In the case of dialogue gospels, their closest companions are naturally canonical gospels, with which they share the same characters and content even if these are interpreted radically differently. The act of comparing and contrasting can help refine our understanding of the dialogue gospel genre, the intertextual relationships between dialogue gospels and New Testament texts, and the individual texts themselves.

Intertextual connections between dialogue gospels and their literary neighbours might be viewed as rhizomatic network. The idea of employing the rhizomatic root system to think with was developed by Deleuze and Guattari in *A Thousand Plateaus*. For Deleuze and Guattari, the rhizome stands in contrast to arborescent systems (exemplified by the way a tree's roots are constructed). The hierarchical and centred nature of the arborescent system of a tree, they argue, 'has dominated Western reality and all of Western thought'.[6] Deleuze and Guattari explain:

> unlike trees or their roots, the rhizome connects any point to any other point … It is composed not of units but of dimensions, or rather directions in motion. It has neither beginning nor end, but always a middle from which it grows and which it overspills … In contrast to centered (even polycentric) systems with hierarchical modes of

[6] Gilles Deleuze and Félix Guattari, *A Thousand Plateaus: Capitalism and Schizophrenia*, trans. Brian Massumi (Minneapolis: University of Minnesota Press, 1980; repr. London and New York: Continuum, 2004), 20.

> communication and pre-established parts, the rhizome is an acentered, nonhierarchical, nonsignifying system.[7]

This model for thinking can be applied to a number of phenomena. Deleuze and Guattari use it as a base for which they write their book (the genre, essentially). Vander Stichele employs it as a useful tool for intertextuality,[8] and for this project, it is an exemplary tool for finding connections within gospel literature, and especially dialogue gospels that are difficult to date. Cavan sees early Christian trade networks as a rhizomatic net of relations. He writes:

> While arborescent maps trade in linear causality, binary oppositions, and clear classifications, a rhizome, with its chaotic and wild offshoots, offers a model for thinking that relies on interconnected and evolving networks of relations that grow, change, dissipate, and expand without a prescribed plan and in response to larger, interrelated forces, like bamboo roots or a Jackson Pollock painting.[9]

Applying this model to early Christian networks, he offers a picture of no centre of command, links between different religious people, ships that carry goods to different centres, religious authorities that might also be slaves or administers – these small Christian networks are interconnected with other non-Christian networks, creating a wider acentered network.

As well as intertextuality, the rhizome model can also be applied to discussions of uniformity and diversity within a genre of texts – for us, the dialogue gospels. Although I will put the Johannine Farewell Discourse as the 'middle' from which the genre grows, the network of resultant literature is both interconnected and disparate and any point can connect to any other point. This model can be expanded to apply to all gospel literature, and in the later discussion, the canonical resurrection narratives and selected Pauline texts will be put into conversation with dialogue gospels. Not all points will fit perfectly within the rhizomatic structure, but it is a useful tool for mapping and thinking about early Christian literature.

[7] Deleuze and Guattari, *A Thousand Plateaus*, 23.

[8] Caroline Vander Stichele, 'The Head of John and its Reception or How to Conceptualize "Reception History"', in *Reception History and Biblical Studies: Theory and Practice*, ed. Emma England and William John Lyons (London and New York: Bloomsbury T&T Clark, 2015), 84–5.

[9] Cavan W. Concannon, *Assembling Early Christianity: Trade, Networks, and the Letters of Dionysios of Corinth* (Cambridge: Cambridge University Press, 2017).

Outline of the Study

The category of dialogue gospels – what it is, which texts belong in this genre, and why an author might write one – is the subject of Part I. Chapter 1 looks specifically at the genre itself and its creation of a new category of early Christian texts in which Jesus engages in dialogue with his disciples. Previous genre definitions have varied widely, resulting in debates regarding both what to call it and which texts are to be included in it, and the taxonomies always suit the interest of the scholar delimiting them. The present work builds on the monographs of Perkins and Hartenstein, among others, who also investigate dialogue gospels but from the viewpoint of 'gnostic' theology or their narrative frame.[10] I aim to show that the dialogue gospel form does not intrinsically share a link to 'gnosticism'; that the narrative frame and dialogue are often not two separate entities glued together (this is certainly not the case in the Gospel of Mary); and that the dialogical form is a fitting vehicle for eschatological revelation. An overview of the thirteen texts selected to construct our genre is then offered, followed by a cursory analysis of the connections between their depictions of the Saviour and eschatology.

Chapter 2 builds on this open categorization of dialogue gospels, asking what themes and issues might have inspired an early Christian author to write one, and reading the texts alongside literature that came to be, or had already been, accorded 'canonical' status. Dialogue gospels have strong and varied intertextual links to the canonical gospels and the Pauline epistles, and their shared themes are the subject of this chapter.[11] I argue that the genre is inspired by the Johannine Farewell Discourse, in both temporal setting and generic form. Other intertextual links are found beyond the Johannine Farewell Discourse and, for the purpose of highlighting

[10] Pheme Perkins, *The Gnostic Dialogue: The Early Church and the Crisis of Gnosticism* (New York: Paulist Press, 1980); Judith Hartenstein, *Die zweite Lehre: Erscheinungen des Auferstandenen als Rahmenerzählungen frühchristlicher Dialoge*, TU 146 (Berlin: de Gruyter, 2000).

[11] The general meaning of the concept of 'intertextuality' is not limited to sources, citations and allusions, nor does it preclude these. To speak of an intertextual connection between the First Apocalypse of James and the Apocryphon of James does not suggest that the First Apocalypse of James is dependent on the Apocryphon of James, nor does it suggest that it is not. The concept of intertextuality allows the conversation to broaden: we can speak of a number of texts (or art, or other sources) without assigning a chronological order to them or focusing on details of dependence. I do suggest that the Johannine Farewell Discourse is a starting point for dialogue gospels, and most likely the dialogue gospels are inspired by the Johannine Farewell Discourse, in whatever form.

these links, themes have been selected from Matthew, Mark, Luke, Acts, John and Pauline epistles, and the differences and similarities between these texts and selected dialogue gospels are discussed. An example of this is the theme of mission shared by Matt 28.19–20, the Gospel of Mary and the Epistle of Peter to Philip, among others. In Matthew, the evangelist does not narrate how the disciples go about enacting the command to 'make disciples of all nations' or how they feel about it. The Gospel of Mary and the Epistle of Peter to Philip fill this gap in the narrative by highlighting the disciples' fear of persecution following Jesus' command to preach. As this small-scale example illustrates, a reason for the composition of later texts in dialogue format possibly was to address perceived deficiencies in earlier gospel literature. By using this comparative approach, Chapter 2 also takes the opportunity for further exegesis on the dialogue gospels themselves.

Whereas the first two chapters cover a wide breadth of dialogue gospels and their intertextual links, Part II takes an in-depth look at the Gospel of Mary. The Gospel of Mary is unique among the dialogue gospels in the extent to which the narrative frame is integrated into the dialogue. Unusually this gospel extends well beyond the departure of Jesus, and the ensuing narrative and dialogue are premised on the new reality of Jesus' absence.[12] It is because of his departure that the disciples worry about being persecuted and quarrel over his words, and it is for the same reason that Mary can come to the fore and explain his eschatological journey and how they can follow him.

Chapter 3 focuses on the narrative frame. There, I explore possibilities for what was contained in the missing six pages of the Berlin Codex that form the beginning of the Gospel of Mary, firmly situating it within the dialogue gospel genre. The extant narrative frame is then divided into three parts: (1) The Saviour's farewell discourse that leads to his final departure, (2) Mary's intervention and (3) the subsequent breach between the disciples and its possible healing. I will argue that the Saviour's farewell discourse encourages the disciples to be active participants in the Christian message of salvation. They must procure Jesus' peace, they are warned against waiting for an apocalyptic Son of Man, and they must find Christ within. They are told to preach the gospel and banned from imposing new

[12] In the Epistle of Peter to Philip and the Gospel of Judas, as examples, Jesus departs but reappears or continues to speak. In the Gospel of Mary, Jesus reappears only indirectly, in the form of Mary explaining her memories of Jesus.

laws of their own devising. Once Jesus has gone, the disciples are left with Mary to comfort them. The section on Mary's intervention focuses on two features of the text's depiction of her character: her relationship with the male disciples and her relationship with Jesus. Attention to the differences between the Greek (POxy 3525; PRyl 463) and Coptic (BG) versions of (parts of) the Gospel of Mary indicate that the Coptic recension heightens antagonism and disunity between Mary and the men. Mary's relationship to Jesus, on the other hand, is one of unity, and I argue that Mary takes on a kind of paraclete role as she 'rises' only as Jesus departs, and she teaches and comforts the other disciples.

The final part of the narrative frame sees the disciples split into two factions, with Mary and Levi on one side and Peter and Andrew on the other. The split is the result of Mary's recollection of the ascent of the soul. Andrew and Peter will not accept this teaching as it is not consistent with what they know of Jesus and because Jesus revealed it to Mary alone. They condemn Mary's revelation as heterodox. By challenging Mary, Peter is cast as an adversary akin to the hostile cosmic powers that attempt to prevent the soul from attaining her eschatological 'rest'. The text gives Levi the last words, and he reminds them all of the Saviour's teaching in his farewell discourse. The Gospel of Mary concludes with the enactment of Jesus' command to preach – although in the Greek Rylands papyrus, Levi preaches alone, whereas in the Coptic MS, there is an ambiguous '*they* departed to preach'. If the narrative frame of the Coptic Gospel of Mary creates greater tension between the male disciples and Mary, does the word 'they' allow for a greater reconciliation between the two parties, or does 'they' refer to Mary and Levi and thus rule out reconciliation altogether? This is explored in light of other textual evidence, especially the Pistis Sophia.

There are two sets of eschatological teachings in the Gospel of Mary – the dissolution of matter, revealed to the group by the Saviour, and the ascent of the soul, revealed alone to Mary who then recounts it to the group. These themes are the focus of Chapters 4 and 5. The cosmic eschatology of the Gospel of Mary is essentially that the created heavens and earth will be restored through dissolution into its original constituent parts. This presupposes a cosmology in which matter is the raw material of the cosmos and has been moulded into the composite created entities called in the Gospel of Mary 'every nature, every form, every creature'. This cosmology does not imply an inferior-demiurgic creator deity, and the author's view of the contingent nature of the material world is shared among many second-century Christian thinkers, including Justin and Irenaeus. Chapter 4 firstly deals with the cosmological make-up of matter, nature, form and creature, and secondly argues that dissolution must occur because humanity lives under sin and death because of its enslavement to passion. This is essentially a Pauline view. I then discuss the christological reading of 'the Good' as the instigator of the cosmic eschaton, and how this relates to the 'Son of Man', whom Jesus proclaims is living within the disciples. The Son of Man in the Gospel of Mary contradicts a parousia theology, in which Jesus will come again to judge and destroy the world. But the Son of Man is still Jesus – just as he can live within his disciples in Paul and John, he lives within his disciples in the Gospel of Mary. There is no expectation of a future external figure, nor need there be one: with Christ's coming, the end time has begun. The Son of Man is within. The Good dissolves the cosmos. Christ is both.

Chapter 5 explores the individual eschatology of the Gospel of Mary, which is narrated through the ascent of the individual and paradigmatic soul to its heavenly 'rest'. I will argue that the anonymous soul is in the first instance Jesus himself: It is the ascension of John 20.17. Yet it is also the disciple's soul, who follows Jesus into heaven. The soul must ascend past malevolent archons who challenge her, and by declaring her heavenly origins, she can overcome them and return home. In the First Apocalypse of James, we see that Jesus' ascension past fearsome archons paves the way for James to follow, and at the time of James' own ascension he must profess his own heavenly ancestry to these archons (cf. the Gospel of Thomas 50). The comparable scheme in the Gospel of Mary extends the ascension reference in John 20.17 to the disciple's salvation.

The characterization of Mary here suggests that she has already (partly) followed Jesus into eternal 'rest'. At the culmination of the ascent, Mary mirrors the soul in her silence. She is called 'blessed', the Saviour loves her more than the other disciples, and she receives private revelation from him. She does not appear to be under the influence of passions, sin and death. I propose that, in the Gospel of Mary, 'rest' can be partly realized in the present Christian experience, much like the Johannine eternal life, and fully attained after death.

Part I

1

WHAT IS A DIALOGUE GOSPEL?

Defining a Genre

Dialogue gospels comprise a great variety of portrayals of Jesus and his disciples, as well as his cosmological, eschatological and soteriological teachings. Yet at the heart of each dialogue gospel stands Jesus as revealer and Saviour. All gospels are inspired by this figure, whether they narrate his life, death and resurrection, recount his sayings, or describe him answering his disciples' questions. Our purpose here is to construct a genre, or literary group, of dialogue gospels as a starting point to find connections that will point to other texts within the genre itself as well as to those outside of it. The term 'genre' here needs some qualification. Collins writes: 'By "literary genre" we mean a group of written texts marked by distinctive recurring characteristics which constitute a recognizable and coherent type of writing.'[1] For our purposes, thirteen texts have been focused on under the premise that to be a dialogue gospel, a text must contain two things: (1) Jesus, the central character, on the verge of departure, and (2) dialogue with one or more of his disciples.

'Dialogue gospels' is a constructed or invented genre: the genre has various names, and each name is indicative of the texts that scholars wish to include within it. Sometimes they are called 'resurrection dialogues', which confines the genre to dialogues with the risen Lord. These might include the Apocryphon of John, the Sophia of Jesus Christ and the Epistula Apostolorum, among others. Sometimes the group's title is prefixed with the label 'gnostic', and so will exclude the Epistula Apostolorum and the Apocalypse of Peter (and arguably the Apocryphon of James). A more inclusive group of texts might be called 'dialogue gospels', expanding the

[1] John J. Collins, 'Introduction: Towards the Morphology of a Genre', *Semeia* 14 (1979): 1. However, as we shall see, some or many of these 'recurring characteristics' may not be 'distinctive' at all but shared with texts in a quite different generic category. In other words, genres are 'open' to one another and overlap; conversely, a single text may inhabit multiple genres.

group to include farewell discourses, such as the Dialogue of the Saviour, the Johannine Farewell Discourse and the Gospel of Judas, alongside resurrection dialogues of any theological persuasion. This chapter will discuss how previous scholarship has construed the genre and ask what work the construction of a genre can do for us.[2] I will propose that for this study, genre is a useful tool for comparison of texts.

The thirteen texts that form our genre of dialogue gospels comprise:

i. *Johannine Farewell Discourse*
ii. *Apocalypse of Peter* (Greek and Ethiopic)
iii. *Apocryphon of James*
iv. *Apocryphon of John*
v. *Book of Thomas*
vi. *Dialogue of the Saviour*
vii. *Epistle of Peter to Philip*
viii. *Epistula Apostolorum*
ix. *First Apocalypse of James*
x. *Gospel of Judas*
xi. *Gospel of Mary*
xii. *Pistis Sophia*
xiii. *Sophia of Jesus Christ*

Following an overview of these thirteen texts, I will analyse how the concepts of the Saviour and eschatology are broadly conceived throughout the genre. The cursory overview will demonstrate the unity and diversity within the genre and exemplify why a rhizomatic lens is a useful way to think about these texts, rather than any binary or structured model.

[2] See the table below. The differences in the collections have been noted by e.g. Petersen: 'Diese Zusammenstellung macht deutlich, daß die Zuordnung einer Schrift zur Gattung des gnostischen Dialogs keineswegs eindeutig ist', Silke Petersen, *Zerstört die Werke der Weiblichkeit! Maria Magdalena, Salome und andere Jüngerinnen Jesu in christlich-gnostischen Schriften*, NHMS 48 (Leiden: Brill, 1999), 37. Dettwiler also notes: 'Die Texte, die von der Forschung zur Gattung des gnostischen Dialogs des Erlösers resp. des gnostischen Offenbarungsdialogs gerechnet werden, sind weder formal noch inhaltlich streng einheitlich. So werden bspw. je nachdem, ob die Dialogstruktur als konstitutiv für eine Schrift angesehen wird oder nur eine spätere literarische Einkleidung einer ursprünglich nichtdialogischen Schrift darstellt, unterschiedlich viele Texte dieser Gattung zugerechnet', Andreas Dettwiler, *Die Gegenwart des Erhöhten: Eine exegetische Studie zu den johanneischen Abschiedsreden (Joh 13,31–16,33) unter besonderer Berücksichtigung ihres Relecture-Charakters* (Göttingen: Vandenhoeck & Ruprecht, 1995), 22.

1.1 'Gnostic Dialogues' and 'Dialogue Gospels'

The Literature

Few scholars have looked at dialogue gospels in their entirety, and those that have reached no consensus regarding what they are (i.e. what genre) or which texts should be included. The two main studies on these dialogues as a 'genre' are Perkins' *The Gnostic Dialogue* and Hartenstein's *Die zweite Lehre*.[3] Perkins includes only those that she considers 'gnostic', and Hartenstein includes only those that contain a narrative frame. Although different interests predominate, both studies build their categories and analysis from earlier scholarship that tended to hold an exacting view of both genre and 'gnosticism'. Recent trends in literary studies tend to advocate a looser and more flexible explanation of how genre is constructed, and for this study, a porous and malleable understanding of genre facilitates a deeper appreciation of the place of dialogue gospels within the rhizome of early Christian literature, as well as the interconnections within the group itself. Furthermore, to my knowledge, since 'gnosticism' as a category has been dismantled or nuanced, no major study on 'dialogue gospels' has been published.[4] The critical evaluation of 'gnosticism' as a failed category also yields to a new way of looking at dialogue gospels, allowing us to see the genre as made up of individual texts that represent divergent theologies, christologies, eschatologies, and so forth.

Two decades after the discovery of the Nag Hammadi codices in 1945, scholars were constructing a group of 'dialogue gospels' that included several texts found at Nag Hammadi alongside works from previously known related codices. Much of the scholarship from the late 1960s to the 1980s stressed identifying literary genres, proposing structural similarities between texts, and then deciding on the antecedent genre. In 1968, Rudolph raised the question of

[3] Pheme Perkins, *The Gnostic Dialogue: The Early Church and the Crisis of Gnosticism* (New York: Paulist Press, 1980); Judith Hartenstein, *Die zweite Lehre: Erscheinungen des Auferstandenen als Rahmenerzählungen frühchristlicher Dialoge*, TU 146 (Berlin: Akademie Verlag, 2000).

[4] Much of the scholarship before Williams' and King's works understands dialogue gospels in terms of non-Christian traditions woven into a Christian narrative framework. For example, Meyer states that the Epistle of Peter to Philip has 'baptized these [non-Christian] traditions as revelatory utterances of the risen Christ', Marvin W. Meyer, *The Letter of Peter to Philip*, SBLDS 53 (Chico, CA: Scholars Press, 1981), 122. In the last twenty years, most scholars working on texts that were once classified as 'gnostic' have become more nuanced and qualify their use of these categories.

the 'gnostic dialogue' as a literary genre, understanding these texts as an independent literary form developed out of older styles such as *erotapokriseis* and Platonic dialogues.[5] The texts he considers are the Apocryphon of John, the Gospel of Mary, the Apocalypse of Paul, the First Apocalypse of James, the Sophia of Jesus Christ, the Pistis Sophia, the Second Book of Jeu and the Manichaean *Kephalaia*. He constructs the genre by identifying features typical to the texts, including the following: the teacher-revealer is the exalted Christ; the students are the apostles; the teacher-student relationship is frozen in a 'Question-Answer Schema'; there is no discussion with opponents; the aim is not primarily polemical but to serve its own '*Sitz im Leben*'; the content is often concerned with exegetical questions; and the characters are fictional 'without flesh and blood'.[6] Mary Magdalene is by far the most popular disciple, appearing sixty-nine times (followed by Peter appearing seven times as a not-so-close second). Within the dialogues, Rudolph sees the characteristics as:

> repeated call for attention,
> self-predication given at the beginning,

[5] Kurt Rudolph, 'Der gnostische "Dialog" als Literarisches Genus', in *Probleme der koptischen Literatur*, ed. Peter Nagel (Halle: Wissenschaftliche Beiträge der Universität Halle-Wittenberg, 1968), esp. 89. Revelation dialogues have continued to be associated with *erotapokriseis* literature, and the question has recently been addressed in a collection of essays from a 2013 volume. Kaler argues against the tendency to link revelatory dialogues too closely to *erotapokriseis* literature as it will overemphasize only one aspect of the revelation dialogue, Michael Kaler, 'Just How Close Are the Gnostic Revelation Dialogues to Erotapokriseis Literature, Anyway?', in *La littérature des Questions et Réponses dans l'Antiquité profane et chrétienne: De l'enseignement à l'exégèse*, ed. Marie-Pierre Bussières, Instrumenta Patristica et Mediaevalia 64 (Turnhout: Brepols Publishers, 2013), 37–49. Piovanelli shows that these are traditions that are in transition and are not static, Pierluigi Piovanelli, 'Entre oralité et (ré)écriture : Le modèle des erotapokriseis dans les dialogues Apocryphes de Nag Hammadi', in *Questions et Réponses*, 93–103. In the same volume, Edwards argues that the First Apocalypse of James 'is not representative of our concept of *erotapokriseis*', as the dialogue is not intended to be didactic or exegetical and is not a one-sided conversation between teacher and student, Robert Michael Edwards, 'The Rhetoric of Authority: The Nature of Revelation in the First Apocalypse of James', in *Questions et Réponses*, 77. I would say that the conversation between James and Jesus in the First Apocalypse of James is both didactic and exegetical and should be no more or less associated with *erotapokriseis* than other dialogue gospels. Zamagni shows that the question-and-answer pattern in early Christianity serves a number of aims and purposes and is far from clearly defined itself, Claudio Zamagni, 'Is the Question-and-Answer Literary Genre in Early Christian Literature a Homogeneous Group?', in *Questions et Réponses*, 241–68.

[6] Rudolph, 'Der gnostische "Dialog"', 89–90.

> consolation of the disciples frightened by his [Jesus'] appearance, praise of particularly well-asked questions or answers, speech without parables that is clear and undisguised.[7]

He argues that the dialogues are written to develop doctrine and convey salvation, and that it is 'through this form of literature that Gnosis seeks to enlighten itself'.[8]

Outlines to this effect are relatively popular in discussions about genre. Puech defines 'gnostic gospels' as having the following features: located on a mountain and set after the resurrection, contains the appearance of the Saviour in supernatural light form, depicts astonishment and fear from the recipients, and begins the dialogue almost immediately. In the dialogues, the resurrected and glorified Christ bestows the highest revelation, revealing mysteries and solving problems about which the disciples are concerned.[9] Krause suggested a simpler outline of the 'revelation dialogue' genre: (1) setting: post-resurrection, (2) question/dialogue, (3) action, (4) conclusion.[10] A different approach was taken by Koester who, instead of listing internal-textual features that define a genre, inserted dialogues into the context of sayings traditions, arguing that the dialogues are a continuation of older sayings collections and offer an interpretation of them. In doing so, he changed the scholarly conversation around these texts; instead of isolating the dialogue gospels from other gospels, he brought them into conversation.[11]

In 1979, Fallon proposed a genre of 'gnostic apocalypses'. The new focus on 'apocalypse', rather than 'dialogue' or 'gospel' pushed him in the direction of categorizing the texts in terms of their eschatology.[12] He created a scheme of those without (Type I) and those

[7] Rudolph, 'Der gnostische "Dialog"', 92–3.

[8] Rudolph, 'Der gnostische "Dialog"', 103.

[9] This is in E. Hennecke and W. Schneemelcher, ed., *Neutestamentliche Apokryphen in deutscher Übersetzung: Evangelien*, 3rd ed. (Tübingen: Mohr Siebeck, 1959), 1:170–71. The 1991 sixth edition advises that several Nag Hammadi texts had not been available to Puech, and so we should be cautious in using his work to define this genre, W. Schneemelcher, *New Testament Apocrypha: Gospels and Related Writings*, Vol. 1, trans. ed. R. McL. Wilson (Louisville: WJK, 1991), 354–5.

[10] Martin Krause, 'Die literarischen Gattungen der Apokalypsen von Nag Hammadi', in *Apocalypticism in the Mediterranean World and the Near East: Proceedings of the International Colloquium on Apocalypticism*, Uppsala, August 12–17, 1979, ed. David Hellholm (Tübingen: Mohr Siebeck, 1983), 621–37.

[11] Helmut Koester, *Ancient Christian Gospels: Their History and Development* (London: SCM Press; Philadelphia: Trinity Press International, 1990).

[12] It should be noted here that ancient authors were perhaps oblivious to the distinctions between genres, say prophecy and apocalyptic, that modern authors

with (Type II) an otherworldly journey and sub-types (i) those with cosmic eschatology and (ii) those with only personal eschatology. The apocalypses divide as:

Otherworldly revelations but no otherworldly journey (Type I)

Cosmic eschatology included (I.i): Melchizedek, Second Apocalypse of James, Gospel of Mary, Hypostasis of the Archons, Pistis Sophia 1–3

Personal eschatology only (I.ii): Apocalypse of Adam, Allogenes, Sophia of Jesus Christ, Apocryphon of John, First Apocalypse of James (Apocryphon of James),[13] Apocalypse of Peter (Coptic), Epistle of Peter to Philip, Pistis Sophia 4, Hypsiphrone

Otherworldly journey (Type II)

Cosmic eschatology included (II.i): Paraphrase of Shem

Personal eschatology only (II.ii): Zostrianos, Apocalypse of Paul

Fallon's classification of these texts as apocalypses encourages a stronger emphasis on their eschatological aspects – a facet which is often overlooked. Although his overview is introductory, for his selected texts the analysis is spot on: he argues that the emphasis is on present salvation through knowledge and eschatological salvation conceived through the ascent of the soul/divine element to the divine realm.[14] However, he continues:

> Occasionally, this interest is accompanied by an interest in the consummation, i.e., the dissolution of the cosmos and the return of all divine elements to the divine realm (e.g. NatArch, PS I-III, ParaShem). Obviously, there is no interest in these gnostic apocalypses in cosmic transformation at the end of time, since the cosmos is in principle evil.[15]

are keen to establish. See e.g. John Barton, *Oracles of God: Perceptions of Ancient Prophecy in Israel after the Exile* (London: Darton, Longman and Todd, 1986), 198–202.

[13] In the introduction to the *Semeia* volume on apocalypticism, Collins writes that: 'The Christian Apocryphon of James from Nag Hammadi, which is not clearly Gnostic, also conforms to this type [Apocalypses with only Personal Eschatology (and no otherworldly journey)]', Collins, 'Introduction', 14. But Fallon places it under 'Christian apocalypse' rather than 'gnostic apocalypse', and so it is not placed alongside the First Apocalypse of James, the Epistle of Peter to Philip, and so forth, Francis T. Fallon, 'Gnostic Apocalypses', *Semeia* 14 (1979): 145.

[14] Fallon, 'Gnostic Apocalypses', 125.

[15] Fallon, 'Gnostic Apocalypses', 125. Another defining characteristic is the dualism between the evil heavens and/or their rulers (which are more developed in later works, such as the Pistis Sophia) and the divine realm above them (126).

In actuality, this is not 'obvious' and dissolution of the cosmos does not have to equate to an evil nature, as we will see in the case of the Gospel of Mary in Chapter 4.

Fallon differentiates these apocalypses from 'gnostic revelatory dialogues' on the basis that in the dialogues '[t]here is no account of the appearance or departure of the revealer and thus no clear presentation of Jesus as a transcendent mediator as in the gnostic apocalypses'.[16] The 'revelatory dialogues' are the Gospel of Thomas, the Book of Thomas, the Dialogue of the Saviour, the First and Second Books of Jeu. This division could benefit from being blurred: 'no clear presentation' does not preclude something from being implied or presumed and the Jesus of the First Apocalypse of James and the Dialogue of the Saviour, as examples, may not be so different. The separation of these two genres is arbitrary: as Collins writes in the introduction to the same *Semeia* volume, '[a]n "apocalypse" is simply that which scholars call an apocalypse'.[17] Saying that, he later offers a definition:

> 'Apocalypse' is a genre of revelatory literature with a narrative framework, in which a revelation is mediated by an otherworldly being to a human recipient, disclosing a transcendent reality which is both temporal, insofar as it envisages eschatological salvation, and spatial insofar as it involves another, supernatural world.[18]

From this definition, many texts could be categorized as a dialogue gospel and as an apocalypse.[19]

The monograph-length studies of Perkins and Hartenstein have been influenced by the discussions of Rudolph, Krause and Koester, especially their outlines of generic characteristics. Perkins sees common features throughout the 'gnostic dialogues'. Common features of the narrative frame are: (1) the risen Saviour, (2) the revealer's appearance as angelic, announcing himself with an 'I am' or rebuking the disciples, (3) reference to opponents, (4) the disciples are to preach gnosis and possibly to face persecution, (5) the revelation has been

[16] Fallon, 'Gnostic Apocalypses', 139.

[17] Collins, 'Towards the Morphology of a Genre', 2.

[18] Collins, 'Towards the Morphology of a Genre', 9.

[19] Many aspects of 'apocalyptic' discourse are related to dialogue gospels. Ashton examines themes of apocalyptic discourse in his analysis of John: these are revelation, mystery and two ages, visions and dreams and two stages, riddles, insiders and outsiders, and correspondence between above and below, Ashton, *Understanding the Fourth Gospel*, 2nd ed. (Oxford: Oxford University Press, 2007), 305–30. Many of these issues will be explored in relation to dialogue gospels later in this chapter and Chapter 2.

hidden, (6) a post-resurrection commission and (7) questions listed or an *erotapokriseis* style. Frequently occurring content includes: (1) the Sophia myth, (2) the necessity of gnosis, (3) asceticism, (4) the ascent of the soul, (5) New Testament interpretation and (6) baptism. Other, less common, topics include Genesis interpretation, the nature of God, the crucifixion and cosmic eschatology.[20] The Sophia myth occurs frequently, but the revelation dialogues 'seem content to paraphrase the myth in order to provide a basis for the redemptive activity of the Gnostic revealer'.[21] This may be why, as Perkins concludes, '[t]he predominant emphasis of the revelation dialogue is on soteriology, not on speculation about the cosmos or doctrine'.[22]

With these characteristics, her 'gnostic dialogue' genre includes thirteen works: the Acts of Peter and the Twelve Apostles, the Apocryphon of James, the Apocryphon of John, the First Apocalypse of James, the Apocalypse of Peter (Coptic), the Book of Thomas, the Dialogue of the Saviour, the Epistle of Peter to Philip, the Gospel of Mary, the Hypostasis of the Archons, the Pistis Sophia and the Sophia of Jesus Christ. The dialogues themselves draw on a variety of models, including philosophical dialogues, Jewish apocalypses, Hermetic teacher/pupil dialogues and *erotapokriseis*.[23] Perkins sees the revelation dialogue as a 'powerful weapon' in the debate between different Christian groups. She argues that this may be inferred from the Gospel of Mary, with Peter representing orthodox Christians acting against Mary who represents gnostic Christians,[24] and the Epistula Apostolorum, 'which seems to be an orthodox attempt to use the genre against Gnostic opponents by presenting the content of post-resurrection revelation as identical with the teaching of the canonical gospels'.[25] But the 'gnostic' dialogues are written for insiders: 'They are not rhetorically designed to persuade the unconverted.'[26]

[20] Perkins, *Gnostic Dialogue*, 68. The forms of speech used are commonly the 'Sophia myth, apocalyptic vision, hymnic or prayer language, sayings of Jesus, exegetical questions – usually about the New Testament – and doctrinal questions' (60).

[21] Perkins, *Gnostic Dialogue*, 66, also 63–5.

[22] Perkins, *Gnostic Dialogue*, 73.

[23] Perkins, *Gnostic Dialogue*, 19–20. On philosophical dialogues, she writes that the gnostic dialogue is not an exchange of ideas, but a way to 'provide the revealer with an opportunity to discharge his mission', and on *erotapokriseis*, she writes that the gnostic dialogues have a 'polemical edge which sets them apart from the more irenic instructional dialogues'. The instructional dialogues are Zostrianos, the Hypostasis of the Archons, the Apocryphon of John and the Sophia of Jesus Christ, 80–98.

[24] Perkins, *Gnostic Dialogue*, 133–7.

[25] Perkins, *Gnostic Dialogue*, 26 n. 2. The Epistula Apostolorum, however, does not present revelation identical with the canonical gospels, as will be discussed later.

[26] Perkins, *Gnostic Dialogue*, 68.

Within the 'gnostic dialogue' genre, Perkins notes the various interests of the texts and divides them into four categories:

(1) 'Gnostic revealer' texts, comprising the Apocryphon of John, the Sophia of Jesus Christ, the Hypostasis of the Archons and Zostrianos. These texts claim esoteric truth and show little evidence of polemical aims.
(2) Thomasine texts, which are ascetic in character and include the Book of Thomas and the Dialogue of the Saviour.[27]
(3) Petrine texts, which are interested in 'Christian problems', such as the passion, christology and apostolic authority (as opposed to cosmology, eschatology and ascesis).[28] These texts claim Peter as their favoured disciple and include the Apocalypse of Peter (Coptic), the Epistle of Peter to Philip and the Acts of Peter and the Twelve Apostles. They do not report new post-resurrection revelation and instead emphasize that true instruction was given to Peter and/or the apostles before Jesus' death.[29]
(4) Non-apostolic texts, which favour either Mary or James rather than Peter or the Twelve. These include the Gospel of Mary, the Pistis Sophia, the First Apocalypse of James and the Apocryphon of James. The James texts 'explicitly acknowledge that gnosis was not preached by the apostolic generation', and the Gospel of Mary and the Pistis Sophia claim that Mary or James respectively was someone 'whom Jesus loves'.[30]

Perkins' constructs these four groups first through the disciple(s) that Jesus privileges for his revelation but then finds thematic connections within the revelations themselves. As well as identifying key points of commonality within the groups, she also helpfully detects connections outside of a text's primary classification: for example, she finds common ground between a Thomasine text and a non-apostolic text in the way that the Book of Thomas and the First Apocalypse of James present Jesus' familial relation to a 'twin' or 'brother' as more important than the Twelve.[31]

[27] These two texts Perkins regards as atypical within the genre: 'Though both make it clear that the revealer is the Risen Lord prior to the ascension, they lack the opening epiphany in response to the disciples' perplexity, which is so typical of revelation dialogues,' Perkins, *Gnostic Dialogue*, 100. Parenthetical references omitted.

[28] Perkins, *Gnostic Dialogue*, 114.

[29] Perkins, *Gnostic Dialogue*, 116.

[30] Perkins, *Gnostic Dialogue*, 132. Perkins does not deal with the fact that James is the brother of the Lord in the First Apocalypse of James (NHC 24,12–14) but appears to be one of the Twelve in the Apocryphon of James (1,22–25).

[31] Perkins, *Gnostic Dialogue*, 101.

While these four groups are useful for answering certain questions, the connections between dialogue gospels and related literature can be expanded significantly. For our purposes, to create preliminary subgroups within the dialogue gospel genre undermines the (non-)structural rhizomatic model of all dialogue gospels beginning on an equal footing, and that connections can be made at any place and any point, without hierarchy.

Hartenstein offers a different approach to the genre, seeing the teachings of the 'dialogue gospels' as divergent in content, but their narrative frames as arranged in parallel. Her scope moves away from 'gnostic dialogues' to 'dialogue gospels', which include the Epistula Apostolorum alongside the Apocryphon of John, the Gospel of Mary, the Epistle of Peter to Philip, the First Apocalypse of James, the Apocryphon of James and the Sophia of Jesus Christ. (The Sophia of Jesus Christ, she argues, is the oldest dialogue and perhaps the form that the others were based on.[32]) To refer to dialogue *gospels* is to understand these texts as not only revelatory dialogues but as *gospels*: Jesus is the central figure, these texts claim to reproduce his words, and their message is largely salvific.[33] Hartenstein's dialogue gospel genre or *Gattung* is clearly defined. As well as the need for a narrative frame, another criterion that she imposes is that the narrative frame must establish a post-resurrection setting.

Hartenstein's focus on the narrative frame draws perceptive connections with the resurrection scenes of the canonical gospels, and she argues that the dialogue gospels presuppose the canonical gospels – they do not intend to replace them, nor could they exist independently of them.[34] Instead, they propound a second, higher teaching ('*die zweite Lehre*') to the well-known, recognized and canonical one(s). Post-Easter was an appropriate setting to impart a higher teaching as Jesus acquired a greater status after his resurrection, although she notes that some dialogue gospels assert continuity

[32] On the Sophia of Jesus Christ as the earliest dialogue gospel, see Hartenstein, *Die zweite Lehre*, 313–14. *Contra* van Os who writes that 'Sophia cannot have been the model for the other early resurrection dialogues, as the other early works are often shorter, less coherent, and less structured,' Bas van Os, 'John's Last Supper and the Resurrection Dialogues', in *John, Jesus, and History: Aspects of Historicity in the Fourth Gospel,* Vol. 2, ed. Paul N. Anderson, Felix Just, and Tom Thatcher (Atlanta, GA: Society of Biblical Literature, 2009), 274.

[33] Hartenstein, *Die zweite Lehre*, 27–8.

[34] But: 'Diese Bezüge lassen sich allerdings nicht durch ein Konzept von literarischer Abhängigkeit, wie es zur Bestimmung des Verhältnisses der Synoptiker entwickelt wurde, erfassen', Hartenstein, *Die zweite Lehre*, 20.

between the message of the earthly and risen Jesus. To bring the Epistula Apostolorum into the conversation allows Hartenstein to argue that, although the texts may be seen as 'gnostic' in their content, they are not 'gnostic' on the basis of their genre.[35]

Much like Perkins, Hartenstein sees the dialogue gospels as addressed to their own '*Trägergruppe*', and on the whole, they are neither suitable nor intended for missionary purposes.[36] These groups had a clear self-conscious understanding of their identity, believing themselves to be the recipients of an in-depth understanding of Jesus' teachings. However, she argues that the group(s) behind the dialogue gospels saw themselves as part of mainstream Christianity, and (with the exception of the Apocryphon of James) they were not esoteric writings.

Her seven texts, she argues, have more in common with each other than with other texts, such as the Gospel of Thomas, the Hypostasis of the Archons or the Dialogue of the Saviour. The commonalities are found within the narrative frame and include an appearance of Jesus and the ratio of questions and answers.[37] Perkins noted the atypicality of the Book of Thomas and the Dialogue of the Saviour within her genre as they lack the appearance of the Saviour, and it is on this basis that Hartenstein excludes them altogether as she sees the absence of a narrative frame to represent a different historical perspective. She writes: 'In my opinion, DialSav, like GThom, avoids temporally embedding the revelations – a situation after the resurrection is not clearly recognizable – and therefore it has a different relationship between text and reality than the dialogue gospels.'[38]

If, however, we want to analyse the *content* of the revelation, rather than the structure of the texts or their generic ancestors, then it is helpful to take a more open view of the genre. There are

[35] Martina Janssen also disagrees with linking gnostic theology or christology to the dialogue genre. She uses a wide range of dialogues, including 'gnostic', 'non-gnostic', Manichaean and Hermetic, and demonstrates that there is a lack of common features (including disunity in the narrative frames) to link all dialogue texts, Martina Janssen, 'Mystagogus Gnosticus? Zur Gattung der "gnostischen Gespräche des Auferstandenen"', in *Studien zur Gnosis*, ed. Gerd Lüdemann, *Studies in the Religion and History of Early Christianity* (Frankfurt am Main: Peter Lang, 1999), 21–260.

[36] 'Aus der Analyse der Schriften ergibt sich aber als Gemeinsamkeit, daß alle in erster Linie der Erbauung, Stützung und Festigung ihrer Trägergruppe beabsichtigen', Hartenstein, *Die zweite Lehre*, 251.

[37] Hartenstein, *Die zweite Lehre*, esp. 255–9.

[38] Hartenstein, *Die zweite Lehre*, 256. In a later article, Hartenstein gives up the title 'Dialogevangelien' and replaces it with the more specific 'Erscheinungsevangelien', Judith Hartenstein, 'Erscheinungsevangelien (Gespräche mit dem Auferstandenen)

as many similarities and differences within Hartenstein's seven-text group as there are with related texts outside of it. The cosmologies of the Apocryphon of John and the Pistis Sophia share much in common, both having a repentant Sophia; the Gospel of Mary and the Dialogue of the Saviour have a similar realized/future eschatological tension; the Apocryphon of James and the First Apocalypse of James do not have a high regard for the Twelve – but neither does the Gospel of Judas; and the Epistula Apostolorum and the Ascension of Isaiah share an angelomorphic christology.

Petersen builds on Hartenstein's work, identifying a group of texts that have an appearance of the resurrected Jesus as a focal point.[39] She names the Sophia of Jesus Christ, the First Apocalypse of James, the Gospel of Mary, the Epistula Apostolorum and the Pistis Sophia as 'appearance gospels'. (Her main focus is on women in these texts.[40]) Yet it is not only the appearance that serves a purpose in these texts: Petersen hypothesizes that their use of dialogue incites dialogue among readers and hearers. She writes:

> Dialogues (as well as other ancient texts) were predominately not privately received, but read aloud, heard and possibly even discussed, whereby the dialogic situation was doubled.[41]

Therefore, the dialogue within the text is important for the transmission of the text's contents within the community of its readers. The fact that these texts were *designed* to be read aloud showed that the intention was to expand the audience for Jesus' revelatory speech. Furthermore, Petersen posits that appearance dialogues summarize their revelation at the end, and this revelation is intended to

im Kontext frühchristlicher Theologie: Anknüpfungspunkte und Besonderheiten der christologischen Vorstellungen', in *The Apocryphal Gospels within the Context of Early Christian Theology*, ed. Jens Schröter (Leuven: Peeters, 2013), 305–32.

[39] Petersen maintains Hartenstein's view on Christianity and 'gnosticism', writing: 'Die Texte dokumentieren eine Vermischung und Durchdringung von Christlichem und Gnostischem, und klare Unterscheidungen zwischen beidem sind in vielen Fällen kaum zu treffen', Petersen, *Zerstört die Werke*, 42.

[40] Petersen, *Zerstört die Werke*, 38. In all of Petersen's selected texts but the First Apocalypse of James, Jesus appears to female disciples either first (as in the Epistula Apostolorum, the Gospel of Mary) or within the group (the Sophia of Jesus Christ, the Pistis Sophia). Although the First Apocalypse of James does not have an appearance to a female disciple, the text identifies a group of women as honoured disciples.

[41] Petersen, *Zerstört die Werke*, 43.

be repeated and learned by its readers.[42] Thus, she links the salvific message contained within the text with the form of the text itself.

There are several points at which my analysis of dialogue gospels diverges from the studies of Perkins and Hartenstein. Principally, the deconstruction of the category of 'gnosticism' allows us to see the variety of theological ideas within the group of texts under discussion without presuppositions. Perkins' view of revelatory dialogues ('gnostic dialogues') may be summed up by her statement that '[t]he revelation dialogue seems to have been as characteristic of Christian Gnostics as the Gospel was of orthodox Christians'.[43] The parallel between genre and 'gnosticism' breaks down at the basic level of the inclusion of the Epistula Apostolorum and the Apocalypse of Peter, but also when we see the variety of theological perspectives within the once so-called 'gnostic' texts. Hartenstein also constructs her analysis through this gnostic/Christian dichotomy, but without linking genre and christology. She sees dialogue gospels as comprising a Christian narrative frame that has been imposed on a gnostic dialogue, and only because she focuses on the Christian narrative frame can she make connections to the canonical gospels: 'At the same time, for some writings the narrative frame is the only part that reveals relationships with other Christian traditions, especially the appearance stories in the final chapters of the canonical gospels.'[44] Although some of what we find in our dialogue gospels may have once circulated as independent sources,[45] someone has put them together to create the text that we have today, and this is how they were read and used. Going forward, I propose to read the texts as coherent and complete works and to destabilize outdated boundaries of 'orthodox' and 'gnostic' in order to recognize dialogue gospels within a rhizomatic network of early Christian literature.

[42] Petersen, *Zerstört die Werke*, 43.

[43] Perkins, *Gnostic Dialogue*, 26. For criticism of this, see Janssen, 'Mystagogus Gnosticus?'. Also, King's extensive footnote: Karen L. King, *The Gospel of Mary of Magdala: Jesus and the First Woman Apostle* (Santa Rosa, CA: Polebridge Press, 2003), 192–3 n. 8.

[44] Hartenstein, *Die zweite Lehre*, 3. Despite the overall rhetoric of the Christian narrative frame and the 'gnostic' teaching being largely incompatible, Hartenstein does attempt to appreciate each text on its own basis without instantly ascribing to it a gnostic worldview. Thus, she notes that '[b]ei den von mir untersuchten Schriften ist allerdings nicht immer eindeutig, ob es sich um gnostische Schriften handelt, da der Weltentstehungsmythos nicht in allen vorkommt' (31).

[45] For example, Eugnostos as an independent source text for the Sophia of Jesus Christ, and the dialogue with the archons that we find in Irenaeus' *Adv. Haer.* 1.21 and the First Apocalypse of James.

The Taxonomies

In the scholarship that has investigated this group of texts (in varying forms), there has been no consensus regarding the name or form of the genre or which texts should belong within it. Rudolph, Koester, Perkins and Hartenstein, among others, are interested in different things and so choose to discuss different texts. Hartenstein is interested in the narrative frame and so excludes the Dialogue of the Saviour and the Book of Thomas from her work, and Perkins is interested in gnosticism and so excludes the Epistula Apostolorum. When these scholars define a genre, they are not coming up with the same title or collection because they are not starting with the same set of questions. The table below shows the differences in the titles and texts of these comparable literary genres.

Hennecke-Schneemelcher, 3rd ed. (1959)[46]	Rudolph (1968)[47]	Perkins (1980)[48]	Schneemelcher, 6th ed. (1990)[49]	Hartenstein (2000)[50]	Tuckett (2005)[51]	Markschies-Schröter (2012)[52]	Bockmuehl (2017)[53]
'Dialogues of Jesus with his disciples after his resurrection'	*'Gnostic "dialogue"'*	*'Gnostic dialogues'*	*'Dialogues of the Saviour'*	*'Dialogue gospels'*	*'Resurrection discourses/dialogues'*	*'Dialogue gospels'*	*'Post-resurrection discourse gospels'*
EpAp	1ApocJas	ActPet12	ApJas	ApJas	ApJas	(Allogenes)	ApJas
Freer Logion	ApJohn	ApJas	1ApocJas	1ApocJas	ApJohn	ApJas	1ApocJas
Gospel-fragment of Strassburg Coptic papyrus	ApocPaul	ApJohn	2ApocJas	ApJohn	(BookThom)	1ApocJas	2ApocJas
'Other gnostic gospels and related literature'[54]	2Jeu	1ApocJas	BookThom	EpAp	(DialSav)	2ApocJas	EpAp
ApJas	GMary	$\text{ApocPet}_{\text{COP}}$	DialSav	EpPetPhil	EpAp	BookThom	EpPetPhil
ApJohn	PistSoph	BookThom	EpAp	GMary	GMary	DialSav	GMary
BookThom	SophJesChr	DialSav	EpPetPhil	SophJesChr	(GThom)	EpAp	GPhil
DialSav	The *Kephalaia*	EpPetPhil	Freer Logion		SophJesChr	EpPetPhil	GThom
Jeu		GMary	*'Other gnostic gospels and related literature'*			Freer Logion	SophJesChr
GJudas		HypArch	ApJas			Fragment of dialogue between John and Jesus	
GMary		PistSoph	ApJohn			GJudas	
PistSoph		SophJesChr	BookThom			GMary	
SophJesChr			DialSav			SophJesChr	
			Jeu				
			GJudas				
			GMary				
			PistSoph				
			SophJesChr				

46 Hennecke and Schneemelcher, *Neutestamentliche Apokryphen in deutscher Übersetzung: Evangelien*, Vol. 1.

47 Rudolph, 'Der gnostische "Dialog"'.

48 Perkins, *Gnostic Dialogue*.

49 W. Schneemelcher, *New Testament Apocrypha*.

50 Hartenstein, *Die zweite Lehre*.

51 Christopher Tuckett, 'Forty Other Gospels', in *The Written Gospel*, ed. Markus Bockmuehl and Donald A. Hagner (Cambridge: Cambridge University Press, 2005), 238–53.

52 Christoph Markschies and Jens Schröter, ed., *Antike christliche Apokryphen in deutscher Übersetzung: Evangelien und Verwandtes*, Vol. 1 pt. 2 (Tübingen: Mohr Siebeck, 2012).

53 Markus Bockmuehl, *Ancient Apocryphal Gospels*, Interpretation (Louisville, KY: Westminster John Knox Press, 2017).

54 This is split into several sections and includes many more texts. I only include here those that are relevant to us. This is also the case with the *New Testament Apocrypha* 1990 edition in the fourth column above. (GJudas there refers to the Gospel of Judas as mentioned by Irenaeus, as Codex Tcachos was only made available in 2006.)

The nature of making a 'collection' of New Testament Apocrypha leaves editors with little choice but to create generic categories, and so in the 1959 and 1990 Hennecke-Schneemelcher editions, 'dialogues' were differentiated from 'gospels'. The difficulties in placing these texts into a single category are apparent in the 1990 edition, in which three texts (the Apocryphon of James, the Dialogue of the Saviour and the Book of Thomas) appear in two lists: 'dialogues with the Saviour' and 'gnostic gospels and related literature'. Markschies-Schröter's 2012 collection takes a different approach, combining the two categories into one ('dialogue gospels') and creating a more substantive list.

In the table above, the scholars are largely dealing with the same body of literature, but the lists are not as uniform as we might expect. The Gospel of Mary and the Sophia of Jesus Christ are the only texts that appear in each column. As we have discussed, Hartenstein omits the Dialogue of the Saviour and the Book of Thomas because they lack the narrative frame, as well as the Gospel of Judas because it does not have a post-resurrection setting. Perkins' focus on gnosticism leads her to include the Hypostasis of the Archons and Zostrianos. It is unclear why Markschies-Schröter and Bockmuehl left out the Apocryphon of John.[55] The genre titles and lists make it quite apparent that they reflect the interests of the modern authors rather than anything about the ancient world. The scholarly endeavour to define and delimit a genre necessitates contrast with contemporaries who are interested in the same texts but place them in different generic categories and alongside different ancient writings on the basis of their own differing interests.

Recently, Tuckett and Bockmuehl have created new taxonomies that are less interested in strict genre definitions than the works discussed previously. Tuckett writes about 'resurrection dialogues' that include the Gospel of Mary, the Apocryphon of James, the Sophia of Jesus Christ, the Apocryphon of John, the Dialogue of the Saviour, the Book of Thomas, the Epistula Apostolorum and the Gospel of Thomas.[56] He notes that the Dialogue of the Saviour and the Book of Thomas do not explicitly have a post-resurrection setting but that it might be implied nonetheless, especially in view of the fragmentary nature of the Dialogue of the Saviour.[57] The Gospel of Thomas is less clear,

[55] Neither appears to offer an explanation for this.
[56] Tuckett, 'Forty Other Gospels'.
[57] Tuckett, 'Forty Other Gospels', 247.

but Tuckett wonders whether the present tense of λέγει in the Greek fragments (as opposed to the atemporal tense of ⲡⲉϫⲉ in the Coptic) suggests a speaker in the present – the risen Jesus.[58] He continues:

> Further, dialogue elements are also present: on occasion followers of Jesus, individually or collectively, pose questions to which Jesus responds (sayings 6, 12, 13, 20, 21 etc.). It may be, then, that the *Gospel of Thomas* is rather more like a 'resurrection dialogue' than might appear at first sight, and that in generic terms, not too large a wedge should be driven between *Thomas* (as an alleged 'sayings gospel') and other resurrection dialogues.[59]

Bockmuehl creates a category named 'post-resurrection discourse gospels', a category in which 'many of the lines of textual, ideological, and genre identification are patently blurred'.[60] In it he includes those texts that are 'unambiguous examples of a post-resurrection setting', including the Epistula Apostolorum, the Sophia of Jesus Christ, the Apocryphon of James, the First Apocalypse of James and the Epistle of Peter to Philip, as well as those that 'strongly presuppose or imply such a narrative setting', such as the Gospel of Mary and the Second Apocalypse of James.[61] He also wants to impose 'extremely fluid' boundaries, expanding the genre to include the Gospel of Thomas and the Gospel of Philip – the latter described as 'a timeless mode of instruction that may only be tenuously identified as the teaching of Jesus'.[62] On the Gospel of Thomas, Bockmuehl sees Christ's title ⲓ̅ⲥ̅ ⲉⲧⲟⲛϩ // ιη̅ς ὁ ζῶν (POxy 654) in the prologue as a 'reference to the

[58] But note that Logion 1 on POxy.654 has εἶπεν.

[59] Tuckett, 'Forty Other Gospels', 248. *Contra*, Klauck insists that nothing in the Gospel of Thomas points to a resurrection dialogue, Klauck, *Apocryphal Gospels*, 146.

[60] Bockmuehl, *Ancient Apocryphal Gospels*, 161.

[61] Bockmuehl, *Ancient Apocryphal Gospels*, 162. Yet the Freer Logion 'cannot be regarded as a dialogue gospel' as it never existed independently of Mark (162–3). Presumably then, neither can the Johannine Farewell Discourse. Bockmuehl argues for the fluid boundaries of his genre, but unfortunately never explains what the boundary limits might be.

[62] Bockmuehl, *Ancient Apocryphal Gospels*, 163. The Gospel of Philip is not a dialogue, nor a narrative, but a theological reflection on Christ, and it is unclear why it would be placed alongside dialogue gospels. Bockmuehl writes that: 'In substance and genre, however, *Philip* seems remote from most of the other texts discussed in this [book]' (183–4). He appears to include it because it stands alongside the Gospel of Thomas in NHC 2: '[I]t must be significant that two such noncanonical gospels are here bound together in the same volume, and indeed that the text of *Philip* begins without any intervening new title' (184). But Coptic titles come at the end of texts (sometimes at the beginning too), and the Gospel of Thomas does conclude with a title that separates the two gospels.

heavenly, eternal as opposed to the earthly Christ'.[63] On the matter of 'timelessness', Bockmuehl also points to the Johannine Jesus:

> One may also usefully compare and contrast the apparent timelessness of John's loquaciously self-referential, supratemporal, descended, and perhaps already ascended Son who seems – particularly in the Farewell Discourses of chapters 14–17 – to speak almost from a viewpoint outside history.[64]

Bringing the Johannine Farewell Discourse into the equation is effective. Not only do these chapters present a picture of a self-referential and supratemporal Jesus comparable to dialogue gospels, but they are also structurally comparable in that Jesus answers the questions of individuals (13.36–14.14) and a larger group (16.17) about his departure and the role of the disciples in his absence. Dettwiler and van Os have also noted the similarities between this text and dialogue gospels,[65] but the latter is generally considered without reference to the former and vice versa. With an 'open' view of genre, in which generic categories are fluid rather than fixed entities, they can be brought into much closer contact, and this will be put into practice in the following work.

This overview serves to demonstrate that, despite repeated attempts at meticulous pigeonholing, texts do not fit into neat genre boxes. The term 'dialogue gospel' in itself may point to flexibility as these texts are both gospel and dialogue. But, as we shall see, they can also be revelations, acts and epistles. They might include visions, farewell discourses or *erotapokriseis*.[66] The title 'apocalypse', 'epistle' or 'evangelion' might appear on the manuscript, or no title at all.

[63] Bockmuehl, *Ancient Apocryphal Gospels*, 164.

[64] Bockmuehl, *Ancient Apocryphal Gospels*, 174–5.

[65] Dettwiler, *Die Gegenwart des Erhöhten*, 21–6; van Os, 'John's Last Supper'. These will be discussed in further detail later.

[66] The concept of discourse mode could be used as an alternative way of constructing a view of these texts; for example, we could say that Mark is a gospel in the apocalyptic mode. However, this would damage the open view of genre as it would reinforce imposing a primary genre onto a text rather than acknowledging that a text can participate in than one genre, and so could be both a gospel and an apocalypse. As Chandler notes, 'One theorist's *genre* may be another's *sub-genre* or even *super-genre* (and indeed what is *technique*, *style*, *mode*, *formula* or *thematic grouping* to one may be treated as a *genre* by another),' Daniel Chandler, 'An Introduction to Genre Theory', 2000 [1997], 1. Available from http://visual-memory.co.uk/daniel/Documents/intgenre/chandler_genre_theory.pdf. In another context, it might be useful to discuss modes employed by dialogue gospels, but for the purpose of comparative analysis, it is better to discuss genres.

1.2 The Genre Question

Genre for Interpretation and Comparison

It has been shown that a definition or agreement on the dialogue gospel genre does not exist, and it has been suggested that it is unhelpful to be prescriptive about the texts included in any certain genre. The question now is how and to what purpose might we create a category of texts. Study of ancient Christian literature should be informed by the way that literary theorists now conceive of genre, which has changed dramatically in the recent past. Genre is increasingly regarded as fluid and dynamic rather than static, rigid and constraining. Derrida's statement has become widely cited: 'Every text participates in one or several genres, there is no genreless text; there is always a genre and genres, yet such participation never amounts to belonging.'[67] Derrida articulates the difficulty and necessity of genre. A text can participate in more than one genre and does not have to be hermeneutically confined by its primary genre. The genres themselves are invented rhetorical categories; they do not exist independently of the scholars who create them.[68] Instead of becoming entangled in the 'theoretical minefield' of genre theory, as Chandler describes it,[69] our discussion of genre in early Christian literature will be seen as a microcosm of the larger field of literary studies.[70]

Some scholars of early Christian literature argue that the genre of a text affects the way we interpret it. For example, Burridge writes that genre is vital as 'the set of conventions and expectations mediating between authors and audiences, guiding both the production and the interpretation of texts',[71] and Stanton warns his readers that 'gospels are not letters' and therefore should not be read as such.[72] He writes:

> The very first step in the interpretation of any writing, whether ancient or modern, is to establish its literary genre.

[67] Jacques Derrida, 'The Law of Genre', *Glyph* 7 (1980): 212.

[68] Tzvetan Todorov, 'The Origin of Genres', in *Modern Genre Theory*, ed. David Duff (New York: Longman, 2000), 193–209.

[69] Chandler, 'An Introduction to Genre Theory', 2.

[70] The change in the way genre is perceived is reflected also in classics, e.g. John Marincola, 'Genre, Convention, and Innovation in Greco-Roman Historiography', in *The Limits of Historiography: Genre and Narrative in Ancient Historical Texts*, ed. C. S. Kraus, Mnemosyne, Bibliotheca Classica Batava: Supplementum 191 (Leiden: Brill, 1999), 281–324.

[71] Richard A. Burridge, 'Who Writes, Why, and for Whom?', in *The Written Gospel*, ed. Markus Bockmuehl and D. A. Hagner (Cambridge: Cambridge University Press, 2005), 112.

[72] Graham N. Stanton, *Jesus and Gospel* (Cambridge: Cambridge University Press, 2004), 193. Perkins also: 'Our perception of the genre of any writing is an important help in interpreting it. The implication of particular details may change radically if we change our view of a writing's genre', Perkins, *Gnostic Dialogue*, 26–7.

> If we make a mistake about the literary genre of the gospels, interpretation will be skewed or even misguided. A decision about the genre of a work and the discovery of its meaning are inextricably inter-related; different types of text require different types of interpretation.[73]

It seems to me that modern genre theory would contest this stance, and instead express the view that generic expectations are formed and can be overturned through the reading process.[74] To determine the genre of a text at the outset goes hand in hand with the 'taxonomic' view of genre as static, formal and inflexible. Texts do not belong to genres but participate in them. Texts are shaped by genres, but they also shape genres.[75]

Rather than seeing genre as a method for interpretation, for our purposes it is more helpful to see it as a heuristic tool for comparison. To create a genre entails identifying texts that have certain similarities and therefore can comfortably be placed in a comparative framework. The genre, then, invites various and, at points, disparate texts to be brought together for analysis. Defining a genre for the purpose of comparison allows the analysis to draw out both similarities and differences within the group, as well as holding the potential for gaining new insights into the unique qualities of the individual texts. However, since genres overlap, equally effective comparisons may also be made across their now-fluid boundaries.

Assigning Genres

For a large proportion of early Christian literature, and particularly that deemed 'apocryphal', the way we assign genre is often both arbitrary and rigid. But in light of developments in literary theory,

[73] Stanton, *Jesus and Gospel*, 192.

[74] One of Chandler's great concerns is to ask: '[I]f we are studying the way in which genre frames the reader's interpretation of a text then we would do well to focus on how readers identify genres rather than on theoretical distinctions,' Chandler, 'An Introduction to Genre Theory', 3. I would argue that, to interpret a text, a reader does not need to identify its literary genre – the act of interpretation is not affected by this identification. Reading a text as a work of fiction or a work of history might produce different results, but that necessitates that there are right and wrong answers in interpretation. Identifying a text as one genre or another simply has the potential to produce different results.

[75] See John Frow, *Genre* (London and New York: Routledge, 2006), esp. 28.

opposition towards pigeonholing texts is increasing. Recently, Smith and Kostopoulos have applied an open view of genre to New Testament writings, arguing that 'ancient texts do not bear the imprints of a rigid system of generic classification', and that the 'restrictive system of generic categorisation' needs to be challenged.[76] Luke-Acts is a particularly striking example and the subject of Smith and Kostopoulos' study. Some scholars have tried to place Luke and Acts in the same genre, but Smith and Kostopoulos argue that 'their efforts to force the two volumes into one generic classification often result in awkward pairing – one volume fits well enough, but the other resembles a round peg wedged into a square hole'.[77] Luke is generally considered to be a *bios* gospel, but Acts has been labelled an apology, an epic, a biography, a history and a novel/romance.[78] Smith and Kostopoulos argue:

> We are not seeking to cast Luke-Acts as the 'texte sans genre', but as a text that indeed participates in (and whose author emulates) multiple literary traditions of the ancient Mediterranean world. The emphasis on 'participation' frees us from the problem of choosing a rigid generic category for Luke-Acts.[79]

Acts is not an apology *or* an epic *or* a biography, but participates in all of the above. In fact, to claim a single genre and to read it solely through that lens might lead to 'misguided' interpretation, in the words of Stanton, whereas to read it as participating in multiple genres may well lead to a more thorough understanding of the text.

A genre does not have to apply to a whole text. A single text can include different sections that participate in different genres. John, for example, is a gospel comprised of narratives, dialogues and monologues, as Dodd argued.[80] Attridge sees these different sections within John as purposefully bending a traditional view of genre: for example, 'John 3 is a paradigmatic revealer discourse, yet no sooner does it make a dramatic revelation than it points to ambiguities and tensions within the terms of that revelation. A revelatory genre is

[76] See Daniel Lynwood Smith and Zachary Lundin Kostopoulos, 'Biography, History and the Genre of Luke-Acts', *NTS* 63.3 (2017): 405.

[77] Smith and Kostopoulos, 'Biography, History and the Genre of Luke-Acts', 391.

[78] See Sean A. Adams, *The Genre of Acts and Collected Biography*, SNTSMS 156 (New York: Cambridge University Press, 2013), 5–22.

[79] Smith and Kostopoulos, 'Biography, History and the Genre of Luke-Acts', 406–7.

[80] C. H. Dodd, *The Interpretation of the Fourth Gospel* (Cambridge: Cambridge University Press, 1955), esp. 133–4.

bent'.[81] The way that the larger 'gospel' genre uses and bends different genres is 'playful',[82] and Attridge suggests that 'in the imagination of the fourth evangelist, genres are bent because words themselves are bent'.[83] Genre, then, is not a fixed entity.

Coming back to the dialogue gospels – the name 'dialogue gospel' already suggests that these texts participate in both dialogue *and* gospel genres.[84] But they can also be letters. And letters can be basically anything.[85] The Book of Revelation and the Epistula Apostolorum are both letters, but could belong to several genres as their comparable openings suggest:

> Ἀποκάλυψις Ἰησοῦ Χριστοῦ ἣν ἔδωκεν αὐτῷ ὁ θεὸς δεῖξαι τοῖς δούλοις αὐτοῦ ἃ δεῖ γενέσθαι ἐν τάχει, καὶ ἐσήμανεν ἀποστείλας διὰ τοῦ ἀγγέλου αὐτοῦ τῷ δούλῳ αὐτοῦ Ἰωάννῃ, ὃς ἐμαρτύρησεν τὸν λόγον τοῦ θεοῦ καὶ τὴν μαρτυρίαν Ἰησοῦ Χριστοῦ ὅσα εἶδεν. Μακάριος ὁ ἀναγινώσκων καὶ οἱ ἀκούοντες τοὺς λόγους τῆς προφητείας καὶ τηροῦντες τὰ ἐν αὐτῇ γεγραμμένα, ὁ γὰρ καιρὸς ἐγγύς. Ἰωάννης ταῖς ἑπτὰ ἐκκλησίαις ταῖς ἐν τῇ Ἀσίᾳ … (Rev 1.1–4)
>
> The revelation of Jesus Christ, which God gave him to show his servants what must soon take place; he made it known by sending his angel to his servant John, who testified to the word of God and to the testimony of Jesus Christ, even to all that he saw. Blessed is the one who reads aloud the words of the prophecy, and blessed are those who hear and who keep what is written in it; for the time is near. John to the seven churches that are in Asia …

[81] Harold W. Attridge, 'Genre Bending in the Fourth Gospel', *JBL* 121.1 (2002): 12–13.

[82] Attridge, 'Genre Bending in the Fourth Gospel', 19.

[83] Attridge, 'Genre Bending in the Fourth Gospel', 21: 'If something quite spectacular happens to flesh when the Word hits it, something equally wondrous happens to ordinary words when they try to convey the Word itself. Revealing words reveal riddles; realistic similitudes become surreal; words of testimony undercut the validity of any ordinary act of testifying; words of farewell become words of powerful presence; words of prayer negate the distance between worshiper and God; words that signify shame, death on a cross, become words that enshrine value, allure disciples, give a command, and glorify God.'

[84] As Smith and Kostopoulos write, '[t]he notion of "mixed genre" may sound like scholarly capitulation … [but it] reflects the reality of ancient literary activity', Smith and Kostopoulos, 'Biography, History and the Genre of Luke-Acts', 394.

[85] For definitions of the literary form of an ancient letter, see Andrew Gregory, 'Non-Canonical Epistles and Related Literature', in *The Oxford Handbook of Early Christian Literature*, ed. Christopher Tuckett and Andrew Gregory (Oxford: Oxford University Press, 2015), 90–114.

> The book of what Jesus Christ revealed to his disciples … John, Thomas, Peter, Andrew, James, Philip, Bartholomew, Matthew, Nathanael, Judas the Zealot and Cephas, we have written to the churches of the east and the west, the north and the south. In proclaiming and declaring to you our Lord Jesus Christ, we write about how we both heard him and touched him after he was raised from the dead, and how he revealed to us what is great and wonderful and true. (EpAp 1.1–2.3)[86]
>
> (Near the beginning of the Coptic manuscript:) ⲉⲧⲃⲉ ⲡⲉ̈ⲓ ⲛ̣̄ⲡⲛⲁⲛⲟ ⲉⲁⲛⲥϩⲉ̈ⲓ ⲛⲏⲧⲛⲉ ⲉⲧⲃⲉ ⲧ[ⲙ]ⲁⲣⲧⲩⲣ[ⲓⲁ] ⲛ̄ⲡⲛ̄ⲥ̄ⲱ̄ⲣ̄ ⲡⲭ̄ⲥ̄ ⲛⲉⲧⲁϥⲉⲟⲩⲉ ⲉⲛⲥⲁⲛⲧ ⲛ̄ⲥⲱϥ ⲁ[ⲟⲩ ⲉ]ⲧⲓ ⲁⲛ ϩⲛ̄ ⲛ̄ⲙⲉⲟ̣ⲩⲉ ⲙⲛ̄ ⲛ̄ϩⲃⲏⲩⲉ (EpAp 7.1)
>
> For this reason we have not hesitated to write to you about the [t]estimo[ny] of our Saviour Christ, the things he did as we watched him, a[nd t]hat are still in (our) thoughts and works.

The opening of Revelation shows that it could be judged to be a revelation or apocalypse (1.1–2), a prophecy (1.3) or a letter (1.4f.), or all of the above.[87] The opening of the Epistula Apostolorum suggests a book, a gospel and a letter, but there is no epistolary ending, and the majority of the text has no trace of the letter-form of its opening. This is comparable to other dialogue gospels: the Apocryphon of James begins with an epistolary greeting, with the recipient asking James for a 'secret book' (ⲁⲡⲟⲕⲣⲩⲫⲟⲛ [1,10]), but the bulk of the text is a dialogue with an epistolary conclusion.[88] The Epistle of Peter to Philip too begins as a letter but then changes to narrative, reminiscent of Acts literature,[89] and dialogues between Jesus and the apostles.

[86] Translation (adapted) of the Ethiopic Epistula Apostolorum provided by Francis Watson, forthcoming.

[87] See Richard Bauckham, *The Theology of the Book of Revelation*, New Testament Theology (Cambridge: Cambridge University Press, 1993), 1–17. Bauckham argues that Revelation belongs in three categories: apocalypse, prophecy and letter.

[88] The term 'book' (ϫⲱⲱⲙⲉ) is used in reference to books that the apostles were writing (2,14–16). Scopello calls its genre 'heterogeneous', and Williams suggests that the letter may be a frame added later to the original content, Marvin Meyer and Madeleine Scopello, 'The Secret Book of James', in *The Nag Hammadi Scriptures: The International Edition*, ed. Marvin Meyer (New York: Harper Collins, 2007), 20; Francis E. Williams, 'The Apocryphon of James – 1,2: 1.1–16:30', in *Nag Hammadi Codex I (The Jung Codex)*, ed. Harold W. Attridge, NHMS 22 (Leiden: Brill, 1985), 17–18. But it is incorrect to assume that anything that looks anomalous from the perspective of genre must be a later addition.

[89] F. Lapham, *Peter: The Myth, the Man and the Writings: A Study of the Early Petrine Text and Tradition* (London and New York: T&T Clark, 2004), 172.

Early Christians used the letter form openly, which meant that a letter could be a gospel too.[90] The Epistula Apostolorum, the Apocryphon of James and the Epistle of Peter to Philip are all examples of this.[91]

Many scholars who work on 'non-canonical gospel-like texts' endorse an inclusive definition of gospel, seeing a 'gospel' as a text that purports to give information about the life and/or teaching of Jesus.[92] The table above shows that some scholars have been using this title with reference to the Apocryphon of John and the Dialogue of the Saviour, among many other texts. Of our dialogue gospels, only the Gospel of Mary and the Gospel of Judas are self-titled 'gospel' in the extant manuscripts. The Coptic BG and Greek PRyl manuscripts of the Gospel of Mary contain the subscript 'gospel', which has left scholars perplexed regarding its genre. The missing beginning causes further ambiguity. Bass asks, 'Is it a Gnostic revelation dialogue, apocalypse, gospel or post-resurrection dialogue?'[93] Following Perkins' characteristics of a 'gnostic revelation dialogue', King and Tuckett write that it fits the characteristics of a post-resurrection revelation dialogue.[94] Tuckett thinks it best not to 'specify the genre of a text like the *Gospel of Mary* too narrowly', as it may foreclose or predetermine interpretative possibilities,[95] and while the Gospel of Mary has its closest parallels with revelation discourses/dialogue gospels,[96] it can be called a gospel 'if one is willing to accept the text's own self-description as a "gospel"'.[97] King, on the other hand, prefers 'post-resurrection dialogue' to 'gospel', as the latter indicates 'the message and promise of the Savior, not the genre of the work'.[98] King sees post-resurrection dialogues as mutually exclusive to

[90] Timo Glaser, 'Liaisons Dangereuses: Epistolary Novels in Antiquity', in *A Companion to the Ancient Novel*, ed. Edmund P. Cueva and Shannon N. Byrne, Blackwell Companions to the Ancient World (Chichester and Malden, MA: Wiley Blackwell, 2014), 252–3; Richard Bauckham, 'Pseudo-Apostolic Letters', *JBL* 107.3 (1988), esp. 474.

[91] Bauckham refers to the Apocryphon of James and the Epistula Apostolorum as '[l]etters with mainly Gospel content', Bauckham, 'Pseudo-Apostolic Letters', 483.

[92] In the wider field, scholars vary in their willingness to apply the term 'gospel' to non-canonical gospels. For the division in scholarship, see Judith A. Diehl, 'What Is a 'Gospel'? Recent Studies in the Gospel Genre', *Currents in Biblical Research* 9.2 (2011): 171–99.

[93] Ardyth L. Bass, 'Composition and Redaction in the Coptic Gospel of Mary' (Milwaukee, WI: PhD Thesis, Marquette University, 2007), 2.

[94] Christopher M. Tuckett, *The Gospel of Mary* (Oxford and New York: Oxford University Press, 2007), 37–8; King, *Mary*, 30.

[95] Tuckett, *Mary*, 31.

[96] Tuckett, *Mary*, 41.

[97] Tuckett, *Mary*, 38.

[98] King, *Mary*, 30.

gospel, whereas Tuckett does not. Luttikhuizen does not agree that the Gospel of Mary is a revelation dialogue at all: 'At first sight, one is tempted to put the first part of the Gospel of Mary on a level with other revelation dialogues … But upon closer examination, this equation seems to be quite problematic'.[99] He argues that *only* Jesus' communication with Mary, rather than his dialogue with Peter and others, can be paralleled to revelation dialogues. This seems counter-intuitive as the dialogue with Mary is a vision whereas the dialogue with Peter (from the little we have of it) appears to be much closer to other dialogue gospels; but Luttikhuizen proposes that because Peter's dialogue with the Saviour leaves the disciples in a state of fear, unable to preach and with unanswered questions, it is not comparable to revelation dialogues.[100] Fallon raises another possibility; namely, that the Gospel of Mary is an apocalypse presented through a dialogue, due to its soteriological concerns and personal eschatology.[101] Denzey Lewis follows this, writing: '*GosMary* is an apocalypse, in which a seer (in this case, Mary) is given a tour of the cosmos by a privileged being (in this case, Jesus as the Savior). This text is *also* a revelation dialogue.'[102] The confusion that the Gospel of Mary causes about where it belongs demonstrates that texts cannot be pigeonholed. The Gospel of Mary is a gospel, a (revelation) dialogue, a dialogue gospel and an apocalypse.

Assigning a text to a genre does not render clear criteria or conclusions. If genre does act as an interpretative tool, as Burridge and Stanton among many others have suggested, then we need to reassess our understanding of genre, making it more elastic and expansive and recognizing the role of the scholar in assigning a genre to a text. The creation, delimitation and use of a 'dialogue gospel' genre brings out the distinctive features of the resulting group of texts, but it needs to remain open to intertextual links across the breadth of early Christian literature and beyond.

1.3 The Dialogue Gospels

On the definition adopted here, to be a 'dialogue gospel' a text must contain two things: (1) Jesus as revealer on the verge of

[99] Gerard P. Luttikhuizen, 'The Evaluation of the Teaching of Jesus in Christian Gnostic Revelation Dialogues', *NovT* 30.2 (1988): 163.

[100] Luttikhuizen, 'Evaluation of the Teaching of Jesus', 163–4.

[101] Fallon, 'Gnostic Apocalypses', 131.

[102] Italics inserted. Nicola Denzey Lewis, *Introduction to 'Gnosticism': Ancient Voices, Christian Worlds* (New York and Oxford: Oxford University Press, 2013), 269.

departure, and (2) dialogue with one or more disciples. These main characteristics can then be modified in various ways. This already rules out the Hypostasis of the Archons, Zostrianos and Allogenes, none of which has a revealer that is recognizably Jesus. The Second Apocalypse of James and the Gospel of Philip are also excluded due to their lack of dialogue.

For our purposes, thirteen main texts have been selected that fit these criteria.[103] The Johannine Farewell Discourse is almost certainly the earliest and the Pistis Sophia is probably the latest, but it is not possible to date the rest chronologically. Most scholars agree that the others can be dated to the late second to early third century, but the texts could easily be earlier or later.[104] The Johannine Farewell Discourse is unique as it is embedded in a longer text that narrates Jesus' ministry and death. It will be argued in the following chapter that it is the forerunner of the other dialogue gospels, but

[103] Those on the periphery include: (1) The Coptic Apocalypse of Peter (NHC 7,3), in which Christ and Peter discuss christology and Jesus' death in the Temple. The reason that it is placed on the periphery of dialogue gospels is that Peter only questions the Lord once. (2) The Books of Jeu (Bruce Codex) opens as a dialogue between the apostles and Jesus, but the majority of the text is an explanation of different treasuries (heavenly levels), with a picture on each page, and a gnostic hymn. (3) The Berlin-Strasbourg Apocryphon, once known as the 'Gospel of the Saviour' (P.Berl.22220), is an extremely fragmentary dialogue between the Saviour and his collective disciples before the passion. Sucui argues that it should be classified as a 'pseudo-apostolic memoir' written no earlier than the fifth century, Alin Suciu, *The Berlin-Strasbourg Apocryphon: A Coptic Apostolic Memoir*, WUNT 370 (Tübingen: Mohr Siebeck, 2017). Although the Berlin-Strasbourg Apocryphon shares features with the dialogue gospels, Suciu's reclassification of the text (as well as its fragmentary nature) preclude it from our discussion. (4) 'Fragments of a Dialogue between John and Jesus' is too fragmentary to classify as a dialogue gospel. (5) The Gospel of Thomas (NHC 2,1; POxy 1; POxy 654; POxy 655) is a collection of Jesus' sayings and questions-and-answers. However, only two of the logia (60, 61) contain more dialogue than a single question and answer. Although I propose an 'open' view of genre, lines need to be drawn somewhere; otherwise we might include the Gospel of Thomas 60, John 3 or the various short conversations in Mark 10. However, as none of these are premised on Jesus' departure, they will not be included in our genre.

[104] As many of these texts are only extant in Coptic but presumed to be translated from Greek, the dating is difficult. The editors of the collections of dialogue gospels are not very interested in the question of date, usually placing them somewhere between mid- to late second century and early third century (with the exceptions of the Johannine Farewell Discourse and the Pistis Sophia). The 'new philology' school prefers to read the Coptic texts as products of the fourth century, acknowledging that some may have been written then or have undergone considerable editing to reach the version that we have today, see e.g. Hugo Lundhaug, 'An Illusion of Textual Stability: Textual Fluidity, New Philology, and the Nag Hammadi Codices', in *Snapshots of Evolving Traditions: Jewish and Christian Manuscript Culture, Textual Fluidity, and New Philology*, ed. Liv Ingeborg Lied and Hugo Lundhaug, TU 175 (Berlin and Boston: de Gruyter, 2017), 20–54.

its context does not preclude it from being included in the genre. It encompasses the main elements of dialogue between Jesus and his disciples that deals with two key themes: Jesus' departure and how the community should act in his absence.

The following outlines are intended as a preliminary survey of these texts. In some cases, connections to other dialogue gospels will be drawn out. The Johannine Farewell Discourse will be first, as it stands at the beginning of the genre, but to underline the rhizomatic way of visualizing the texts within the genre, the rest will be arranged alphabetically in order to demonstrate a random approach.

(i) The ***Johannine Farewell Discourse*** (John 13.31–17.1) is at the same time a revelation dialogue, a farewell discourse and part of a *bios* gospel.[105] In 13.31, following Judas' exit, Jesus begins to speak about his own imminent departure, and a select group of disciples (Peter, Thomas, Philip and Judas 'not Iscariot') ask him about his destination and the possibility of following him there (13.36–37), the way he will take (14.5), the revelation of the Father (14.9), and his secret manifestation (14.22). Jesus answers their questions, also telling them about the eschatological dwelling place and promising them the coming of the paraclete. There is a narrative break at 14.31, in which Jesus says, 'Rise, let us be on our way' (Ἐγείρεσθε, ἄγωμεν ἐντεῦθεν), but a lengthy monologue follows. In the monologue, Jesus speaks about the vine, the Father, the disciples needing to abide in him, love, the hostility of the world, his departure and the paraclete. The cryptic saying, 'A little while and you will no longer see me, and again a little while and you will see me' (Μικρὸν καὶ οὐκέτι θεωρεῖτέ με, καὶ πάλιν μικρὸν καὶ ὄψεσθέ με [16.16]), prompts the disciples to ask what Jesus meant, also referring back to his earlier words about going to the Father (16.17–18). The disciples put these questions *to each other* (πρὸς ἀλλήλους [16.17]), however, being seemingly afraid to address them directly to Jesus although wishing to do so; but Jesus answers them anyway (16.19–24). He promises them that in the near future he will speak clearly about the Father, and the disciples then claim that he is *now* speaking openly and no longer in figures of speech (16.25–30). He finishes the dialogue by warning the disciples that they will face persecution in the world, but that he has

[105] There is debate on the unity and structure of the Johannine Farewell Discourse as at the end of chapter 14, Jesus says, 'Rise, let us be on our way' (Ἐγείρεσθε, ἄγωμεν ἐντεῦθεν [14.31]), but then continues to speak for another two chapters. For an overview of the various compositional theories, see Raymond E. Brown, *The Gospel According to John, XIII–XXI*, ABRL (New York: Yale University Press, 1970), 581–603.

conquered the world (16.33). The discourse finishes with a narratival interjection: 'After Jesus had spoken these things' (ταῦτα ἐλάλησεν Ἰησοῦς [17.1]).

(ii) The ***Apocalypse of Peter*** is missing from other lists of dialogue gospels, but it belongs here in view of the requests, questions or comments addressed to Jesus in its opening and closing sections – mostly stemming from Peter. It exists in two Greek fragments[106] and a longer Ethiopic version (in two manuscripts) that is thought to be a relatively reliable translation of the original text.[107] The temporal setting is not specified at the beginning, but a post-resurrection setting is assumed in view of Jesus' ascension at the end.[108] However, the ascension account in the Apocalypse of Peter seems closer to the transfiguration account than to the canonical resurrection appearances. For example, the final scene takes place on 'the holy mountain' (15.1), paralleling the transfiguration account in 2 Pet 1.18.[109]

The Ethiopic text begins with Christ on the Mount of Olives and the apostles asking him about the parousia, the eschaton and the mission. Jesus interprets the parable of the fig tree and declares that he will come again and that the dead will be resurrected to be judged. There follows a particularly vivid description of the fiery destruction and eternal torments for those who have fallen from faith or sinned. The punishments are specific to the crime – blasphemers are hung by their tongues, adulterers are hung up by their loins, those that lent money with interest are hung up by their knees, and disobedient

[106] Akhmim (P. Cair. 10759) and Rainer, see Thomas J. Kraus and Tobias Nicklas, *Das Petrusevangelium und die Petrusapokalypse: Die griechischen Fragmente mit deutscher und englischer Übersetzung* (Berlin and New York: de Gruyter, 2004).

[107] On the manuscripts of the Apocalypse of Peter, see Dennis D. Buchholz, *Your Eyes will be Opened: A Study of the Greek (Ethiopic) Apocalypse of Peter* (Atlanta, GA: Scholars Press, 1988), 119–55; Robert C. Helmer, '"That We May Know and Understand": Gospel Tradition in the Apocalypse of Peter' (Milwaukee, WI: PhD Thesis, Marquette University, 1998), 14–17.

[108] Helmer writes: 'Since the setting on the Mount of Olives for a post-resurrection dialogue is a common one among the apocryphal writings, it is probable that the chronological setting of Apoc. Pet, is likewise post-resurrection', Helmer, 'Gospel Tradition in the Apocalypse of Peter', 55. Also, Bauckham regards it as post-resurrection due to the ascension and the command to preach the gospels, Richard Bauckham, 'The Two Fig Tree Parables in the Apocalypse of Peter', *JBL* 104.2 (1985): 275. *Contra* Janssen who argues that the setting is unclear, Janssen, 'Mystagogus Gnosticus?', 128.

[109] For the parallels between the Apocalypse of Peter 15.1–16.1 and the transfiguration accounts in Matt 17.1–9, Mark 9.2–10, Luke 9.28–36 and 2 Pet 1.18, see Helmer, 'Gospel Tradition in the Apocalypse of Peter', 135–6. He concludes: 'The major difference is that in Apoc. Pet., it is not Jesus who is transfigured, but rather Moses and Elijah' (136).

slaves will chew their tongues forever. There are also birds that eat flesh and insomniac worms that eat entrails.

Jesus then leads the apostles to a second mountain, where, in the Akhmim MS only, the Twelve ask to meet one of the deceased righteous ones. In the Greek, Jesus reveals heaven before hell. In both the Greek and Ethiopic, two of the righteous appear in a beautiful and radiant form. In the Ethiopic version, they are named as Moses and Elijah. Peter asks Jesus where the others are (named Abraham, Isaac and Jacob in the Ethiopic), and he shows him a paradisiacal garden. The ending is only preserved in the Ethiopic, in which Jesus ascends with Moses and Elijah. The disciples descend the mountain, praising God who has written the names of the righteous in heaven in the book of life.

(iii) The ***Apocryphon of James*** (NHC 1,2) is a letter penned by James to an unknown recipient,[110] containing a revelation that Jesus disclosed to James and Peter in secret. James writes that the revelation should not be communicated to many people; in fact, it is so covert that Jesus did not want all of his twelve disciples to receive it, and James has encrypted it by using the Hebrew alphabet. However, those who receive it and believe will be saved. James begins the story with the Twelve recalling and writing what the Saviour had taught them 'whether in secret or openly' (ⲉⲓⲧⲉ ⲙ̄ⲡⲉⲧⲑⲏⲡ· ⲉⲓⲧⲉ ⲙ̄ⲡⲉⲧⲟⲩⲁⲛϩ̄ [2,13–14]). While James writes, Jesus appears. He tells the Twelve that only those who are filled can enter the kingdom of heaven, and he takes James and Peter aside to 'fill them' (ⲙⲁϩⲟⲩ [2,35]). The ensuing text is a dialogue between Jesus and James and Peter, with instruction about being filled and lacking, believing in the cross, an exhortation to martyrdom and parables about the kingdom of heaven.

Following the dialogue, Jesus departs, and James and Peter send their hearts up to heaven, presumably to follow him. The other disciples, apparently witnessing this, call to Peter and James, asking what Jesus said and where he went. The interruption from the other disciples causes James and Peter to come back down to earth; they never reach the highest heaven, described here as 'the Majesty'. James and Peter explain that Jesus showed them a future generation of believers who will surpass and save them. The other disciples do not appreciate this, and James disperses them around the world,

[110] There is a lacuna where the name of the recipient would have stood: [----]ⲑⲟⲥ. Williams (among others) suggests Cerinthus, F. E. Williams, 'The Apocryphon of James (I, 2)', in *The Nag Hammadi Library in English*, ed. James M. Robinson (Leiden and New York: Brill, 1996), 29–31.

while he goes to Jerusalem praying that he will participate in the salvation of the generation to come.

The Apocryphon of James refers to another 'apocryphon' that James has sent the recipient, one that Jesus revealed to James alone (as opposed to James and Peter). There are several instances in which the Apocryphon of James refers to a past revelation from Jesus to James (1,28–35; 8,31–36; 13,38–14,1). In 8,31–36, this previous revelation was about salvation, James' succession and what to say before the archons. Hartenstein suggests that the Apocryphon of James is referring to the First Apocalypse of James: in both texts, James is the guarantor of a tradition that propagates martyrdom and a tradition that sees the Twelve as lesser than James, and knowledge of the First Apocalypse of James is the only way to make sense of these statements in the Apocryphon of James.[111] If she is correct, then James must be a composite James, as he appears to be the James who belongs to the Twelve in the Apocryphon of James (1,23–25), but James is the brother of Jesus in the First Apocalypse of James (NHC 24,13–14). Perkins, however, argues that in spite of these connections, 'the picture of martyrdom and of the death of Christ in ApocryJas comes from a different and more orthodox tradition than that behind [the First Apocalypse of James]'.[112] Without closer analysis, all that can be said is that these two James texts have close connections in the intertextual web of gospel literature, while interpreting shared traditions in different ways and even applying them to different James-characters.

(iv) The ***Apocryphon of John*** (NHC 2,1; NHC 3,1; NHC 4,1; BG 2) is a dialogue between the risen Saviour and John, son of Zebedee, which is preserved in four versions – two short (NHC 3; BG) and two long (NHC 2; NHC 4).[113] It is considered 'one of the most coherent and

[111] Hartenstein, *Die zweite Lehre*, 229–32. Because of this, she argues that whereas the other dialogue gospels know and use the canonical gospels, the Apocryphon of James represents a third stage in that it knows the canonical texts *and* later dialogue gospels (232). This could also be said for the Pistis Sophia and also perhaps any dialogue gospel that refers to the Sophia myth.

[112] Perkins, *Gnostic Dialogue*, 147. See also Pheme Perkins, 'Johannine Traditions in Ap. Jas. (NHC 1,2)', *JBL* 101.3 (1982): 403.

[113] The two copies of the longer version are virtually identical, whereas the two copies of the shorter version have substantive variants. The longer versions include a lengthy citation from the *Book of Zoroaster* and a concluding monologue from 'Pronoia: Forethought'. The three versions in the Nag Hammadi Codices each appear at the beginning of their respective codex, potentially demonstrating the text's importance, see Williams, *Rethinking 'Gnosticism'*, 235–62, 306–10. The version in BG follows the Gospel of Mary.

comprehensive narrations of the revelatory account traditionally labelled as "Gnostic"'.[114]

The text begins with an introductory scene, set in the Temple, with a Pharisee telling John that the 'Nazorene' has deceived him and turned him away from the traditions of his fathers. An upset John leaves the Temple and goes to a mountain, where the risen Jesus appears to him in three forms – a child, old person and servant. Jesus announces that he has come to teach John '[what] is and [what was] and what will come to pass, that you [may know] the things that are not manifest [and the things that are] manifest, and to teach you about the Perfect [Man]' (ⲧ[ⲉⲛⲟⲩ ⲁⲉⲓⲉⲓ] ⲉⲧⲟⲩⲛⲟⲩⲉⲓⲁⲧⲕ ⲉⲃ̣[ⲟⲗ ϫⲉ ⲟⲩ ⲡⲉ]ⲧϣⲟⲟⲡ ⲁⲩⲱ ⲟⲩ ⲡⲉ̣[ⲛⲧⲁϥϣⲱ]ⲡⲉ ⲁⲩⲱ ⲟⲩ ⲡⲉⲧⲉϣ̣[ϣⲉ ⲉⲧⲣⲉϥ]ϣⲱⲡⲉ ϫⲉⲕⲁⲁⲥ ⲉⲕ̣[ⲉⲉⲓⲙⲉ ⲉ]ⲛⲓⲁⲧⲛⲁⲩ (ⲉ) ⲉⲣⲟⲟⲩ ⲙ[ⲛⲛ ⲛⲉⲧⲟⲩ̇]ⲛⲁⲩ ⲉⲣⲟⲟⲩ ⲁⲩⲱ ⲉⲧ[ⲟⲩⲛⲉⲓⲁⲧⲕ] ⲉⲃⲟⲗ ⲉⲧⲃⲉ ⲡⲓⲧⲉⲗⲓ[ⲟⲥ ⲛⲣⲱⲙⲉ] [$_{\text{BG}}$ 22,2–9]). John does not ask a question directly, but simply asks to know it, and the subsequent revelation includes a lengthy monologue from Jesus that explains the transcendent deity as the source of everything; his emanation of a chain of aeons (or light beings) including Sophia and Christ; the birth of Yaldabaoth, begotten from Sophia without a consort, resulting in a monstrous form and jealous nature; and an alternative version of Gen 1–9, retelling the early history of humankind as being entombed in material bodies.[115] This includes the famous boast: 'I am a jealous God, and there is no other God beside me' (ⲁⲛⲟⲕ ⲁⲛⲕ ⲟⲩⲛⲟⲩⲧⲉ ⲛ̄ⲣⲉϥ ⲕⲱϩ ⲁⲩⲱ ⲙⲛ̄ ⲕⲉⲛⲟⲩⲧⲉ ⲛ̄ⲥⲁⲃⲗ̄ⲗⲁï [$_{\text{NHC2}}$ 13,8–9]), to which the narrator responds, 'If there were no other God over him, of whom would he be jealous?' (ⲉⲛⲉⲙ̅ⲛ̅ ⲕⲉⲟⲩⲁ ⲅⲁⲣ ϣⲟⲟⲡ ⲛⲉ ⲛⲓⲙ ⲡⲉⲧϥⲛⲁⲕⲱϩ ⲉⲣⲟϥ [$_{\text{NHC2}}$ 13,12–13]). Yaldabaoth and the archons make various attempts to detain and deceive humanity, which results in countermoves from the heavens to rescue humanity.[116] In this extensive protological discourse, John intervenes only three times ($_{\text{BG}}$ 45,6–7; 58,1–3, 14–15),

[114] Zlatko Pleše, *Poetics of the Gnostic Universe: Narrative and Cosmology in the Apocryphon of John*, NHMS 52 (Leiden and Boston: Brill, 2006), 1. Turner calls the Apocryphon of John '[t]he Sethian Revelation *par excellence*', John D. Turner, *Sethian Gnosticism and the Platonic Tradition*, BCNH:E 6 (Québec: Les Presses de l'Université Laval, 2001), 69.

[115] A useful chart showing the levels of existence in the cosmological narrative can be found in Karen L. King, *The Secret Revelation of John* (Cambridge, MA and London: Harvard University Press, 2006), 87. King's description and analysis of the narrative of the Apocryphon of John is helpful. She splits the text into four parts: the ideal (the divine realm), the problem (rupture), the result (the situation of humanity in the world) and the solution (salvation), see 85–156.

[116] King sees the Apocryphon of John as a series of 'Moves and Countermoves', King, *Secret Revelation of John*, 96–7.

and at every point it is to ask a question of clarification regarding a teaching from the Jewish scriptures.

The section that follows takes a dialogue form and deals with eschatological issues (BG 64,13–71,5). John asks questions about the fate of different souls, in both terms of protology (whether the spirit entered them) and morality (whether they did evil). The Saviour's answers here are not much longer than John's questions. To John's final question on the counterfeit spirit, Jesus offers another long speech regarding Yaldabaoth and the creation of ignorance and fate, with reference to Noah and the archons procreating with human women.

(v) The ***Book of Thomas*** (NHC 2,7) is a dialogue between Jesus and Judas Thomas, who is described as Jesus' 'twin' (ⲥⲟⲉⲓϣ [138,8]). The text is ascribed to Mathaias, who was listening to the conversation between the two of them. The dialogue has no narrative frame, but the reference to Jesus' impending ascension in 138,23 indicates that it is set after Jesus' resurrection. Thomas requests that Jesus tell him about the hidden and invisible things so he can preach them. The central concern in the dialogue is with asceticism: Jesus teaches Judas Thomas that the elect must abandon the fiery passions of the bestial body that destroy the soul. The body is part of the visible cosmos, and it is only through an ascetic life that one can find truth of the invisible heavenly world. The dialogue moves onto a monologue about coming judgement, heaven and hell, including woes and beatitudes, and polemic against non-ascetic Christians who have 'baptized … [their] souls in the water of darkness' (ⲁⲧⲉⲧⲛ̄ⲱⲙⲥ̄ … ⲛ̄ⲯⲩⲭⲏ ϩⲙ̄ ⲡⲙⲟⲟⲩ ⲙ̄ⲡⲕⲁⲕ[ⲉ] [144,1]).

(vi) The ***Dialogue of the Saviour*** (NHC 3,5) is primarily a dialogue between Jesus and three named disciples, Matthew, Judas and Mary; however, a larger group of disciples appears at certain points. The very fragmentary text has no narrative frame and so there is no reference to the time or location of the dialogue. A main point within the discourse is Jesus opening the way (ϩⲓⲏ [120,24]) to the heavenly world, which reflects the Johannine reference to him as the ὁδός (14.6); thus the Dialogue of the Saviour may be intended as a farewell discourse.[117] The text begins with a monologue from the Saviour, teaching about 'rest' and how to overcome the archons, as well as prayer to the Father. Four pages in, the dialogue begins, with Jesus

[117] Létourneau sees it as a farewell discourse in the Johannine model with an ambiguous chronological location, Pierre Létourneau, *Le Dialogue du Sauveur (NH III,5)*, BCNH:T 29 (Louvain: Peeters, 2003), 15. Pagels and Koester argue that it is not possible to determine whether it is meant to be a pre- or post-resurrection

answering the disciples' questions. In the dialogue, we find a Genesis-based creation myth (with the highest Father as creator). There is also a fragment of an apocalyptic vision of the Son of Man, heaven, and hell, which the Saviour shows to Judas, Mary and Matthew.

(vii) The ***Epistle of Peter to Philip*** ($_{\text{NHC}}$ 8,2; $_{\text{CT}}$ 1) consists of an epistolary opening, meetings of the apostles, their dialogue with Christ, several appearances of Jesus and a Pentecost scene. The opening has Peter inviting Philip to rejoin the apostles following a separation, and when Philip receives the letter, he gladly consents. After this point, there is no reference to the letter, and the text does not conclude in epistolary form.

The group of apostles gather on the mountain, where they pray to the Father of light as well as the Son of life and immortality. Jesus appears as a voice emanating from a form of light. The apostles take their chance to ask him about cosmology, the human condition and salvation. Their questions are presented as a unit, in a block quote. Jesus answers with a short paraphrase of a Sophia myth and explains that he is the fullness and was sent down to the world where he was not recognized (cf. John 1.1–18).[118] The apostles then ask how to overcome the archons that fight the inner man and Jesus responds. Jesus' revelation is not new; on three occasions he reminds the disciples that they have already heard this information.

The Epistle of Peter to Philip's narrative frame is unusual in including multiple appearances of Jesus with narrative in between. After the first dialogue, he is taken up into heaven with a clap of thunder and a bolt of lightning, and the apostles begin to return to Jerusalem. While they are on the road, they discuss suffering, and Jesus appears again as a voice to tell them that their suffering is necessary. He responds to the apostles' discussion, but they do not engage in conversation with him. After this second epiphany, the disciples heal a crowd and teach in the Temple. Peter is filled with the Holy Spirit and preaches a sermon on Jesus' incarnation, crucifixion and resurrection.[119] The apostles then separate. The third and final epiphany in the letter occurs after the apostles have gathered again.

dialogue, but that it is 'best seen as a compilation of various sources and traditions, or as the elaboration and expansion of an older dialogue', Helmut Koester and Elaine Pagels, 'Introduction', in *Nag Hammadi Codex III, 5: The Dialogue of the Savior*, NHMS 26 (Leiden: Brill, 1984), 1.

[118] The Sophia myth is not fully or comprehensively explained, which may imply that the audience would have been familiar with it.

[119] Meyer notes the christological tension in Peter's sermon as he affirms the Passion of Christ whilst professing his divinity that is able to transcend suffering, Meyer, *Letter of Peter to Philip*, 156.

Jesus greets them with peace and instructs them to depart without fear, telling them that he will be with them forever. Here, he is not responding to any questions or anxieties. The apostles then leave each other, going out to preach the gospel.

(viii) The ***Epistula Apostolorum*** exists as a full text in a number of Ethiopic manuscripts, a partial version in a Coptic MS and a small Latin fragment. The gospel begins with a short epistolary greeting from the eleven apostles writing to the churches of the world, followed by a creed-like passage and a short description of miracles performed by the incarnate Lord. The authors declare that the letter was written because of Simon and Cerinthus, the enemies of Jesus, and this is followed by a confessional declaration that the Lord was crucified by Pontius Pilate and Archelaus, and buried.[120] Then, the Easter story begins: Mary (or Sarah in Ethiopic), Martha and Mary Magdalene go to the empty tomb, and Jesus appears. He instructs the women to tell the apostles that he has risen, but the male disciples do not believe them. Together with the women, Jesus himself now visits the disciples, who touch him and are persuaded that he is not a ghost. At 12.3, the revelatory dialogue starts. From this point on, the women are long forgotten – presumably they are not present, but their departure is not narrated. The sizeable dialogue comprises a number of questions from the apostles, who always feature as a unified 'we', on topics including the incarnation, the parousia, the judgement, mission, keeping commandments, and an interpretation of the story of the ten virgins. The text concludes with an account of Jesus' ascension.

The Epistula Apostolorum is often seen as 'different' to other dialogue gospels. It has been viewed as a 'proto-orthodox' dialogue gospel that adopted the genre from 'gnostics' in order to criticize them.[121] The claim that the text polemizes against 'gnostics' is based on its opposition to the arch-heretics Simon and Cerinthus, and

[120] The Coptic passage runs: 'This one [to whom we] bear witness is the Lord, who was [crucifi]ed by Pontius Pilate [and A]rchelaus between the two robbe[r]s [and wa]s buried in a place which is called [Sku]ll' (9.1). This follows the apostles' comment on the reason for writing.

[121] Klauck, *Apocryphal Gospels*, 159. Others who think that the Epistula Apostolorum borrowed the genre to combat its opponents include Manfred Hornschuh, *Studien zur Epistula Apostolorum*, Patristische Texte und Studien 5 (Berlin: de Gruyter, 1965), 4–8; Ron Cameron, *The Other Gospels: Non-Canonical Gospel Texts* (Philadelphia, PA: Westminster John Knox Press, 1982), 131–2; J. K. Elliott, *The Apocryphal New Testament: A Collection of Apocryphal Christian Literature in an English Translation* (Oxford: Oxford University Press, 2005), 555; Bruce M. Metzger, *The Canon of the New Testament: Its Origin, Development and*

the fact that the first virgin to be locked out of heaven is named ⲅⲛⲱⲥⲓⲥ (43.16).[122] Yet the Epistula Apostolorum also includes typically 'gnostic' elements, such as the Ogdoad and a cosmology that includes multiple heavens.[123] While the argument that the Epistula Apostolorum consciously used the dialogue gospel form against its 'gnostic' creators might be standard opinion, there is little sign that the Epistula Apostolorum has a greater polemical purpose than other texts within the genre.

(ix) The ***First Apocalypse of James*** (NHC 5,3; CT 2) recounts two dialogues between Jesus and James, described as non-physical brothers, followed by a lengthy explanation that Jesus' teaching is to be kept secret for several generations. The first dialogue is set before Jesus' crucifixion, and the second half after his resurrection. There is no narrative to commence the text, but the setting is explained through the narrative passage in which Jesus departs, James mourns, comforts his disciples and prays, and Jesus returns. This is complemented by narrative at the end, in which James is arrested and stoned. Jesus' death is not narrated but referred to in the dialogue.

The topics of conversation are mostly the same before and after Jesus' death and resurrection. These include God (the pre-existent One), femaleness (Sophia and the seven female disciples) and cosmology (a body of seventy-two archons), but the key theme throughout both dialogues is James' concern about his own impending suffering at the hands of both the earthly rulers and the heavenly toll-collectors who demand souls. Jesus instructs James how to attain eschatological salvation by telling the toll-collectors that he belongs to the pre-existent Father. The two dialogues include a number of questions from James, most of which Jesus answers straightforwardly.

The Codex Tchacos recension, published several decades after the Nag Hammadi version, reveals a third revelatory section (one hidden behind lacunae in the Nag Hammadi text), which states that the revelation is to be handed down to Addai, then to Manael, then to Levi and finally to Levi's son who will finally communicate it to

Significance (Oxford: Clarendon Press, 1989), 182. *Contra* Bauckham who argues that the 'discourse of the risen Christ to his disciples was a popular genre among the writers of post-canonical Gospel material and was used by orthodox writers as well as (and probably before) Gnostic writers', Bauckham, 'Two Fig Tree Parables', 276.

[122] On the virgin named 'gnosis' and other possible instances of polemic throughout the text, see Hartenstein, *Die zweite Lehre*, 103–4.

[123] See esp. Hartenstein, *Die zweite Lehre*, 105–7.

others.[124] James plays no part in this succession discourse, but he then asks three questions about the seven women and spirits of prophecy. The text concludes with a narrative about James preaching to the disciples and then being arrested and killed.

(x) The ***Gospel of Mary*** ($_{BG}$ 1, POxy 3525; PRyl 463) begins following six missing pages that once opened the Berlin Codex. The first page of the extant text opens with a conversation between Peter (and presumably other disciples) and the Saviour about matter, nature and sin. A page later, after a short self-contained 'farewell discourse', Jesus departs, and Mary arises to take his place. She comforts the weeping disciples, who are identified as Peter, Andrew and Levi, allaying their fears about potential persecution and reminding them that Jesus will protect them. As the male disciples debate the interpretation of Jesus' words, Mary responds to a request from Peter by recounting how 'the Lord' appeared to her in a vision, in which he responded to her questions about the vision and taught her about the ascent of the personified soul through hostile cosmic powers. Following another four-page hiatus and the finale of the recollection of vision, the narrative frame continues and Peter and Andrew challenge Mary's teaching. Previously silent Levi jumps in to defend her, belittling Peter and ultimately reminding them all of the Saviour's instructions to preach the gospel. The text ends with disciples going out to fulfil those instructions, though there is considerable ambiguity regarding who is included in the group. (See the analysis of the interpretative and textual issues in Chapter 3.)

(xi) The ***Gospel of Judas*** ($_{CT}$ 3) is a 'secret discourse' (λογο[ς] ετϩηπ [33,1]) that Jesus reveals to Judas shortly before Judas betrays him. The text opens with a short summary of Jesus' activity on the earth but depicts part of this activity as appearing in different forms and passing freely between the heavens and earth. Then a setting is specified: in Judea, Jesus finds the disciples gathered together. It is unclear whether Jesus arrives in a 'divine appearance' as such.[125] The disciples and Jesus engage in dialogue, and Jesus laughs at the Twelve for their foolish interpretation of the eucharist and tells them that they do not understand his true identity. Namely, he is not the son of 'their God', and they are not from the immortal holy race. As in the Apocryphon

[124] Not a lot of scholarship on the First Apocalypse of James has been published since CT has been available to us.

[125] According to Gathercole, Jesus came to the disciples in a 'sudden and mysterious appearance', Simon Gathercole, *The Gospel of Judas: Rewriting Early Christianity* (Oxford and New York: Oxford University Press, 2007), 67.

of James and the First Apocalypse of James, Jesus proclaims that the apostolic generation will not understand him.

Judas recognizes Jesus' true identity, and so Jesus takes him aside and answers his cosmological and eschatological questions about the holy race and personal eschatology. Jesus reveals a cosmological myth featuring the holy and imperishable race of Seth. At the end of the text, either Judas or Jesus ascends into a cloud,[126] and then Judas betrays Jesus to the Jewish authorities for money. After the publication of the Gospel of Judas in 2006, there was debate over whether the gospel narrated Judas as saved or damned (depending partly on whether Jesus or Judas ascended into the cloud).[127] It is now generally accepted that Judas was subject to a negative fate.[128]

(xii) The ***Pistis Sophia*** (Askew Codex) is a post-resurrection dialogue in which the risen Jesus has spent eleven years explaining the mysteries to the disciples. At the beginning, Jesus tells them that he had previously taught only in general terms and that there were many things he had not explained. The Pistis Sophia consists of four 'books', separated by titles on the MS.[129] The first two books mostly comprise an account of the repentances of the Pistis Sophia, largely told through interpretation of Psalms. The disciples ask Jesus a number of questions, but also answer questions themselves through their recollection or interpretation of Psalms, the Psalms of Solomon and the Odes of Solomon. Books Three and Four contain Jesus answering the questions of his disciples, with a focus on the different levels of salvation for different souls. The afterlife souls will

126 Ambiguities regarding the ascension will be discussed in Chapter 2.

127 The disagreement over whether Judas was saved or damned, and whether Jesus instructed Judas to betray him, has resulted in a number of publications on this work – perhaps more than any in the Nag Hammadi Codices or Berlin Codex, barring the Gospel of Thomas. Unfortunately, the other texts in Codex Tchacos have been somewhat neglected.

128 For example, April D. DeConick, ed., *The Codex Judas Papers: Proceedings of the International Congress on the Tchacos Codex Held at Rice University, Houston, Texas, March 13–16, 2008*, NHMS 71 (Leiden and Boston: Brill, 2009); Lance Jenott, *The Gospel of Judas: Coptic Text, Translation, and Historical Interpretation of 'the Betrayer's Gospel'*, STAC 64 (Tübingen: Mohr Siebeck, 2011); Nicola Denzey Lewis, *Cosmology and Fate in Gnosticism and Graeco-Roman Antiquity: Under Pitiless Skies*, NHMS 81 (Leiden and Boston: Brill, 2013).

129 As in Carl Schmidt, *Pistis Sophia*, trans. Violet MacDermot, NHMS 4 (Leiden: Brill, 1978), xiv. Evans challenges the assumption that there were four books, writing that 'Schmidt's fourth book has a lacuna of eight pages, and the contents, themes, and even assumed cosmologies differ dramatically before and after the gap, suggesting they are parts of separate works', Erin Evans, *The Books of Jeu and the Pistis Sophia as Handbooks to Eternity: Exploring the Gnostic Mysteries of the Ineffable*, NHMS 89 (Leiden and Boston: Brill, 2015), 95.

attain depends on which mysteries they had been initiated into and whether they continued to sin. Book Four opens with a ritual prayer of Jesus after his resurrection and includes prayer and ritual alongside dialogue.[130] Throughout the books, there is a heavy emphasis on forgiveness of sins and the sacraments.

The Pistis Sophia is usually dated later than other dialogue gospels, and it is only on the basis of its late date that Hartenstein excludes it from her analysis, despite acknowledging that it is an 'appearance dialogue'.[131] At four books, it is also much longer than other dialogue gospels, and at points it can be rather obscure and extremely repetitive. Burkitt goes as far as to call it a 'dreary Egyptian book'![132] But in my opinion, it adds volumes to our understanding of the ways in which early Christians conceived of their world, and it should be referred to much more frequently in such discussions.[133] The Pistis Sophia is particularly interesting for the intertextual relationship between dialogue gospels and canonical texts as it contains quotations from Matthew, Luke and Romans, as well as numerous Psalms, Isaiah, and the Psalms and Odes of Solomon. Furthermore, it has connections to other texts within the dialogue gospel genre, including a variation of the Sophia myth of the Apocryphon of John (where Sophia repents – although in the Pistis Sophia she belongs to the material cosmos) and Andrew's incomprehension of the ascent of the soul, as in the Gospel of Mary.

(xiii) The ***Sophia of Jesus Christ*** ($_{\text{NHC}}$ 3,4; $_{\text{BG}}$ 3; POxy 1081[134]) opens with the twelve disciples and seven women on a mountain in Galilee,

[130] Evans understands the first part of Book Four as 'serv[ing] as a preparatory tool for someone about to undergo the first baptism', Evans, *The Books of Jeu and the Pistis Sophia*, 96.

[131] Hartenstein, *Die zweite Lehre*, 12, 257. *Contra* Bockmuehl who writes that it 'does not present itself as a gospel', presumably because it is instead an 'elaborate disquisition about gnostic mythology', although he does not offer further explanation, Bockmuehl, *Ancient Apocryphal Gospels*, 194. It is unclear why Bockmuehl would categorize the Gospel of Philip as a 'post-resurrection discourse gospel' but not the Pistis Sophia.

[132] F. C. Burkitt, 'Pistis Sophia Again', *JTS* 26.104 (1925): 391.

[133] With me on this is van der Vliet: 'The neglect of the *Pistis Sophia* is one of the riddles of modern Gnostic studies. W. C. van Unnik's authoritative opinion that in the *Pistis Sophia* "nicht nur Wahnsinn vorliegt, wie es beim oberflächlichen Lesen den Anschein hat" and that rather "man durch sorgfältige Einzelexegese Einblicke bekommt in die Bildung gnostischer Systeme" has hardly met with any response. Nevertheless, this compendious volume of Christian Gnostic teaching is a treasure-trove of ideas on soteriology, cosmology, eschatology and biblical exegesis', Jacques van der Vliet, 'Fate, Magic and Astrology in Pistis Sophia, Chaps 15–21', in *The Wisdom of Egypt: Jewish, Early Christian and Gnostic Essays in Honour of Gerard P. Luttikhuizen*, ed. A. Hilhorst and G. H. van Kooten, AGJU 59 (Leiden and Boston: Brill, 2005), 519–20.

[134] The two Coptic MSS are fairly similar but BG has more preserved.

wondering about the universe, the arrangement (ⲟⲓⲕⲟⲛⲟⲙⲓⲁ) of the cosmos, the powers and the Saviour. The Saviour appears in a form of great light that only pure, perfect flesh could bear, and he greets them with his peace. Five named disciples – Philip, Matthew, Thomas, Mary and Bartholomew – or his disciples as a collective, ask him short questions including about the make-up of the cosmos and their own origins. In contrast to the short questions, the Saviour gives lengthy replies, explaining the intricate and detailed cosmic structure, the deficiency of philosophers, the nature of truth, the One who is Ineffable, the perishable and the imperishable, Yaldabaoth and the cosmos, and the disciples' origins and salvation. Jesus explains a threefold pantheon: the transcendent God (which is the focus of the first part), Man (representing both saved and fallen humanity), and the Son of Man–Christ.[135] The dialogue leaves no room for narratival interjections, until the end, when having their questions answered, the disciples go out with joy to preach the gospel.[136]

1.4 Eschatology and the Saviour

Our thirteen texts share a number of commonalities and differences, and any point can connect to any other point. Here, we will discuss how the concepts of the Saviour and eschatology are employed throughout the genre. This is where the rhizomatic image is of particular importance: dialogue gospels demonstrate a network of connections that are non-linear, non-bifurcated, non-homogenous and non-hierarchical.

[135] As suggested by René Falkenberg, 'Matthew 28:16–20 and the Nag Hammadi Library: Reception of the Great Commission in the Sophia of Jesus Christ', in *Mark and Matthew II: Comparative Readings, Reception History, Cultural Hermeneutics, and Theology*, ed. Eve-Marie Becker and Anders Runesson, WUNT 304 (Tübingen: Mohr Siebeck, 2013), 99–100. Man and the Father are merged into one divinity.

[136] The usual conversation around the Sophia of Jesus Christ presupposes that it is a Christian narrative frame imposed on the non-Christian dialogue Eugnostos (NHC 3,3; 5,1). The short questions posed by the disciples only serve to move the narrative along, and nothing would be lost without the appearance, the disciples or Jesus' departure. However, the supposition concerning the manner in which the Sophia of Jesus Christ has been 'imposed' on Eugnostos may be too simplistic, and an alternative to the simplistic 'christianization' argument is seeing Christ as fulfilling the role of 'the interpreter who was sent' (ⲡⲣⲉϥⲃⲱⲗ ⲛ̄ⲧⲁⲩⲧⲁⲟⲩⲟϥ [BG 94,16–17]) in Eugnostos, as suggested in D. M. Parrott, *Nag Hammadi Codices III,3–4 and V,1, with Papyrus Berolinensis 8502,3 and Oxyrhynchus Papyrus 1081: Eugnostos and the Sophia of Jesus Christ* (Leiden and New York: Brill, 1991), 4. Hartenstein, however, is hesitant to identify the 'interpreter' with Christ, Hartenstein, *Die zweite Lehre*, 38 n. 22. The 'christianization' assumption may need to be readdressed, but this is not my purpose here, and we will not deal further with Eugnostos.

The overlaps and connections in their teachings demonstrate how problematic it is to taxonomize these texts into particular theological groups. This is meant to be a preliminary comparative survey of these main themes, and it is far from my intention to present a comprehensive analysis of these themes in all thirteen texts. The broad, sweeping overviews are intended only to show the diversity at the point of commonality within the genre and that the dialogue gospel genre cannot and should not be thought to display only linear patterns.

The Saviour

The whole point of a dialogue with Jesus is for him to impart knowledge to his disciples. Dialogue gospels see knowledge as a means of salvation, whether it be knowledge of one's origins, knowledge of how to act properly or knowledge that Jesus is revealer and Saviour. And thus, the texts' soteriological messages are interwoven with the genre. However, although each dialogue gospel is centred around Jesus as Saviour, it is not a given that every depiction of Jesus was remotely the same. Each gospel, both canonical and non-canonical, offers a new interpretation of Jesus.[137] In Chapter 2, we will look at the differences in the portrayal of the appearance of Jesus, but here we will focus on christological titles.

Christological titles are often used to denote Jesus' identity: he is the Christ, the Lord, the Saviour and the Son of God. Dialogue gospels, in general, predominately use the names Saviour and Lord, with Jesus (Christ) being comparatively rare. ⲥⲱⲧⲏⲣ and ϫⲟⲉⲓⲥ are generally employed in *dialogue*, particularly in the introductory formulae 'the Saviour said' and 'the Lord said'. As examples, the two names are alternated in the Dialogue of the Saviour, the Epistula Apostolorum, the Sophia of Jesus Christ, the Apocalypse of Peter (alongside Jesus Christ) and the Book of Thomas (alongside Jesus). The First Apocalypse of James does not use Saviour at all, only Lord

[137] As Watson writes: 'As Luke indicates to Theophilus, each attempt to write the gospel represents a new answer to the question who Jesus is on the assumption that the answers embodied in earlier gospels are either inadequate or misleading', Francis Watson, *Gospel Writing: A Canonical Perspective* (Grand Rapids, MI and Cambridge: Eerdmans, 2013), 8. Conversely, Perkins argues that '[t]he Nag Hammadi writings have developed their picture of the Savior from traditions quite different from those which underlie New Testament christological assertions', Pheme Perkins, 'Gnostic Christologies and the New Testament', *CBQ* 43.4 (1981): 606. However, King points out that the Saviour in 'gnostic' texts is depicted in radically different ways, Karen L. King, *What Is Gnosticism?* (Cambridge, MA: Harvard University Press, 2005), 208–10.

(and Rabbi as an address). The Pistis Sophia, by far the longest of the dialogue gospels, uses Jesus and Saviour alternately in Book Three, whereas in Books One and Four he is Jesus, and in Book Two he is generally called the First Mystery but Jesus at the end.

The title Lord is very common in early Christian literature and multifaceted in meaning;[138] however, the title Saviour has been mistakenly associated with 'gnostic' ideology. This most likely stems from Irenaeus' rebuke of the so-called gnostics' preference for Saviour ('For this reason, they say, the Saviour – they refuse to call him Lord – spent thirty years without doing anything in public' [*Adv. Haer.* 1.1.3]) and has led certain scholars to incorrectly assume that texts that employ this title are 'gnostic'. For example, POxy 840 is similar to the canonical gospels in style and tone and deals with an encounter between the Saviour and a Pharisee about ritual cleanliness and baptism; it is just a small fragment of a text but uses σωτήρ exclusively. Bovon argued that this christological title was evidence of intra-Christian polemic, writing that the 'use of the title Savior and the absence of the name Jesus suggest a location for the fragment within a Gnostic or Manichaean milieu using apocryphal tradition'.[139] However, the title Saviour occurs throughout a wide range of early Christian literature, and in numerous texts that we might imagine Irenaeus would have approved of. As well as the Epistula Apostolorum and the Apocalypse of Peter, Ignatius frequently refers to Jesus Christ as Saviour,[140] and Justin hardly shies away from it, telling us that 'the name Jesus in the Hebrew language means Σωτήρ in the Greek tongue' (*1 Apol.* 33.7).[141] The 'Saviour' title then need

[138] See Larry W. Hurtado, *Lord Jesus Christ: Devotion to Jesus in Earliest Christianity* (Grand Rapids, MI and Cambridge: Eerdmans, 2003), 108–17; Ferdinand Hahn, *The Titles of Jesus in Christology: Their History in Early Christianity*, trans. Harold Knight and George Ogg, Library of Theological Translations (Cambridge: James Clarke Co., 2002), 68–128; Wilhelm Bousset, *Kyrios Christos: A History of the Belief in Christ from the Beginnings of Christianity to Irenaeus*, trans. John E. Steely, 5th ed. (Nashville, TN and New York: Abingdon Press, 1970), 121–52.

[139] François Bovon, 'Fragment Oxyrhynchus 840, Fragment of a Lost Gospel, Witness of an Early Christian Controversy over Purity', *JBL* 119.4 (2000): 728. *Contra* Kazen who argues against POxy 840 being closer to Christian 'gnostic' or Manichaean ideas than the synoptics and Jewish texts regarding purity. See Thomas Kazen, 'Sectarian Gospels for Some Christians? Intention and Mirror Reading in the Light of Extra-Canonical Texts', *NTS* 51.4 (2005): 575. Kruger simply argues that this title places the gospel in the second century, Michael J. Kruger, *The Gospel of the Savior: An Analysis of P.Oxy. 840 and Its Place in the Gospel Traditions of Early Christianity*, TENT 1 (Leiden: Brill, 2005), esp. 203–4.

[140] Epistles to the *Ephesians* 1.1; *Magnesians* 1.1; *Philadelphians* 9.2; *Smyrnaeans* 7.1.

[141] Furthermore, 2 Peter and the Pastoral Epistles employ it frequently (2 Pet 1.1, 11; 2.20; 3.2, 18; Tit 1.3, 4; 2.10, 13; 3.4, 6; 1 Tim 1.1; 2.3; 4.10 and 2 Tim 1.10).

not imply any particular theology. It is more appropriate to suggest that the title refers to Jesus' *saving* capacity – through his death and resurrection in the case of Ignatius, through purity in the case of POxy 840 and through revelation in the case of dialogue gospels such as the Sophia of Jesus Christ.

Although Irenaeus' criticism is incorrect, for his opponents' texts do wish to call Jesus 'Lord', he is right to point out that it is possible to use or reject certain christological titles on theological grounds.[142] In some dialogue gospels, christological titles are important in delimiting the identity of the Saviour and certain titles were not appropriate. This is evident in the scribal changes we see in the recensions of the Sophia of Jesus Christ and the Apocryphon of John. In both recensions of the Sophia of Jesus Christ (BG, NHC 3) it is the 'Saviour' who appears to the disciples, and he is usually called 'the perfect Saviour' in the dialogues. However, in the NH version, Philip, Thomas and Mary address him as 'Lord' (ϫ̅ⲥ̅),[143] whereas the parallel passages in BG use 'Christ' (ⲭ̅ⲥ̅).[144] The Coptic nomina sacra used for 'Christ' and 'Lord' are very similar, with just a single line difference (ϫ̅ⲥ̅ and ⲭ̅ⲥ̅), which may suggest that the variation is a simple mistake or misreading. However, it later becomes clear that human error is not the explanation. The Saviour is teaching the disciples, and we read:

> ⲧⲙⲛ̄ⲧⲉⲣⲟ ⲇⲉ ⲧⲁ ⲡϣⲏⲣⲉ ⲙⲡⲣⲱⲙⲉ ⲧⲉ ⲉⲧⲉ ϣⲁⲩⲙⲟⲩⲧⲉ ⲉⲣⲟϥ ϫⲉ ⲡⲉⲭ̅ⲥ̅ (BG 101,6–9).
>
> Now the kingdom is that of the Son of Man, who is called 'Christ'.
>
> ⲧⲙⲛ̄ⲧⲣ̄ⲣⲟ ⲧⲏⲣⲥ̄ ⲙ̄ⲡϣⲏⲣⲉ ⲙ̄ⲡⲣⲱⲙⲉ ⲡⲉⲧⲉϣⲁⲩⲙⲟⲩⲧⲉ ⲉⲣⲟϥ ϫⲉ ⲡϣⲏⲣⲉ ⲙ̄ⲡⲛⲟⲩⲧⲉ (NHC 105,19–21).
>
> The whole kingdom of the Son of Man, who is called 'Son of God'.

The change from Christ to Son of God, or vice versa, cannot be explained as a misreading of ⲭ and ϫ. It must be more intentional.

[142] We can assume the Apocryphon of John represents a text of Irenaeus' opponents due to the close parallels between the Apocryphon of John and *Adv. Haer.* 1.29–30, and the First Apocalypse of James due to its parallels with 1.21.5. This is not to say that Irenaeus knows or refers to these exact texts.

[143] BG 86,7; 87,9; 90,1–2.

[144] NHC3 95,19; 96,15; 98,10. In the BG, ⲡⲉϫⲁϥ ⲛⲁϥ ⲛ̄ϭⲓ ⲙⲁⲑⲁⲓⲟⲥ ϫⲉ ⲡⲱⲥ ⲁϥⲟⲩⲱⲛϩ ⲉⲃⲟⲗ ⲛ̄ϭⲓ ⲡⲣⲱⲙⲉ (Matthew said to him, 'How was Man revealed?' [BG 93,12–15])

In the Apocryphon of John, we see the same thing. John repeatedly addresses Jesus as 'Christ' in BG and 'Lord' in NHC 2 and 3.[145] Yet, except in direct address, he is called the 'Saviour'. The scribal activity behind the Berlin Codex suggests that Christ was an appropriate title for the Saviour, whereas that of Nag Hammadi Codices 2 and 3 pushes against this identification.[146]

As we mentioned above, the name 'Christ' is less common in dialogue gospels than other early Christian literature. This may be due to the association with the Jewish Messiah. Whether this was the reasoning behind the change from Christ to Lord, or vice versa, in the Sophia of Jesus Christ and the Apocryphon of John is impossible to say. The Apocryphon of John denies any possibility that Jesus is the Jewish Messiah as the text is in active contradiction with Jewish scripture and its God, and the titles in the Nag Hammadi versions might seek to reinforce this. However, there are many dialogue gospels that do not actively oppose Jewish scripture and its God, and so their exclusion of the name Christ is not necessarily advocating or opposing the identification of Jesus with the Messiah (e.g. the Epistle of Peter to Philip, the First Apocalypse of James, the Apocryphon of James, the Gospel of Mary, the Book of Thomas, the Dialogue of the Saviour, the Sophia of Jesus Christ). This lack of interest might be compared to Colossians, which never quotes the Jewish scriptures nor shows much interest in the role of Jesus as fulfilling them. There was simply no need to profess Jesus' identity as the Christ[147] – rather, it was more useful to stress the novelty of Jesus as Saviour.

follows the exact same format as the other questions, but there is no address. NHC 3, on the other hand, does have an address: ⲡⲉϫⲁϥ ⲛⲁϥ ⲛ̄ϭⲓ ⲙⲁⲑⲑⲁⲓⲟⲥ ϫⲉ ⲡϫⲟⲉⲓⲥ ⲡⲥⲱⲧⲏⲣ· ⲡⲱⲥ ⲁⲡⲣⲱⲙⲉ ⲟⲩⲱⲛϩ ⲉⲃⲟⲗ (Matthew said to him, 'Lord, Saviour, how was Man revealed?' [100,16–19]).

[145] For example, BG 46,6 // NHC 2 13,18; BG 58,2 // NHC 2 22,10 // NHC 3 28,18. There are many more instances of this. In some cases, it is unclear whether ⲭ̅ⲥ̅ is in reference to Christ or Goodness since he anointed him with his ⲙⲛ̄ⲧⲭ̅ⲥ̅ (Christhood Χριστός, or goodness χρηστός) ($_{BG}$ 30,15)

[146] This was probably not a conscious choice if they simply inherited Coptic versions of the Sophia of Jesus Christ and the Apocryphon of John, and this is not the case for other texts in NHC 2 and 3. The Gospel of Philip in NHC 2 and the Gospel of the Egyptians in NHC 3 use 'Christ'.

[147] One reason for this may be that they were written primarily for a Gentile audience. This is one of the two main possible reasons that Foster proposes for the lack of Scriptural citations in Colossians (likewise 1 Thessalonians); the other reason is that the author did not know the Jewish biblical texts (or that Paul did not have access to them while he was in prison), see Paul Foster, *Colossians*, Black's New Testament Commentaries (London: Bloomsbury, 2016), 52–60.

It is often the case in the dialogue gospels that the reason for Jesus' incarnation/descent/appearance is novel revelation. The Sophia of Jesus Christ repeatedly asserts that *Christ came to reveal*, without mention of any other motive (such as an atoning death): 'The perfect Saviour said, "I came from the Infinite that I might teach you all things"' (ⲡⲉϫⲁϥ ⲛϭⲓ ⲡⲧⲉⲗⲓⲟⲥ ⲛ̄ⲥⲱ̄ⲣ̄ ϫⲉ ⲁⲛⲟⲕ ⲁïⲉ̂ⲓ ⲉⲃⲟⲗ ϩⲙ̄ ⲡⲓⲁⲡⲉⲣⲁⲛⲧⲟⲛ ϫⲉ ⲉⲉⲓⲉⲧⲥⲉⲃⲉ ⲧⲏⲩⲧⲛ̄ ⲉⲛ̄ⲕⲁ ⲛⲓⲙ [SophJesChr, $_{BG}$ 87,12–15]). The revelatory teaching can either be instigated by Jesus or by the disciples questioning him, but in every dialogue gospel, it is prevalent and explicit:

Johannine Farewell Discourse	Ταῦτα ἐν παροιμίαις λελάληκα ὑμῖν· ἔρχεται ὥρα ὅτε οὐκέτι ἐν παροιμίαις λαλήσω ὑμῖν, ἀλλὰ παρρησίᾳ περὶ τοῦ πατρὸς ἀπαγγελῶ ὑμῖν (16.25)
	I have said these things to you in figures of speech. The hour is coming when I will no longer speak to you in figures, but will tell you plainly of the Father.
Apocalypse of Peter	The second coming of Christ and resurrection of the dead, which Christ revealed to Peter … And these things he pondered so that he might understand their mystery. (incipit)
Apocryphon of James	ⲁϩ̣[ⲓⲣ] ϣⲁⲣⲡ̣ ⲉⲉⲓϣⲉϫⲉ ⲛⲙ̄ⲙⲏⲧⲛ̄ ϩⲣⲏï ϩⲛ̄ ϩⲙ̄ⲡⲁⲣⲁⲃⲟⲗⲏ · ⲁⲩⲱ ⲛⲉⲣⲉⲧⲛ̄ⲣ ⲛⲟⲉⲓ ⲉⲛ · ϯ[ⲛ]ⲟⲩ ⲁⲛ ϯϣⲉϫⲉ ⲛⲙ̄ⲙⲏⲧ̣[ⲛ ϩ]ⲛ̄ ⲟⲩⲱⲛϩ̄ ⲁⲃⲁⲗ (7,1–5)
	At first I spoke to you in parables, and you did not understand. N[o]w I speak to yo[u] openly.
Apocryphon of John	ⲧ[ⲉⲛⲟⲩ ⲁⲉⲓⲉⲓ] ⲉⲧⲟⲩⲛⲟⲩⲉⲓⲁⲧⲕ ⲉⲃ̣[ⲟⲗ ϫⲉ ⲟⲩ ⲡⲉ]ⲧϣⲟⲟⲡ ⲁⲩⲱ ⲟⲩ ⲡⲉ̣[ⲛⲧⲁϥϣⲱ]ⲡⲉ ⲁⲩⲱ ⲟⲩ ⲡⲉⲧⲉϣ[ϣⲉ ⲉⲧⲣⲉϥ]ϣⲱⲡⲉ ϫⲉⲕⲁⲁⲥ ⲉⲕ̣[ⲉⲉⲓⲙⲉ ⲉ]ⲛⲓⲁⲧⲛⲁⲩ (ⲉ) ⲉⲣⲟⲟⲩ ⲙ̣[ⲛⲛ ⲛⲉⲧⲟⲩ]ⲛⲁⲩ ⲉⲣⲟⲟⲩ ⲁⲩⲱ ⲉⲧ[ⲟⲩⲛⲉⲓⲁⲧⲕ] ⲉⲃⲟⲗ ⲉⲧⲃⲉ ⲡⲓⲧⲉⲗⲓ[ⲟⲥ ⲛⲣⲱⲙⲉ] ($_{BG}$ 22,2–9[148]).
	[Now I have come] to teach you [what] is, and [what was] and what will come to pass, that you [may know] the things that are not manifest [and the things that are] manifest, and to teach you about the Perfect [Man].
Book of Thomas	ⲥⲱⲧⲙ̄ ⲉⲣⲟï ⲛ̄ⲧⲁϭⲱⲗⲡ ⲛⲁⲕ ⲉⲃⲟⲗ ⲉⲧⲃⲉ ⲛⲉⲛⲧⲁⲕ ⲙⲉⲉⲩⲉ ⲉⲣⲟⲟⲩ ϩⲣⲁï ϩⲙ̄ ⲡⲉⲕ ϩⲏⲧ (138,6–8)
	Listen to me, and I will reveal to you the things you have pondered in your mind.
Dialogue of the Saviour	ϯⲛⲁⲧⲥⲁⲃⲱⲧⲛ̄ (122,1–2)
	I will teach you.

148 Largely reconstructed from NHC 4.

Epistula Apostolorum	ⲧⲱ̣[ⲛⲉ ⲁ]ⲟⲩ ϯⲛⲁϭⲱⲗ(ⲡ) ⲛⲏⲧⲛⲉ ⲁⲃⲁⲗ ⲛ̄ⲛⲉⲧⲙ̄ⲡⲥⲁ[ϩ]ⲣ̣ⲉ̣ ⲛ̄ⲛ̄ⲡⲏⲩⲉ ⲙⲛ̄ ⲛⲉⲧϩⲛ̄ ⲛ̄ⲡⲏⲩⲉ ⲁⲟⲩ ⲧⲉⲧⲛ̄ⲁ̣ⲛⲁⲡⲁⲩⲥⲓⲥ ⲉⲧϩⲛ̄ ⲧⲙⲛ̄ⲧⲣ̄ⲣⲟ ⲛ̄ⲡⲏⲩⲉ (12.3) Ri[se, a]nd I will reveal to you the things abo[v]e the heavens and the things in the heavens and your rest, which is in the kingdom of the heavens.
Epistle of Peter to Philip	ⲛ̄ⲧⲱⲧ̣ⲛ̄ ⲟⲩⲁⲧ ⲧⲏⲩⲧⲛ̄ ⲉⲧⲣ̄ ⲙ̄ⲛ̄ⲧⲣⲉ ϫⲉ ⲁⲓⲉϫⲉ ⲛⲁï ⲧⲏⲣⲟⲩ ⲛⲏⲧⲛ̄ ⲁⲗ̣[ⲗ]ⲁ [ⲉ]ⲧ̣ⲃⲉ ⲧⲉⲧ̄ⲛ̄ⲙ̄ⲛ̄ⲧ̄ ⲁⲧ ⲛⲁϩⲧⲉ ϯ[ⲛ]ⲁϣⲁϫⲉ ⲛ̄ⲕⲉⲥⲟⲡ· ($_{NHC}$ 135,4–8) It is you yourselves who witness that I spoke all these things to you. But because of your unbelief, I will speak again.
First Apocalypse of James	[ⲉⲓⲥ] ϩⲏⲧⲉ ϯⲛⲁ ϭⲱⲗⲡ̄ ⲛⲁⲕ ⲉⲃⲟⲗ ⲙ̄ⲡⲉⲕⲥⲱⲧⲉ̣ ($_{NHC}$ 32,29–33,1) [Behold], I shall reveal to you your redemption.
Gospel of Judas	ⲁ̣ϥⲁⲣⲭ̣[ⲉⲓ] ⲛϣⲁ[ϫⲉ] ⲛⲙ̄ⲙⲁⲩ ⲉⲙ̄ⲙ[ⲩⲥ]ⲧⲏⲣⲓ[ⲟ]ⲛ̣ ⲉⲧϩⲓ ϫⲛ̄ ⲡⲕⲟⲥⲙⲟⲥ ⲁⲩⲱ ⲛⲉⲧⲛⲁϣ̣ϣⲡ̣ⲉ̣ ϣ̣ⲁⲃⲟⲗ (33,15–18) And he beg[an] to spe[ak] with them about the m[ys]teri[e]s above the world and what will happen up to the end.
Gospel of Mary	ⲡⲉⲑⲏⲡ ⲉⲣⲱⲧⲛ̄ ϯⲛⲁⲧⲁⲙⲁ ⲧⲏⲩⲧⲛ̄ ⲉⲣⲟϥ (10,8–9) What is hidden from you, I will proclaim to you.
Pistis Sophia	ϫⲓⲛ ⲡⲟⲟⲩ ϭⲉ ⲉⲃⲟⲗ ϯⲛⲁϣⲁϫⲉ ⲛ̄ⲙ̄ⲙⲏⲧ̄ⲛ̄ ϩ̄ⲛ̄ ⲟⲩⲡⲁⲣⲣⲏⲥⲓⲁ ϫⲓⲛ ⲧⲁⲣⲭⲏ ⲛ̄ⲧⲁⲗⲏⲑⲉⲓⲁ ϣⲁ ⲡⲉⲥϫⲱⲕ · ⲁⲩⲱ ϯⲛⲁϣⲁϫⲉ ⲛ̄ⲙ̄ⲙⲏⲧ̄ⲛ̄ ⲛ̄ϩⲟ ϩⲓ ϩⲟ ⲁϫ̄ⲛ̄ ⲡⲁⲣⲁⲃⲟⲗⲏ · (1.6 [8,23–9,2])[149] From today on, I will speak with you openly from the beginning of the truth until its completion. And I will speak with you face to face, without parable.
Sophia of Jesus Christ	ⲙⲁⲧⲥⲁⲃⲟⲛ ϩⲛ̄ⲛ ⲟⲩⲱⲛϩ ⲉⲃⲟⲗ ($_{BG}$ 102,8–9) | ⲡⲁⲗⲓⲛ ⲛⲉϥⲙⲁⲑⲏⲧⲏⲥ ⲡⲉϫⲁⲩ ϫⲉ ⲙⲁⲧⲁⲙⲟⲛ ϩⲛ̄ ⲟⲩⲱⲛϩ ⲉⲃⲟⲗ ($_{NHC}$ 106,9–11) Teach us openly. | Again, his disciples said: ‘Tell us openly.’

The theme is the same, but the details vary. Some of these quotations reveal that the teaching will be redemptive, some appear simply to placate the disciples’ worries or questions, some reveal what was previously hidden, and in some it is the disciples who ask Jesus to educate them. In the Gospel of Mary quotation above, it is Mary who speaks – she is the one who will pass on the Saviour’s teachings.

The theme of revelation goes hand in hand with understanding. Jesus often speaks about those who have not understood (e.g. ‘he who spoke concerning this scripture had a limited understanding’

149 References to the Pistis Sophia follow the format of (chapter,section [page,verse]) as some chapters are very long. This follows the page and line numbers in Schmidt, *Pistis Sophia*.

[πετα`ϥ΄ϣαϫε ϩα τεϊγραφη ⲛ̄ταϥϲοογⲛ ϣα πεϊⲙα, 1ApocJas $_{NHC}$ 26,6–7]), as well as rejoicing at the disciples' questions when they demonstrate comprehension (e.g. 'Then he rejoiced when I asked him this, and he said to me: "Truly, you are blessed for you have understood"' [τοτε αϥραϣε ⲛ̄ταριϫⲛογϥ επαϊ αγω πεϫαϥ ⲛαϊ ϫε αληθωϲ ⲛ̄τκ ογⲙακαριοϲ επιδη ακⲣ̄ⲛοει, ApJohn $_{NHC2}$ 27,14–17]).

In several of these dialogues, the disciples are confused or upset as they do not understand Jesus' teachings:

> πετροϲ ⲛ̄ϫε αϥογωϣⲃ̄ ⲛ̄ⲛαϩⲣⲛ̄ ⲛεει πα[ϫ]εϥ ϫε ϩⲛ̄ϲαπ ⲙεⲛ κⲣ̄ προτρεπε ⲙ̄ⲙαⲛ αϩογⲛ ατⲙⲛ̄τⲣ̄ρο ⲛ̄ⲙ̄πηγε ϩενκεϲαπ αⲛ κϲτο ⲙ̄ⲙαⲛ αβαλ· πϫαειϲ ϩⲛ̄ϲαπ· ⲙεⲛ κⲣ̄ πιθε αγω κϲωκ· ⲙ̄ⲙαⲛ αϩογⲛ ατπιϲτιϲ αγω κϣπωπ ⲛεⲛ ⲙ̄πωⲛϩ̄ ϩⲛκεϲαπ αⲛ κϩβαρβⲣ̄ ⲙ̄ⲙαⲛ αβαλ ⲛ̄τⲙⲛ̄τερο ⲛ̄ⲙ̄πηγε (ApJas 13,25–36)
>
> Then Peter replied to these words and said, 'Sometimes you urge us toward the kingdom of heaven, and at other times you turn us back. Lord, sometimes you persuade and draw us to faith and promise us life, and at other times you cast us forth from the kingdom of heaven.'

Incomprehension is an especially pressing problem in the dialogue gospels due to Jesus' imminent absence. We frequently find the idea that the disciples feel that it is *necessary* to question Jesus, either for purposes of salvific understanding or mission:

> ερτⲙ̄τεογ[α ειⲙε ϫεⲛ̄] ταπκωϩτ· ϣωπε ⲛ̣̄[α]ϣ ⲛ̣̄ϩ[ε] ϥⲛαρωκϩ ⲛ̄ϩραϊ ⲛ̄ϩητϥ̄· εβ̣[ολ] ϫεⲛ̄ϥϲοογⲛ αⲛ ⲛ̄τεϥⲛογⲛε̣̄ (DialSav 134,1–4)
>
> If [one] does not [understand how] fire came into existence, he will burn in it because he does not know its root.
>
> παλιⲛ̣ [αⲛ] παϫεⲛ ⲛεϥ ϫε πϫαειϲ ογαⲛαγκη γαρ ⲛεⲛ τε ατⲛ̄ϣιⲛε αβαλ ϩιτοοτκ αβαλ ϫε κογαϩϲαϩⲛε ⲛεⲛ ατⲛ̄ταϣεαειϣ (EpAp 23.1)
>
> Again we said to him, 'Lord, it is necessary for us to question you, for you command us to preach.'

The Pistis Sophia develops this, referring to a synoptic passage (Matt 7.7 // Luke 11.9). Mary says:

> παϫοειϲ ⲙ̄πⲣ̄ϭωⲛ̄τ εροϊ ε̈ιϣιⲛε ⲙ̄ⲙοκ · ϫε εⲛϣιⲛε ⲛ̄ϲα ϩωβ ⲛιⲙ ϩ̄ⲛ̄ ογωⲣ̄ϫ̄ ⲙ̄ⲛ̄ ογαϲφαλια · ακϫοοϲ γαρ εροⲛ ⲙ̄πιογοειϣ · ϫε ϣιⲛε ταρετⲛ̄ϭιⲛε αγω τωϩⲙ̄ταρογογωⲛ ⲛητⲛ̄ ϫε ογοⲛ

> ⲅⲁⲣ ⲛⲓⲙ ⲉⲧϣⲓⲛⲉ ϥⲛⲁϭⲓⲛⲉ · ⲁⲩⲱ ⲟⲩⲟⲛ ⲛⲓⲙ ⲉⲧⲧⲱϩ̄ⲙ̄ ⲉϩⲟⲩⲛ · ⲥⲉⲛⲁⲟⲩⲱⲛ ⲛⲁϥ · ⲧⲉⲛⲟⲩ ϭⲉ ⲡⲁϫⲟⲉⲓⲥ ⲛⲓⲙ ⲡⲉϯⲛⲁϭⲛ̄ⲧϥ̄ ⲏ ⲛⲓⲙ ⲡⲉⲧⲛ̄ⲛⲁⲧⲱϩ̄ⲙ̄ ⲉⲣⲟϥ · ⲏ ⲛⲓⲙ ⲛ̄ⲧⲟϥ ⲡⲉⲧⲉ ⲟⲩⲛ̄ϣϭⲟⲙ ⲙ̄ⲙⲟϥ ⲉϫⲱ ⲉⲣⲟⲛ ⲛ̄ⲧⲁⲡⲟⲫⲁⲥⲓⲥ ⲛ̄ⲛ̄ϣⲁϫⲉ ⲉⲧⲛ̄ⲛⲁϣⲛ̄ⲧⲕ̄ ⲉⲣⲟⲟⲩ · ⲏ ⲛⲓⲙ ⲛ̄ⲧⲟϥ ⲡⲉ ⲉⲧⲥⲟⲟⲩⲛ ⲛ̄ⲧϭⲟⲙ ⲛ̄ⲛ̄ϣⲁϫⲉ ⲉⲧⲛ̄ⲛⲁϣⲓⲛⲉ ⲛ̄ⲥⲱⲟⲩ … ⲉⲃⲟⲗ ϫⲉ ⲛⲉ̈ⲓϣⲓⲛⲉ ⲁⲛ ⲛ̄ⲥⲁ ⲑⲉ ⲉⲧⲟⲩϣⲓⲛⲉ ⲙ̄ⲙⲟⲥ ⲛ̄ϭⲓ ⲛ̄ⲣⲱⲙⲉ ⲛ̄ⲧⲉ ⲡⲕⲟⲥⲙⲟⲥ · ⲁⲗⲗⲁ ⲉⲛϣⲓⲛⲉ ⲁⲛⲟⲛ ϩ̄ⲙ̄ ⲡⲥⲟⲟⲩⲛ̄ ⲛ̄ⲧⲉ ⲡϫⲓⲥⲉ ⲡⲁ̈ⲓ ⲉⲛⲧⲁⲕⲧⲁⲁϥ ⲛⲁⲛ ⲁⲩⲱ ⲉⲛϣⲓⲛⲉ ⲟⲛ ϩ̄ⲙ̄ ⲡⲧⲩⲡⲟⲥ ⲛ̄ⲧϭⲓⲛϣⲓⲛⲉ ⲉⲧⲟⲩⲟⲧ̄ⲃ̄ · ⲧⲁ̈ⲓ ⲛ̄ⲧⲁⲕⲧⲥⲁⲃⲟⲛ ⲉⲣⲟⲥ ⲉⲧⲣⲉⲛϣⲓⲛⲉ ⲛ̄ϩⲏⲧⲥ̄ · ⲧⲉⲛⲟⲩ ϭⲉ ⲡⲁϫⲟⲉⲓⲥ ⲙ̄ⲡⲣ̄ϭⲱⲛ̄ⲧ ⲉⲣⲟ̈ⲓ· ⲁⲗⲗⲁ ϭⲱⲗ̄ⲡ̄ ⲛⲁ̈ⲓ ⲉⲃⲟⲗ ⲙ̄ⲡϣⲁϫⲉ ⲉϯⲛⲁϣⲛ̄ⲧⲕ̄ ⲉⲣⲟϥ· (2.83 [184,8–19; 185,2–9])

> My Lord, be not angry with me that I question you, for we question all things with assurance and certainty. For you once said to us, 'Seek and you shall find, and knock and it shall be opened to you, for everyone who seeks will find, and to everyone who knocks, it will be opened to him.' Now at this time, my Lord, whom will I find, or to whom shall we knock, or rather who is able to say to us the answer to the words on which we question you, or rather who knows the power of the words which we will question? … For we do not question in the way that the people of the world question, but we question with the knowledge of the height that you have given to us, and we question with the type of the superior questioning that you have taught us, that we should question therewith. Now at this time, my Lord, do not be angry with me, but reveal to me the subject on which I will question you.

Jesus responds and says that he is glad to answer her questions since she has asked them in the right way (i.e. with assurance).

The request for the revelatory teaching that Jesus must provide can be relentless (especially when the disciples never quite grasp the point). In the quotation above, Mary twice asks Jesus not to be angry with her for her questions, and she even attempts to justify her own questioning methods. The disciples of the Epistula Apostolorum explain that they need answers because Jesus has commanded them to preach (23.1), but he still gets infuriated by their relentless questioning:

> [ⲁϥⲃ]ⲱⲗⲕ ⲁⲣⲁⲛ ⲉϥϫⲟⲩ ⲙ̄ⲙⲁⲥ ⲛⲉⲛ ϫⲉ ⲱ ⲛⲁⲧⲡⲓ[ⲥⲧⲓⲥ]ϩⲏⲙ ϣⲁ ⲉϩ ⲛ̄ϩⲟⲟⲩⲉ ⲉⲧⲉⲧⲛ̄ϣⲓⲛⲉ (EpAp 24.4)

> [He was a]ngry with us, saying to us, 'O you of little faith, how long will you question?'

In spite of all the differences in the theological content of the revelations, the dialogue gospels depict a similar relationship between Jesus and his disciple(s). Jesus is the revealer and Saviour, and the disciples desperately need him to reveal the truths of their salvation before he leaves them

Eschatology

The revelations of Jesus in the dialogue gospels are generally concerned with the broad concepts of eschatology and soteriology. In these texts, eschatology and soteriology are not easily distinguished as salvation is the eschatological aim of humanity. In order to encompass both the cosmic and individual 'end', our discussion will be conceived in terms of 'eschatology'. Even the texts that focus on one's origins are soteriological and often eschatological, as in many dialogue gospels salvation is a return to one's root.[150] Hartenstein notes that the form of the dialogue gospel, especially the lists of questions, mirrors its concern with revelatory salvation: 'The popularity of the lists of questions is to be understood in the context of gnostic theology. Since knowledge [*Erkenntnis*], especially the knowledge [*Wissen*] about one's own origin, signifies salvation, searching and questioning have high priority; it may even have its own soteriological quality.'[151]

As we saw earlier, Fallon divided the 'gnostic apocalypses' into those that include cosmic eschatology and those that include only personal. The dialogue gospels do not neatly bifurcate into these two categories, as in several texts a cosmic eschatology can at least be inferred – although it is not a primary concern of the text, it is in the background. Often it is simply said that the cosmos is perishable (e.g. SophJesChr $_{BG}$ 89,9–12, GJudas 50,11–14). Other texts deal with this theme more explicitly. In the Gospel of Mary the disciples ask about the dissolution of matter (7,1–2), and Jesus explains that it will return to its root. In the Pistis Sophia, it is said that 'world matter' (ⲑⲩⲗⲏ ⲙ̄ⲡⲕⲟⲥⲙⲟⲥ) will 'dissolve completely' (ϥⲛⲁⲃⲱⲗ ⲉⲃⲟⲗ ⲉⲡⲧⲏⲣ̄ϥ) (2.93 [212,22–23]). The disciples see this dissolution as the work of Jesus, as when he ascends to heaven an earthquake occurs and the disciples

[150] For an analysis of the range of eschatological perspectives in 'gnostic' texts, see Tobias Nicklas, 'Gnostic "Eschatologies"', in *Eschatology of the New Testament and Some Related Documents*, ed. J. van der Watt, WUNT II 315 (Tübingen: Mohr Siebeck, 2011), 601–28.

[151] Hartenstein, *Die zweite Lehre*, 278.

wonder if the world will 'be rolled up' (ⲉⲩⲛⲁϭ̄ⲗ̄-ⲡⲕⲟⲥⲙⲟⲥ [1.3 (6,14)]) and whether Jesus will 'dissolve all places' (ⲛⲁⲃⲱⲗ ⲉⲃⲟⲗ ⲛ̄ⲛ̄ⲧⲟⲡⲟⲥ ⲧⲏⲣⲟⲩ [1.4 (7,4)]). The Apocryphon of John, which is concerned primarily with origins over eschatology, sees a protological end: 'It is because of you [the Invisible Spirit] that all things have come into being, and (it is) to you (that) all things will return' (ⲉⲧⲃⲏⲧⲕ ⲁⲡⲧⲏⲣϥ ϣⲱⲡⲉ ⲁⲩⲱ ⲉⲣⲉⲡⲧⲏⲣϥ ⲛⲁⲛⲁⲩϩϥ ⲉⲣⲟⲕ [$_{\text{NHC2}}$ 9,7–8]). The Dialogue of the Saviour refers to the 'time of dissolution' (ⲡⲉⲟⲩⲟⲉⲓϣ ⲙ̄ⲡⲃⲱⲗ ⲉⲃⲟⲗ [122,3]) and later to 'weeping and [gnashing] of teeth over the end of a[ll] these things' (ⲡⲣⲓⲙⲉ ⲙⲛ̄ [ⲡ…] ⲛ̣̄ⲛ̄ⲟⲃϩⲉ ⲉϫⲛ̄ⲑⲁϩ ⲛ̄ⲛⲁϊ ⲧⲏ[ⲣⲟⲩ] [127,17–19]). The Apocalypse of Peter also refers to the whole creation dissolving (5.7), which brings judgement and the parousia. On the whole, cosmic eschatology is a less pressing concern in the dialogue gospels than individual salvation; however, sometimes they are complementary. In the background of Jesus' teaching about the resurrection of the flesh to be judged, or the ascent of the soul through the archons, is a dissolving cosmos.

On the topic of salvation, Hartenstein groups together the Apocryphon of John, the Sophia of Jesus Christ, the Gospel of Mary and the First Apocalypse of James (and to an extent the Epistle of Peter to Philip), arguing that they have a similar cosmology and report similar conditions of the creation of humankind:

> These mythological explanations are to be understood against the background that knowledge of the heavenly events and, above all, about one's own origin has a redeeming effect. Such knowledge allows the ascension of the person or their soul, which is explicitly addressed in the Sophia of Jesus Christ (BG p.122,5–125,10 par.) and the Apocryphon of John (BG p.64,14–71,2 par.). In the Gospel of Mary and the First Apocalypse of James, there is a focus on an aspect of the ascension, which means only a shift in the thematic focus. The dialogue gospels as a genre appear to have such an affinity to questions of (gnostic) soteriology.[152]

The Sophia of Jesus Christ explains that Jesus has broken the bonds of the archons by teaching humanity about the Immortal Man. Having this knowledge, humans can 'ascend to the One Who Is' (ⲃⲱⲕ ⲉϩⲣⲁϊ ⲉⲡⲉⲧϣⲟⲟⲡ [$_{\text{BG}}$ 122,13–15]). The Apocryphon of John also discusses how knowledge and action allow the soul to ascend.

[152] Hartenstein, *Die zweite Lehre*, 260.

In short, the Apocryphon of John conjectures a transcendent God whose divine essence is protologically given to humans made in its image. Once humans understand their divine heritage, they become free from 'fate' and can be saved (unlike Judas in the Gospel of Judas whose fate dooms him beyond salvation[153]). In the First Apocalypse of James, Jesus explains how James will ascend through the archons by declaring his divine heritage, and in the Gospel of Mary we see a comparable ascent of an individual soul narrated. Each of these texts understands salvation and personal eschatology as protological: the person returns to their origins. This group may be extended to include the Pistis Sophia, in which all souls ascend at the end of age, but the individual soul will only reach the realm according to which it has received the mysteries. The ascent is therefore conditional and hierarchical. In the Apocryphon of John and the Pistis Sophia, souls that have not received the mysteries or correct knowledge, or that have acted out of accordance with them, face the prospect of reincarnation.

The Apocryphon of James presupposes knowledge of this kind of journey-through-archons eschatology, although the text is not interested in reproducing that teaching:

> ⲉⲧⲃⲉ ⲡⲉⲉⲓ ϯϫⲟⲩ ⲙ̄ⲙⲁⲥ ⲛ̄ⲛⲏⲧⲛ̄ ϫⲉ ⲉⲣⲓ ⲛⲏⲫⲉ· ⲙ̄ⲡⲱⲣ· ⲁⲣ̄ⲡⲗⲁⲛⲁ ⲁⲩⲱ ϩⲁϩ ⲛ̄ⲥⲁⲡ ⲁϩⲓ̈ϫⲟⲟⲥ ⲛⲏⲧⲛ̄ ⲙⲛ̄ ⲛⲉⲧⲛ̄ⲉⲣⲏⲩ· ⲁⲩⲱ ⲁⲛ ⲛ̄ⲧⲁⲕ ⲟⲩⲁⲉⲉⲧⲕ̄· ⲱ ⲓ̈ⲁⲕⲕⲱⲃⲟⲥ ⲁϩⲓ̈ϫⲟⲟⲥ ϫⲉ ⲟⲩϫⲉⲉⲓ· ⲁⲩⲱ ⲁϩⲓ̈ϩⲱⲛ ⲁⲧⲟⲟⲧⲕ̄· ⲁⲧⲣⲉⲕⲟⲩⲁϩⲕ̄ ⲛ̄ⲥⲱⲉⲓ ⲁⲩⲱ ⲁϩⲓ̈ⲧⲥⲉⲃⲉ ⲉⲓⲉⲧⲕ ⲁⲃⲁⲗ ⲁⲑⲩⲡⲟⲑⲉⲥⲓⲥ ⲛ̄ⲛⲁϩⲣⲛ̄ ⲛ̄ⲛⲁⲣⲭⲱⲛ ⲉⲛⲉⲩ ϫⲉ ⲁⲛⲁⲕ ⲁϩⲓ̈ⲉ̅ⲓ̅ ⲁⲡⲓⲧⲛ̄ ⲁⲩⲱ ⲁϩⲓ̈ϣⲉϫⲉ ⲁⲩⲱ ⲁϩ<ⲓ̈>ⲣ̄ ⲥⲕⲩⲗⲗⲉ ⲙ̄ⲙⲁⲉⲓ· ⲁⲩⲱ ⲁϩⲓ̈ϥⲓ ⲙ̄ⲡⲁⲕⲗⲁⲙ· ⲛ̄ⲧⲁⲣⲓⲛⲟⲩϩⲙ̄ ⲙ̄ⲙⲱⲧⲛ̄ ⲁϩⲓ̈ⲉⲓ ⲅⲁⲣ ⲁⲡⲓⲧⲛ̄ ⲁⲧⲣⲁⲟⲩⲱϩ ⲛⲙ̄ⲙⲏⲧⲛ̄ ϫⲉⲕⲁⲥⲉ· ⲉ<ⲣⲉⲧ>ⲛⲁⲟⲩⲱϩ ⲛⲙ̄ⲙⲏⲓ̈ ϩⲱⲧ· ⲧⲏⲛⲉ (ApJas 8,26–9,4)
>
> This is why I say to you: Be sober; do not be deceived. And many times have I said to you all together, and also to you alone, James, have I said 'Be saved'. And I have commanded you to follow me, and I have taught you what to say before the archons. Observe that I have descended and have spoken and undergone tribulation and carried off my crown after

[153] According to Denzey Lewis, the Gospel of Judas does not propound escape from astral fatalism, in contrast to the Apocryphon of John; see Denzey Lewis, *Cosmology and Fate*, 165–80. On the Apocryphon of John's understanding of fate, King writes, 'despite the oft-repeated cliché that Gnostics felt themselves to be enslaved by fate, in fact, the *Secret Revelation of John* affirms that spiritual humanity was always under the care of the true Pronoia', King, *Secret Revelation of John*, 108.

> saving you. For I came down to dwell with you so that you in turn might dwell with me.

Reading the Apocryphon of James alone, it is unclear who or what the archons are. But reading it in light of texts such as the Gospel of Mary and the First Apocalypse of James, it can be assumed that they are the cosmic powers that the human (soul) must conquer on its way to heaven, mirrored in the earthly realm as authorities that persecute Christians. The Apocryphon of James explicitly links this to its incarnation theology: Jesus has descended from the heavens and been crucified in order that Christians can dwell with him in the heavens, presumably after producing the necessary verbal declarations to pass the cosmic powers.

This cosmic/earthly powers parallelism is typical of the 'martyrdom' dialogue gospels. Alongside the Apocryphon of James, these are the First Apocalypse of James and the Epistle of Peter to Philip.[154] In the First Apocalypse of James, James must be martyred, and the text concludes with his death by stoning at which he imitates Jesus, crying: 'Forgive them, for they do (not) [know] what they are doing' (ⲕⲱ ⲛⲁⲩ ⲉⲃⲟⲗ ⲛ̣ⲥ̣[ⲉⲥⲟⲟⲩ]ⲛⲉ ⲅⲁⲣ (ⲁⲛ) ⲇⲉ ⲉⲩⲣ ⲟⲩ [$_{\text{CT}}$ 30,25–26]). Jesus prepares James for his impending death by teaching him about the heavenly realms and, as Haxby argues, 'by focusing so deeply on the revelation which James receives, *1ApocJas* narrates a martyrdom which focuses far more on the transmission of knowledge than on the testing and trial of the hero martyr'.[155] In the Epistle of Peter to Philip, the apostles ask Jesus to 'give us our power, for they seek to kill us' (ⲙⲁϯ ⲛⲁⲛ ⲛⲛⲟⲩϭⲁⲙ ⲉⲡ̣ⲓⲇⲏ ⲥⲉⲕⲱⲧⲉ ⲛⲥⲱⲛ ⲉϩⲟⲧⲃⲛ [$_{\text{NHC}}$ 134,8–9]). Throughout the text, Jesus tells them that their suffering is necessary. The potential persecution is related to mission, but there are also cosmic powers that they must fight against. The earthly martyrdom, in which the disciple battles the authorities and dies, is paralleled in the cosmos, where the disciple battles the archons and gains immortality.[156]

[154] These are both found in Codex Tchacos, and King proposes that, along with the Gospel of Judas, these texts could be read together as preparation for martyrdom, Karen L. King, 'Martyrdom and Its Discontents in the Tchacos Codex', in *The Codex Judas Papers: Proceedings of the International Congress on the Tchacos Codex Held at Rice University, Houston, Texas, March 13–16, 2008*, ed. April D. DeConick, NHMS 71 (Leiden and Boston: Brill, 2009), 23–42.

[155] Mikael Haxby, 'The First Apocalypse of James: Martyrdom and Sexual Difference' (Cambridge, MA: PhD Thesis, Harvard University Press, 2013), 14. He focuses on how James prepares for martyrdom through gaining knowledge about the heavens and femaleness, and thus sees it as a 'non-standard martyrdom'.

[156] For a deeper analysis of these themes in the First Apocalypse of James, see Sarah Parkhouse, 'Identity, Death and Ascension in the Gospel of John and the First Apocalypse of James', forthcoming.

In the Epistula Apostolorum, the Book of Thomas and the Apocalypse of Peter, humankind must face judgement and heaven or hell. In the Epistula Apostolorum and the Apocalypse of Peter, judgement is linked with the parousia.[157] In the Apocalypse of Peter, Jesus says that he will return 'on a cloud of heaven with great power and in my glory, my cross going before my face … shining seven times more than the sun … that I might judge the living and the dead' (1.6–7). In the Epistula Apostolorum, he says:

> ϯⲛⲏⲩ ⲅⲁⲣ ⲛ̄ⲧⳉⲉ ⲛ̄ⲡⲣⲓ ⲉⲧⲡⲣ̄ⲓⲱⲟⲩ ⲁⲟⲩ ⲉⲉⲓⲉ ⲛ̄ⲟⲩⲁⲉⲓⲛⲉ ⲛ̄ⲥⲁⳉϥ ⲛ̄ⲕⲱⲃ ⲡⲁⲣⲁⲣⲁϥ ⳉⲛ̄ ⲡⲁⲉⲁⲩ ⲉⲛⲧⲛ̄ϩ ⲛ̄ⲕⲗⲟⲟⲗⲉ ϩ̣ⲓ̣[ⲟⲩⲥ]ⲁⲡ̣ⳉⲁⲣⲁï ⳉⲛ̄ ⲟⲩⲉⲁⲩ ⲉⲡⲥⲏⲙⲉⲓ̣ⲟ̣ⲛ [ⲛ̄ⲡⲥ]ⲧ̣ⲁⲩⲣⲟⲥ ϩⲓⲧⲁⲉϩⲓ ⲁⲟⲩ ϯⲛⲏⲩ ⲁⳉⲣⲏï ⲁϫⲛ̄ ⲡⲕⲁϩ ⲧⲁϯϩⲉⲡ ⲁⲛⲉⲧⲁⲛⳉ ⲙⲛ̄ ⲛⲉⲧⲙⲁⲩⲧ (EpAp 16.3–5)
>
> I am coming like the sun that shines, and the light will be seven times greater than it, in my glory. On the wings of clouds, I shall be carried in glory, the sign of the cross before me. And I am coming down upon the earth, and I give judgement to the living and the dead.

Both texts describe clouds, glory, the cross and light seven times more powerful than the sun, and combine these images with the portrayal of Christ as the 'judge of the living and the dead'.[158]

In the Epistula Apostolorum and the Apocalypse of Peter, judgement is linked with fleshly resurrection (EpAp 21.6; ApocPet 1.8, 4.1, 4.12). In the Book of Thomas, there is a passing reference to 'the day of judgement' (143,7), but without explanation. It must be conceived differently to the Epistula Apostolorum and the Apocalypse of Peter as the idea of bodily resurrection is contested – in the Book of Thomas, it is the soul alone that is punished. The text makes it clear that flesh will never rise again: 'Now that which changes will decay and perish, and has no hope of life from then on, since that body is bestial' (ⲡⲉⲧϣⲓⲃⲉ ⲇⲉ ϥⲛⲁⲧⲉⲕⲟ ⲛ̄ϥⲱϫⲛ̄ ⲁⲩⲱ ⲙⲛ̄ⲧⲉϥ ϩⲉⲗⲡⲓⲥ ⲛ̄ⲱⲛϩ ϫⲙ̄ ⲡⲓⲛⲁⲩ ϫⲉ ⲡⲓⲥⲱⲙⲁ ⲅⲁⲣ ⲟⲩⲧⲃ̄ⲛⲏ ⲡⲉ [139,4–6]), and 'the vessel of their flesh will dissolve' (ⲡⲥⲕⲉⲩⲟⲥ ⲅⲁⲣ ⲛ̄ⲧⲟⲩⲥⲁⲣⲝ ⲛⲁⲃⲱⲗ

[157] The question of dependency (the Epistula Apostolorum on the Apocalypse of Peter) has been raised, but as Bauckham writes: 'the *Epistle of the Apostles* seems to show no other sign of dependence on the *Apocalypse of Peter*. It is at least equally likely that both works reflect common traditional descriptions of the parousia', Bauckham, 'Two Fig Tree Parables', 274.

[158] Helmer writes that 'judge of the living and the dead' 'quickly became codified as a stock phrase in the creedal formulas of the early Church', Helmer, 'Gospel Tradition in the Apocalypse of Peter', 82. In the NT, it is found in Acts 10.42, 2 Tim 4.1 and 1 Pet 4.5.

ⲉⲃⲟⲗ [141,6–7]). Humans love the material world made of fire, but it is the fire that will consume those who loved it.

The all-consuming fire is an intertextual motif between the Book of Thomas and the Apocalypse of Peter:

> ϩⲉⲛ ⲫⲣⲁⲅⲉⲗⲗⲟⲩ ⲛ̄ⲥⲁⲧⲉ ⲉⲩⲛⲉϫ ϯⲕ̄ ⲧⲕ̄ ⲉⲃⲟⲗ ⲉϩⲟⲩ(ⲛ) [ϩ]ⲛ̣̄ ⲫⲟ ⲙ̄ⲡⲉⲧⲟⲩⲡⲏⲧ ⲛ̄ⲥⲱϥ ⲉϥⲡⲏⲧ ⲁⲡⲁⲙⲛⲧⲉ ⲉϥϭⲓ[ⲛ]ⲉ ⲛ̄ⲧⲁⲥⲁⲧⲉ ⲉϥϣⲁⲛⲕⲧⲟϥ ⲁⲣⲏⲥ ⲉϥϭⲛⲧⲥ̄ ⲟⲛ̄ ⲙ̄ⲙⲁⲩ ⲉ̣ϥϣⲁⲛⲕⲧⲟϥ ⲁϩⲏⲧ ϣⲁⲥⲧⲱⲙⲧ ⲉⲣⲟϥ ⲁⲛ ⲛ̄ϭⲓ ⲧⲁⲡⲓⲗⲏ ⲛ̄ⲥⲁⲧⲉ ⲉⲥⲃⲣ̄ⲃⲣ̄ ⲙⲁϥϭⲓⲛⲉ ⲇⲉ ⲛ̄ⲧⲟϥ ⲛ̄ⲑⲓⲏ ⲙ̄ⲡⲁⲉⲓⲃ̄ⲧⲉ ⲁⲡⲱⲧ ⲉⲙⲁⲩ ⲛ̄ϥⲟⲩ ϫⲁⲉⲓ ⲙ̄ⲡⲉϥϭⲛⲧⲥ̄ ⲅⲁⲣ ⲙ̄ⲫⲟⲟⲩ ⲉϥϩⲛ̄ ⲥⲱⲙ̣[ⲁ] ϫ̣ⲉⲕⲁⲁⲥ ⲉϥⲛⲁϭⲛⲧⲥ̄ ⲙ̄ⲫⲟⲟⲩ ⲛ̄ⲧⲕⲣⲓⲥⲓⲥ (BookThom 143,1–7)
>
> fiery scourges that cast a shower of sparks into the face of the one who is pursued. If he flees westward, he finds the fire. If he turns southward, he finds it there as well. If he turns northward, the threat of seething fire meets him again. Nor does he find the way to the east so as to flee there and be saved, for he did not find it in the day he was in the body, so that he might find it in the day of judgement.
>
> And so as soon as the whole creation dissolves, the men that are in the east shall flee to the west, and those who are in the west to the east; those in the south shall flee to the north, and those who are in the north to the south. And in all places shall the wrath of a fearful fire overtake them; and an unquenchable flame driving them shall bring them to the judgement of wrath, to the stream of unquenchable fire that flows, flaming with fire, and when its waves part themselves one from another, burning, there shall be a great gnashing of teeth among the children of men. (ApocPet 5.7–9)[159]

The extensive fire acts as a barricade in both of these texts, also being linked with judgement. The Book of Thomas uses this motif to promote its ascetic ideology: non-ascetic Christians are pursued by fire as a reflection of their desire for material things. In the Apocalypse of Peter, fire acts to drive sinners towards judgement.

Torments of hell is another common thread within the theme of eschatology in the Book of Thomas, the Apocalypse of Peter and the Epistula Apostolorum. In the Book of Thomas, those who love

[159] This translation is taken from J. K. Elliott, 'The Apocalypse of Peter', in *The Apocryphal New Testament: A Collection of Apocryphal Christian Literature in an English Translation* (Oxford: Clarendon Press, 1993), 593–612.

their beastly nature and those who sneer at the Christian message will be thrown down to the abyss and tormented, not being able to move, and if they try to flee, they will be met with fire (141,33–35; 142,26–143,13). Here there is a long list of 'woe' proclamations to those who have not understood the true nature of the material world. In the Apocalypse of Peter, the bulk of the text is a vision of the punishments of sinners, as described earlier. The Epistula Apostolorum's focus is not on the fate of sinners, yet we do find the teaching that the one who did not keep Jesus' commandments will remain outside the kingdom, and 'he will be terribly tortured and lacerated and torn apart with a great punishment, [and he will] be in agony' (44.4).[160] The three texts have largely different emphases and diverge in key theological teachings, and yet we find certain points of convergence regarding teachings of judgement, fire and torments.

Another text that incorporates torments is the Apocryphon of John, which present them as an alternative to the ascending soul or reincarnation. It is said of the souls that knew the All but turned away from it:

> ⲛ̄ⲥⲉⲁⲣⲉϩ ⲉⲣⲟⲟⲩ ⲉⲡⲉϩⲟⲟⲩ ⲉⲧⲟⲩⲛⲁⲕⲟⲗⲁⲍⲉ ϩⲣⲁ̈ⲓ ⲛϩⲏⲧϥ̄ ⲟⲩⲟⲛ ⲛⲓⲙ ⲛ̄ⲧⲁϥϫⲉ ⲟⲩⲁ ⲉⲡⲉⲡ̅ⲛ̅ⲁ̅ ⲉⲧⲟⲩⲁⲁⲃ ⲥⲉⲛⲁⲃⲁⲥⲁⲛⲓⲍⲉ ⲙⲙⲟⲟⲩ ϩⲛ ⲟ̣ⲩ̣ⲕⲟⲗⲁⲥⲓⲥ ⲛ̄ϣⲁ ⲉⲛⲉϩ ($_{BG}$ 70,16–71,2)
>
> They will be kept for the day on which everyone who has blasphemed the Holy Spirit will be punished. They will be tortured with eternal punishment.

The inclusion of this sentiment in the Apocryphon of John shows how wide-ranging the idea of post-mortem punishment is in early Christian literature. Torment is not exclusively reserved for flesh nor souls, as either can be subjected to eternal woes, and thus the theme of punishment is not linked to any particular stance towards materiality, nor theology nor christology.

The Apocalypse of Peter and the Epistula Apostolorum may appear to be more similar to each other than to other dialogue gospels, in their confirmation of judgement, torments and fleshly resurrection; however, the two texts present diametrically opposed depictions of 'heaven'. In the Apocalypse of Peter, the Akhmim

[160] The translation follows the Ethiopic text. The Coptic corresponds, but there are lacunae: ⲥⲉ[ⲛⲁ]ⲧ̣ϩ̣ⲙ̣ⲕⲟ ⲛ̄ⲙⲁϥ ⲕⲁⲕ ⲓⲛⲁ ⲁϥ[ⲛⲁ .. ⲁⲟⲩ ⲥⲉⲛⲁⲣ̄ⲕⲟⲗⲁⲍⲉ] ⲛ̄ⲙⲁϥ ϩⲛ̄ ϩⲛ̄ⲛⲁϭ̣ [ⲛ̄ⲕⲟⲗⲁⲥⲓⲥ ⲁⲟⲩ ϥⲛⲁ]ϩ̣ⲱ ⲡⲉ ϩ̣ⲁ ⲃⲁⲥⲁⲛⲟⲥ (37.5–8). Schmidt's restoration of the Coptic text does not sufficiently take the Ethiopic into account, and so his reconstructions are often unreliable.

fragment describes a large, light, sunny place. It is a great sensory experience, with a powerful scent of unfading flowers, spices and fruit plants. The inhabitants are dressed in shining clothes and walk among angels (15–20). Conversely, the picture of heaven in the Epistula Apostolorum is devoid of sensory experience – it is described in terms of being a place without eating or drinking, sorrow or singing, earthly clothing or decay (19.13–15). It is described as 'rest' (ⲁⲛⲁⲡⲁⲩⲥⲓⲥ [12.3, 19.14, 26.5]), which aligns salvation in the Epistula Apostolorum with salvation in the Gospel of Mary (17,15), the Epistle of Peter to Philip ($_{\text{NHC}}$ 137,10), the Dialogue of the Saviour (120,5–8) and the Book of Thomas (145,8–16).

Certain eschatological themes arise repeatedly throughout the diverse group of dialogue gospels, and this brief overview of selected themes in selected texts has served to show that they are variable and capricious. Dialogue gospels cannot be categorized into 'types' of eschatology. Each is concerned with individual salvation, whether it be ascension, reincarnation or resurrection.[161] Some include judgement and a fiery punishment, but this is not conditional on their stance towards materiality or the body. Often a dissolving cosmos is in the background, which may directly affect the individual or play two separate parts of a larger eschatological scheme. The eschatologies of dialogue gospels do not form binary oppositions; rather, they relate a web of interconnected networks and are best seen through a rhizomatic model. With all their divergences, the texts converge in their focus on Jesus as the way to salvation: Christ is the middle from which the varying eschatologies grow.

1.5 Conclusion

The thirteen dialogue gospels chosen to be part of our genre have as much and as little in common with each other as they do with other early Christian literature. 'Dialogue gospels' is a constructed genre, or group, which is always constructed around the interests of the constructor. For our purposes, the genre was created for the purpose of comparison, to highlight the similarities and differences within a group of thirteen texts that have (1) Jesus, as the central character, on the verge of departure, and (2) dialogue (broadly conceived) with one or more of his disciples. To bring these thirteen texts together allows

[161] A point that we have not touched on is the varying views of resurrection. For this, see Outi Lehtipuu, *Debates over the Resurrection of the Dead*, Oxford Early Christian Studies (Oxford and New York: Oxford University Press, 2015).

us to uncover and analyse connections that resist binary opposition or strict organization. As with the model of a rhizome, any point within a dialogue gospel can connect to any other within the same text, a different dialogue gospel or a text outside of the genre. We must remain flexible and open towards genre, as pigeonholing texts into one category or another hinders the discovery of links between texts that might not otherwise be obvious. As demonstrated through the cursory discussion of the depictions of the Saviour and eschatology within the dialogue gospel genre, there are multiple points of connections and divergences within the group, which can sometimes be quite unexpected and sometimes cause us to view the text in a new light.

2

WHY WRITE A DIALOGUE GOSPEL?

Themes from the New Testament

Dialogue gospels do not exist in isolation. They are part of the wider network of literary texts and traditions that shaped Christianity. They share a number of intertextual motifs with the canonical gospels and Pauline epistles. A broad overview of the themes, thoughts, motifs and linguistic connections shared between certain dialogue gospels and certain New Testament texts will be the subject of this chapter.

Why one might write a dialogue gospel is a difficult question to answer. Any number of personal, sociological and theological reasons could be proposed. But looking to the texts that came to be in the New Testament might act as a starting point for seeing how the dialogue gospels developed. Hartenstein's view that the dialogue gospels presupposed the canonical gospels and were intended as a 'second teaching' to supplement or surpass them is a helpful starting point.[1] Issues of dependence are not at stake here,[2] but rather the question will be framed around the concerns shared between the canonical texts and dialogue gospels and how they are answering the same questions similarly or differently. These concerns might be about Jesus' departure and its consequences, the nature of his resurrection or how to overcome the powers and principalities that dwell between earth and heaven. Comparisons between the two groups of texts can be made in general or specific ways, and both similarities and differences may be highlighted so as to establish connections

[1] It is not correct to presume that all of the dialogue gospels knew any number of canonical gospels, Paul's letters or other 'canonical' writings. For questions regarding sources, each dialogue gospel would have to be taken on its own terms and analysed in relation to the New Testament texts. However, it may be assumed that dialogue gospels are later than the canonical gospels and Pauline epistles and show evidence of sharing select traditions within them.

[2] For studies with this aim, see e.g. Christopher M. Tuckett, *Nag Hammadi and the Gospel Tradition: Synoptic Tradition in the Nag Hammadi Library* (Edinburgh: T&T Clark, 1986); Lorne R. Zelyck, *John among the Other Gospels: The Reception of the Fourth Gospel in the Extra-Canonical Gospels*, WUNT II 347 (Tübingen: Mohr Siebeck, 2013).

between dialogue gospels and canonical texts. Such comparisons may also result in new exegetical insights into the individual texts.

2.1 The Johannine Farewell Discourse (John 13.31–17.1)

As was shown in the previous chapter, the Johannine Farewell Discourse resembles other dialogue gospels so much so that it was included in our genre. To exclude it on the basis that it is also part of a *bios* gospel would be detrimental to the 'open' view of genre desirable for comparative analysis. Yet the Johannine Farewell Discourse may also be considered a precursor to other texts written in a question-and-answer format that are similarly concerned with Jesus' departure and how to act in his absence. On the whole, we might say that the dialogue gospel genre stemmed from John 13.31–17.1, and the latter inspired the themes and issues of the former.

Inspiration for the Genre

A connection between post-resurrection dialogues and the Johannine Farewell Discourse is often noted. In addition to Bockmuehl's observation, quoted in the last chapter, that the Jesus of the Johannine Farewell Discourse is similar to the Jesus of 'post-resurrection discourse gospels',[3] Dettwiler argues for similarities between the Johannine Farewell Discourse and post-resurrection dialogues, such as the Apocryphon of John, the Dialogue of the Saviour and the Gospel of Mary. He argues that such similarities lie in the character configuration of Jesus and his disciples, the sequence of dialogue, the rhetorical device of the misunderstanding disciples, selected sayings of Jesus and the function of the dialogues. He sees the Johannine discourse and post-resurrection dialogues as written for the purpose of exhortation and comfort within the community itself. He writes that the basic pragmatic function of both texts is to assure and strengthen their own theological beliefs.[4]

[3] Bockmuehl, *Ancient Apocryphal Gospels*, 174–5.

[4] Dettwiler, *Die Gegenwart des Erhöhten*, 21–6. Van Os argues that the Johannine farewell discourse is the model to which the post-resurrection dialogues were based on, citing the Epistula Apostolorum as evidence: 'The idea of a resurrection dialogue written by a "conservative" author can be explained as a counterattack on the gnostic resurrection dialogue. But the idea that such an author would dare to do so is better understood if there was a precedent in the Johannine tradition,' van Os, 'John's Last Supper', 277. As discussed in Chapter 1, it is unhelpful to characterize dialogue gospels as 'orthodox' (as opposed to 'gnostic'), let alone 'conservative'. It might be more helpful to say that the precedent for the genre in the Johannine tradition gave rise to the spectrum of teachings that we find in the other dialogue gospels.

The previous discussions have overlooked one glaring aspect in comparisons between the Johannine Farewell Discourse and other dialogue gospels: the shared overriding theme of Jesus' imminent departure. It is Jesus' looming exit from the world that necessitates eschatological revelation and instructions to the community. The Johannine Jesus makes this clear by saying, 'I did not say these things to you from the beginning, *because I was with you*; but now I am going to him who sent me' (ταῦτα δὲ ὑμῖν ἐξ ἀρχῆς οὐκ εἶπον, ὅτι μεθ' ὑμῶν ἤμην νῦν δὲ ὑπάγω πρὸς τὸν πέμψαντά με [16.4–5]). Taking this as a self-contained sentence, it is clear that there are teachings that Jesus did not tell the disciples until he had to. And νῦν is the final opportunity to ensure the salvation of his followers and their community.

Of our dialogue gospels, all but the fragmentary Dialogue of the Saviour narrate or indicate Jesus' departure in one way or another. Jesus frequently exits via ascension into heaven following post-resurrection teachings. In spite of this apparent inconsistency with the Johannine departure by death, dialogue gospels employ the departure theme in the same way: it is the last opportunity for revelatory dialogue. In most cases, the temporal setting of the departure is transposed from the Johannine last supper to after the resurrection, and this may be because the risen Jesus is considered to carry more authority than the incarnate Jesus. Often, the new nature of Jesus is said to be the reason that a post-resurrection dialogue might be inscribed. As the risen Jesus, he is privy to heavenly truths.[5] But so is the Johannine Jesus who has been glorified in 13.31. As John blurs resurrection, ascension and glorification, it does not matter too much that Jesus has not yet risen after his death or up on the cross. The more likely reason for the transposition from pre-death to post-resurrection is that Christians came to expect the narrative of the disciples meeting Jesus again after his crucifixion, and so there would be another opportunity for dialogue. To set the dialogue after the resurrection renders his departure to be imminent and final.

It is undeniable that the Johannine Farewell Discourse is different from other dialogue gospels: It is within a *bios* gospel. However, that does not mean that it did not give rise to the genre of dialogue gospel. It might be useful here to think in terms of macro-genres and micro-genres (or sub-genres).[6] To use Engberg-Pedersen's language: 'The

[5] See e.g. Hartenstein, *Die zweite Lehre*.

[6] 'The classification and hierarchical taxonomy of genres is not a neutral and "objective" procedure. There are no undisputed "maps" of the system of genres within any medium (though literature may perhaps lay some claim to a loose consensus).

gospel genre as created by Mark should itself be seen as a macro-genre which allows for the inclusion of several micro-genres: speeches, parables, and many more. In John we may find even more micro-genres to be included.'[7] The Farewell Discourse may be seen as a micro-genre in John, but new genres are often created from micro-genres. As Chandler writes, 'Each new work within a genre has the potential to influence changes within the genre or perhaps the emergence of new sub-genres (which may later blossom into fully-fledged genres).'[8]

In order to talk about the Johannine Farewell Discourse, the previous discussion about the necessity of an open and fluid concept of genre is particularly pertinent. Attridge, mentioned earlier, writes of John 'bending' particular genres, and this article has been widely cited since. He writes that: 'The farewell discourses present the greatest complexity for formal analysis',[9] and many scholars now see the Farewell Discourse as betraying a 'polyphony' of genres. However, Attridge still claims a primary influence of testamentary genre, due to 'the strong thematic insistence on the imminent departure of Jesus'.[10] Ashton combines the testament genre with the commission form, and he argues that the Farewell Discourse is to be understood as a 'bent' version of these combined genres.[11] Sheridan, however, criticizes him for having a 'taxonomic' approach to John's 'genre mosaic'.[12] She takes a more open view of genre, writing that the 'sub-genre [of the farewell discourse] alone is said to contain within itself a myriad of other micro-genres, and to "play" upon a generic field broad enough to call into question the validity of categorizing these chapters in terms of a single, over-arching genre'.[13]

Furthermore, there is often considerable theoretical disagreement about the definition of specific genres ... One theorist's genre may be another's sub-genre or even super-genre (and indeed what is technique, style, mode, formula or thematic grouping to one may be treated as a genre by another),' Chandler, 'An Introduction to Genre Theory', 1.

[7] Troels Engberg-Pedersen, 'A Question of Genre: John 13–17 as Paraklesis', in *The Gospel of John as Genre Mosaic*, ed. Kasper Bro Larsen, Studia Aarhusiana Neotestamentica 3 (Göttingen: Vandenhoeck & Ruprecht, 2015), 285. Unusually, Engberg-Pedersen understands John to be 'genre-bending' in order to provide the fullest clarity to its readers. He writes, 'Let us stop talking about "riddles", "enigmas", and the like in the Fourth Gospel. This text aims at achieving clarity for the benefit of its readers,' 285.

[8] Chandler, 'An Introduction to Genre Theory', 3.

[9] Attridge, 'Genre Bending in the Fourth Gospel', 17.

[10] Attridge, 'Genre Bending in the Fourth Gospel', 17. Cf. Chandler sees themes as an inadequate basis for defining genres since any theme can appear in any genre, Chandler, 'An Introduction to Genre Theory', 1.

[11] Ashton, *Understanding the Fourth Gospel*, 420–53.

[12] Ruth Sheridan, 'John's Gospel and Modern Genre Theory: The Farewell Discourse (John 13–17) as a Test Case', *Irish Theological Quarterly*, 75.3 (2010): 292.

[13] Sheridan, 'John's Gospel and Modern Genre Theory', 288.

It is my proposal that the writers of other dialogue gospels were so inspired by the Johannine 'dialogue gospel' that they did not just take on the themes of departure, consolation, theology, eschatology and soteriology, but they also took on the form of John 13.31–17.1. This may have been a conscious or sub-conscious decision, or even the result of many small decisions.[14] The micro-genre of the Johannine Farewell Discourse, once within the macro-genre of the *bios*, then becomes a macro-genre itself (although 'dialogue gospels' can also be apocalypses, epistles, gospels, and so forth). In these texts, Jesus engages in conversation with one or more of his disciples, on the eve of his departure, to give revelation. He can impart lengthy monologues (Apocryphon of John, Pistis Sophia), akin to John 15. Each dialogue gospel revises the themes and the form in different ways to produce a wide range of literature within the genre: there are instances of repetition and difference.[15] Yet each is inspired, in some way, by the themes and form found in the Johannine Farewell Discourse.

Specific Links

The relationship between the Johannine Farewell Discourse and other dialogue gospels is not just generic but includes thematic overlaps associated with Jesus' departure and what will happen to the disciples following it.[16] Here, I present a few of the many examples of connections that one might spot between the Johannine Farewell Discourse and dialogue gospels in order to highlight the collective interest in the ramifications of Jesus' exit from the world.

Perkins sees particularly close parallels between the Johannine Farewell Discourse and the Apocryphon of James, arguing that the Apocryphon of James is 'very much dependent upon the Johannine farewell discourses to answer orthodox objections [to its theology]'.[17]

[14] Patristic commentaries did not tend to differentiate between John 13.31–17.1 and the rest of the gospel, and so it is wrong to imagine ancient readers consciously thinking that they particularly liked the Farewell Discourse.

[15] Chandler cites Steve Neale, who declares that 'genre are instances of repetition and difference' and that 'difference is absolutely essential to the economy of genre', Chandler, 'An Introduction to Genre Theory', 2.

[16] There are also verbal overlaps such as the peace saying of John 14.27 (εἰρήνην ἀφίημι ὑμῖν, εἰρήνην τὴν ἐμὴν δίδωμι ὑμῖν) that occurs in the Sophia of Jesus Christ (BG 79,10–12) and the Gospel of Mary (8,14–15). The differences between the nuances of the saying in the Gospel of Mary and John are discussed in Chapter 3.

[17] Perkins, *Gnostic Dialogue*, 151. She sees similarities too with the First Apocalypse of James, in that the First Apocalypse of James describes Jesus' relationship with the highest God, his mission in making God known and his ascent and return. In both texts

The Apocryphon of James does appear to counter another Christian narrative (essentially condemning the apostolic generation [15,34–16,1]), but Perkins' claim that the author 'creates a *gnostic* farewell discourse'[18] is not so helpful. Earlier scholarship did not regard the Apocryphon of James as 'gnostic', in view of its christological narrative, disdain for prophecy (6,21–31) and enthusiasm for martyrdom (4,23–6,18)[19] – and that was at a time when 'gnosticism' still seemed an unproblematic category. It is better to understand it, as Brakke does, not as 'gnostic', Valentinian or as belonging to the Thomasine Syrian tradition (the categories into which much of the NHC has been split), but instead as an example of 'unclassified Christian apocrypha' with links to the hermeneutics and soteriology of Clement and Origen.[20]

At the beginning of the conversation between the risen Jesus and the Twelve in the Apocryphon of James, we find clear analogies to the Johannine Farewell Discourse:[21]

Apocryphon of James	John
ⲡⲁϫⲉⲛ ⲛⲉϥ ϫⲉ ⲁⲕⲃⲱⲕ ⲁⲕⲟⲩⲁⲉⲓⲉ ⲁⲣⲁⲛ (2,22)	Λέγει αὐτῷ Σίμων Πέτρος· κύριε, ποῦ ὑπάγεις; (13.36)
We said to him, 'Have you gone and departed from us?'	Simon Peter said to him, 'Lord, where are you going?'
ⲓⲏⲥ ⲇⲉ ⲡⲁϫⲉϥ ϫⲉ ⲙⲡⲉ· ⲁⲗⲗⲁ ϯⲛⲁⲃⲱⲕ ⲁⲡⲧⲟⲡⲟⲥ ⲛ̄ⲧⲁϩⲉⲓ̈ⲉⲓ ⲙ̄ⲙⲉⲩ (2,23–24)	πορεύομαι πρὸς τὸν πατέρα (14.28)
Jesus said, 'No, but I will go to the place from which I came.'	I am going to the Father.
	νῦν δὲ ὑπάγω πρὸς τὸν πέμψαντά με, καὶ οὐδεὶς ἐξ ὑμῶν ἐρωτᾷ με· ποῦ ὑπάγεις; (16.5)
	But now I am going to him who sent me.
	ἐξῆλθον παρὰ τοῦ πατρὸς καὶ ἐλήλυθα εἰς τὸν κόσμον· πάλιν ἀφίημι τὸν κόσμον καὶ πορεύομαι πρὸς τὸν πατέρα. (16.28)
	I came from the Father and have come into the world; again, I am leaving the world and am going to the Father.

Jesus warns the disciples that they will suffer and speaks of a paraclete figure (which is James himself in the First Apocalypse of James), Perkins, *Gnostic Dialogue*, 143.

[18] Perkins, 'Johannine Traditions in Ap. Jas.', 408.

[19] See W. C. van Unnik, 'The Origin of the Recently Discovered "Apocryphon Jacobi"', *VC* 10.3 (1956): 149–56. He argues that the Apocryphon of James originates from a small village church in Egypt that has not been affected by 'gnosticism'.

[20] David Brakke, 'Parables and Plain Speech in the Fourth Gospel and the Apocryphon of James', *JECS* 7.2 (1999): 203.

[21] For an extensive chart of these parallels, see Perkins, 'Johannine Traditions in Ap. Jas.', 408–10.

ϣⲡⲉ ⲧⲉⲧⲛ̄ⲟⲩⲱϣⲉ· ⲉⲉⲓ̂ ⲛⲙ̄ⲙⲏⲉⲓ̂ ⲁⲙⲏⲧⲛ̄ (2,25–26) If you wish to come with me, come.	ὅπου ὑπάγω οὐ δύνασαί μοι νῦν ἀκολουθῆσαι, ἀκολουθήσεις δὲ ὕστερον (13.36) Where I am going, you cannot follow me now; but you will follow afterward.
	πάλιν ἔρχομαι καὶ παραλήμψομαι ὑμᾶς πρὸς ἐμαυτόν, ἵνα ὅπου εἰμὶ ἐγὼ καὶ ὑμεῖς ἦτε. καὶ ὅπου [ἐγὼ] ὑπάγω οἴδατε τὴν ὁδόν. (14.3b–4) I will come again and will take you to myself, so that where I am, there you may be also. And you know the way where I am going.
ⲁϩⲟⲩⲱϣⲃ̄ ⲧⲏⲣⲟⲩ ⲡⲁϫⲉⲩ ϫⲉ ϣⲡⲉ ⲕⲣ̄ ⲕⲉ̣ⲗⲉⲩⲉ ⲛⲉⲛ ⲧⲛ̄ⲛ̄ⲏⲟⲩ (2,26–28) They all answered and said: 'If you command us, we come.'	λέγει αὐτῷ [ὁ] Ἰησοῦς· ἐγώ εἰμι ἡ ὁδὸς καὶ ἡ ἀλήθεια καὶ ἡ ζωή· οὐδεὶς ἔρχεται πρὸς τὸν πατέρα εἰ μὴ δι' ἐμοῦ. (14.6) Jesus said to him: 'I am the way, and the truth, and the life. No one comes to the Father except through me.'
ⲡⲁϫⲉϥ ϫ̣[ⲉ] ϩⲁⲙⲏⲛ ϯϫⲟⲩ ⲙ̄ⲙⲁⲥ ⲛⲏⲧⲛ̄ ϫ̣[ⲉ] ⲙⲏ ⲗⲁⲁⲩⲉ ⲁⲛⲏϩⲉ ⲛⲁⲃⲱⲕ ⲁϩⲟⲩ(ⲛ) ⲁⲧⲙⲛⲧⲣ̄ⲣⲟ ⲛⲙ̄ⲡⲏⲩⲉ· ⲉⲉⲓϣⲁⲛ̣(ⲣ) ⲕⲉⲗⲉⲩⲉⲓ ⲛⲉϥ ⲁⲗⲗⲁ ⲁⲃⲁⲗ ϫⲉ̣ ⲧⲉⲧⲛ̄ⲙⲏϩ ⲛ̄ⲧⲱⲧⲛ̄· (2,28–33) He said: 'Truly I say to you, no one will ever come into the kingdom of heaven if I command him – but because you yourselves are full.'	αἰτεῖτε καὶ λήμψεσθε, ἵνα ἡ χαρὰ ὑμῶν ᾖ πεπληρωμένη. (16.24) Ask and you will receive, so that your joy may be fulfilled. νῦν δὲ πρὸς σὲ ἔρχομαι καὶ ταῦτα λαλῶ ἐν τῷ κόσμῳ ἵνα ἔχωσιν τὴν χαρὰν τὴν ἐμὴν πεπληρωμένην ἐν ἑαυτοῖς. (17.13) But now I am coming to you, and I speak these things in the world so that they may have my joy fulfilled in themselves.

A major shared theme between the Johannine Farewell Discourse and the Apocryphon of James is the disciples' concern about how to follow Jesus after his final departure.[22] Jesus tells them that he is going home to his Father (John 16.28 corresponds perfectly to the Apocryphon of James 2,23–25) and that the disciples can accompany him – but conditionally. The Johannine disciples can follow Jesus into the kingdom (or to the Father) when they understand that he is the way (14.6) and that they are connected to the Father through Jesus (14.20). In the Apocryphon of James, Jesus tells the Twelve that they can only enter the 'kingdom of heaven' if they are 'full' (ⲙⲏϩ). Perkins conceives this parallel as a difference: 'The issue in the dialogue contrasts entering

22 As we have seen in the previous chapter, the Apocryphon of James and the First Apocalypse of James are closely connected.

the kingdom at Jesus' command (impossible) or by "becoming full" (a gnostic).'[23] However, becoming 'full' in the Apocryphon of James probably equates to the need for comprehension in the Johannine Farewell Discourse. In John, it is from Jesus' fullness (πλήρωμα) that humanity has received grace (1.16), and joy can be fulfilled (πεπλήρωται), as John the Baptist discovers when he hears the voice of the bridegroom (3.29). In the Farewell Discourse, Jesus promises the disciples a day when their joy will be fulfilled (πεπληρωμένη) by asking and receiving (16.24). That day is the day when Jesus no longer speaks in figures (16.25, cf. 17.13) – and thus the disciples will be filled with joy the day they come to understanding.[24] Therefore, instead of the Johannine/gnostic contrast that Perkins proposes, to understand that Jesus is the way to the Father in John is closely related to being filled in the Apocryphon of James.[25] This is demonstrated through the narrative: in the Apocryphon of James, Jesus takes James and Peter away to 'fill them', but what ensues is a revelatory dialogue from which the receptive disciple will gain understanding.[26]

The Apocryphon of John, likewise, has been compared to the Johannine Farewell Discourse as an explanation of how to follow Jesus into heaven. In John 14.2–4, Jesus promises his disciples that he will prepare a place for them with his Father and that he will return and show them the way there. King writes, '[t]he fact that the entire Secret Revelation of John is framed as the return of Christ to complete his revelation and show the way back to the Divine Realm makes it possible to read it as the completion of Christ's revelation in the Gospel of John [14.2–4]'.[27] Turner agrees, writing that '[t]he Fourth Gospel's farewell dialogues … concerning his promised return to the Father are now supplemented by John's post-ascension encounter with the very Savior who had indeed already returned to the Father just as he had predicted'.[28] He argues that the veiled references to the

[23] Perkins, 'Johannine Traditions in Ap. Jas.', 407.

[24] See Brakke, 'Parables and Plain Speech', 196–7.

[25] This may also be connected with the disciples being 'perfected' (τετελειωμένοι) in unity (17.23). *Contra* Hill who sees the Apocryphon of James as contradicting John 14.6: 'Against the testimony of Jesus in the Fourth Gospel, the author of *Ap. Jas.* does away with the need to come to the Father through Jesus. He who is "full" can enter on his own,' Charles E. Hill, *The Johannine Corpus in the Early Church* (Oxford: Oxford University Press, 2004), 255.

[26] This will be discussed further below. See also Brakke, 'Parables and Plain Speech'.

[27] King, *Secret Revelation of John*, 237–8.

[28] John D. Turner, 'The Johannine Legacy: The Gospel and Apocryphon of John', in *The Legacy of John: Second-Century Reception of the Fourth Gospel*, ed. Tuomas Rasimus, NovTSup 132 (Leiden and Boston: Brill, 2010), 139–40.

'many rooms' in John 14.2–3 are clarified in the Apocryphon of John as the four aeons, which Jesus himself had prepared before the world came into existence. To read the Apocryphon of John in this way means that the later dialogue gospel was written in order to answer what was left unanswered in John.

However, in spite of Jesus' promise to take his disciples to his Father, there still remains a period of time when the disciples must continue the Christian message without their leader. The questions that the dialogue gospels grapple with are not just about following Jesus to heaven but also what the disciples are to do in his absence. Throughout the Johannine Farewell Discourse, and in the prayer following, the disciples take on the characteristics of Jesus. They are sent into the world (17.18) to bear witness (15.27), they have received 'the words' that Jesus received (17.8), as well as the glory (17.22) and love (17.26), and they are hated by the world (15.18; 17.16). Come the end of the Farewell Discourse, they can pray directly to the Father (16.23), as Jesus does in chapter 17, and the Father gives 'everything' to Jesus (17.7), which now Jesus gives to the disciples (16.23). Because of Jesus' departure, the disciples are commissioned to do greater works than Jesus himself (14.12), leading Woll to envisage the disciples 'as successor-agents of the works of the Son, and as bearers of the presence of Father and Son'.[29] This role is comparable to the portrayal of the disciples in the Sophia of Jesus Christ, in which the relationship between the Father, the Son and the disciples parallels John:

> καθὼς ἐμὲ ἀπέστειλας εἰς τὸν κόσμον, κἀγὼ ἀπέστειλα αὐτοὺς εἰς τὸν κόσμον (John 17.18)
>
> As you have sent me into the world, so I have sent them into the world.
>
> ⲛ̄ⲧⲱⲧⲛ̄ ⲁⲩⲧⲛ̄ⲛⲟⲟⲩ ⲧⲏⲩⲧⲛ̄ ⲉⲃⲟⲗ ϩⲓ̈ⲧⲟⲟⲧϥ ⲙ̄ⲡϣⲏⲣⲉ ⲛ̄ⲧⲁⲩⲧⲛ̄ⲛⲟⲟⲩϥ (SophJesChr $_{BG}$ 105,14–17)
>
> You yourselves were sent by the Son who was sent.

Although the relationship of sender and sent corresponds, the contexts are different. In the Sophia of Jesus Christ, the disciples are sent by the Son to receive light and escape the realm of forgetfulness. This should probably be read alongside: 'All who come into the world have been sent by him, like a drop from the light, to the

[29] D. Bruce Woll, 'The Departure of "The Way": The First Farewell Discourse in the Gospel of John', *JBL* 99.2 (1980): 234.

world of the Pantocrator, to guard it through him' (ⲟⲩⲟⲛ ⲛⲓⲙ ⲉⲧⲛⲏⲩ ⲉⲡⲕⲟⲥⲙⲟⲥ ⲁⲩⲧⲛ̄ⲛⲟⲟⲩⲥⲉ ⲉⲃⲟⲗ ϩⲓ̈ⲧⲙ̄ ⲡⲁⲉⲓ ⲛ̄ⲑⲉ ⲛ̄ⲛⲟⲩⲧⲗ̄ϯⲗⲉ ⲉⲃⲟⲗ ϩⲙ ⲡⲟⲩⲟⲓ̈ⲛ ⲉⲡⲕⲟⲥⲙⲟⲥ ⲙⲡⲡⲁⲛⲧⲟⲕⲣⲁⲧⲱⲣ ⲉⲁⲣⲉϩ ⲉⲣⲟϥ ⲉⲃⲟⲗ ϩⲓ̈ⲧⲟⲟⲧϥ [BG 103,10–26]).[30] The concepts of mission appear very different in the two texts. Yet the texts converge again as the disciples 'who are sent' bear the divine presence (light) in the world but do not belong to it (cf. John 17.16).[31] It seems that the Johannine Farewell Discourse and the Sophia of Jesus Christ are grappling with the same idea but approaching it from different perspectives.

In John, the chain of authority also encompasses the paraclete – the spirit that the Johannine Jesus sends to teach and comfort the disciples, and who will only arrive after Jesus' departure. The paraclete mirrors Jesus as it is sent into the world (17.18), and the world will not receive it (15.18). Martyn argues that these actions also apply to the Christian witness.[32] The disciple as a successor of Jesus in a paraclete-type role is encountered in dialogue gospels, as when James is presented as the 'second teacher' (ⲡⲙⲉϩ ⲥⲁϩ̄) and 'comfort' (ⲥⲟⲗⲥⲓⲗ̄) in the First Apocalypse of James (CT 17,13–15) and Mary stands in for Jesus in the Gospel of Mary.[33] Nowhere in the dialogue gospels does Jesus promise a Johannine-style paraclete sent from the Father – the disciples must take on this role themselves, becoming Jesus' successors on earth as he abides in heaven.[34]

[30] The version in NHC 3 reads ϫⲉ ⲉⲩⲉϩⲁⲣⲏϩ ⲉⲣⲟⲟⲩ ⲉⲃⲟⲗ ϩⲓ̈ⲧⲟⲟⲧϥ̄ (that they may be guarded through him [107,4–5]) instead of ⲉⲁⲣⲉϩ ⲉⲣⲟϥ ⲉⲃⲟⲗ ϩⲓ̈ⲧⲟⲟⲧϥ (to guard it through him). The Brill edition translates 'by him' instead of 'through him' and considers the BG version to be corrupt, *Nag Hammadi Codices III,3–4*, 129. But 'through him' makes better sense as those entering the world protect it from the Pantocrator (the Demiurge) through the agency of the highest God. The two recensions provide different interpretations, with the disciples in BG having an active role in guarding the world.

[31] For this and further parallels to the Johannine concept of sending in the Apocryphon of John, the Apocryphon of James and other texts, see Johan Ferreira, *Johannine Ecclesiology*, LNTS 160 (Sheffield: T&T Clark, 1998), 166–200, esp. 183–90.

[32] J. Louis Martyn, *History and Theology in the Fourth Gospel*, 3rd ed., New Testament Library (Louisville, KY and London: Westminster John Knox Press, 2003), 141–2.

[33] The Father–Jesus–disciples hierarchy is also explicit in the First Apocalypse of James. See Edwards, 'The Rhetoric of Authority', 65–79. Edwards writes: 'While Jesus is a reflection of the "One Who Is", somehow the same and also second, the same dynamic exists between Jesus and James' (73). He also notes interesting parallels between Jesus' and James' martyrdoms in the First Apocalypse of James, such as James being found not guilty but condemned by a crowd (75). More will be said on Mary's paraclete-type role in the Gospel of Mary in the next chapter.

[34] But cf. ApJas 11,11–13, 'Woe to you who lack a paraclete!' (ⲟⲩⲁⲉⲓ ⲛⲏⲧⲛ̄ ⲱ ⲛⲉⲧϣⲁⲁⲧ· ⲛ̄ⲛⲟⲩⲡⲁⲣⲁⲕⲗⲏⲧⲟⲥ), where the paraclete is probably the ascended Jesus interceding for his disciples (11,4–6; cf. 1 John 2.1).

2.2 Canonical Resurrection Appearances

The four canonical gospels each end with a risen Jesus coming to speak with his disciples, Acts opens with the risen Jesus teaching them about the kingdom of God over the course of forty days (1.3), and Paul writes of multiple but limited appearances of the risen Lord (1 Cor 15.5–8). This section will select a theme in each of these texts and examine its treatment in the dialogue gospels. A number of other themes might have been selected, such as the nature of ὤφθη in 1 Corinthians 15.5–8, the journey narrative in Mark LE and Luke 24 or the role of the Johannine beloved disciple. The selected themes cannot be confined to individual texts; for example, the ambiguous treatment of Jesus' physicality in John 20 is comparable to Luke 24.

1 Corinthians 15 and the Hierarchy of Disciples

Dialogue gospels show clear favourites among the disciples. Jesus may select one or more specific disciples to receive his teachings. He may select, for example, John, Peter or James alone, or he may prefer to speak the Twelve altogether.[35] Either way, this suggests a hierarchy of disciples. The question of a hierarchy, predicated on who is the main or first recipient of Jesus' revelation, may be comparable to whom the risen Jesus appears to in 1 Corinthians 15.5–8. Paul divides the appearances of the risen Jesus into six:

1. And that he appeared to Cephas (καὶ ὅτι ὤφθη Κηφᾷ)
2. then to the Twelve (εἶτα τοῖς δώδεκα)
3. then he appeared to more than five hundred brothers (and sisters) at once, of whom the majority remain until now, but some have fallen asleep (ἔπειτα ὤφθη ἐπάνω πεντακοσίοις ἀδελφοῖς ἐφάπαξ, ἐξ ὧν οἱ πλείονες μένουσιν ἕως ἄρτι, τινὲς δὲ ἐκοιμήθησαν)
4. then he appeared to James (ἔπειτα ὤφθη Ἰακώβῳ)
5. then to all the apostles (εἶτα τοῖς ἀποστόλοις πᾶσιν)
6. and last of all, he appeared to me, as to the untimely birth (ἔσχατον δὲ πάντων ὡσπερεὶ τῷ ἐκτρώματι ὤφθη κἀμοί)

[35] There is a fair amount of scholarship on individual disciples that engages with dialogue gospels. A few examples include: Bart D. Ehrman, *Peter, Paul, and Mary Magdalene: The Followers of Jesus in History and Legend* (New York: Oxford University Press, 2006); Ismo Dunderberg, *The Beloved Disciple in Conflict? Revisiting the Gospels of John and Thomas* (New York: Oxford University Press, 2006); Ann Graham Brock, *Mary Magdalene, The First Apostle: The Struggle for Authority* (Cambridge, MA: Harvard University Press, 2003).

Although chronology is an issue, Paul's formula places Peter and James in dominant positions, using parallelism in the pairings of 'Cephas – the Twelve' and of 'James – all the apostles' within the format of the εἶτα – ἔπειτα – ἔπειτα – εἶτα construction. So, although Jesus appears to the Twelve before James, Paul's syntax places James' authority above that of the Twelve.

The dialogue gospels are not concerned with whom Jesus appears to *first*: the revelation is not that Jesus has risen, but the question is with whom he engages in revelatory dialogue. There are clearly dominant and privileged disciples. In the Book of Thomas, Jesus speaks to Judas Thomas alone, addressing him as 'my twin and true friend' (ⲡⲁⲥⲟⲉⲓϣ ⲁⲩⲱ ⲡⲁϣⲃⲣ̄ⲙ̄ⲏⲙⲉ [138,7–8]).[36] The Apocryphon of John sees John as the chosen disciple, and the Gospel of Mary chooses Mary. The First Apocalypse of James describes James as a teacher with his own disciples. The Epistle of Peter to Philip, the Apocalypse of Peter and the Epistula Apostolorum see the Twelve (or Eleven) as an apostolic union, but the Epistle of Peter to Philip and the Apocalypse of Peter have Peter leading. The Epistula Apostolorum begins with 'John and Thomas and Peter … to the churches' (2.1–3), suggesting that John and Thomas may have a greater role than Peter.[37] The Gospel of Judas and the Apocryphon of James, on the other hand, propose that there is a problem with the apostolic generation. In the Gospel of Judas, Jesus laughs at the stupidity of the Twelve, and in the Apocryphon of James, the apostles' salvation is dependent on the generation to come. The Dialogue of the Saviour has Jesus teaching Matthew, Judas and Mary, and the Sophia of Jesus Christ may be the most inclusive of the texts as Jesus appears there to the Twelve and seven women and does not separate any from the rest of the group. Of all the texts discussed, Paul is only included in the Epistula Apostolorum, in which Jesus comes to him in a separate

[36] Schenke equates this to the beloved disciple in John: 'One is thus justified in supposing a Greek original with this meaning "you are … my true friend" behind the Coptic. Transposed into a form parallel with that of the Gospel of John, this would read "you are the one I truly love", or, in the third person singular, "he is the one whom Jesus truly loved",' Hans-Martin Schenke, 'Function and Background of the Beloved Disciple', in *Der Same Seths: Hans-Martin Schenkes kleine Schriften zu Gnosis, Koptologie und Neuem Testament*, ed. Gesine Schenke Robinson, Gesa Schenke, and Uwe-Karsten Plisch (Leiden and Boston: Brill, 2012), 611.

[37] See Francis Watson, 'A Gospel of the Eleven: The Epistula Apostolorum and the Johannine Tradition', in *Connecting Gospels: Beyond the Canonical/Non-Canonical Divide*, ed. Francis Watson and Sarah Parkhouse (Oxford: Oxford University Press, 2018), 189–215.

appearance: 'and he will hear my voice from heaven with astonishment, fear and trembling' (31.1).

Harnack argued that the lists in 1 Corinthians 15 came into being from a rivalry between the Peter-party and the James-party in the early Church,[38] and in view of the dialogue gospels, there may be some truth in this claim. Peter is a contested figure in the dialogue gospels – he is likened to an 'adversary' (ⲁⲛⲧⲓⲕⲉⲓⲙⲉⲛⲟⲥ [18,10]) in the Gospel of Mary and so paralleled to the cosmic powers named Desire, Ignorance and Wrath (16,5–13). In contrast, the Epistle of Peter to Philip presents him as the leader of the apostles, the first to receive the Holy Spirit and communicate the Christian message. He writes to Philip to ask him to return to the group, and Philip willingly goes as requested. As Meyer writes: 'Philip ultimately is submissive to the will of the apostle Peter ... Hence in the *Ep. Pet. Phil.*, as in Acts, the day belongs to Peter. His is the preeminent authority, and the letter and tractate champion his cause.'[39] In the First Apocalypse of James, there is a stark contrast between James' role and that of the Twelve. James is instructed to 'hide (Jesus' revelation) [wi]thin you and be silent' (ⲉⲕⲉϩⲱⲡ <ⲙ̄ⲙⲟⲟⲩ> ϩⲣ[ⲁ̈ⲓ̈ ⲛ̄]ϩ̣ⲏⲧⲕ̄· ⲉⲕⲉϣⲱⲡⲉ ⲇⲉ ⲉⲕⲕ̣ⲱ ⲛ̄ⲣⲱⲕ [$_{\text{NHC}}$ 36,13–14]). The revelation will only be made public several generations later ($_{\text{NHC}}$ 37,20–23). The Epistle of Peter to Philip and the First Apocalypse of James are striking in how much they emphasize the authority of their protagonists. In both texts, it may be said that Peter and James have their own 'disciples' (ⲛⲉϥⲙⲁⲑⲏⲧⲏⲥ [EpPetPhil $_{\text{NHC}}$ 139,10; 1ApocJas $_{\text{CT}}$ 17,11]).[40]

The Apocryphon of James, conversely, prioritizes James *and* Peter, suggesting that any perceived rivalry is not quite as stark as a Peter-party and a James-party. However, they are not equals, nor are they flawless. Peter shows his ignorance in his questions, and James refers to a secret book that contained teachings that the Saviour had revealed to him alone (1,28–35; cf. 1ApocJas) but states that this one, the Apocryphon of James, has been revealed to him and to Peter. Like the First Apocalypse of James, the Apocryphon of

[38] See Reginald H. Fuller, *The Formation of the Resurrection Narratives* (Philadelphia, PA: Fortress Press, 1980), 28, citing Adolf Harnack, 'Die Verklärungsgeschichte Jesu, der Bericht des Paulus (I Kor. 15, 3ff) und die beiden Christusvisionen des Petrus', *Sitzungsberichte der Königlich Preussischen Akademie der Wissenschaften zu Berlin* (1922): 62–80.

[39] Meyer, *Letter of Peter to Philip*, 96.

[40] According to Meyer, it is ambiguous in the Epistle of Peter to Philip whether 'his disciples' refers to Peter speaking to *his disciples* or Peter speaking to *Jesus' disciples*, see Meyer, *Letter of Peter to Philip*, 150. There is a lacuna in the CT version. The same interpretative problem might be raised for the First Apocalypse of James.

James too contains teachings that ‘the Saviour did not wish to tell all of us, his twelve disciples’ (ⲉⲧⲉ·ⲙ̄ⲡⲉⲡⲥⲱⲣ ⲟⲩⲱϣ· [ⲁ]ϫⲟⲟϥ ⲁⲣⲁⲛ ⲧⲏⲣⲛ̄ ⲡϥⲙⲛ̄ⲧⲥⲛⲁⲩⲥ ⲙ̄ⲙⲁⲑⲏⲧⲏⲥ [1,22–25]). The other disciples are presented as flawed – they write books about the Saviour without being filled (2,8–15, 33–39), and they become jealous of the coming blessed generation (16,2–5).[41]

The disparagement of the apostles and the apostolic age in the Apocryphon of James actually includes James and Peter, which becomes clear on the final pages. James and Peter ascend through the heavens but cannot reach the highest one: ‘We were not permitted to see or hear anything, *for the other disciples called us*’ (ⲙ̄ⲡⲟⲩⲕⲁⲁⲛ· ⲁⲛⲉⲩ· ⲟⲩⲧⲉ ⲁⲥⲱⲧⲙ̄ ⲁⲗⲁⲩⲉ· ϩⲁⲡⲕⲉϣⲱϫⲡ̄ ⲅⲁⲣ ⲙ̄ⲙⲁⲑⲏⲧⲏⲥ ⲙⲟⲩⲧⲉ ⲁⲣⲁⲛ [15,26–29]). It seems then that James and Peter are constrained by the other disciples; their calling them acts as a reminder that they belong within the limits of the apostolic age. The letter continually looks backward and forward; back to the error and ignorance of the apostolic generation and forward to a new generation of children who will secure the salvation of humankind. Jesus pronounces woe on those who have seen the Son of Man, but blessings for those who have not (3,11–23), and points to the future generation:

> ϩⲙ̄ⲙⲁⲕⲁⲣⲓⲟⲥ ⲛ̄ϣⲁⲙⲛ̄ⲧ ⲛ̄ⲥⲁⲡ ⲛⲉ[[ⲉⲓ]] ⲛⲉⲉⲓ̣ ⲛⲧ[ⲁϩⲟⲩ]ⲧⲁϣⲉ ⲁⲉⲓϣ ⲙ̄ⲙⲁⲩ ϩⲓ̈ⲧⲛ̄ ⲡϣⲏ̣[ⲣⲉ] ⲉⲙⲡⲁⲧⲟⲩϣⲱⲡⲉ· ϫⲉⲕⲁⲥⲉ ⲉⲣ̣[ⲉ]ⲟⲩⲙⲉⲣⲟⲥ ϣⲱⲡⲉ ⲛⲏⲧⲛ̄ ⲛⲙ̄ⲙⲉⲩ (14,41–15,5)
>
> Three times blessed are they who [were] proclaimed by the So[n] before they came to be, that you might have a portion among them.

The notion that the apostolic generation is inadequate may stem from Thomas’ doubt in seeing the risen Jesus in John 20. Thomas needs Jesus to invite him to touch his wounds to believe that he has risen, and only then does he profess Jesus as his Lord and God. Jesus replies: ‘Have you believed because you have seen me? Blessed are those who have not seen and yet have come to believe’ (ὅτι ἑώρακάς με πεπίστευκας; μακάριοι οἱ μὴ ἰδόντες καὶ πιστεύσαντες [20.29]). Although John is not necessarily referring to a future generation, the μακάριοι language of those that have not seen mirrors the praise of the ‘blessed’ (ⲙⲁⲕⲁⲣⲓⲟⲥ) future generation in the Apocryphon of James, whereas Thomas represents disbelief and doubt.

[41] For this and also the potentiality of the Twelve writing their gospels before receiving gnosis, see Perkins, ‘Johannine Traditions in Ap. Jas.’, 404, 406. On the books, see Brakke, ‘Parables and Plain Speech’.

The Apocryphon of James takes this further than simply stating the superiority of the future generations: the text claims that James and Peter will be saved only through this future generation. James writes:

> ⲁϥϭⲱⲗⲡ ⲛⲉⲛ ⲁⲃⲁⲗ ⲛ̄ϩⲛ̄ϣⲏⲣⲉ ⲉⲩⲛ̄ⲛⲏⲩ ⲙⲛ̄ⲛ̄ⲥⲱⲛ ⲉⲁϥⲣ̄ ⲕⲉⲗⲉⲩⲉ [ⲛⲉⲛ] ⲁ[ⲧⲣ]ⲉ̣ⲛⲙⲉⲣⲓⲧⲟⲩ ϩⲱⲥ ⲉⲛⲁⲟ̣[ⲩϫ]ⲉ̣[ⲉⲓ] ⲉⲧⲃⲉ ⲛⲉⲧⲙ̄ⲙⲉⲩ (15,38–16,2)
>
> He revealed to us children who are to come after us, bidding [us] love them, as we would be [saved] because of them.[42]

James then prays that he might obtain a portion among these children (16,9–11) and refers to a faith that will be greater than his. In the text James (and Peter) are not the targets of polemic, but they are certainly understood as belonging to an apostolic age that is inferior to the future generation and can only be saved through them.

Another answer to the question of which disciples Jesus addresses, and one that is omitted by Paul and the texts prioritizing Peter, James or Thomas, is to include women. The Gospel of Mary, the Sophia of Jesus Christ, the Dialogue of the Saviour, the Pistis Sophia and the Epistula Apostolorum all do so, but in varying ways.[43] The Gospel of Mary presents Mary as lead disciple and privy to previously unknown eschatological teachings, the Sophia of Jesus Christ includes seven women on the mountain with the Twelve, the Dialogue of the Saviour involves Mary in the dialogue, the Pistis Sophia involves several women in the dialogue, and the Epistula Apostolorum has Jesus appearing first to Mary, Martha and Mary Magdalene (or Sarah, Martha and Mary Magdalene in the Ge'ez version).[44] The inclusion of female disciples in a post-resurrection context contrasts with the account in 1 Corinthians, but comes closer to the canonical gospels in which all but Luke narrate the risen Jesus appearing first to a group of women or Mary alone.

[42] The Brill translation reads: '[he] revealed to us children who are to come after us, after bidding [us] love them, as we would be [saved] for their sakes', Williams, 'The Apocryphon of James – 1,2: 1.1–16:30', 53. This translation implies that James and the apostles will be saved in order to help the children, rather than being saved because of their superiority. My translation is similar to Rouleau's. See Louise Roy and Donald Rouleau, *L'Épître apocryphe de Jacques (NH I,2) suivi de l'Acte de Pierre (BG 4)*, BCNH:T 18 (Québec: Les Presses de l'Université Laval, 1987), 90–1.

[43] Petersen focuses on the presentation of the women in these texts, Petersen, *Zerstört die Werke*.

[44] The Coptic actually reads 'Mary of Martha (ⲙⲁⲣⲓⲁ ⲧⲁⲙⲁⲣⲑⲁ) and Mary Magdalene' (9.2), but presumably this is a mistake, as is the preceding reference to 'a th[ird w]oman' (ⲉⲩⲙⲁϩ[ϩⲁⲙⲧⲉ ⲛ̄ⲥ]ϩⲓⲙⲉ); Ge'ez: 'three women'.

The hierarchy of disciples is not just a hierarchy among the Twelve – it may include Mary or Martha, James the Just or Judas. The selection of disciples may demonstrate criticism of the Twelve. Earlier texts left unanswered the question of who has authority in Jesus' absence – and, as the Gospel of Mary makes clear, apostolic authority was a key issue of contestation, as Jesus' followers had different interpretations of his teachings. The convergence and contrasts between the characters in the dialogue gospels demonstrate how the role of disciples were in flux in the early centuries, and the texts are attempting to answer the issue of who was the most reliable witness of Jesus in his absence.

Matthew 28 and the Mission Charge

At the end of Matthew, the risen Jesus commissions the Eleven to make disciples of all nations, and the mission charge marks a transition point from the teaching of Jesus to the activity of the disciples.[45]

> πορευθέντες οὖν μαθητεύσατε πάντα τὰ ἔθνη, βαπτίζοντες αὐτοὺς εἰς τὸ ὄνομα τοῦ πατρὸς καὶ τοῦ υἱοῦ καὶ τοῦ ἁγίου πνεύματος, διδάσκοντες αὐτοὺς τηρεῖν πάντα ὅσα ἐνετειλάμην ὑμῖν: καὶ ἰδοὺ ἐγὼ μεθ' ὑμῶν εἰμι πάσας τὰς ἡμέρας ἕως τῆς συντελείας τοῦ αἰῶνος (28.19–20)
>
> Therefore, go and make disciples of all nations, baptizing them in the name of the Father and of the Son and of the Holy Spirit, and teaching them to obey everything that I have commanded you. And behold I am with you always, to the very end of the age.

What the disciples are supposed to do is clear; how they are supposed to do it is not. Matthew shows no evidence that Jesus has provided the

[45] Hartenstein, *Die zweite Lehre*, 297. Hartenstein sees Matt 28.16–20 as the most influential of the canonical gospel passages on the dialogue gospels (292). In Matthew, Jesus' resurrection is accepted without question, unlike Luke or John. Instead of confirming his resurrection, Matthew simply allows Jesus to give his instructions to the disciples – a starting point for many dialogue gospels. Furthermore, the appearance in Matthew is the '*himmlischste*' of all the canonical resurrection accounts, with the mountain setting and no description of Jesus' appearance (293–4). She writes of the Sophia of Jesus Christ, the Apocryphon of James and the Gospel of Mary that they are '[b]esonders stark matthäisch geprägt' (292), and that the Sophia of Jesus Christ is an extension or alternative to the Matthean commission scene (57–8). On Matt 28 and the Sophia of Jesus Christ, see also Falkenberg, 'Matthew 28:16–20 and the Nag Hammadi Library', 93–104. On Matt 28 and the Apocalypse of Peter, see Helmer, 'Gospel Tradition in the Apocalypse of Peter', esp. 67.

capability, knowledge or means to enact his instruction. While in Luke-Acts and John he equips his disciples with the spirit, in Matthew there are just the relatively impractical words: 'I am with you always.' In dialogue gospels, where the command to preach is either explicit or implicit, the lack of training and education leads to mission anxiety. Thomas in the Book of Thomas and the Eleven in the Epistula Apostolorum worry about not having enough information: how can the disciples evangelize if they do not fully understand the Christian message themselves?

> ⲡⲁⲗⲓⲛ̣ [ⲁⲛ] ⲡⲁϫⲉⲛ ⲛⲉϥ ϫⲉ ⲡϫⲁⲉⲓⲥ ⲟⲩⲁⲛⲁⲅⲕⲏ ⲅⲁⲣ ⲛⲉⲛ ⲧⲉ ⲁⲧⲛ̄ϣⲓⲛⲉ ⲁⲃⲁⲗ ϩⲓⲧⲟⲟⲧⲕ ·ⲁⲃⲁⲗ ϫⲉ ⲕⲟⲩⲁϩⲥⲁϩⲛⲉ ⲛⲉⲛ ⲁⲧⲛ̄ⲧⲁϣⲉⲁⲉⲓϣ · ϫⲉⲕⲁⲁⲥ ⲁⲛⲛⲁⲙ̄ⲙⲉ ϩⲟⲩⲟⲩⲛⲉ ⳉⲛ̄ ⲟⲩⲱⲣϫ [ⲁ]ⲃⲁⲗ ϩⲓⲧⲟⲟⲧⲕ ⲁⲟⲩ ⲧⲛ̄ⳉⲱⲡⲉ ⲛ̄ⲣⲉϥⲧⲁϣⲉⲁⲉⲓϣ ⲉϥⲣ̄ϣⲉⲩ ⲁⲟⲩ ⲛⲉⲧⲛⲁⲧⲥⲉⲃⲟ ⲁⲃⲁⲗ ϩⲓⲧⲟⲟⲧⲛⲉ ⲥⲉⳉⲱⲡⲉ ⲉⲩⲣ̄ⲡⲓⲥⲧⲉⲩⲉ ⲁⲣⲁⲕ ⲉⲧⲃⲉ ⲡⲉⲓ̈ ⲧⲁⲣⲛ̄ϣⲛ̄ⲧⲕ ⲛ̄ϩⲁϩ ⲛ̄ⲥⲁⲡ (EpAp 23.1–3)
>
> Again, we said to him, 'Lord, it is necessary for us to question you, for you command us to preach; so that we ourselves may know with certainty through you and be useful preachers, and [that] those who will teach through us may believe in you. That is why we question you so much!'
>
> ⲡⲁϫⲉⲛ ⲇⲉ ⲛⲉϥ [ϫⲉ ⲡϫⲁ]ⲉⲓⲥ ⲛⲓⲙ ⲡⲉⲧⲛⲁ̣ⲣ̄ⲡⲓⲥⲧⲉⲩⲉ ⲛⲉ̣ⲛ ⲏ [ⲛⲓⲙ ⲡⲉⲧ]ⲛⲁⲥⲱⲧⲙⲉ ⲁⲣⲁⲛ (EpAp 30.1)
>
> We said to him: '[Lo]rd, who will believe us, or [who] will listen to us?'
>
> ⲡⲁϫⲉϥ ⲇⲉ ⲛ̄ϭⲓ ⲑⲱⲙⲁⲥ ⲙ̄ⲡϫⲟⲉⲓⲥ ϫⲉ ⲉⲧ̣ⲃⲉ ⲡⲁⲉⲓ ϭⲉ ϯⲥⲟⲡⲥ̄ ⲙ̄ⲙⲟⲕ ϫⲉⲕⲁⲁⲥ ⲉⲕⲛⲁϫⲱ ⲛⲁⲓ̈ [ⲛ̄ⲛ]ⲉϯϣⲓⲛⲉ ⲙ̄ⲙⲟⲕ ⲉⲣⲟⲟⲩ ϩⲁ ⲑⲏ ⲛ̄ⲧⲉⲕ ⲁⲛⲁⲗⲏⲙ ⲯⲓⲥ [ⲁⲩ]ⲱ ϩⲟⲧⲁⲛ ⲉⲉⲓϣⲁⲛ ⲥⲱⲧⲙ̄ ⲉⲃⲟⲗ ϩⲓⲧⲟⲟⲧⲕ ϩⲁ ⲡⲣⲁ ⲛⲛ̣ⲉⲑⲏⲡ ⲧⲟⲧⲉ ⲟⲩⲛ̄ ϭⲟⲙ ⲙ̄ⲙⲟⲉⲓ ⲉϣⲁϫⲉ ⲉⲧⲃⲏ ⲧ[ⲟ]ⲩ ⲁⲩⲱ ⲥⲟⲩⲟⲛϩ ⲉⲃⲟⲗ ⲛⲁⲉⲓ ϫⲉ ⲧⲙⲏⲉ ⲥⲙⲟⲕϩ ⲁ ⲁ[ⲥ] ⲛ̄ⲛⲁϩⲣⲛ̄ ⲛ̄ⲣⲱⲙⲉ (BookThom 138,21–27)
>
> Now Thomas said to the Lord, 'Therefore I beg you to tell me what I ask you before your ascension, and when I hear from you about the hidden things, then I can speak about them. And it is obvious to me that the truth is difficult to perform before men.'
>
> ⲁⲗⲗⲁ ⲛⲓϣⲁ[ϫⲉ ⲉ]ⲧⲕϫⲱ ⲙ̄ⲙⲟⲟⲩ ⲛⲁⲛ ϩⲉⲛⲥⲱⲃⲉ ⲛⲉ ⲙ̄ⲡⲕⲟⲥ[ⲙⲟ]ⲥ ⲁⲩⲱ ϩⲛ̄ⲗ̄ⲕ ϣⲁⲉⲓ ⲛ̄ⲥⲱⲟⲩ ⲛⲉ ⲉⲡⲓⲇⲏ ⲥⲉⲥⲟ[ⲟⲩ]ⲛⲉ ⲙ̄ⲙⲟⲟⲩ ⲁⲛ ⲛ̄ⲁϣ ϭⲉ ⲛ̄ⲣⲏⲧⲉ ⲉⲛⲛⲁϣⲃⲱⲕ ⲁ[ⲧⲁ]ϣ̣ⲉⲟⲉⲓϣ ⲙ̄ⲙⲟⲟⲩ ⲉⲡⲓⲇⲏ ϫⲉ ⲥⲉⲱⲡ ⲙ̄ⲙⲟⲛ [ⲁⲛ ϩ]ⲙ̄ ⲡⲕⲟⲥⲙⲟⲥ (BookThom 142,21–26)

> But these words that you speak to us are ridiculous and contemptible to the world since they are misunderstood. So how can we go and preach them since we are [not] esteemed [in] the world?

While these two texts otherwise have drastically different priorities – the former focusing on the fleshly nature of the resurrection and the latter on an ascetic message of contempt for the flesh – they converge at the point of the disciples' concern about mission. The Jesus of the Epistula Apostolorum relieves the disciples' trepidation, assuring them that he will give them his peace and spirit and that they will prophesy (30.2). In the Book of Thomas, Jesus' reassurance takes a different approach: he responds to Thomas' concerns by saying that those who sneer or smirk at the Christian message will go to hell (142,24–37).

A comparable mission anxiety is articulated in the Gospel of Mary and the Epistle of Peter to Philip, where the anxiety stems from fear of persecution rather than fear of ridicule or failure. Jesus has commanded the disciples to preach, and the disciples appreciate that this might lead to their suffering:

> ⲁⲩⲣⲓⲙⲉ ⲙ̄ⲡⲱⲁ ⲉⲩϫⲱ ⲙⲙⲟⲥ ϫⲉ ⲛⲛⲁϣ ⲛ̄ϩⲉ ⲉⲛⲛⲁⲃⲱⲕ ϣⲁ ⲛϩⲉⲑⲛⲟⲥ ⲛ̄ⲧⲛ̄ⲧⲁϣⲉⲟⲉⲓϣ ⲛ̄ⲡⲉⲩⲁⲅⲅⲉⲗⲓⲟⲛ ⲛⲧⲙⲛ̄ⲧⲉⲣⲟ ⲙⲡϣ`ⲏ´ⲣⲉ ⲙⲡⲣⲱⲙⲉ ⲉϣϫⲉ ⲡⲉⲧⲙ̄ⲙⲁⲩ ⲙ̄ⲡⲟⲩϯⲥⲟ ⲉⲣⲟϥ ⲛⲁϣ ⲛ̄ϩⲉ ⲁⲛⲟⲛ ⲉⲩⲛⲁϯⲥⲟ ⲉⲣⲟⲛ (GMary 9,6–12)

> They wept much, saying, 'How shall we go to the nations and preach the gospel of the kingdom of the Son of Man? If they did not spare him, how will they spare us?'

> ⲉϣϫⲉ ⲛⲧⲟϥ ⲡⲉⲛϫⲟ̣ⲉ̣[ⲓⲥ] ⲁϥϫⲓ ⲙⲕⲁϩ ϩⲓⲉ ⲁⲟⲩⲏⲣ ϭⲉ ⲁⲛⲟⲛ (EpPetPhil $_{\text{NHC}}$ 138,15–16)

> If he, our Lor[d], suffered, then how much (must) we (suffer)?

In both texts, the concern is voiced as the disciples speak with each other about Jesus' words after he has departed. In Jesus' final instructions, he had told them to preach. Following this, Jesus reappears to confirm that they must suffer in the Epistle of Peter to Philip, and Mary comforts her brothers by reminding them that Jesus will protect them in the Gospel of Mary. Their fears must be allayed as the narratives conclude with the disciples going out to preach.

The support promised to the disciples in their anxiety differs in these two gospels. In the Gospel of Mary, Mary acts as a comforter to remind them that Jesus will protect them. The disciples are instructed to find the Son of Man within and put on the Perfect Man (8,18–20; 18,16), and so being armed with Christ they can preach the gospel. In the Epistle of Peter to Philip, they are to become 'illuminators', but they also receive the Holy Spirit ($_{\text{NHC}}$ 140,1–13). In its christological focus and in Mary's assurance that 'his grace will be with you all' (ⲧⲉϥⲭⲁⲣⲓⲥ ⲅⲁⲣ ⲛⲁϣⲱⲡⲉ ⲛⲙ̄ⲙⲏⲧⲛ̄ ⲧⲏⲣ<ⲧ>ⲛ̣ [9,16–17]), the Gospel of Mary comes close to the Matthean 'I am with you always' (Matt 28.20), but the Gospel of Mary uses the Pauline language of 'putting on' (Rom 13.14; Gal 3.27) and 'Perfect Man' (Col 1.28; Eph 4.13) to express this point. The Epistle of Peter to Philip combines repeated allusions to Matt 28.20 (134,17–18; 138,1–3; 140,22–22) with unmistakeable echoes of Acts 2, as the exalted Lord bestows the spirit on Peter and the other disciples to empower them for mission (139,14; 140,5–10).

The Matthean commission is about more than just making disciples; it is about going to πάντα τὰ ἔθνη. The Epistle of Peter to Philip, the Epistula Apostolorum, the Pistis Sophia, the Gospel of Mary and the Apocalypse of Peter likewise advocate a worldwide mission. In the Apocalypse of Peter, Jesus commands Peter to 'send my message into the whole world in peace' (14.5). As we have seen, in the Gospel of Mary the disciples worry about preaching to the ϩⲉⲑⲛⲟⲥ. In the Pistis Sophia, Jesus says, 'when I have gone to the light, preach to the whole world' (ⲉ̈ⲓϣⲁⲛⲃⲱⲕ ⲉⲡⲟⲩⲟⲉⲓⲛ ⲕⲏⲣⲩⲥⲥⲉ ⲙ̄ⲡⲕⲟⲥⲙⲟⲥ ⲧⲏⲣϥ̄ [3.102 (256,2–3)]) and the text closes with the disciples going out in threes to preach the gospel in the four directions (4.148).[46] Likewise, the disciples of the Epistula Apostolorum are commissioned to preach to the East, West, North and South (30.1), and in the Epistle of Peter to Philip, it is said that the disciples went 'out in four words' (ⲉϩⲣⲁ̈ⲓ ⲉⲡⲓϥⲧⲟⲟⲩ ⲛ̄ϣⲁϫⲉ [140,25]).[47]

In the brief examination of the mission charge in selected dialogue gospels, it is clear that the texts go beyond the Matthean narrative by narrating the disciples' reactions to the charge and overcoming their anxieties. In none of these texts is it assumed that the Eleven on the mountain in Galilee were thrilled by Jesus' instruction to make disciples of all nations. Rather, they appreciate that the disciples might have had some concerns.

[46] This conclusion is a later addition.

[47] Meyer questions whether this could be amended to four directions, but also proposes that we could read in it Irenaeus' conception of four directions corresponding to four gospels (*Adv. Haer*. 3.11.8), Meyer, *Letter of Peter to Philip*, 160.

The Longer Ending of Mark and the Description: 'In Another Form'

Mark has four different endings in the MS tradition. Mark 16.9–20 (the 'longer ending') is not in the earliest manuscripts, and Eusebius' *ad Marinum* tells us that the 'accurate copies' (τὰ ἀκριβῆ τῶν ἀντιγράφων) do not include it.[48] The 'accurate' text concludes at 16.8 with the women fleeing from the tomb, for 'terror and amazement had seized them, and they said nothing to anyone, for they were afraid' (εἶχεν γὰρ αὐτὰς τρόμος καὶ ἔκστασις καὶ οὐδενὶ οὐδὲν εἶπαν ἐφοβοῦντο γάρ). The 'shorter ending' follows from verse 8 and states that the women did report what they had been told to Peter and his companions, and that after this Jesus himself sent out the proclamation of eternal salvation through the disciples. (The fourth ending, the 'Freer Logion', will be briefly discussed in the next section.) The 'longer ending' (LE) adds Jesus' appearances to Mary Magdalene, to two disciples walking in the country, and to the Eleven. Never in the dialogue gospels do the male or female disciples stay silent from fear, but a strong connection with Mark LE can be found in the unfamiliar appearance of Jesus.

When Jesus appears to the two disciples walking in the country, the post-Markan author-editor writes that he manifests himself 'in another form' (ἐν ἑτέρᾳ μορφῇ [16.12]). The idea that the risen Jesus differs from his pre-crucifixion self is reflected in the resurrection scene of Luke, in which Jesus vanishes from sight (αὐτὸς ἄφαντος ἐγένετο ἀπ' αὐτῶν [24.31]), and John, in which Jesus can appear through locked doors (20.19, 27), and, even more strangely, when he appears to one of his closest followers, she does not recognize him (20.14–15). A difference in form is also anticipated in the transfiguration accounts (Matt 17.1–9 and pars.). Matthew has nothing to suggest an unfamiliar form, unless it is implied by his reference to the disciples' doubt (Matt 28.17).

In Mark LE, the three appearances of Jesus use the verb φαίνω (16.9, 12, 14), which can have luminosity connotations.[49] It is

[48] See James A. Kelhoffer, 'The Witness of Eusebius's ad Marinum and Other Christian Writings to Text-Critical Debates Concerning the Original Conclusion to Mark's Gospel', in his *Conceptions of 'Gospel' and Legitimacy in Early Christianity*, WUNT 324 (Tübingen: Mohr Siebeck, 2014), 121–64.

[49] Φαίνω generally means bring to light or cause to appear, but it can mean 'give light' or 'shine'. For example, 'God kindled a light which now we call the sun, to the end that it might shine, so far as possible, throughout the whole heaven (ἵνα ὅτι μάλιστα εἰς ἅπαντα φαίνοι τὸν οὐρανὸν),' *Tim.* 39b. For more examples, see Liddell, Scott, and Jones, eds. *A Greek-English Lexicon*, 9th ed. (Oxford, 1843; 1940), 1912–3.

common for dialogue gospels to begin with an appearance of Jesus in a different form, and this form is often characterized by its luminosity.[50] The Sophia of Jesus Christ and the Pistis Sophia emphasize a brightness that makes Jesus hyper-recognizable as the risen Saviour. The Sophia of Jesus Christ begins: 'The Saviour appeared to them not in his previous form but in the invisible spirit, and his likeness resembled *a great angel of light*' (ⲁϥⲟⲩⲱⲛϩ ⲉⲣⲟⲟⲩ ⲛ̄ϭⲓ ⲡⲥⲱⲧⲏⲣ ϩⲛ̄ ⲧⲉϥϣⲟⲣⲡ ⲙ̄ⲙⲟⲣⲫⲏ ⲁ(ⲛ) ⲁⲗⲗⲁ ϩⲣⲁï ϩⲙ̄ ⲡⲓⲁϩⲟⲣⲁⲧⲟ(ⲛ) ⲙ̅ⲡ̅ⲛ̅ⲁ̅ ⲡⲉϥⲉⲓⲛⲉ ⲇⲉ ⲛⲉ ⲡⲉⲓⲛⲉ ⲡⲉ ⲛ̄ⲛⲟⲩⲛⲟϭ ⲛ̄ⲁⲅⲅⲉⲗⲟⲥ ⲛⲧⲉ ⲡⲟⲩⲟⲉⲓⲛ [BG 78,11–79,2]). According to the Pistis Sophia,

> ⲙ̄ⲡⲛⲁⲩ ⲛ̄ϫⲡ̄ⲯⲓⲧⲉ ⲙ̄ⲡⲉϥⲣⲁⲥⲧⲉ ⲁ ⲙ̄ⲡⲏⲩⲉ ⲟⲩⲱⲛ ⲁⲩⲱ ⲁⲩⲛⲁⲩ ⲉⲓ̅ⲥ̅ ⲉϥⲛⲏⲩ ⲉⲡⲉⲥⲏⲧ' · ⲉϥⲣ̄ⲟⲩⲟⲉⲓⲛ ⲉⲙⲁϣⲟ ⲉⲙⲁϣⲟ · ⲉⲙ̅ⲛ̅·ϣⲓ ⲉⲡⲉϥⲟⲩⲟïⲛ ⲉⲧϥ̄ϣⲟⲟⲡ ⲛ̄ϩⲏⲧϥ̄ · ⲛⲉϥⲣ̄ⲟⲩⲟⲉⲓⲛ ⲅⲁⲣ ⲛ̄ϩⲟⲩⲟ ⲉⲡⲛⲁⲩ ⲉⲛⲧⲁϥⲃⲱⲕ ⲉϩⲣⲁï ⲉⲙ̄ⲡⲏⲩⲉ · ϩⲱⲥⲧⲉ ⲛⲉⲙ̅ⲛ̅ϣϭⲟⲙ ⲛ̅ⲣ̅ⲙ̅ⲛ̅ⲕⲟⲥⲙⲟⲥ ⲉϣⲁϫⲉ ⲉⲡⲟⲩⲟⲉⲓⲛ ⲉⲛⲉϥϣⲟⲟⲡ ⲙ̄ⲙⲟϥ · ⲁⲩⲱ ⲛⲉϥⲛⲉϫⲁⲕⲧⲓⲛ ⲛ̄ⲟⲩⲟⲉⲓⲛ ⲉⲃⲟⲗ ⲡⲉ ⲉⲙⲁⲧⲉ ⲉⲙⲁⲧⲉ ⲉⲙ̅ⲛ̅ϣⲓ ⲉⲛⲉϥⲁⲕⲧⲓⲛ · ⲁⲩⲱ ⲛⲉⲣⲉ ⲡⲉϥⲟⲩⲟⲉⲓⲛ ⲛⲉϥϣⲏϣ ⲁⲛ ⲡⲉ ⲙ̅ⲛ̅ⲛⲉϥⲉⲣⲏⲩ · ⲁⲗⲗⲁ ⲛⲉϥⲟ' ⲙ̄ⲙⲓⲛⲉ ⲙⲓⲛⲉ ⲡⲉ … (PistSoph 1.4 [7,6–14])
>
> On the ninth hour of the following day the heavens opened, and they saw Jesus coming down, giving light exceedingly, and there was no measure to the light in which he was. For he gave more light than in the hour that he went up to heaven, so that the people of the world were not able to speak of the light which was his, and he cast forth very many rays of light, and there was no measure to his rays. And his light was not equal throughout, but it was of different kinds …

The description continues with different types of light. Chapter 7 explains Jesus' garment of light – he received it after his crucifixion, and through it he will reveal the truth to humanity

[50] See Perkins, *Gnostic Dialogue*, 49–52. Fallon sees the light-form epiphany as typical: 'The epiphany of the revealer is presented. It is frequently but not always associated with light, involved with a self-predication, and placed upon a mountain,' Fallon, 'Gnostic Apocalypses', 125. In addition to the Sophia of Jesus Christ and the Pistis Sophia, the Epistle of Peter to Philip has Jesus as a light and voice. Also, although the Book of Thomas does not have an appearance narrative, according to Turner the resurrected Saviour reveals himself to be 'the light that is about to withdraw back to the heavenly essence of light. As the light, he serves to illumine the secrets of darkness', John D. Turner, *The Book of Thomas the Contender from Codex II of the Cairo Gnostic Library from Nag Hammadi (CG II, 7): The Coptic Text with Translation, Introduction and Commentary*, SBLDS 23 (Missoula, MT: SBL Scholars Press, 1975), 4–5.

(1.7 [9,22–10,17]).[51] The form of great light is connected both with the resurrected Christ and his role as revealer. There is likely a Johannine element here, as there Jesus is the light in the darkness (John 8.12, 9.5, 12.46), but the form of the risen Christ as light may also be inspired by Mark LE's use of φαίνω.

A different way of visualizing the Markan ἑτέρα μορφή is found in the polymorphous Christ of the Apocryphon of John:

> ⲁ[ⲓ̈ⲣ ϩⲟⲧⲉ … ⲁⲩⲱ ⲉⲓⲥϩⲏⲏⲧⲉ ⲁⲓ̈]ⲛⲁⲩ ϩⲣⲁⲓ̈ ϩⲙ̅ ⲡⲟⲩⲟⲉ̣ⲓ̣ⲛ̣ [ⲉⲩⲁⲗⲟⲩ ⲁϥⲁϩⲉ ⲇⲉ] ⲉ̣ⲣⲁⲧϥ ⲛⲁⲓ̈ ⲛ̅ⲧⲁⲣⲓⲛⲁ[ⲩ ⲉⲣⲟϥ ⲁϥϣⲱⲡ]ⲉ̣ ⲉϥⲟ ⲛ̅ⲑⲉ ⲛ̅ⲟⲩⲛⲟϭ ⲁⲩⲱ ⲛⲁϥⲕ̣ⲱ̣[ⲧⲉ ⲙⲡⲉ]ϥ̣ⲥⲙⲁⲧ ⲉϥⲟ ⲛⲑⲉ ⲛ̅ⲟⲩϩ̣ⲁ̣ⲗ ⲛ̅ⲛⲁⲩ[ⲟ ⲛϩⲁϩ ⲁⲛ ⲙ]ⲡⲁⲙ̅ⲧ̣ⲟ ⲉⲃⲟⲗ ⲁⲩⲱ ⲛⲉⲟⲩⲛ ⲟ[ⲩⲉⲓ]ⲛ̣ⲉ ⲉ̣[ϥⲟ ⲛ]ϩⲁϩ ⲙ̅ⲙⲟⲣⲫⲏ ϩⲣⲁⲓ̈ ϩⲙ̅ ⲡⲟⲩⲟ̣[ⲉⲓⲛ] ⲁⲩⲱ ⲛ̣[ⲓⲥⲙⲁⲧ] ⲛⲁⲩⲟⲩⲟⲛϩ ϩⲓⲧⲛ̅ ⲛⲉⲩⲉⲣⲏ̣ⲩ ⲁ̣[ⲩⲱ] ⲡⲉ̣[ⲥⲙⲁ]ⲧ̣ ⲛⲁϥⲟ ⲛ̅ϣⲟ[ⲙ]ⲧ[ⲉ] ⲙ̅ⲙⲟⲣⲫⲏ ($_{\text{NHC2}}$ 2,1–9)
>
> [I was … afraid and behold, I] saw in the lig[ht a child, and he stoo]d by me. While I loo[ked at him, he became] like an old man. And he tur[ned] his form, becoming like a servant. There [was not a plurality] before me, but there was a [like] ness [with] many forms in the light, and th[e forms] appeared through each other a[nd] the [for]m has thr[e]e forms.[52]

Foster argues that polymorphic appearances often occur in post-resurrection contexts as 'they were a way of communicating Jesus' transcendence over the realm of death'.[53] However, different appearances of Jesus are not limited to his resurrected body as in the transfiguration scene, where Jesus is manifest in his true glory (Matt 17.1–8 + par.), and the Gospel of Judas. Set before the crucifixion,

[51] Robinson suggests that the risen Jesus appeared in a luminous form in the earliest resurrection accounts, James M. Robinson, 'Jesus from Easter to Valentinus (Or to the Apostles' Creed)', *JBL* 101.1 (1982): esp. 11–14.

[52] The BG version is slightly different. It begins with a child (ⲟⲩⲁⲗⲟⲩ) and the old man (ϩⲗ̅ⲗⲟ) ($_{\text{BG}}$ 21,4–5). The text reads that it had three faces (ⲛ̅ϣⲟⲙ `ⲧ´ ⲛ̅ϩⲟ) [$_{\text{BG}}$ 21,13]), but there is no servant as in NHC 2.

[53] Paul Foster, 'Polymorphic Christology: Its Origins and Development in Early Christianity', *JTS* 58.1 (2007): 67. In the Apocryphon of John, however, the reason for the three forms is unclear. Pleše proposes that it was read in various ways: 'For some, multiformity has more to do with different spiritual capacities of recipients than with Christ's real nature. For others, it proved that Christ was, in fact, without any form and above all determinations. For some, again, polymorphy was the visible expression of Christ's multiple potencies, virtues, or perfections (ἐπίνοιαι), in contrast with the unity, simplicity, and ineffability of the transcendent Father. For others, it was the symbol of Christ's paradoxical status, of his being one with and, at the same time, different from the other members of the divine triad', Pleše, *Poetics of the Gnostic Universe*, 32–3.

the Gospel of Judas tells how 'a number of times he did not reveal himself to his disciples, but could be found as a child[54] in their midst' (ⲟⲩⲏⲡⲉ ⲇⲉ [ⲛ]ⲥⲟⲡ' ⲙⲁ̣ϥⲟⲩⲟⲛϩϥ̄ ⲉⲛⲉϥⲙⲁⲫⲏⲧⲏⲥ ⲁⲗⲗⲁ ⲛ̄ϩⲣ̄ⲟⲧ ϣⲁ{ⲕ}<ⲩ>ϩ̄ⲉ̄ ⲉⲣⲟϥ ϩⲛ̄ ⲧⲉⲩⲙⲏⲧⲉ [33,18–21]). To have Jesus appearing as a 'child' in the Gospel of Judas seems to have the opposite purpose to his appearance in the transfiguration narratives and the Sophia of Jesus Christ and the Apocryphon of John: rather than showing his glory, he is hiding himself. ⲙⲁϥⲟⲩⲟⲛϩϥ̄ suggests concealment.

The tradition of Christ appearing in a different and often luminous form reflects early Christian concerns over christology and resurrection. Each time that a text includes a description of the form of Jesus, it is attempting to answer questions about Jesus' identity. The Sophia of Jesus Christ, the Pistis Sophia and the Apocryphon of John are grappling with the same question that we find in Mark, Luke and John: What did the risen Jesus who appeared to his disciples look like? The Sophia of Jesus Christ and the Pistis Sophia converge with Mark 16.12, especially if Mark too implies a luminous or radiant form, as at the transfiguration. The Apocryphon of John takes a different approach, freeing the risen Jesus from the confines of the (un-morphable) flesh and highlighting his multiple identities.

The Freer Logion

The fourth variation in the MS tradition of the ending of Mark is found in the fourth- or fifth-century Codex Washingtonianus, in which a dialogue known as the 'Freer Logion' is incorporated into the Longer Ending.[55] It reads:

> κἀκεῖνοι ἀπελόγουντε λέγοντες ὅτι ὁ αἰὼν οὗτος τῆς ἀνομίας καὶ τῆς ἀπιστίας ὑπὸ τὸν σατανᾶν ἔστιν ὁ μή ἐῶν τὰ ὑπὸ τῶν πν[ευμ]άτων ἀκάθαρτα τὴν ἀλήθειαν τοῦ θ[εο]ῦ καταλάβεσθαι δύναμιν διὰ τοῦτο ἀποκάλυψόν σου τὴν δικαιοσύνην ἤδη ἐκεῖνοι ἔλεγον τῷ χ[ριστ]ῷ καὶ ὁ χ[ριστὸ]ς ἐκείνοις προσέλεγεν ὅτι πεπλήρωται ὁ ὅρος τῶν ἐτῶν τῆς εξουσίας τοῦ σατανᾶ ἀλλά ἐγγίζει ἄλλα δινὰ καὶ ὑπὲρ ὧν ἐγὼ ἁμαρτησάντων

[54] The meaning of ⲛ̄ϩⲣ̄ⲟⲧ is unclear. It may be a form of the word 'child' in the Bohairic or Old Coptic dialect, or ϩⲟⲣⲧϥ̄ or ϩⲟⲣⲧ 'apparition' or 'phantom'. Jenott argues that 'child' is the most plausible translation due to fluctuation between Coptic dialects and the tradition of Jesus appearing as a child (e.g. the Apocryphon of John), Jenott, *Gospel of Judas*, 189–90.

[55] Frey thinks that this might have been inserted in the latter half of the second century as an edifying expansion of Mark LE, Jörg Frey, 'Zu Text und Sinn des Freer-Logion', *ZNW* 93.1–2 (2002): 13–34.

> παρεδόθη(ν) εἰς θάνατον ἵνα ὑποστρέψωσιν εἰς τὴ(ν) ἀλήθειαν καὶ μηκέτι ἁμαρτήσωσιν ἵνα τὴν ἐν τῷ οὐρανῷ πν[ευματ]ικὴν καὶ ἄφθαρτον τῆς δικαιοσύνης δόξαν κληρονομήσωσιν.[56]
>
> And they began defending themselves and said, 'This lawless and unbelieving age is under Satan, the one who does not permit the things made unclean by the spirits to receive powerfully the truth of God. Because of this reveal your righteousness now!' They kept on saying this to Christ, and Christ began to respond to them, 'The limit of the years of the authority of Satan is fulfilled, but other fearful things draw near and for the sake of those who sinned I was handed over to death, in order that they may return to the truth and no longer sin, in order that they may inherit the spiritual and imperishable glory of righteousness in heaven.'

This passage is inserted between the references to Jesus rebuking the disciples for their lack of faith (16.14) and telling them to preach the gospel to all creation (16.15).

The Freer Logion has been included in lists of post-resurrection dialogue gospels in the *New Testament Apocrypha*, as seen in the last chapter. Hartenstein sees it as different from the others, as 'the Freer Logion shows no relationship to gnostic thought'.[57] Bockmuehl notes that it cannot be seen as a dialogue gospel because it never existed independently of Mark.[58]

The Freer Logion is important in many ways – although it may be the work of a single scribe,[59] it tells us that post-resurrection narratives were being edited and expanded, that early Christians thought it was appropriate for the risen Jesus to engage in dialogue with his disciples, and that the disciples wanted answers from him. Also, it blurs the divide between canonical and 'apocryphal'

[56] Greek and translation (adapted) from Thomas R. Shepherd, 'Narrative Analysis as a Text Critical Tool: Mark 16 in Codex W as a Test Case', *JSNT* 32.1 (2009): 84. Nomina sacra taken from Bruce M. Metzger, *Manuscripts of the Greek Bible: An Introduction to Greek Palaeography* (Oxford and New York: Oxford University Press, 1981), 82.

[57] Judith Hartenstein, 'Dialogische Evangelien', in *Antike christliche Apokryphen in deutscher Übersetzung: Band in zwei Teilbänden: Evangelien und Verwandtes*, ed. Christoph Markschies and Jens Schröter, Vol. 2 (Tübingen: Mohr Siebeck, 2012), 1052.

[58] Bockmuehl, *Ancient Apocryphal Gospels*, 162–3.

[59] Jörg Frey, 'Das Freer-Logion', in *Antike christliche Apokryphen in deutscher Übersetzung: Band in zwei Teilbänden: Evangelien und Verwandtes*, ed. Christoph Markschies and Jens Schröter, Vol. 2 (Tübingen: Mohr Siebeck, 2012), 1060.

resurrection dialogues by showing that the former could be amended and elaborated.

Luke 24 and the Hidden Sense of Scripture

In Luke, after Jesus' resurrection, his first appearance is to Cleopas and his unnamed companion on the road to Emmaus. Jesus 'comes near' (ἐγγίσας [24.15]), 'but their eyes were kept from recognizing him' (οἱ δὲ ὀφθαλμοὶ αὐτῶν ἐκρατοῦντο τοῦ μὴ ἐπιγνῶναι αὐτόν [v.16]). It is within this narrative that we find one of the recurring themes in the dialogue gospels: the revelation of the previously concealed meaning of scripture, which then becomes a key for understanding the significance of Jesus himself. In the dialogue between Jesus and the two travellers (24.14–15, 17–21, 25–27), Jesus reveals the scriptural testimony to the Messiah's death and resurrection, which is repeated in his later appearance in Jerusalem:

> καὶ ἀρξάμενος ἀπὸ Μωϋσέως καὶ ἀπὸ πάντων τῶν προφητῶν διερμήνευσεν αὐτοῖς ἐν πάσαις ταῖς γραφαῖς τὰ περὶ ἑαυτοῦ (24.27)
>
> Then beginning with Moses and all the prophets, he interpreted to them the things about himself in all the scriptures.
>
> τότε διήνοιξεν αὐτῶν τὸν νοῦν τοῦ συνιέναι τὰς γραφάς (24.45)
>
> Then he opened their mind to understand the scriptures.

Luke is the only canonical gospel in which the risen Jesus explicitly reveals what has previously been concealed from the disciples.[60] The concealment is also emphasized in Luke's version of the second and third passion predictions:

> θέσθε ὑμεῖς εἰς τὰ ὦτα ὑμῶν τοὺς λόγους τούτους· ὁ γὰρ υἱὸς τοῦ ἀνθρώπου μέλλει παραδίδοσθαι εἰς χεῖρας ἀνθρώπων. οἱ δὲ

[60] The concept is also found in John, in which the true interpretation of scripture can only be understood after Jesus' glorification/resurrection. In 2.20, the disciples recall Jesus' message about the Temple and only then do they correctly interpret and believe the scripture; and in 12.14–16, Jesus quotes Zech 9.9, and the disciples do not understand. 12.16 states that 'only after Jesus was glorified did they realize that these things had been written about him and that these things had been done to him' (ἀλλ' ὅτε ἐδοξάσθη Ἰησοῦς τότε ἐμνήσθησαν ὅτι ταῦτα ἦν ἐπ' αὐτῷ γεγραμμένα καὶ ταῦτα ἐποίησαν αὐτῷ). At 7.39, the evangelist must explain that the spirit, or the paraclete, will only come after Jesus' glorification, thus explaining Jesus' use of scripture here. On these and more, see Ashton, *Understanding the Fourth Gospel*, 339–41.

> ἠγνόουν τὸ ῥῆμα τοῦτο καὶ ἦν παρακεκαλυμμένον ἀπ᾽ αὐτῶν ἵνα μὴ αἴσθωνται αὐτό, καὶ ἐφοβοῦντο ἐρωτῆσαι αὐτὸν περὶ τοῦ ῥήματος τούτου (9.44–45)
>
> 'Let these words sink into your ears: The Son of Man is going to be betrayed into human hands.' But they did not understand this saying; its meaning was *concealed* from them, so that they could not perceive it. And they were afraid to ask him about this saying.
>
> καὶ αὐτοὶ οὐδὲν τούτων συνῆκαν καὶ ἦν τὸ ῥῆμα τοῦτο κεκρυμμένον ἀπ᾽ αὐτῶν καὶ οὐκ ἐγίνωσκον τὰ λεγόμενα (18.34)
>
> But they understood nothing about all these things; in fact, what he said was *hidden* from them, and they did not grasp what was said.

In Luke, even the most astute disciple could not have understood Jesus' predictions about his death and resurrection as in each case the concealment is an action from God.[61] Luke's concept of 'once hidden/now revealed' corresponds to a ministry or post-resurrection chronological setting. A similar schema occurs in Matthew and Mark, where it is said that the revelation of Jesus' identity at the transfiguration is to be kept secret until after the resurrection (Mark 9.9 // Matt 17.9).[62] In some dialogue gospels, it is after the resurrection that Jesus finally reveals soteriological truths. For example, the disciples of the Epistula Apostolorum comment on the fact that hidden things were revealed only after Jesus' resurrection:

> Lord, what great things you have spoken to us and revealed to us, things never yet spoken, and in everything you have comforted us and been gracious to us! For after your resurrection you revealed all this to us, so that we might truly be saved. (34.1–2)

A similar sentiment is found at the start of the Pistis Sophia, in which Jesus tells his disciples that there are many things that he has not yet disclosed, but 'From today on, I will speak with you openly

[61] Tannehill notes that Luke 24 'emphatically repeats themes which have already been expressed in the passion prophecies of Jesus', Robert C. Tannehill, *The Narrative Unity of Luke-Acts: A Literary Interpretation; Volume 1, The Gospel according to Luke* (Philadelphia, PA: Fortress Press, 1986), 277. Also, Joseph A. Fitzmyer, *The Gospel According to Luke X–XXIV*, AB 28A (New York: Doubleday, 1985), 1563.

[62] Luke omits the passage in which the disciples descend from the mountain in Mark 9.9–13.

from the beginning of the truth until its completion. And I will speak with you face to face, without parable' (ϫⲓⲛ ⲡⲟⲟⲩ ϭⲉ ⲉⲃⲟⲗ ϯⲛⲁϣⲁϫⲉ ⲛ̄ⲙ̄ⲙⲏⲧⲛ̄ ϩⲛ̄ ⲟⲩⲡⲁⲣⲣⲏⲥⲓⲁ ϫⲓⲛ ⲧⲁⲣⲭⲏ ⲛ̄ⲧⲁⲗⲏⲑⲉⲓⲁ ϣⲁ ⲡⲉⲥϫⲱⲕ · ⲁⲩⲱ ϯⲛⲁϣⲁϫⲉ ⲛ̄ⲙ̄ⲙⲏⲧⲛ̄ ⲛ̄ϩⲟ ϩⲓ ϩⲟ ⲁϫⲛ̄ ⲡⲁⲣⲁⲃⲟⲗⲏ · [1.6 (8,23–9,2)]). In all these cases, it is the post-resurrection setting that is the moment for full disclosure.

In Luke, it is explicitly the true meaning of scripture that Jesus reveals after his resurrection; however, we are not told what scriptures Jesus explains and what he says. Morris suggests that 'Jesus began a systematic Bible study … [Luke] makes it clear that the whole Old Testament was involved'.[63] In reality, this is not remotely clear, but the Lukan Jesus probably does explain a range of Hebrew Bible passages. The Apocryphon of John has the risen Jesus doing exactly that: the text narrates the risen Christ explaining and interpreting the early history of humankind as found in Gen 1–7 from the beginning to the flood, as the context for his own role as Saviour.[64] In spite of the major ideological differences between Luke and the Apocryphon of John in relation to the Jewish scriptures, both writers agree that a correct interpretation of scripture is a prerequisite for understanding the coming of Jesus.

In the Apocryphon of John the links to Genesis are more than just a re-telling of the story: there are direct links to the text of LXX Genesis. Following Yaldabaoth's boast that there is no God beside him, a voice comes from above saying: 'The Man exists and the Son of Man' (ϥϣⲟⲟⲡ ⲛ̄ϭⲓ ⲡⲣⲱⲙⲉ ⲁⲩⲱ ⲡϣⲏⲣⲉ ⲙⲡⲣⲱⲙⲉ [$_{\text{BG}}$ 47,14–16]). As King notes:

> This statement is almost a direct quotation from the Greek translation of *Genesis* 1.3, in which God says (in Hebrew), '"Let there be light" and there was light'. The Hebrew term for light is translated into Greek as *phos,* which spells two Greek words depending upon how they are accented, either φῶς ('light') or φώς ('human'). Since most ancient

[63] Leon Morris, *Luke: An Introduction and Commentary*, Tyndale New Testament Commentaries (Grand Rapids, MI and Cambridge: Eerdmans, 1988), 370. Tannehill, more sensibly, writes that Luke's 'sweeping language seems to point beyond a limited number of scriptural predictions to something that is central to Scripture as such', Tannehill, *Narrative Unity*, 1:286.

[64] Pleše concurs: 'Christ's hermeneutical strategy, as described in Luke [24.27], is therefore not much different from the Savior's exegesis of *Genesis* [in the Apocryphon of John],' Pleše, *Poetics of the Gnostic Universe*, 17. On Genesis in the Apocryphon of John, see Gerard P. Luttikhuizen, *Gnostic Revisions of Genesis Stories and Early Jesus Traditions*, NHMS 58 (Leiden and Boston: Brill, 2006).

> manuscripts are not accented, the Greek could be translated either as 'Let there be light and there was light' or 'Let the human exist and the human exists.' The *Secret Revelation of John* exploits this ambiguity in order to make a pun identifying the image of the First Human who appears in the waters below with the primordial light of *Genesis* 1.3.[65]

As the Apocryphon of John retells the Genesis story, Christ explains to John that Moses' interpretation was wrong: 'it is not as Moses said' (ⲕⲁⲧⲁ ⲑⲉ ⲛ̄ⲧⲁⲙⲱⲩ̈ⲥⲏⲥ ⲁⲛ ϫⲟⲟⲥ [$_{\mathrm{BG}}$ 58,16–17, cf. also 45,8–10; 73,4–5]). As Pleše writes, '[t]he Savior's hermeneutical stance is polemical and revisionary. What he contests is not the facticity of events recorded by Moses, but the perspective from which they are told – that is, the authority of Moses as a reliable witness and narrator'.[66] In spite of this explicit undermining of Moses, the Jesus of the Apocryphon of John does not dismiss Genesis entirely. The Apocryphon of John is still concerned to reveal the true meaning concealed behind these Jewish writings.

Correct interpretation of Moses within a post-resurrection setting also features in the Pistis Sophia, although here the concern is not with prophecy (as in Luke) or the primeval narrative (as in the Apocryphon of John) but with the commandments of the law. These need to be interpreted correctly and in light of Jesus' teachings.[67] In the course of a long discourse about fate and the archons, the Saviour says:

> ⲉⲧⲃⲉ ⲡⲁ̈ⲓ ϭⲉ ⲟⲩⲛ ⲁ̈ⲓϫⲟⲟⲥ ⲉⲣⲱ̅ⲧ̅ⲛ̅ ⲙ̄ⲡⲓⲟⲩⲟ̈ⲓϣ ϫⲉ ⲡⲉⲧⲉ ⲛ̅ϥ̅ⲛⲁⲕⲁ ⲉⲓⲱⲧ ⲁⲛ ϩⲓ ⲙⲁⲁⲩ ⲛ̄ⲥⲱϥ ⲛ̅ϥ̅ⲉⲓ' ⲛ̅ϥ̅ⲟⲩⲁϩ̅ϥ̅ ⲛ̄ⲥⲱ̈ⲓ ⲡⲁ̈ⲓ ⲛ̅ϥ̅ⲙ̅ⲡ̅ϣ̅ⲁ̅ ⲙ̄ⲙⲟ̈ⲓ ⲁⲛ · ⲛ̄ⲧⲁ̈ⲓϫⲟⲟⲥ ⲟⲩⲛ ⲙ̄ⲡⲉⲩⲟⲉⲓϣ ⲉⲧⲙ̄ⲙⲁⲩ ϫⲉ ⲉⲧⲉ̅ⲧ̅ⲛ̅ⲉⲕⲱ ⲛ̄ⲥⲱ̅ⲧ̅ⲛ̅ ⲛ̄ⲛⲉ̅ⲧ̅ⲛ̅ⲉⲓⲟⲧⲉ ⲛ̄ⲁⲣⲭⲱⲛ · ⲧⲁⲣ̄ⲧⲏⲩ̅ⲧ̅ⲛ̅ ⲛ̄ϣⲏⲣⲉ ⲙ̄ⲡⲓϣⲟ̅ⲣ̅ⲡ̅ ⲙ̄ⲙⲩⲥⲧⲏⲣⲓⲟⲛ ⲛ̄ϣⲁⲉⲛⲉϩ (1.131 [337,18–25])

> Now concerning this, I have said to you once: 'The one who does not leave father and mother and come and follow me is not worthy of me.' Now I said at that time: 'You should

[65] King, *Secret Revelation of John*, 98. Greek characters inserted.

[66] Pleše, *Poetics of the Gnostic Universe*, 67. Recently, Creech has argued that the challenges to Moses were inserted later and in reaction to conflict with the 'orthodox' church, David Creech, *The Use of Scripture in the Apocryphon of John: A Diachronic Analysis of the Variant Versions*, WUNT II 441 (Tübingen: Mohr Siebeck, 2017).

[67] The Pistis Sophia also makes reference to other Old Testament material, such as several Psalms (1.32–2.82) as well as discussing the afterlife of the prophets and patriarchs (3.135).

> leave your fathers, the archons, so that I make you sons of the First Mystery for ever.'

Here Jesus cites one of his own sayings, in a form influenced by Gen 2.24: 'The one who does not leave [καταλείψει] …', rather than 'the one who loves [φιλῶν] father and mother more than me …' (Matt 10.37), or 'the one who does not hate [οὐ μισεῖ] his father and mother …' (Luke 14.26). An apparent contradiction of the law of Moses causes confusion for Salome, who asks:

> ⲡⲁϫⲟⲉⲓⲥ ⲉϣϫⲉ ⲛⲉⲛⲉⲓⲟⲧⲉ ⲛⲉ ⲛ̅ⲁⲣⲭⲱⲛ ⲉⲓ̈ⲉ ⲡⲱⲥ ⲥⲏϩ ϩ̅ⲙ̅ ⲡⲛⲟⲙⲟⲥ ⲙ̅ⲙⲱⲩ̈ⲥⲏⲥ ϫⲉ ⲡⲉⲧⲛⲁⲕⲱ ⲛ̅ⲥⲱϥ ⲙ̅ⲡⲉϥⲉⲓⲱⲧ ⲙ̅ⲛ̅ ⲧⲉϥⲙⲁⲁⲩ ϩ̅ⲛ̅ ⲟⲩⲙⲟⲩ ⲙⲁⲣⲉϥⲙⲟⲩ · ⲉⲓ̈ⲉ ⲟⲩⲕⲟⲩⲛ ⲛ̅ⲧⲁ ⲡⲛⲟⲙⲟⲥ ϣⲁϫⲉ ⲁⲛ ϩⲁⲣⲟϥ (3.132 [338,2–6])

> My Lord, if our fathers are the archons, how is it written in the law of Moses: 'He who shall leave his father and his mother shall die the death.' Did the law not therefore speak of it?

Mary Magdalene asks Jesus if she can respond, and it is she who offers the correct interpretation of Moses' commandment:

> ⲛ̅ⲧⲁ ⲡⲛⲟⲙⲟⲥ ⲁⲛ ϫⲉ ⲡⲁⲓ̈ ⲉⲧⲃⲉ ⲧⲉⲯⲩⲭⲏ ⲟⲩⲧⲉ ⲉⲃⲧⲉ ⲡⲥⲱⲙⲁ ⲟⲩⲧⲉ ⲉⲧⲃⲉ ⲡⲁⲛⲧⲓⲙⲓⲙⲟⲛ ⲙ̅ⲡ̅ⲛ̅ⲁ̅ · ϫⲉ ⲛⲁⲓ̈ ⲅⲁⲣ ⲧⲏⲣⲟⲩ ⲛ̅ϣⲏⲣⲉ ⲛⲉ ⲛ̅ⲧⲉ ⲛ̅ⲁⲣⲭⲱⲛ · ⲁⲩⲱ ϩⲉⲛⲉⲃⲟⲗ ⲛ̅ϩⲏⲧⲟⲩ ⲛⲉ · ⲁⲗⲗⲁ ⲛ̅ⲧⲁ ⲡⲛⲟⲙⲟⲥ ϫⲉ ⲡⲁⲓ̈ ⲉⲧⲃⲉ ⲧϭⲟⲙ ⲛ̅ⲧⲁⲥⲉⲓ' ⲉⲃⲟⲗ ϩⲙ̅ ⲡⲥⲱⲧⲏⲣ ⲧⲁⲓ̈ ⲉⲧⲟⲛ̅ⲣ̅ⲙ̅ⲛ̅ⲟⲩⲟⲉⲓⲛ ⲡⲉⲛϩⲟⲩⲛ ⲙ̅ⲡⲟⲟⲩ · ⲛ̅ⲧⲁ ⲡⲛⲟⲙⲟⲥ ⲟⲛ ϫⲟⲟⲥ ϫⲉ ⲟⲩⲟⲛ ⲛⲓⲙ ⲉⲧⲛⲁϭⲱ ⲡⲃⲟⲗ ⲙ̅ⲡⲥⲱⲧⲏⲣ ⲙ̅ⲛ̅ ⲛⲉϥⲙⲩⲥⲧⲏⲣⲓⲟⲛ ⲛⲉϥⲉⲓⲟⲧⲉ ⲧⲏⲣⲟⲩ · ⲟⲩⲙⲟⲛⲟⲛ ϫⲉ ϩ̅ⲛ̅ ⲟⲩⲙⲟⲩ ϥⲛⲁⲙⲟⲩ · ⲁⲗⲗⲁ ϩ̅ⲛ̅ ⲟⲩⲧⲁⲕⲟ ϥⲛⲁⲧⲁⲕⲟ (3.132 [338,20–339,4])

> The law has not said this concerning the soul, nor concerning the body, nor concerning the spirit counterpart, for all these are sons of the archons and come from them, but the law has said this concerning the power which came forth from the Saviour, which is the man of light within us today. The law has thus said: 'Everyone who will remain outside the Saviour and his mysteries, all his fathers, not only will he die the death, but he will be destroyed with destruction.'

The passage from the law that Salome quotes and Mary interprets is based on Exod 21.16 LXX, also cited in Mark and Matthew: 'For Moses said: "Honour your father and your mother", and "The one who speaks evil of father or mother must surely die"' (Μωϋσῆς γὰρ εἶπεν, Τίμα τὸν πατέρα σου καὶ τὴν μητέρα σου, καί, Ὁ κακολογῶν πατέρα ἢ μητέρα θανάτῳ τελευτάτω [Mark 7.10; cf. Matt 15.4]). True interpretation of scripture is here carried out by a disciple but still lies within a post-resurrection setting.

Luke 24, the Apocryphon of John and the Pistis Sophia all present the risen Christ as giving or enabling an interpretation of scripture in the light of his own coming. Luke sets the precedent here. The three texts employ a two-era schema of concealment and revelation: before Jesus the true meaning of Moses' words was hidden, and only after the resurrection is their true meaning revealed.

Acts 1 and the Ascension

Luke's ending parallels Acts' beginning: the risen Christ teaches and ascends. Luke's narration of the ascension differs from the disappearance at Emmaus and indicates that his departure is final. The beginning of Acts tells us that Jesus appeared over a period of forty days, with convincing proofs and teaching about the kingdom of God (1.3), and then he ascended. In both texts, the ascension marks the end of his teaching. Jesus' final departure in dialogue gospels is told in different ways, but here we will look at how the motif of a (final) ascension is depicted.[68]

The ascension in Acts is narrated differently to Luke, with more emphasis on a visible event:

> καὶ ἐγένετο ἐν τῷ εὐλογεῖν αὐτὸν αὐτοὺς διέστη ἀπ' αὐτῶν καὶ ἀνεφέρετο εἰς τὸν οὐρανόν (Luke 24.51)
>
> While he was blessing them, he withdrew from them and was carried up into heaven.
>
> καὶ ταῦτα εἰπὼν βλεπόντων αὐτῶν ἐπήρθη, καὶ νεφέλη ὑπέλαβεν αὐτὸν ἀπὸ τῶν ὀφθαλμῶν αὐτῶν. καὶ ὡς ἀτενίζοντες ἦσαν εἰς τὸν οὐρανὸν πορευομένου αὐτοῦ, καὶ ἰδοὺ ἄνδρες δύο παρειστήκεισαν αὐτοῖς ἐν ἐσθήσεσιν λευκαῖς, οἳ καὶ εἶπαν, Ἄνδρες Γαλιλαῖοι, τί ἑστήκατε [ἐμ]βλέποντες εἰς τὸν οὐρανόν; οὗτος ὁ Ἰησοῦς ὁ ἀναλημφθεὶς ἀφ' ὑμῶν εἰς τὸν οὐρανὸν οὕτως ἐλεύσεται ὃν τρόπον ἐθεάσασθε αὐτὸν πορευόμενον εἰς τὸν οὐρανόν (Acts 1.9–11)

[68] This is different to Jesus' ascension to the Father, from which he returns soon after and tells his disciples about it (e.g. John 20, the Gospel of Mary, the First Apocalypse of James, which will be discussed in Chapter 5).

> When he had said this, as they were watching, he was lifted up, and a cloud took him out of their sight. While he was going, and they were gazing up toward heaven, suddenly two men in white robes stood by them. They said, 'Men of Galilee, why do you stand looking up toward heaven? This Jesus, who has been taken up from you into heaven, will come in the same way as you saw him go into heaven.'

Jesus' ascension in dialogue gospels is told in different ways. The Apocryphon of James (15,6) uses the low-key term ⲁϥⲃⲱⲕ ('he departed'). In the Apocryphon of James, ⲁϥⲃⲱⲕ clearly implies an ascension as Jesus has previously referred to it (14,20–21), and James and Peter follow him up through the heavens where they encounter apocalyptic images of wars, trumpets and angelic jubilation. In comparison, ⲁϥⲃⲱⲕ in the Gospel of Mary (9,5) and the Gospel of Judas (44,14) simply refers to a departure, but not necessarily an ascension. In the case of the Gospel of Mary, commentators have wondered whether this terse statement necessarily implies a final departure,[69] but the disciples' ensuing anguish and conflict indicate that this is the case. In the Gospel of Judas, on the other hand, it is used for a temporary departure. 'He departed' ends the line in the codex, followed by a space equivalent to about five letters, but the next line begins with Judas asking Jesus a question. It is a clear but not a climactic departure.

At another point in the text, the Gospel of Judas reports a potential ascension, but it occurs before the crucifixion. The text reads:

> ⲓ̈ⲟⲩⲇⲁⲥ ⲇⲉ ⲁϥϥⲓⲁⲧ︦ϥ︦ ⲉϩ︦ⲣ︦ⲁⲉⲓ ⲁϥⲛⲁⲩ ⲉⲧϭⲏⲡⲉ ⲛ̄ⲟⲩⲟⲓⲛ ⲁⲩⲱ ⲁϥϥⲱⲕ ⲉϩ︦ⲟ︦ⲩⲛ ⲉⲣⲟⲥ (57,22–24)

> Judas raised his eyes, he saw the luminous cloud, and he entered it.

A voice comes from the cloud, followed by five lines of lacunae (from which all we can decipher of the voice's message is a possible reference to the great race), and then the words: 'Then Judas stopped looking [at J]esus' (ⲁⲩⲱ ⲁ︤ⲓ̈ⲟⲩⲇⲁⲥ ⲗⲟ ⲉϥⲛⲁⲩ [ⲉ︦ⲓ︦]ⲏ︦ⲥ︦ [58,5–6]). It is unclear who has ascended. Schenke Robinson argues that the ⲁⲩⲱ allows Jesus to be the subject of ⲁϥϥⲱⲕ, and so the scene depicts Jesus' spiritual self entering the cloud, leaving his body behind to be crucified.[70] Jenott

[69] Hartenstein notes that it could refer to a mundane departure, a miraculous vanishing or an ascension, Hartenstein, *Die zweite Lehre*, 145. Tuckett sees a final parting, Tuckett, *Mary*, 161.

[70] Gesine Schenke Robinson, 'The Relationship of the Gospel of Judas to the New Testament and to Sethianism', *Journal of Coptic Studies* 10 (2008): 65–8.

leans more towards the possibility that it is Judas entering the cloud, but also disagrees that the text narrates a final departure of Jesus: '[I]t may simply indicate the end of the vision'.[71] According to Jenott, the scene is close to Moses' entering a cloud on Mount Sinai (Exod 24.18–25.1) or to the Lukan transfiguration scene (Luke 9.34–35) due to the revelatory voice.[72] Both Judas and Jesus are on earth after the voice speaks. However, as Jesus' ascension is such a common subject throughout early Christian literature, the Gospel of Judas may well also imply ascension of some kind.

The Epistle of Peter to Philip also has Jesus (in the form of light) ascending, but then reappearing. The ascension seems to be final:

> [ⲧ]ⲟⲧⲉ̣ ⲁⲥϣⲱⲡⲉ ⲛϭⲓ ⲟⲩⲉⲃⲣⲏϭⲉⲥ ⲙⲛ ⲟⲩϩⲣⲟⲩⲙⲡⲉ ⲉⲃⲟⲗ ϩⲛ ⲧⲡⲉ· ⲁⲩⲱ ⲁⲩⲧⲱⲣⲡ ⲙⲡⲉⲧⲁϥⲟⲩⲱⲛϩ ⲛⲁⲩ ⲉⲃⲟⲗ ⲙⲡⲓⲙⲁ ⲉⲧⲙⲙⲁⲩ ⲉϩⲣⲁ̈ⲓ ⲉⲧⲡⲉ (138,3–7)
>
> Then there came lightning and thunder from heaven, and what appeared to them there was taken up to heaven.

However, later we read: 'Jesus appeared to them' (ⲁϥⲟⲩⲱⲛϩ ⲉⲃⲟⲗ ⲛϭⲓ ⲓ̅ⲥ̅ [140,16]) with the peace greeting familiar from bodily appearances elsewhere. This ascension imagery does not presuppose finality: 'What appeared to them there' that was taken up to heaven refers to the Lord in the form of a voice in a light rather than a bodily Jesus.[73] Jesus speaks on two further occasions, first just as a voice (138,21) but then in a further appearance when the disciples have come together again after going out to preach. The Epistle of Peter to Philip shows that early Christians had a flexible understanding of ascension, and so it is quite possible that in the Gospel of Judas Jesus ascends (in some sense) even before his crucifixion.

The Epistula Apostolorum describes a cinematic ascension that is an observable, historical event. The final pages of the text have not survived in the Coptic MS, but the Ge'ez reads:

> And when he had said this and finished speaking with us, he said to us again, 'Behold, on the third day, at the third hour, the one who sent me will come so that I may go with him.' And as he spoke there was thunder and lightning and an earthquake, and the heavens were torn asunder, and a

[71] Jenott, *Gospel of Judas*, 17.

[72] Jenott, *Gospel of Judas*, 17.

[73] Although the language used compares to that of Acts, Meyer rightly notes that '[t]he author of *Ep. Pet. Phil.* is not fighting the theological battles of Luke, and operates with a different scenario', Meyer, *Letter of Peter to Philip*, 144.

> bright cloud came and took him. And we heard the voice of many angels as they rejoiced and blessed and said, 'Gather us, O priest, to the light of glory!' And when they drew near to the firmament of heaven, we heard him saying, 'Go in peace!' (51.1–4)

The Epistula Apostolorum's depiction of Jesus' ascension mirrors its depiction of the resurrection in that they are both very physical understandings of divine events. In the Epistula Apostolorum, the more ambiguously corporeal elements of Jesus' resurrection in the canonical accounts, such as appearing in locked rooms, are eliminated in favour of the tangible form of a Jesus whose feet are firmly on the ground. The dramatic depiction of Jesus' departure with its apocalyptic imagery is out of keeping with his low-key appearance to the women at the tomb, which simply reads 'the Lord appeared to them' (ⲁⲡϫⲁⲉⲓⲥ ⲟⲩⲱⲛϩ [ⲛⲉ]ⲩ ⲁⲃⲁⲗ [10.1]).[74] There are several apocalyptic images shared between the ascension narrative of the Epistula Apostolorum and Acts 1, such as the cloud as a symbol of both Jesus' departure (EpAp 51.2) and return (EpAp 16.3; Acts 1.9–11).

Apocalyptic imagery is also found in the ascension account of the Apocalypse of Peter, and there too the cloud has an active part to play: 'A large cloud, very white, came over our heads, and it carried away our Lord, Moses, and Elijah' (17.2). But the narrative in the Apocalypse of Peter does more than narrate – it affirms that the righteous are fleshly in heaven: 'We watched, and the heavens were opened. We saw people in the flesh who came and welcomed our Lord and Moses and Elijah, and they went into the second heaven' (17.3). The narrative also refers to fear and trembling in heaven and then to heaven being closed (17.5–6). Unlike other departure narratives, however, the scene opens with a voice from heaven declaring: 'This is my beloved son, with whom I am pleased. Obey him' (17.1). Here the Apocalypse of Peter links the voice from the synoptic transfiguration to the post-resurrection ascension – if the author understood the two events in this differentiated way.[75]

An ascension is one way to narrate Jesus' (final) departure and mark the end of his presence with his disciples, which is a main

[74] As Hartenstein writes, it would be more appropriate to parallel it with Christ's descent through the heavens into Mary's womb in chapter 13, and with the description of the parousia in chapter 16, Hartenstein, *Die zweite Lehre*, 116–17.

[75] Helmer rightly sees this reference to Jesus' ascension as further confirmation of the Apocalypse of Peter's post-resurrection setting, Helmer, 'Gospel Tradition in the Apocalypse of Peter', 151.

concern of dialogue gospels. These texts reported ascension in diverse ways, whether they use apocalyptic and cinematic or low-key imagery or present it as temporary or final. The early Christian understanding of ascension was clearly alterable and inconsistent, and ascension could be depicted and understood in line with a text's own agenda.

John 20–21 and the Issue of 'Physicality'

The risen Jesus in John 20 is both physical and not. He shows the disciples his wounds and invites Thomas to touch them and even to insert his hand into the laceration (20.27). Yet this same physical entity can appear in rooms through locked doors (20.19, 27), and possibly in a less-than-recognizable form (20.14–15). In stark contrast to what he offers Thomas, he tells Mary Magdalene: 'Do not touch me, for I have not yet ascended to the Father' (μή μου ἅπτου, οὔπω γὰρ ἀναβέβηκα πρὸς τὸν πατέρα [20.17]).[76] Why Jesus tells Mary not to touch him has caused endless confusion for John's readers – Brown refers to at least nine possible interpretations.[77] Many scholars read ἅπτομαι as referring to an emotional grasp, as in 'stop clinging to me'.[78] But other uses of the word ἅπτομαι in the

[76] Some MSS add και προσεδραμεν αψασθαι αυτου before Jesus' prohibition, demonstrating the peculiarity of the original text.

[77] Although he notes that some of these arguments are ridiculous: 'One wonders which is worse: the utterly banal explanation that Jesus does not want to be touched because his wounds are still sore, or Belser's fanciful thesis that, having heard of the eucharistic meal on Thursday evening, Mary Magdalene sees Jesus risen and is holding onto him, pleading that he give her holy communion,' Brown, *The Gospel According to John, XIII–XXI*, 992–3. For a deeper analysis of John 20.17, see Reimund Bieringer, '"I Am Ascending to My Father and Your Father, to My God and Your God" (John 20:17): Resurrection and Ascension in the Gospel of John,' in *The Resurrection of Jesus in the Gospel of John*, ed. Helmut Koester and Reimund Bieringer, WUNT I 222 (Tübingen: Mohr Siebeck, 2011), 209–35.

[78] As ἅπτομαι may imply either the physical act of touching or the emotional sense of clinging onto Jesus, the present imperative form has been taken to imply a sense of 'stop doing what you are doing', which suggests 'a persistent clinging that fits the emotional character of the encounter', as in Craig S. Keener, *The Gospel of John: A Commentary*, Vol. 1 (Grand Rapids, MI: Baker Academic, 2003), 1193; Brown, *The Gospel According to John, XIII–XXI*, 992. Dodd writes that it 'might mean "Do not cling to me", without any necessary implication that Mary was doing so (since μή with the present imperative may simply negative the specific meaning of that tense)', Dodd, *Interpretation of the Fourth Gospel*, 443 n. 2. Although Ridderbos largely agrees with this, he also notes that '[w]e should think of the supernatural character of Jesus' coming as the Risen One, as a result of which contact with him was unlike a natural encounter with the senses', Herman Ridderbos, *The Gospel of John: A Theological Commentary*, trans. John Vriend (Grand Rapids, MI and Cambridge: Eerdmans, 1997), 636.

canonical gospels do not refer to clinging: Jesus does not *emotionally cling* to the slave's ear to heal it (Luke 22.51).[79] The use of ἅπτομαι tends to refer to a healing touch (e.g. Matt 8.3, 8.15), as shown by the declaration of the haemorrhaging woman: 'If I only touch his cloak, I will be made well' (ἐὰν μόνον ἅψωμαι τοῦ ἱματίου αὐτοῦ σωθήσομαι [Matt 9.21]).[80] There is little reason to assume John 20.17 uses ἅπτομαι differently. It therefore seems that Jesus is telling Mary not to *touch* him, in contrast to the women touching and holding (κρατέω) Jesus' feet in Matthew (28.9).[81] In light of John 20, the same ambiguity about the physicality of the risen Jesus might be seen in John 21. When Jesus appears in the near distance, the disciples do not recognize him (21.4), and only the beloved disciple knows that it is the Lord once he has instructed them how to catch fish (21.6–7). The beloved disciple may only be able to identify Jesus because he has special insight. Peter only *hears* that it is the Lord; he does not see or recognize him (21.7).[82] As the disciples approach him, it is said that 'none of the disciples dared to ask him, "Who are you?" because they knew it was the Lord' (οὐδεὶς δὲ ἐτόλμα τῶν μαθητῶν ἐξετάσαι αὐτόν, Σὺ τίς εἶ; εἰδότες ὅτι ὁ κύριός ἐστιν [21.12]). Here, τολμάω suggests that although they did not have the courage to ask, they wanted to; presumably, his identity was not clear. There is nothing to indicate that the man who manifests himself in locked rooms is here straightforwardly recognizable or tangible.

The uncertainty about Jesus' physicality in John is much like Luke. Luke presents the risen Jesus as fleshly and fish-eating, yet vanishing and ascending. After a short dialogue and recognition through bread-breaking, Jesus vanishes from sight: αὐτὸς ἄφαντος ἐγένετο ἀπ' αὐτῶν (21.31). This suggests that he is not in the same, recognizable, bodily form that he was before his death. Jesus must then prove to the disciples that he is not a πνεῦμα, which he does through physical actions (Luke 24.37–43). Yet the Jesus of Luke 24 is different to the Jesus of Luke 1–23: his words 'while I was with

[79] 'But Jesus answered (and) said, "No more of this". And he touched his ear and healed him' (ἀποκριθεὶς δὲ ὁ Ἰησοῦς εἶπεν, Ἐᾶτε ἕως τούτου, καὶ ἁψάμενος τοῦ ὠτίου ἰάσατο αὐτόν).

[80] There are many uses of ἅπτομαι in the Synoptics, for example healing lepers by touch (Matt 8.3) and healing fever by touching a woman's hand (Matt 8.15).

[81] Schnackenburg, for example, points to the connection with Matthew, Rudolf Schnackenburg, *The Gospel according to John: Vol. 3. Commentary on Chapters 13–21*, trans. David Smith and G. A. Kon (Kent: Burns & Oates, 1988), 318.

[82] As Brown writes, '[s]eemingly he still could not recognize Jesus visually', Brown, *The Gospel According to John, XIII–XXI*, 1072.

you' (ἔτι ὢν σὺν ὑμῖν [24.44]) shows that his presence now is different to his presence before. The risen Jesus appears and disappears and reveals hidden truths.[83]

The majority of dialogue gospels are not so concerned with the issue of physicality. As we have seen, the Apocryphon of John, the Sophia of Jesus Christ and the Pistis Sophia depict Jesus in a different form. Others, such as the Dialogue of the Saviour, the Book of Thomas and the Apocalypse of Peter, do not describe the form in which Jesus manifested himself and perhaps thought it to be of little importance.

The Epistula Apostolorum, on the other hand, is extremely concerned to show the physicality of Jesus:

> ⲉⲧⲃⲉ ⲟ ⲧⲉⲧⲛ̄ⲣ̄ⲇⲓⲥⲧⲁⲍⲉ ⲉⲧⲓ ⲧⲉⲧⲛ̄ⲉ ⲛ̄ⲁⲧⲛⲁϩⲧⲉ ⲁⲛⲁⲕ ⲡⲉ ⲡⲉⲓ̈ ⲉⲧⲁϩϫⲟⲟⲥ ⲛⲏⲧⲛⲉ ⲉⲧⲃⲉ ⲧⲁⲥⲁⲣⲝ ⲙⲛ̄ ⲡⲁⲙⲟⲩ ⲙⲛ̄ ⲡⲁⲧⲱⲛⲉ ϫⲉⲕⲁⲁⲥ ⲁⲧⲉⲧⲛⲁⲙ̄ⲙⲉ ϫⲉ ⲁⲛⲁⲕ ⲡⲉ · ⲡⲉⲧⲣⲉ ⲧⲱⲕⲉ ⲛ̄ⲛⲉⲕϯⲃⲉ ⲁⲛⲉⲓϥⲧ ⲛ̄ⲛⲁϭⲓϫ ⲁⲟⲩ ⲛ̄ⲧⲁⲕ ϩⲟⲩⲟⲩⲕ ⲑⲱⲙⲁⲥ ⲧⲱⲕⲉ ⲛ̄ⲛⲉⲕϯⲃⲉ ⲁⲛⲥⳉⲛ̄ⲗⲟⲅⲭⲏ ⲛⲡ̄ⲁⲥⲡⲓⲣ ⲛ̄ⲧⲁⲕ ⲇⲉ ⲁⲛⲇⲣⲉⲁⲥ ⲙⲟⲩⳉ ⲁⲛⲁⲟⲩⲣⲏⲧⲉ ⲕⲛⲟ ϫⲉ ⲥⲉⲧⲱⲙⲉ ⲉⲛ ⲁⲡⲕⲁϩ ϥⲥⲏⳉ ⲅⲁⲣ ⳉⲛ̄ ⲡⲡⲣⲟⲫⲏⲧⲏⲥ ϫⲉ ⲟⲩⲫⲁⲛⲧⲁⲥⲓⲁ ⲛ̄ⲇⲁⲓⲙⲟⲛ ⲙⲁ[ⲣⲉ]ⲣⲉⲧ̄ϥ̄ ⲧⲟⲩⲙⲉ ϩⲓϫⲛ̄ ⲡⲕⲁϩ ⲁⲛⲁⲛ ⲇⲉ ⲁ̣[ⲛϭⲁⲙ]ϭⲙⲉ ⲁⲣⲁϥ ϫⲁⲛⲁ̄ⲙⲙⲉ ⲛⲁⲙⲓⲉ ϫⲉ ⲛⲉ ⲁ[ϥⲧⲱⲛⲉ] ⳉⲛ ⲥⲁⲣⲝ ⲁⲟⲩ ⲁⲛⲡⲁⳉⲧⲛⲉ ⲁϫⲛ̄ [ⲡ]ⲛ̣̄[ϩⲟ ⲉⲛⲣ̄] ⲉⲝⲟⲙⲟⲗⲟⲅⲉⲓ ⲛ̄ⲛ̄ⲛⲁⲃⲉ ϫⲉ ⲁⲛⳉⲱⲡⲉ ⲛ̣̄[ⲁⲧⲛⲁ]ϩⲧⲉ (11.6–12.2)
>
> Why do you still doubt, you unbelievers? It is I, this one who told you about my flesh and my death and my resurrection. So that you will know it is I, Peter, thrust your fingers to the nail [marks] in my hands, and Thomas, thrust your fingers into the spear [wounds] in my side, and Andrew, look at my feet and see if they do not join to the ground. For it is written in the prophet that 'a demonic ghost does not ha[ve] his foot joined to the ground'. W[e touch]ed him so that we might truly know that h[e had risen] in the flesh, and we bowed [our faces], confess[ing] our sins, for we had been [without] faith.

The proof of the risen Jesus' corporeality comes in two ways: touching his wounds and seeing that his feet touch the ground.[84] To have feet

[83] '[T]he Risen One is portrayed on the one hand precisely as if he were still the earthly Jesus: he walks with his disciples, he accepts an invitation to supper in their home, and he breaks the bread before them as he had done during his earthly ministry … Yet on the other hand he is a mysterious "divine man," who appears and disappears at will,' Fuller, *Formation of the Resurrection Narratives*, 106.

[84] The prophecy that refers to a demonic ghost is nowhere to be found. A similar phrase does occur in Ignatius' *Epistle to the Smyrnaeans* (οὐκ εἰμὶ δαιμόνιον ἀσώματον [3.2]), which has much in common with this narrative in the Epistula Apostolorum.

on the ground seems to be an alternative to the Lukan account of confirmation by eating. Luke, John and the Epistula Apostolorum all have confirmation through touch. Yet whereas Luke and John 'are emphasizing the corporeal continuity between the earthly and the risen Jesus',[85] the Epistula Apostolorum takes their accounts further. The most prominent difference is that the Epistula Apostolorum has a single appearance of the risen Jesus. He 'appears' (ⲟⲩⲱⲛϩ) just once. There is no separate appearance to the Eleven – he appears to the women and goes with them to find the men. He does not materialize in locked rooms. Moreover, any hint in the canonical gospels that his resurrected form is unrecognizable or different to the crucified body is resolutely stamped out.

Koester contrasts the Epistula Apostolorum's emphasis on the physical reality of Jesus' resurrection with the christophanies of other 'revelation gospels'.[86] The dichotomy between the Epistula Apostolorum and other dialogue gospels is needless, and the Epistula Apostolorum could just as well be contrasted with the canonical gospels. Dialogue gospels are varied, and most do not engage with the issue. Some, however, clearly assume that the risen Jesus has a physical body. The First Apocalypse of James is one example:

> ⲁϥⲟⲩⲟⲛϩ̄ ⲉⲣⲟϥ ⲛ̄ϭⲓ ⲡϫⲟⲉ̣[ⲓⲥ] ⲛ̄ⲧⲟϥ ⲇⲉ ⲁϥⲕⲁ ⲧⲉⲡⲣⲟⲥⲉⲩⲭ[ⲏ] ⲉⲃⲟⲗ ⲁϥⲙⲁⲗϩ̄ϥ̄ ⲛ̄ϩⲏⲧϥ̄· ⲁϥϯ ⲡⲓ ⲉⲣⲱϥ ($_{\text{NHC}}$ 31,2–5)
>
> The Lord appeared to him. Then he [James] ceased praying; he embraced him and kissed him.

The significance of this reception by James is emphasized as Jesus specifically comments on it ($_{\text{NHC}}$ 32,1–8). The First Apocalypse of James further affirms the corporeal form of the risen Jesus as he sits on a rock with James ($_{\text{NHC}}$ 32,15–16). In spite of the text's presentation of salvation as overcoming the 'bond of the flesh' ($_{\text{CT}}$ 13,22–24), these narrative inserts demonstrate that the risen Lord is not a disembodied spirit or soul.[87] The First Apocalypse of James, which narrates a post-mortem ascension through cosmic archons, is like the Epistula Apostolorum in that Jesus returns not as a theophany of light or a polymorphous ghost but as a touchable and huggable human being.

[85] Raymond E. Brown, *The Virginal Conception and Bodily Resurrection of Jesus* (New York: Paulist Press, 1973), 89.

[86] Helmut Koester, 'One Jesus and Four Primitive Gospels', *HTR* 61.2 (1968): 245.

[87] See Parkhouse, 'Identity, Death and Ascension'.

2.3 The Pauline Influence

A resurrection-orientated christology and soteriology in an archon-dwelling cosmos is one way to sum up the impact of Pauline thought in dialogue gospels.

The Risen Christ

A focus on the risen Christ occurs in most, though not all, of the dialogue gospels, and this emphatic focus on the risen Christ appears to stem from Paul. As Paul writes, 'If indeed we once knew Christ according to the flesh, we know [him] no longer' (εἰ καὶ ἐγνώκαμεν κατὰ σάρκα Χριστόν, ἀλλὰ νῦν οὐκέτι γινώσκομεν [2 Cor 5.16]). For Paul, without Jesus' resurrection, there is no point in proclaiming his message, and neither is there salvation:

> εἰ δὲ Χριστὸς οὐκ ἐγήγερται, κενὸν ἄρα [καὶ] τὸ κήρυγμα ἡμῶν, κενὴ καὶ ἡ πίστις ὑμῶν ... εἰ δὲ Χριστὸς οὐκ ἐγήγερται, ματαία ἡ πίστις ὑμῶν, ἔτι ἐστὲ ἐν ταῖς ἁμαρτίαις ὑμῶν (1 Cor 15.14, 17)
>
> If Christ has not been raised, then our proclamation is in vain, and your faith is in vain ... If Christ has not been raised, your faith is futile, and you are still in your sins.[88]

The focus on Jesus' salvific resurrection is evident in dialogue gospels – although at points the salvation comes through revelation, and the resurrection is blurred with ascension. In the Epistula Apostolorum, as in Paul, Jesus' resurrection is the precondition for the disciples': 'Truly I say to you, as my Father raised me from the dead, so also you too will be raised and taken above the heavens' (21.1). The resurrection is followed by ascension in the Epistula Apostolorum; and in the Pistis Sophia, the Gospel of Mary and the First Apocalypse of James, Jesus' ascension through the heavens paves the way for Christians to follow him there.

Paul and the dialogue gospels have in common a lack of attention paid to the ministry of Jesus. Paul renders it unnecessary for the

[88] 1 Cor 15 was referred to by more early Christians than any other section of a Pauline letter, Jennifer R. Strawbridge, *The Pauline Effect: The Use of the Pauline Epistles by Early Christian Writers*, SBR 5 (Berlin: de Gruyter, 2015), 97. As Pagels notes, among its users were 'Naassene and Valentinian exegetes [who] cite this passage frequently; Irenaeus says it is the Valentinians who insist on introducing texts from 1 Corinthians 15 to support their own position against the "orthodox" [*Adv. Haer.* 5.9.1]; the Gospel of Philip demonstrates such an exegesis [104,26–105,3],' Elaine H. Pagels, '"The Mystery of the Resurrection": A Gnostic Reading of 1 Corinthians 15', *JBL* 93.2 (1974): 277. References added from the footnotes.

earthly Jesus to be a focus; he himself has only seen him after his resurrection, and yet he can claim the same status as those who followed him from Galilee.

> Οὐκ εἰμὶ ἐλεύθερος; οὐκ εἰμὶ ἀπόστολος; οὐχὶ Ἰησοῦν τὸν κύριον ἡμῶν ἑόρακα; οὐ τὸ ἔργον μου ὑμεῖς ἐστε ἐν κυρίῳ (1 Cor 9.1)
>
> Am I not free? Am I not an apostle? Have I not seen Jesus our Lord? Are you not my work in the Lord?

Paul claims that he is in no way to be outranked by the disciples who knew Jesus when he was on the earth, and thus he implicitly devalues pre-Easter traditions.[89] A dialogue with the risen Christ, in which the ministry of the earthly Jesus is relegated to the background and in which Christ as Saviour teaches and appoints apostles, could be regarded as a *Pauline gospel.*

The Ephesian Cosmos

Many of the dialogue gospels present Jesus as salvation from an archon-inhabited cosmos, which is an idea found in certain Pauline texts and also explicated particularly in Ephesians.[90] While Ephesians can depict believers as already seated with Christ in heaven (1.21; 2.6), malevolent cosmic powers remain a threat to be combatted (6.12). The Ephesian image of the powers is quoted (glossed with a phrase from Colossians 1.13) from 'the great apostle' in the Hypostasis of the Archons, a Nag Hammadi text close in content to the Apocryphon of John and the Sophia of Jesus Christ, but without the character Jesus.[91]

> ⲉⲧⲃⲉ ⲑⲩⲡⲟⲥⲧⲁⲥⲓⲥ ⲛ̄ⲛ̄ⲉⲝⲟⲩⲥⲓⲁ ϩⲙ̄ ⲡⲡ̄ⲛ̄ⲁ̄ ⲙ̄ⲡⲉⲓⲱⲧ ⲛ̄ⲧⲙⲉ ⲁϥϫⲟⲟⲥ ⲛⲁⲛ ⲛ̄ϭⲓ ⲡⲛⲟϭ ⲛ̄ⲁⲡⲟⲥⲧⲟⲗⲟⲥ ⲉⲧⲃⲉ ⲛⲉⲝⲟⲩⲥⲓⲁ ⲙ̄ⲡⲕⲁⲕⲉ ϫⲉ ⲡⲛ̄ϣⲱϫⲉ ϣⲟⲟⲡ ⲁⲛ ⲟⲩⲃⲉ ⲥⲁⲣⲝ ϩⲓ [ⲥⲛⲟ]ϥ̣ ⲁⲗⲗⲁ ⲉϥⲟⲩⲃⲉ ⲛⲉⲝⲟⲩⲥⲓⲁ ⲙ̄ⲡⲕⲟⲥ[ⲙⲟⲥ] ⲙ̣ⲛ̄ ⲙ̄ⲡⲛⲉⲩⲙⲁⲧⲓⲕⲟⲛ ⲛ̄ⲧⲡⲟⲛⲏⲣⲓⲁ [ⲁⲉⲓ]ϫⲉⲛⲉ ⲛⲁⲉⲓ ⲉⲕϣⲓⲛⲉ ⲉⲧⲃⲉ ⲑⲩⲡⲟⲥⲧⲁ[ⲥⲓⲥ ⲛ̄]ⲉⲝⲟⲩⲥⲓⲁ (86,20–27)
>
> On account of the nature of the powers, (inspired) by the spirit of the Father of truth, the great apostle – referring

[89] Cf. Robinson, 'Jesus from Easter to Valentinus', 21.

[90] For early exegetes, Ephesians was written by Paul, and so we will often refer to Paul as its author. See Strawbridge, *Pauline Effect*, 57–8.

[91] Hartenstein sees 'erstaunliche Parallelen in den Gattungsmerkmalen' and groups the Hypostasis of the Archons together with the Apocryphon of John and the Sophia of Jesus Christ due to their similar cosmology and anthropology, Hartenstein, *Die zweite Lehre*, 258, 260.

> to the powers of darkness – told us that our contest is not against flesh and [blood]; but against the powers of the cosmos and spirits of wickedness. [I have] sent (you) this because you inquire about the natu[re of the] powers.

A number of dialogue gospels understand comparable wicked archons to be connected to the cosmic entities that separate humanity from God: death, life, angels, rulers, things present, things to come, powers, height, depth or anything else in creation (Rom 8.38–39). In Ephesians, Paul is concerned with cosmology; the phrase 'in the heavens' (ἐν τοῖς ἐπουρανίοις) appears five times (1.3, 20; 2.6; 3.10; 6.12) and must refer to the realm beyond the world where both Jesus and malevolent archons dwell.[92] This realm clearly has different levels as Christ sits 'above every ruler and power and authority and dominion and every name being named, not only in this age but in the coming one' (ὑπεράνω πάσης ἀρχῆς καὶ ἐξουσίας καὶ δυνάμεως καὶ κυριότητος καὶ παντὸς ὀνόματος ὀνομαζομένου οὐ μόνον ἐν τῷ αἰῶνι τούτῳ ἀλλὰ καὶ ἐν τῷ μέλλοντι [Eph 1.20–21]). A similar picture of the cosmos is accepted in the First Apocalypse of James and the Gospel of Mary, among others, which have Jesus or the disciple travelling through hostile heavenly spheres to reach 'rest' or salvation. The Epistula Apostolorum paints a comparable picture of cosmic spheres, with Jesus descending through different cosmic levels to reach Mary's womb (13.1–14.6), but here the heavenly beings are cast as angels who appear to pose no threat to the descending Christ.

In Ephesians, the 'plan' (οἰκονομία) for bringing harmony to the disunited cosmos is eschatological: 'Paul' writes that God has made known a plan for 'the fullness of time, to gather up all things in Christ, things in heaven and things on earth, in him' (τοῦ πληρώματος τῶν καιρῶν, ἀνακεφαλαιώσασθαι τὰ πάντα ἐν τῷ Χριστῷ, τὰ ἐπὶ τοῖς οὐρανοῖς καὶ τὰ ἐπὶ τῆς γῆς ἐν αὐτῷ [1.10]).[93] A comparable idea is found in the Gospel of Mary, in which Jesus has come to restore the unstable cosmos to stability, through dissolution, rendering the harmonization eschatological.[94] The πλήρωμα language in Ephesians 1.10 connects the completion of time to the fullness of Christ;

[92] *Contra* Talbert who reads it as 'the realm of transcendence', Charles H. Talbert, *Ephesians and Colossians*, Paideia (Grand Rapids, MI: Baker Academic, 2007), 44.

[93] The overriding theme of the letter is God's plan to bring unity to the cosmos through Christ, and from this, '[o]ne may infer … that the unity and harmony of the cosmos have suffered serious dislocation, on earth and in the heavenlies', Talbert, *Ephesians and Colossians*, 47.

[94] This will be explored further in Chapter 4.

cosmology, christology and eschatology are not easily distinguishable in Ephesians. Paul writes about 'the fullness of the one filling all in all' (τὸ πλήρωμα τοῦ τὰ πάντα ἐν πᾶσιν πληρουμένου [1.23]). The Greek here is tricky, but Paul seems to use πλήρωμα to refer to the body/church, while τοῦ τὰ πάντα ἐν πᾶσιν πληρουμένου refers to Christ.[95] Yet in Colossians Christ comprises the πλήρωμα: 'For in him [Christ] the whole fullness of deity dwells bodily' (ὅτι ἐν αὐτῷ κατοικεῖ πᾶν τὸ πλήρωμα τῆς θεότητος σωματικῶς [2.9]).[96] Later in Ephesians, πλήρωμα is used to describe an attainable state of being:

> μέχρι καταντήσωμεν οἱ πάντες εἰς τὴν ἑνότητα τῆς πίστεως καὶ τῆς ἐπιγνώσεως τοῦ υἱοῦ τοῦ θεοῦ, εἰς ἄνδρα τέλειον, εἰς μέτρον ἡλικίας τοῦ πληρώματος τοῦ Χριστοῦ (4.13)
>
> until all of us come to the unity of the faith and the knowledge of the Son of God, to a Perfect Man, to the measure of the maturity with reference to the fullness of Christ.

Ephesians has Jesus as the one filling, and fullness as the pinnacle state. Read alongside Col 2.9, that pinnacle state is becoming Christlike. These concepts connect the deutero-Pauline language of 'fullness' to certain dialogue gospels. The Apocryphon of James focuses on the idea of fullness, as Jesus takes Peter and James aside 'to fill them' (ⲙⲁϩⲟⲩ [2,35]). It is only by becoming full that they can enter the kingdom of heaven (2,29–33).[97] Read alongside John in Chapter 1, it was suggested that 'fullness' is associated with understanding. The Apocryphon of John uses the πλήρωμα language differently, as it refers to the entirety of the heavenly, eternal beings. Ephesians likens the fullness of Christ to becoming a Perfect Man – an idea we find in the Gospel of Mary, where Levi exhorts the disciples to put on 'the Perfect Man' (ⲡⲣⲱⲙⲉ ⲛⲧⲉⲗⲓⲟⲥ [18,16]).

Paul also invites the Ephesians to 'put on the full armour of God' (ἐνδύσασθε τὴν πανοπλίαν τοῦ θεοῦ [6.11; cf. v.13]) in order to defeat the 'rulers' (ἀρχάς), 'powers' (ἐξουσίας), 'world rulers of this darkness'

[95] For this reading, see e.g. John Muddiman, *A Commentary on the Epistle to the Ephesians*, Black's New Testament Commentaries (London and New York: Continuum, 2001), 94–6: 'the Church is the fullness of the all-filling Christ' (96).

[96] 'In Colossians, the christological referent of the word πλήρωμα is beyond question', Muddiman, *Ephesians*, 95.

[97] Hedrick sees the concept of fullness as a 'common gnostic motif' which has been attached to a 'traditional saying' about who can enter the kingdom (cf. Mark 10.15), Charles W. Hedrick, 'Kingdom Sayings and Parables of Jesus in the Apocryphon of James: Tradition and Redaction', *NTS* 29.1 (1983): 20. On πλήρωμα as a favourite term of 'gnostics', see also Meyer, *Letter of Peter to Philip*, 129–30.

(κοσμοκράτορας τοῦ σκότους τούτου) and 'evil spiritual beings in the heavens' (πνευματικὰ τῆς πονηρίας ἐν τοῖς ἐπουρανίοις) (6.12). The armour includes the breastplate of righteousness, the equipment of the gospel, the shield of faith, the helmet of salvation and the sword of the spirit. The Epistle of Peter to Philip employs military imagery akin to Ephesians in its discussion about the powers, as well as christological and cosmological motifs:

ⲏ̄ ⲡⲱⲥ ⲟⲩⲛ̄ⲧⲁⲛ [ⲛ̄ϯⲉⲝⲟ]ⲩⲥⲓⲁ ⲛ̄ⲧⲉ ϯⲡⲁ̣ⲣϩⲏⲥⲓⲁ· (134,26–135,1) Again, how do we have [the] authority of *boldness*?	This was in accordance with the eternal purpose that he has carried out in Christ Jesus our Lord, in whom we have access to God *in boldness and access* (ἔχομεν τὴν παρρησίαν καὶ προσαγωγὴν) in confidence through faith in him. (3.11–12)
[ⲏ̄] ⲉⲧ̣ⲃ̣ⲉ ⲟⲩ ⲛⲓϭⲟⲙ ⲥⲉϯ ⲛⲙⲙⲁⲛ (135,2) [And] why do the *authorities fight* against us? ⲁⲩⲱ ⲁϥⲕⲱ ⲛ̄ϩⲉⲛϭⲟⲙ ⲉϩⲣⲁ̈ⲓ ⲉϫⲱϥ ⲙ̄ⲛ̄ ϩⲉⲛⲉⲝⲟⲩⲥⲓⲁ· ⲁⲩⲱ [ⲁ]ϥϥⲟⲗ̄ϥ̄ ⲉϩⲟⲩⲛ ⲉⲛⲓⲉⲱ̣ⲛ ⲉⲧ ⲙⲟ̣[ⲟ]ⲩⲧ · ⲁⲩⲱ ⲁⲩⲣⲁϣⲉ ⲛ̄ϭⲓ ⲛⲓϭⲟⲙ ⲧⲏⲣⲟⲩ ⲛ̄ⲧⲉ ⲡⲕⲟⲥⲙⲟⲥ ϫⲉ ⲁⲩϫⲡⲟⲟⲩ · (135,23–28) And he [the Arrogant One] placed authorities over it and powers. And he enclose[ed] it in the aeons that are d[e]ad. And all the *powers of the world* rejoiced that he had been begotten.	For our struggle is not against blood and flesh, but against the rulers (ἀρχάς), against the powers (ἐξουσίας), against the cosmic rulers (κοσμοκράτορας) of this present darkness, against the spiritual forces of evil in the heavens. (6.12) following the ruler of the power of the air (τὸν ἄρχοντα τῆς ἐξουσίας τοῦ ἀέρος) (2.2)
ⲧⲛ̄ⲟⲩⲱϣ ⲉⲉⲓⲙⲉ ⲉ ⲡϣⲱ̣ⲱⲧ ⲛ̄ⲧⲉ ⲛⲉⲱⲛ ⲙ̄ⲛ̄ ⲡⲉ[ⲩ]ⲡⲗⲏⲣⲱⲙⲁ (134,21–23) We wish to know the deficiency of the aeons and [their] *fullness*. ⲉⲧⲃⲉ ⲡⲓⲡⲗⲏⲣⲱⲙⲁ ⲇⲉ ⲁⲛⲟⲕ ⲡⲉⲧ̣ⲉ̣ⲁⲩⲧⲛ̄ⲛⲟⲟⲩⲧ ⲉϩⲣⲁ̈ⲓ ϩ̄ⲙ̄ ⲡⲥⲱⲙⲁ ⲉ̣ⲧⲃⲉ ⲡⲓⲥⲡⲉⲣⲙⲁ ⲉⲧⲉⲁϥϩⲉ ⲉⲃⲟⲗ (136,16–18) But concerning the *fullness*, I am the one who was sent down in the body because of the seed, which had fallen away.	the *fullness* (πλήρωμα) of the one filling all in all (1.23) the unity of the faith and the knowledge of the Son of God; to a Perfect Man (ἄνδρα τέλειον); to the measure of the maturity with reference to the *fullness* (πληρώματος) of Christ. (4.13)
ⲛⲓⲁⲣⲭⲱⲛ ⲅⲁⲣ ⲉⲩϯ ⲙ̣̄ⲛ̄ ⲡⲓⲣⲱⲙⲉ ⲉⲧ ⲥⲁϩⲟⲩⲛ (137,21–22) For the archons are fighting against the *inner man*.	I pray that … he may grant that you may be strengthened in your *inner man* (εἰς τὸν ἔσω ἄνθρωπον) with power through his spirit (3.16)
ⲁⲩⲱ ⲛ̄ⲧⲱⲧ̄ⲛ̄ ϩⲱⲕⲧⲏⲩⲧ̄ⲛ̄ ⲛ̄ϩⲣⲁ̈ⲓ ϩ̄ⲛ̄ ϯϭⲟⲙ ⲛ̄ⲧⲉ ⲡⲁ̣[ⲉ]ⲓⲱⲧ (137,25–28) And you arm yourselves with the *strength* of my *[F]ather*	Put on the whole *armour* of *God* (6.11)

Both texts articulate the need to take up the armour of the Father and to strengthen the inner Man to defeat cosmic powers. To get these ideas across, terms such as παρρησίαν/ⲡⲁⲣϩⲏⲥⲓⲁ and πλήρωμα/ⲡⲗⲏⲣⲱⲙⲁ are used. The question 'how do we have [the] authority of boldness?' in the Epistle of Peter to Philip is surrounded by questions about cosmology, eschatology and salvation, and so, although Meyer sees ⲡⲁⲣϩⲏⲥⲓⲁ as referring to boldness in preaching, it is more likely to have the sense of boldness needed to overcome the hostile powers.[98] In many ways, it has a similar meaning to παρρησία in Ephesians, which describes Christians' access to God. Thielman sees παρρησία and προσαγωγή being used to describe a close relationship in which Christians can speak freely with God and with each other,[99] but Lincoln reads it in reference to the powers: '[T]he access can be seen as no longer impeded by the menace of hostile principalities and authorities'.[100] In the Epistle of Peter to Philip, it appears to employ both senses.

The language of 'fullness' arose in our earlier discussion of the Johannine Farewell Discourse and the Apocryphon of James, in which the disciples must 'become full' to enter the kingdom. Here we meet this language again, now connecting Ephesians and the Epistle of Peter to Philip.[101] In the Epistle of Peter to Philip ($_{\text{NHC}}$ 134,22–23), the fullness refers to the aeons, but a scribe corrected it from 'your fullness' (ⲡⲉⲕⲡⲗⲏⲣⲱⲙⲁ) to 'their fullness' (ⲡⲉⲩⲡⲗⲏⲣⲱⲙⲁ). As Meyer writes, 'it is easy to see how ⲡⲉⲕⲡⲗⲏⲣⲱⲙⲁ could be a desirable reading, since the Savior identifies himself with the fullness at 136,16. Yet as the answer suggests, the restoration of the fullness of others is the purpose of the work of the Savior'.[102] Either ⲡⲉⲕ- or ⲡⲉⲩ- would work: '[T]he orientation of the question was merely changed from the Savior to the aeons, or from Christology to soteriology'.[103] This directly links 'fullness' in the Epistle of Peter to Philip to its use in the Apocryphon of James and Ephesians: Christ is the one who fills humanity.[104]

[98] Meyer, *Letter of Peter to Philip*, 114.

[99] Frank Thielman, *Ephesians*, BECNT (Grand Rapids, MI: Baker Academic, 2010), 218–19.

[100] Andrew T. Lincoln, *Ephesians*, World Biblical Commentary 42 (Waco, TX: Word, 1990), 191.

[101] The indirect question 'we wish to know the deficiency of the aeons and their pleroma' links to the same queries in the Dialogue of the Saviour: 'What is the fullness and what is the deficiency?' (ⲟⲩ ⲡⲉ ⲡⲉⲡⲗⲏⲣⲱⲙⲁ ⲁⲩⲱ ⲟⲩ ⲡⲉ ⲡϣⲱⲱⲧ [139,14–15]).

[102] Meyer, *Letter of Peter to Philip*, 171.

[103] Meyer, *Letter of Peter to Philip*, 113. Meyer's use of the word 'merely' here is interesting. In dialogue gospels, christiology and soteriology are so closely linked, and this idea informs my reading of the Gospel of Mary in Part II.

[104] Meyer also notes the link with Ephesians and Col 1.19, Meyer, *Letter of Peter to Philip*, 129.

The battle language in the Epistle of Peter to Philip is strongly reminiscent of Ephesians 6.10–20.[105] Meyer sees that both texts are concerned with fighting cosmic powers and that therefore 'their weaponry ought to be correspondingly spiritual'.[106] The 'power of my Father' in the Epistle of Peter to Philip is comparable to the 'whole armour of God' in Ephesians. For early Christian exegetes, the armour was conceived in terms of baptism (Ignatius and Origen), wisdom and courage (Clement) or prayer (Tertullian and Origen).[107] In the Epistle of Peter to Philip, the disciples conquer the powers by stripping off the corruptible (i.e. the mortal body) (137,6–9).[108] But they are also to fight the archons by coming together and teaching the world (137,22–25), tying in with the theme of apostolic unity and preaching that runs throughout the letter. Both texts have unity as an overarching theme: Ephesians has cosmic unity and church unity, while the Epistle of Peter to Philip accentuates apostolic unity, with Peter calling Philip to rejoin the apostolic group. In the Epistle of Peter to Philip, once the disciples have stripped off the flesh, they become 'illuminators' (ⲫⲱⲥⲧⲏⲣ [137,8]) – a term that the Epistle of Peter to Philip also applies to Christ (133,27) and that Paul applied to his addressees in Philippi (τέκνα θεοῦ ἄμωμα μέσον γενεᾶς σκολιᾶς καὶ διεστραμμένης, ἐν οἷς φαίνεσθε ὡς *φωστῆρες* ἐν κόσμῳ [Phil 2.15]).[109] It is *because* the disciples have become illuminators that they can fight the powers, but the *how* is through unity and preaching. They must become Christlike to preach. The same military language is used in both the Epistle of Peter to Philip and Ephesians to emphasize overcoming cosmic powers and unity.

We have examined just a small sample of motifs, ideas and language found in both Pauline texts and dialogue gospels. Naturally, there will be similarities and intertextual connections between such authors as they are all grappling with closely related theological questions regarding Christ and the cosmos, and to read these texts together may shed light on the kinds of concerns that the authors

[105] This passage was widely received in the ancient Christian world. Strawbridge investigates this and argues that early Christians discerned their need to defend themselves against spiritual forces most frequently in contexts either of baptism or persecution, Strawbridge, *Pauline Effect*, 57–96.

[106] Meyer, *Letter of Peter to Philip*, 142.

[107] Strawbridge, *Pauline Effect*, 78–82.

[108] This has parallels throughout early Christian literature, as we will see in Chapter 5.

[109] As Meyer writes, 'Just as Christ is a fullness and an illuminator, so also the Gnostics can become fullnesses and illuminators. Christ's fate is their fate, his lot their lot,' Meyer, *Letter of Peter to Philip*, 139.

of dialogue gospels were facing. In the end, Paul's historical context pushes him away from dialogue gospels, as he focuses on the relation of Gentiles to the Jewish law, whereas the majority of dialogue gospels are concerned with cosmology and eschatology. Much of the common ground is related to the new conceptuality introduced in Ephesians and Colossians, in which the Pauline concern with Gentiles and the Law is less visible. The narrative frame of dialogue gospels, in which the (risen) Jesus speaks with his immediate followers, and not those of later generations, produces a close literary correlation between dialogue gospels and the resurrection scenes of the canonical gospels; however, the emphasis on the importance of the risen Christ and the understanding of a cosmos inhabited by archons and powers makes the dialogue gospels appear markedly Pauline.

2.4 Parables, Mysteries and Weaning

Parables

Although Jesus says a lot in the canonical gospels, he leaves so much unanswered. The disciples are often left in a state of confusion, especially after parables. Despite the argument of many scholars that the parables had a life-changing and earth-shattering effect on Jesus' audience, clearly not all early Christians understood them.[110] Clement of Alexandria says that only a select few intelligent people could understand parables through divine teaching (*Strom.* 2.2.7.2), the Epistula Apostolorum depicts the disciples complaining that Jesus is again speaking to them in parables that they cannot understand (32.3),[111] and the Jesus of the Pistis Sophia promises to speak openly instead of in parables and no longer to conceal anything (1.6; 2.85). John prefers the term 'riddles' or 'figures of speech' to parables, and the Johannine disciples can only claim to grasp Jesus' message when he gives up his parabolic style (John 16.29).

[110] For criticism of the claim that Jesus' parables had 'a profound and life-changing effect on his audiences', see Mary Ann Beavis, 'The Power of Jesus' Parables: Were They Polemical or Irenic?', *JSNT* 82 (2001): 3–30. She argues that there is no evidence for the claims that parables were 'imbued with a transformative efficacy'.

[111] Hills rightly sees this as illustrating the assumption that the earthly Jesus spoke parabolically as opposed to the risen Lord who does not, Julian V. Hills, *Tradition and Composition in the Epistula Apostolorum*, HTS 57 (Cambridge, MA: Harvard University Press, 2008), 33.

The synoptic Jesus tells the disciples that he speaks in parables so that those outside his inner circle will not be able to understand his teachings:

> Καὶ ὅτε ἐγένετο κατὰ μόνας, ἠρώτων αὐτὸν οἱ περὶ αὐτὸν σὺν τοῖς δώδεκα τὰς παραβολάς. καὶ ἔλεγεν αὐτοῖς· ὑμῖν τὸ μυστήριον δέδοται τῆς βασιλείας τοῦ θεοῦ· ἐκείνοις δὲ τοῖς ἔξω ἐν παραβολαῖς τὰ πάντα γίνεται, ἵνα βλέποντες βλέπωσιν καὶ μὴ ἴδωσιν, καὶ ἀκούοντες ἀκούωσιν καὶ μὴ συνιῶσιν, μήποτε ἐπιστρέψωσιν καὶ ἀφεθῇ αὐτοῖς (Mark 4.10–12 // Matt 13.10–15, Luke 8.9–10)
>
> When he was alone, those who were around him along with the Twelve asked him about the parables. And he said to them, 'To you has been given the mystery of the kingdom of God, but for those outside everything[112] comes in parables, in order that they might look but not perceive and might listen but not understand, so that they might not turn again and be forgiven.'

Mark draws a clear distinction between the 'inside' circle who have been given the mysteries and those 'outside' to whom everything remains concealed.[113] The same idea is found in Luke where Peter wants to clarify whether another of Jesus' parables is 'for us' (πρὸς ἡμᾶς) or 'for everyone' (πρὸς πάντας) (12.41). The distinction between open and hidden teaching is picked up in the Apocryphon of James, as the disciples recall and write books about 'the things that the Saviour had said to each of them, whether in a hidden or open manner' (ⲛ̄ⲚⲈⲚⲦⲁϩⲁⲡⲥⲱⲧⲏⲣ ϫⲟⲟⲩ ⲁⲡⲟⲩⲉⲉⲓ ⲡⲟⲩⲉⲉⲓ· ⲙ̄ⲙⲁⲩ ⲉⲓⲧⲉ ⲙ̄ⲡⲉⲧⲑⲏⲡ· ⲉⲓⲧⲉ ⲙ̄ⲡⲉⲧⲟⲩⲁⲛϩ̄ ⲁⲃⲁⲗ [2,11–14]).[114] The same idea is found

112 Ashton makes an interesting suggestion that τὰ πάντα here should be translated as 'the universe' ('but for those outside the entire universe comes in riddles'), Ashton, *Understanding the Fourth Gospel*, 320. See also John Ashton, 'The Transformation of Wisdom: A Study of the Prologue of John's Gospel', *NTS* 32.2 (1986), 161–86, 184 n. 37.

113 This hard-line distinction generates anxieties in certain exegetes, such as France, who writes: 'Few have been content to believe that Jesus really meant to say just that, and there are sufficient ambiguities or obscurities in the wording to allow wide scope for scholarly ingenuity to discover a more appropriate intent,' R. T. France, *The Gospel of Mark: A Commentary on the Greek Text*, NIGTC (Grand Rapids, MI and Cambridge: Eerdmans, 2002), 193. According to France, the point is that whether the parable produces a response depends on the 'condition of the hearer … Thus the same parable which to some brings an understanding of the secret of God's kingship will leave others cold. They are the ones who remain ἔξω' (198–99). Beavis, on the other hand, argues that Mark's ancient audience would have had a positive response to the idea of esoteric teaching to an in-group, Mary Ann Beavis, *Mark's Audience: The Literary and Social Setting of Mark 4.11–12*, JSNTSup 33 (Sheffield: JSOT Press, 1989).

114 Brakke argues that, 'rather than indicating the existence of two distinct kinds of gospels (obscure and plain), this scene more likely characterizes other known

in the Gospel of Mary as the Lord appears to Mary in a vision to teach her different things than those that he taught the wider group – things that are 'hidden' (ϩⲏⲡ) from the 'brothers' (10,8). When Mary recalls this teaching, Andrew declares it heterodox (ϩⲛ̄ⲕⲉⲙⲉⲉⲩⲉ [17,15]).

As we have already seen, there are strong links between the Apocryphon of James and the Johannine Farewell Discourse. What we did not discuss above is the parallelism between Jesus' use of parabolic language in the two texts.

> Ταῦτα ἐν παροιμίαις λελάληκα ὑμῖν· ἔρχεται ὥρα ὅτε οὐκέτι ἐν παροιμίαις λαλήσω ὑμῖν, ἀλλὰ παρρησίᾳ περὶ τοῦ πατρὸς ἀπαγγελῶ ὑμῖν (John 16.25)
>
> I have said these things to you in figures of speech; the hour is coming when I shall no longer speak to you in figures but tell you in plain speech of the Father.
>
> ⲁϩ̣[ⲓⲣ] ϣⲁⲣⲡ̣ ⲉⲉⲓϣⲉϫⲉ ⲛⲙ̄ⲙⲏⲧⲛ̄ ϩⲣⲏï ϩⲛ̄ ϩⲙ̄ⲡⲁⲣⲁⲃⲟⲗⲏ· ⲁⲩⲱ ⲛⲉⲣⲉⲧⲛ̄ⲣ ⲛⲟⲉⲓ ⲉⲛ· ϯ[ⲛ]ⲟⲩ ⲁⲛ ϯϣⲉϫⲉ ⲛⲙ̄ⲙⲏⲧ̣[ⲛ ϩ]ⲛ̄ ⲟⲩⲱⲛϩ̄ ⲁⲃⲁⲗ ⲁⲩⲱ ⲛ̄ⲧⲉ̣ⲧ̣ⲛ̄ⲣ ⲁⲓⲥⲑⲁⲛⲉ ⲉⲛ (ApJas 7,1–6)
>
> At first I spoke to you in parables and you did not understand. No[w] I speak to yo[u] openly, and you do not perceive.

The Johannine Farewell Discourse and the Apocryphon of James share the idea of movement from parables to open teaching. In John, Jesus tells his disciples that open speech will come in the future (16.25). Four verses later, the disciples claim that he is speaking frankly (ἐν παρρησίᾳ) and not in figures of speech (παροιμίαν) (16.29), suggesting that the time for plain or frank speech has arrived. In the preceding verse, Jesus tells them that he is from the Father and will return to the Father (16.28), which suggests to the reader that Jesus' words may not have changed but that the disciples claim to finally understand them. Whether the disciples actually understand is not clear.[115]

Jesus literature as similar to *Ap. Jas.* itself in being a mixture of "secret" and "open" teachings', Brakke, 'Parables and Plain Speech', 206. However, it is possible that the Apocryphon of James shares the same idea as *4 Ezra,* in which God orders Ezra to 'Make public the twenty-four books that you wrote first and let the worthy and the unworthy read them; but keep the seventy that were written last in order to give them to the wise among your people. For in them is the spring of understanding, the fountain of wisdom, and the river of knowledge' (14.45–47).

[115] Brown argues that the disciples are simply 'being impetuous' and that 'they are not much closer to true understanding than they were when they asked

We assume from the declarations in the Epistula Apostolorum and the Pistis Sophia that the risen Jesus will no longer speak in parables, but in the Apocryphon of James Jesus speaks both openly and parabolically 550 days after his resurrection. There is no chronological progression from parabolic to open teaching. He refers to past parables named 'the shepherds', 'the seed', 'the lamps of the virgins', 'the wage of the labourers' and 'the didrachmae' (8,6–10), but also introduces new parables about the kingdom and a palm shoot, the word as a grain of wheat, and the word as an ear of grain (7,22–35; 8,11–27; 12,20–30). If the former parables were teachings from Jesus' earthly life, his resurrection has not brought a new, definitive mode of speech. As Brakke writes, '*Ap. Jas.* does not rigidly assign parabolic speech to the life of the earthly Jesus and plain speech to appearances of the risen Jesus; rather, it presents all of Jesus' discourse as a combination of these two.'[116]

Furthermore, the parables in the Apocryphon of James are not associated with concealment either before or after the resurrection. The astute disciple understood the parables the first time simply by hearing them (7,35–8,10). Peter and James lack such insight and continue to struggle with Jesus' teachings:

> ⲡⲉⲧⲣⲟⲥ ⲛ̄ⲇⲉ ⲁϥⲟⲩⲱϣⲃ̄ ⲛ̄ⲛⲁϩⲣⲛ̄ ⲛⲉⲉⲓ ⲡⲁ[ϫ]ⲉϥ ϫⲉ ϩⲛ̄ⲥⲁⲡ ⲙⲉⲛ ⲕⲣ̄ ⲡⲣⲟ̣ⲧⲣⲉⲡⲉ ⲙ̄ⲙⲁⲛ ⲁϩⲟⲩⲛ ⲁⲧⲙⲛ̄ⲧⲣ̄ⲣⲟ ⲛ̄ⲙ̄ⲡⲏⲩⲉ ϩⲉⲛⲕⲉⲥⲁⲡ ⲁⲛ ⲕⲥⲧⲟ ⲙ̄ⲙⲁⲛ ⲁⲃⲁⲗ· ⲡϫⲁⲉⲓⲥ ϩⲛ̄ⲥⲁⲡ· ⲙⲉⲛ ⲕⲣ̄ ⲡⲓⲑⲉ ⲁⲩⲱ ⲕⲥⲱⲕ· ⲙ̄ⲙⲁⲛ ⲁϩⲟⲩⲛ ⲁⲧⲡⲓⲥⲧⲓⲥ ⲁⲩⲱ ⲕϣⲡⲱⲡ ⲛⲉⲛ ⲙ̄ⲡⲱⲛϩ̄ ϩⲛⲕⲉⲥⲁⲡ ⲁⲛ ⲕϩⲃⲁⲣⲃⲣ̄ ⲙ̄ⲙⲁⲛ ⲁⲃⲁⲗ ⲛ̄ⲧⲙⲛ̄ⲧⲉⲣⲟ ⲛ̄ⲙ̄ⲡⲏⲩⲉ (ApJas 13,25–36)

> Then Peter replied to these words and said, 'Sometimes you urge us toward the kingdom of heaven, and at other times you turn us back. Lord, sometimes you persuade and draw us to faith and promise us life, and at other times you cast us forth from the kingdom of heaven.'

naïve questions earlier in the Discourse', Brown, The Gospel According to John, XIII–XXI, 732. Dunderberg refers to Jesus' 'biting remark ('Is it now that you believe?'), followed by his prediction that the disciples will soon leave him alone (John 16:31–32) … warns against taking at face value the disciples' self-styled claim to finally understanding Jesus', Ismo Dunderberg, 'Secrecy in the Gospel of John', in *Mystery and Secrecy in the Nag Hammadi Collection and Other Ancient Literature: Ideas and Practices*, ed. Christian H. Bull, Liv Ingeborg Leid, and John D. Turner (Leiden: Brill, 2012), 229.

[116] Brakke, 'Parables and Plain Speech', 206. In the First Apocalypse of James too, Jesus begins the higher teaching before the crucifixion but will leave some to be revealed afterwards.

Brakke regards the Apocryphon of James to be working within the Platonic doctrine of 'intellectual understanding' and 'sense perception', used also by Clement and Origen. The Apocryphon of James, he argues, 'presents Jesus' parables as means to "intellectual understanding" and thus superior to Jesus' plain speech, which offers merely "sense perception"'.[117] The text places the focus on the disciples rather than Jesus – the disciples must work to understand the meaning of the parables.

Overall, dialogue gospels appear to respond to the problem of Jesus' perplexing teachings by presenting Jesus as responding to the disciples' questions with clear and often lengthy revelations. The Epistula Apostolorum refers to parabolic teaching as a thing of the past, suggesting that, like Luke, the risen Lord will reveal what was previously concealed or misunderstood.[118] However, the Apocryphon of James demonstrates that the earthly-parables/risen-open dichotomy is not a division that works in every case. Just as the Johannine Jesus speaks openly before his crucifixion, the Jesus of the Apocryphon of James speaks in parables after his resurrection. Neither suggests that the disciples do or do not understand: the disciples may understand parables, as in the Apocryphon of James, or may not understand open speech, as is a plausible reading of John.[119] The stronger connection between these texts is not sequential modes of revelation, but the continuation of the themes of hidden/open teachings and the disciples' ongoing attempts to understand Jesus' message.

Mysteries

As we have seen, Mark links parables and mystery, contrasting those that are given the mystery with those who receive parables (4.11).

[117] Brakke, 'Parables and Plain Speech', 207–8.

[118] Parables are also discussed and explained in the Pistis Sophia and the Apocalypse of Peter. The Pistis Sophia paraphrases Matt 10.12–13, referring to it as a 'parable' that Jesus once spoke. Jesus then interprets the instruction to bestow his peace on worthy households as their reception of the mysteries (3.107 [247,7–248,11]). The Apocalypse of Peter reformulates the parable of the fig tree in Matt 24.32–35 and Luke 13.6–9, replacing 'the summer' in Matt 24.32 with the parousia: 'as soon as its shoots have gone forth and its boughs have sprouted, the end of the world will come' (2.1). Peter needs an explanation, and Jesus tells him that the tree is the House of Israel and that when its boughs sprout false messiahs will come and there will be martyrs (2.2,7–10). On this, see Bauckham, 'Two Fig Tree Parables'; Julian V. Hills, 'Parables, Pretenders, and Prophecies: Translation and Interpretation in the Apocalypse of Peter 2', *Revue Biblique* 98.4 (1991): 560–73.

[119] Dunderberg, 'Secrecy in the Gospel of John'.

Mystery language permeates early Christian literature and usually refers to hidden things, although it can be used in a very loose sense.[120] Lang studies the mystery language in Paul and states that in the majority of the undisputed letters the term 'mystery' refers to

> some newly revealed and plainly stated eschatological or christological fact … [T]he term designates some important truth of Christian theology or eschatology that was previously hidden and has now been made known.[121]

Dialogue gospels purport to reveal Jesus' mysteries. A mere three examples are the Apocryphon of John, the Dialogue of the Saviour and the First Apocalypse of James. The Apocryphon of John begins by proclaiming itself as containing '[t]he teaching [of the Saviour and] the re[vel]ation of mysteries [and the th]ings hidden in silence' (ⲧⲉⲥⲃⲱ [ⲛⲧⲉ ⲡⲥⲱⲧⲏⲣ ⲁⲩⲱ] ⲡ̣ϭ̣[ⲱⲗ]ⲡ ⲉⲃⲟⲗ ⲛ̄ⲙ̣̄ⲙ̣ⲩⲥⲧⲏⲣⲓⲟⲛ [ⲙⲛ ⲛⲉ]ⲧϩⲏⲡ ϩⲛ̄ ⲟⲩⲙ̄ⲛ̄ⲧⲕⲁⲣⲱϥ [$_{\text{NHC2}}$ 1,1–4]). Although this opening only occurs in Codex 2, all recensions end with the recollection that John received the 'mystery' from the Saviour, as well as references to mysteries throughout. The term appears to encompass the teachings of the text as a whole in addition to specific mysteries such as the 'mystery of their life' (ⲡⲙⲩⲥⲧⲏⲣⲓⲟⲛ ⲙ̄ⲡⲉⲩⲱⲛϩ [$_{\text{BG}}$ 56,8–9]), which is an interpretation of Gen 2–3.[122] The Dialogue of the Saviour refers to the 'mystery of truth' (ⲡⲙⲩⲥⲧⲏⲣⲓⲟⲛ̣ ⲛ̄ⲧⲙⲏⲉ [143,8]) in a passage that Létourneau understands as a reference to 'receiving the revelation from the Savior ("to stand or be established in the mystery of truth") [which] allows the elect to recognize themselves and make themselves known to humanity'.[123] Mystery and revelation are also connected in both recensions of the First Apocalypse of James:

> ⲉⲓⲥ ϩⲏⲧⲉ ϯⲛⲁϭⲱⲗⲡ̄ ⲛⲁⲕ ⲉⲃⲟⲗ ⲛ̄ϩⲱⲃ ⲛⲓⲙ ⲙ̄ⲡⲓⲙⲩⲥⲧⲏⲣⲓⲟⲛ ($_{\text{NHC}}$ 25,5–7)

[120] As noted by Strousma, the word μυστήριον 'has obviously a very broad semantic spectrum in late antiquity, and is more often than not ambivalent or used in a metaphoric or at least a rather loose sense', Guy G. Stroumsa, *Hidden Wisdom: Esoteric Traditions and the Roots of Christian Mysticism*, 2nd ed. (Leiden and Boston: Brill, 2005), 64.

[121] T. J. Lang, *Mystery and the Making of a Christian Historical Consciousness: From Paul to the Second Century*, BZNW 219 (Berlin: de Gruyter, 2015), 40.

[122] On this and mystery/mysteries more generally in the Apocryphon of John, see Karen L. King, 'Mystery and Secrecy in The Secret Revelation of John', in *Mystery and Secrecy in the Nag Hammadi Collection and Other Ancient Literature: Ideas and Practices*, ed. Christian H. Bull, Liv Ingeborg Leid, and John D. Turner, NHMS 76 (Leiden and Boston: Brill, 2012), 61–86.

[123] Pierre Létourneau, 'The Dialogue of the Savior as a Witness to the Late Valentinian Tradition', *VC* 65.1 (2011): 90.

Behold, I shall reveal to you everything of this mystery.

ⲉⲓⲥ ϩⲏⲧⲉ ⲁ̈ⲓϭⲱⲗⲡ ⲛⲁⲕ ⲉⲃ̣ⲟⲗ ⲙ̣̄ⲡ̣ⲙ̣ⲩⲥⲧⲏⲣⲓⲟⲛ ($_{\text{CT}}$ 11,8–9)

Behold, I have revealed to you the mystery.

Jenott sees a major christological difference in the two recensions as the future tense in the Nag Hammadi version points the reader to the mystery in the discourse that follows, whereas the past tense in Codex Tchacos identifies the mystery with the foregoing christological discourse, marked by a paragraphus between the two instructions to 'behold'.[124] This previous discourse has explained that Jesus came to show James the highest deity and his own identity ($_{\text{CT}}$ 10,8–11,8). Thus, by revealing the mystery, Jesus reveals to James his salvation. The future tense in the NHC version, on the other hand, 'casts Jesus' opening discourse as an introduction to the rest of the treatise, so that the reader expects to learn "each part" of the mystery in what follows'.[125] The beginning of the First Apocalypse of James reveals the nature of the relationship between Jesus, James and the 'One Who Is' – for CT this is the mystery, but for NHC this is just an introduction to the mystery of James' salvation through the archons.

Who Can Be Weaned?

Mysteries are often associated with secrecy – and secrecy is widespread in dialogue gospels. The titles 'apocryphon' or 'apocalypse' both pertain to secrecy.[126] To whom mysteries can be disclosed is a matter of contestation and brings us back to Paul and John. The secret and concealed nature of mysteries is clear in 1 Corinthians 2:

> σοφίαν δὲ λαλοῦμεν ἐν τοῖς τελείοις, σοφίαν δὲ οὐ τοῦ αἰῶνος τούτου οὐδὲ τῶν ἀρχόντων τοῦ αἰῶνος τούτου τῶν καταργουμένων

[124] Lance Jenott, 'Reading Variants in James and the Apocalypse of James: A Perspective from New Philology', in *Snapshots of Evolving Traditions: Jewish and Christian Manuscript Culture, Textual Fluidity, and New Philology*, ed. Liv Ingeborg Leid and Hugo Lundhaug (Berlin and Boston: de Gruyter, 2017), 76. On the paragraphus: 'At the beginning of the discourse, just where Jesus says "Listen" (CT 10.8), the scribe marked the passage with a paragraphus in the left-hand margin, and on the next page punctuated its logical conclusion with a series of diplai (>>>) inside the textual column (CT 11.7), thus demarcating the entire passage in an inclusio. Because of the infrequency of the paragraphus in CT (there are only three extant instances in the codex: pp. 10, 61, 63) it was apparently used to mark passages which the scribe regarded as especially significant' (76).

[125] Jenott, 'Reading Variants in James', 76.

[126] On the title 'apocalypse', for the First Apocalypse of James in NHC 5, Jenott writes: 'The function of the term "apocalypse" in the title can therefore be understood

ἀλλὰ λαλοῦμεν θεοῦ σοφίαν ἐν μυστηρίῳ τὴν ἀποκεκρυμμένην, ἣν προώρισεν ὁ θεὸς πρὸ τῶν αἰώνων εἰς δόξαν ἡμῶν, ἣν οὐδεὶς τῶν ἀρχόντων τοῦ αἰῶνος τούτου ἔγνωκεν (1 Cor 2.6–8)

But wisdom we do speak among the perfect, but a wisdom not of this age nor of the rulers of this age who are passing away. But rather we speak in a mystery the wisdom of God, which has been hidden, which God ordained before the ages for our glory, which none of the rulers of this age have known.[127]

Who are the perfect? The 'perfect' who speak the wisdom of God are later equated with the spiritual: 'And we speak of these things in words not taught by human wisdom but taught by the spirit, interpreting spiritual things to those who are spiritual' (ἃ καὶ λαλοῦμεν οὐκ ἐν διδακτοῖς ἀνθρωπίνης σοφίας λόγοις ἀλλ' ἐν διδακτοῖς πνεύματος, πνευματικοῖς πνευματικὰ συγκρίνοντες [2.13]) who have the 'mind of Christ' (νοῦν Χριστοῦ [v.16]). The Corinthians do not make the cut:

Κἀγώ, ἀδελφοί, οὐκ ἠδυνήθην λαλῆσαι ὑμῖν ὡς πνευματικοῖς ἀλλ' ὡς σαρκίνοις, ὡς νηπίοις ἐν Χριστῷ. γάλα ὑμᾶς ἐπότισα, οὐ βρῶμα· οὔπω γὰρ ἐδύνασθε. ἀλλ' οὐδὲ ἔτι νῦν δύνασθε, ἔτι γὰρ σαρκικοί ἐστε (1 Cor 3.1–3)

And so, brothers and sisters, I could not speak to you as spiritual people, but rather as people of the flesh, as infants in Christ. I fed you with milk, not solid food, for you were not ready for solid food. Even now you are still not ready, for you are still of the flesh.

The Corinthians are not able (or ready) to be weaned onto Paul's solid food.

Although these verses are considered favourites of the 'secretive gnostics', no one could more explicitly endorse this idea than Ignatius:

Μὴ οὐ δύναμαι ὑμῖν τὰ ἐπουράνια γράψαι; ἀλλὰ φοβοῦμαι, μὴ νηπίοις οὖσιν ὑμῖν βλάβην παραθῶ καὶ συγγνωμονεῖτέ

as a mode of religious advertising insofar as it promises to offer the reader secret truths, now revealed, which Jesus had originally delivered to James, and which were later recorded and transmitted for posterity. Simultaneously, the title enhances the religious self-esteem of the reader as someone privileged enough to receive such revelation him- or herself,' Jenott, 'Reading Variants in James', 66.

[127] Translation from Lang, adapted. On translation points here, see Lang, *Mystery and the Making*, 55–6.

> μοι, μήποτε οὐ δυνηθέντες χωρῆσαι στραγγαλωθῆτε (*Ep. Trall.* 5.1)
>
> Am I not able to write to you about heavenly things? But I am afraid that I may harm you who are still infants. Grant me this concession – otherwise you may choke, not being able to swallow.

Ignatius continues by telling the Trallians that he is unlike them as he is able 'to understand the heavenly realms and angelic realms and hierarchies of the cosmic rulers, both visible and invisible' (δύναμαι νοεῖν τὰ ἐπουράνια καὶ τὰς τοποθεσίας τὰς ἀγγελικὰς καὶ τὰς συστάσεις τὰς ἀρχοντικάς, ὁρατά τε καὶ ἀόρατα [*Ep. Trall.* 5.2]). The Pauline association continues, as Ignatius urges his readers to eat only Christian food as foreign foods are heresy (6.1). Ignatius' rhetoric emerges here as a blend of Paul's reference to infants who cannot consume solid food and what we find Jesus saying to Nicodemus in John 3.[128] Nicodemus is not able (or ready) to receive higher teaching: Jesus says to him, 'If I told you about the earthly things and you do not believe, how can you believe if I tell you about the heavenly things?' (εἰ τὰ ἐπίγεια εἶπον ὑμῖν καὶ οὐ πιστεύετε, πῶς ἐὰν εἴπω ὑμῖν τὰ ἐπουράνια πιστεύσετε; [John 3.12]). To use Pauline language, Nicodemus is not able to eat solid food.

The concept of two levels of knowledge is also found in the Book of Thomas, and here we find the earthly-heavenly division described through the language visible and invisible:

> ⲁϥ ⲟⲩⲱϣⲃ̄ ⲛ̄ϭⲓ ⲡ︦ⲥ︦ⲱ︦ⲣ︦ ⲉϥϫⲱ ⲙ̄ⲙ̣[ⲟ]ⲥ ϫⲉ ⲉϣⲡⲉ ⲛⲉⲧⲟⲩⲟⲛϩ ⲉⲃⲟⲗ ⲛⲏⲧⲛ̄ ⲥⲉϩⲏⲡ ⲛ̣̄[ⲛ]ⲁ̣ϩⲣⲛ̄ ⲧⲏⲛⲉ ⲛ̄ϩⲉ ⲉⲩⲛ̄ ϭⲁⲙ ⲙ̄ⲙⲱⲧⲛ̄ ⲁⲥⲱⲧⲙ̄ ⲁⲛⲉⲧⲉ ⲛ̄ⲥⲉⲟⲩⲟⲛϩ ⲉⲃⲟⲗ ⲁⲛ (BookThom 138,27–30)
>
> The Saviour answered, saying, 'If the things that are visible to you are obscure to you, how can you hear about the things that are not visible?'

The invisible things are not just out of sight; they are 'hidden things' (ⲡⲣⲁ ⲛⲛ̣ⲉⲑⲏⲡ [128,24–25]). The Book of Thomas does not answer the question of who can be weaned: Thomas is concerned with

[128] It continues to be debated whether Ignatius knew John, see Hill, *Johannine Corpus*, 421–43; Paul Foster, 'The Epistles of Ignatius of Antioch and the Writings That Later Formed the New Testament', in *The Reception of the New Testament in the Apostolic Fathers*, ed. Andrew Gregory and Christopher M. Tuckett (Oxford: Oxford University Press, 2005), 159–86. The quotation above from *Ep. Trall.* may not be a direct allusion to John 3.

preaching, perhaps suggesting that this revelation is not to be hidden from anyone. A more overt answer is found in other dialogue gospels that indicate that solid food is given to 'those who are worthy'. The secrecy and revelation theme is often linked to 'gnostic inner-circles' associated with 'the aura of novelty and exclusiveness';[129] but basic and advanced theological teaching was common in many ancient schools of thought, including the Christians behind the *Apostolic Tradition*, attributed to Hippolytus, in which pre-baptismal training took three years, as well as Clement of Alexandria and Origen, who both proposed higher teachers for the spiritually mature.[130]

Claims of exclusiveness and 'gnostic inner-circles' conflict with an appeal to universal mission, which was popular in dialogue gospels, as seen in our discussion of Matthew 28 earlier in this chapter. In all versions of the Apocryphon of John, a text titled an 'apocryphon', a secret book, we find a declaration that John is to write down all that the Saviour has told him 'and give them to your fellow spirits in secret' (ⲚⲄⲦⲀⲀⲨ ⲚⲚⲈⲔϨⲞⲘⲞⲠⲚⲀ ϨⲘ ⲠⲠⲈⲐⲎⲠ [$_{BG}$ 75,6–9]). John then goes to 'his fellow disciples' (ⲚⲈϤϢⲂⲢ ⲘⲀⲐⲎⲦⲎⲤ [$_{BG}$ 77,1–2]) and tells them what he has heard. The term 'apocryphon' along with 'fellow spirits' has led some to see the Apocryphon of John to be written for a limited '*Empfängerkreis*'[131] or 'chosen few'.[132] But King rightly interprets the language that the Apocryphon of John uses in the same way that similar language is employed in the canonical gospels and Paul. She writes: 'There, too, Jesus is depicted as a heavenly Savior, who imparts secret teaching to a chosen few.'[133] She identifies the problem of presuming that the language of secret revelation 'must necessarily correlate to a socially exclusive group', when '[s]cholars have in fact argued the opposite in the case of the gospels and Paul'.[134] She writes:

> Indeed nothing in the mere use of such themes suggests that this 'pattern' of secrecy, when deployed by some Christians, is distinctively 'Gnostic' and indicates a secret society whose membership is limited to an elite, while the same pattern

[129] Pleše, *Poetics of the Gnostic Universe*, 8.

[130] On the issue of being sufficiently educated, or spiritually mature, in early Christianity in relation to Valentinian schools, see Ismo Dunderberg, *Beyond Gnosticism: Myth, Lifestyle, and Society in the School of Valentinus* (New York: Columbia University Press, 2008), 191–5.

[131] Hartenstein, *Die zweite Lehre*, 64.

[132] Pleše, *Poetics of the Gnostic Universe*, 7.

[133] King, 'Mystery and Secrecy', 70.

[134] King, 'Mystery and Secrecy', 71.

> used by 'canonical' Christians supposedly indicates exoteric tradition and presumably a correspondingly open (non-elite) social group. All these cases combine claims of secret revelation with practices of universal mission.[135]

We might take this further – clearly the 'fellow spirits' to whom John is to give Jesus' teaching are the 'disciples', and there is no indication that there are Christians who could not become disciples. In fact, the text itself says that the spirit is in every human or they would not be able to stand ($_{\text{BG}}$ 67,4–7), but some are led astray by the counterfeit spirit ($_{\text{BG}}$ 67,14–18). Perhaps John's 'fellow spirits' are all humans,[136] but secrecy is necessary so the spiritually immature do not attempt to chew before they are ready; or secrecy may be in order to keep this knowledge hidden from the evil archons. In either of these cases, the Apocryphon of John appears to be no more restrictive than Paul's letters to the Corinthians (for which Lang suggests 'the spiritual' means the 'ethically sound' Christians rather than an exclusive group[137]).

The idea that the teachings of the Apocryphon of John were intended to be delivered universally may be a stretch too far, but it does appear that it saw the mature who were able to digest solid food in a comparable way to other Christian writings. So on the question of who could be weaned, the 'gnostic' dialogue gospels are not dissimilar from other early Christian texts. The overriding attitude towards the question of who could be weaned is nicely summed up by the Gospel of Thomas:

> ⲡⲉϫⲉ ⲓ̣ⲥ̅ ϫⲉ ⲉⲓ̈ϫⲱ ⲛ̄ⲛⲁⲙⲩⲥⲧⲏⲣⲓⲟⲛ ⲛ̄ⲛⲉ̣[ⲧⲙ̄ⲡϣⲁ] ⲛ̣̄[ⲛⲁ]ⲙ̣ⲩⲥⲧⲏⲣⲓⲟⲛ (GThom 62)
>
> Jesus said, 'I tell my mysteries to those who are [worthy] of [my] mysteries.'

In the dialogue gospels, Jesus' departure indicates the beginning of the time of the disciples' own independent agency. The departure

[135] King, 'Mystery and Secrecy', 71.

[136] See also Michael A. Williams, 'Secrecy, Revelation, and Late Antique Demiurgical Myths', in *Rending the Veil: Concealment and Secrecy in the History of Religions*, ed. Elliot R. Wolfson (New York: Seven Bridges Press, 1999), 50. The external evidence backs this up: the teachings of the Apocryphon of John appear to be relatively widely known. The Apocryphon of John is found today in four recensions, was known to Irenaeus (in some form), and promulgated in at least two languages (see 37–41).

[137] Lang, *Mystery and the Making*, 66.

of Jesus enacts a division between past and future, and the disciples are the future. And, in most cases, this is the time of disclosure. This finds its antecedent in Paul, who sees himself and other disciples of Christ as administrators of the mysteries (1 Cor 4.1)[138] that are to be disclosed (1 Cor 15.51–52). The secrecy and revelation theme then is not novel in the dialogue gospels, nor does it pertain to 'gnostic' exclusivity. Rather, it connects a wide range of Christian traditions, including the canonical gospels and Paul.

2.5 Conclusion

There is a plethora of intertextual connections between dialogue gospels and the texts that came to be in the New Testament, particularly the canonical gospels and the Pauline epistles. Dialogue gospels were not written or read in isolation. They belong in a wider context of broader traditions narrating events around Jesus' departure and resurrection, asking who is to be left in charge and how to enact the mission charge. It is these traditions and themes, which are found in the New Testament, that influenced and shaped the dialogue gospels.

The Johannine Farewell Discourse is integral to understanding other texts in the genre as it acts as their precursor and companion: focused on Jesus' departure, select disciples ask Jesus how to follow him in both life and death and what they should do in his absence. Yet in John, Jesus returns after his farewell dialogue and can continue to engage in dialogue. A final revelation, then, can only come after his resurrection, and thus it is after the resurrection that we find the temporal setting of most dialogue gospels. Similar themes and concerns are found in the dialogue gospels, the resurrection accounts of the canonical gospels, Acts 1 and 1 Corinthians 15 – among these themes and concerns are the question of the leading disciple, the mission charge, the form of Jesus' resurrection body, the primacy of post-resurrection revelation, and the question of whether the risen Jesus could and should be touched. Dialogue gospels present these various issues differently. They might choose a key disciple, they might allay fears about mission, they might depict Jesus as a luminous being, they might reveal previously hidden things, and/or they might affirm the physicality of the risen Christ. However much the depictions of Jesus within the dialogue gospels

[138] For 1 Cor 4.1, Lang writes that 'the apostles' standing as "administrators of the mysteries of God" is correlated with their identity as "servants of Christ"', Lang, *Mystery and the Making*, 34.

contrast with one another, they may be seen to have a similar range to those that we find within the canonical resurrection narratives.

Although dialogue gospels have closer textual links with the canonical gospels than other texts of the New Testament, there is a firm influence from the Pauline and the deutero-Pauline epistles. There are a number of possible topics that could have been discussed here, but three have provided the main focus: (1) the emphasis on the risen Lord, at the expense of the earthly Jesus, (2) the Ephesian view of liberation from the cosmic powers through Christ and (3) mysteries that must be withheld from the immature. The Pauline thought-world disclosed by these three topics is continuous with what we find in many of the dialogue gospels. Paul's interest in mysteries that cannot be taught to those that are not ready stands alongside Mark's view of parabolic teaching for those 'outside' and John's depiction of Nicodemus' lack of ability to perceive higher teaching. I have argued that we find similar ideas in the dialogue gospels, but those that have been viewed as 'gnostic' have been interpreted in an esoteric way, in contrast to Paul, Mark and John. Yet the canonical and non-canonical texts converge at this point: Jesus' mysteries will be revealed to those who are worthy – his Christian followers. The Matthean 'great commission' is also echoed in a number of these dialogue gospels, suggesting that they were intended for general circulation and not just for the elite – much like the New Testament texts.

The broad trends that link the texts within the dialogue gospel genre relate to those in the canonical gospels and Paul, and there are many cases of more pointed textual or thematic links. This discussion of the genre and its relation to the New Testament has been framed in a way to highlight the fact that dialogue gospels are a part of the same literary world as other gospels and early Christian literature more generally. This wide-ranging demonstration of intertextual connections has been far from comprehensive, but it may serve to draw attention to a body of literature from which useful comparisons can be drawn that illuminate aspects of the concerns, inspirations and motivations of early Christian authors.

To sharpen the discussion and to engage in more sustained exegetical work, we now turn our attention to a single text: the Gospel of Mary.

Part II

3

THE NARRATIVE FRAME OF THE GOSPEL OF MARY

The basic outline of the format of the Gospel of Mary is a series of dialogues enclosed by a narrative frame.[1] The beginning six pages of the Gospel of Mary are no longer extant, but we can assume that there was a short narrative there in order to set the scene. This is followed by a dialogue between the Saviour and his disciples, of which only the final two questions survive. A separate farewell discourse concludes Jesus' teachings, which we include in the narrative frame as it is essential to the narrative that follows. Without Jesus' departure, the rest of the material would not make sense. As Jesus departs, Mary arises, comforts the disciples and reminds them of Jesus' teaching, and only because Jesus has departed can the disciples squabble over Mary's revelation. This chapter will examine how she is portrayed in relation to the male disciples and in relation to Jesus. Four pages are missing from Mary's teaching, but it starts with a vision that she has of Jesus and finishes with a narrative of a personified soul ascending through the heavens, and this leads on to the next part of the narrative frame: the breach between the disciples. Peter and Andrew cannot accept what Mary has said and accuse the revelation of being strange and secretive. Levi jumps in, likening Peter to the hostile cosmic powers that the soul has overcome; this leads to a rather inconclusive ending – one or more disciples go out to preach the gospel, but the question of who differs between the Greek and Coptic versions.[2] The narrative frame encompasses

[1] My understanding of the narrative frame is the same as Hartenstein's, who includes 8,11–10,16 and 17,7–19,2, Judith Hartenstein, *Die zweite Lehre: Erscheinungen des Auferstandenen als Rahmenerzählungen frühchristlicher Dialoge*, TU 146 (Berlin: Akademie Verlag, 2000), 137–42. The two revelatory dialogues (between the Saviour and his disciples and Mary's recollection of her vision) are separate from the narrative frame.

[2] Hartenstein divides the Gospel of Mary into four parts: (1) the beginning and no longer extant appearance and dialogue; (2) Jesus' final instructions, his disappearance and the reaction of the disciples; (3) the disciples gathered together, arguing about his words; and (4) the post-vision disciples and departure, Hartenstein, *Die zweite Lehre*,

the missing beginning, the Saviour's farewell speech and departure, Mary consoling the male disciples, the ensuing argument and the breach following Mary's teaching. This chapter follows this outline.

Despite the genre of 'dialogue gospel', the narrative frame is as integral to understanding the message of the Gospel of Mary as the eschatological teachings in the dialogues. In fact, the dialogue and the narrative frame are more integrated in the Gospel of Mary than in other dialogue gospels.[3] The Sophia of Jesus Christ, for example, looks to be a narrative frame imposed on a pre-existing dialogue (which equates largely to Eugnostos). In the Gospel of Mary, the Saviour's departure is necessary for the following text, and Mary's teaching leads to the argument between the disciples.

3.1 The Beginning of the Gospel of Mary: The Missing Pages

There are six missing pages at the beginning of *Papyrus Berolinensis 8502* (BG). Based on a papyrological analysis of the Greek papyrus fragment, PRyl.GM, in comparison to BG, it is safe to assume that these six pages were the opening of the Gospel of Mary. The extant BG is paginated 7–10 and 15–19 and the recto (→) and verso (↓) of PRyl.GM are numbered 21 and 22. PRyl.GM covers 17,4 to 19,5 (the end) of BG. It can be assumed that the Rylands codex contained a single text, as was typical of gospel codices in the second and third centuries, and so the Gospel of Mary must have taken up the whole 22 pages.[4] As PRyl.GM contains the end of the Gospel of Mary, the BG Gospel of Mary is likely to be the *entire* 19 pages.[5]

142. An alternative way of structuring the Gospel of Mary is provided by King, who writes: 'It is structured as a series of dialogues and departures: 1) the dialogue between the Savior and the disciples, followed by the Savior's departure; 2) the dialogue among the disciples, followed by their departure (or at least Levi's departure) to preach the gospel; 3) the dialogue between the Savior and Mary, ending in her silence; and 4) the dialogues between the soul and the Powers, culminating in the soul's departure from the world to its final resting place,' Karen L. King, *The Gospel of Mary of Magdala: Jesus and the First Woman Apostle* (Santa Rosa, CA: Polebridge Press, 2003), 30.

[3] Despite Hartenstein's general assumption that dialogue gospels can be separated into a Christian narrative frame and non-Christian teachings in the dialogues, for the Gospel of Mary she rejects all earlier hypotheses of disunity and redaction, stating that 'das EvMar ist eine durchaus kohärente und in seiner jetzigen Form verständliche Schrift', Hartenstein, *Die zweite Lehre*, 137. On the general assumption, see her introduction and pp. 280–3.

[4] In the *editio princeps*, Roberts writes, on a palaeographical basis, that '463 can hardly be later than the middle of the third century and probably is considerably earlier', C. H. Roberts, '463: The Gospel of Mary', in *Catalogue of the Greek Papyri in the John Rylands Library*, 3 (Manchester: Manchester University Press, 1938), 20.

[5] This problem has been noted by Tuckett who concludes that the Gospel of Mary was probably the first text of the codex, Christopher M. Tuckett, *The Gospel of Mary*

It is appropriate then to begin a discussion of the narrative frame by asking what was written in the beginning six pages. This poses a number of questions, including: did the text contain a passion or resurrection narrative? Where did Jesus appear, and what were the disciples doing? What is the purpose of the text? Working within the limitations of the fragmentary state of the Gospel of Mary, these questions can only begin to be answered by examining comparable sources. As we have seen with Perkins and Hartenstein in Chapter 1, dialogue gospels often begin with a narrative setting, which introduces and sometimes authenticates the revelation. Although it is impossible to be certain how the Gospel of Mary begins, suggestions can be made.

In the body of dialogue gospels, the extant Gospel of Mary is one with more narrative throughout. The text narrates the Saviour's departure, Mary's rising, her weeping and the disciples' departure. It would be odd, then, if there was no narrative at the beginning. Based on Perkins' argument that the 'opening narratives [of revelation dialogues] are more uniformly stylized than the concluding ones',[6] and by employing a comparative approach and focusing on the teachings of the gospel, several possibilities for pages 1–6 can be suggested. In the discussion that follows, some texts offer a more useful comparison than others, for their setting, their dialogue form, or, in most cases, both – especially the Sophia of Jesus Christ, the Johannine Farewell Discourse, the Pistis Sophia, and the resurrection accounts in John 20, Matt 28 and Mark LE. Other, less frequent, comparisons will be drawn from the Apocryphon of John, the First Apocalypse of James, the Dialogue of the Saviour and the Epistle of Peter to Philip. A common feature of these texts is that the dialogue takes place after Jesus' resurrection (with the exception of the first part of the First Apocalypse of James[7]), indicating that the Gospel of Mary is a post-resurrection dialogue.

As a preliminary point of caution, all dialogue gospels are unique. The Gospel of Mary is unlike existing texts of this genre as the narrative continues extensively beyond the Saviour's departure

(Oxford and New York: Oxford University Press, 2007), 6 n. 8. Till, however, suggests that the complete Rylands version may have been longer than the Coptic, Walter C. Till, *Die gnostischen Schriften des koptischen Papyrus Berolinensis 8502*, TU 60, 2nd ed. (Berlin: Akademie Verlag, 1972), 25.

[6] Pheme Perkins, *The Gnostic Dialogue: The Early Church and the Crisis of Gnosticism* (New York: Paulist Press, 1980), 41.

[7] The Dialogue of the Saviour is not explicitly post-resurrection, but it is likely to be, as discussed in Chapter 1.

(although he makes another appearance in Mary's recollection). Therefore, any suggestions regarding the missing material based on the genre are highly speculative. In fact, basing a reconstruction on relatively similar material could be a serious error of judgement. If the genealogy of Matthew had been lost and we were to base a reconstruction on the Lukan infancy narrative, due to the gospels being the same *bios* genre and subsequently sharing a lot of the same material, we would be so far from the gospel text that it would be more useful to omit a reconstruction altogether. Therefore, the following proposals do not pretend to act as a reconstruction but instead to highlight the teachings in the extant text and to situate the Gospel of Mary within the body of dialogue gospel literature.

A Resurrection Account?

Despite clear differences between the Gospel of Mary and the canonical gospels, it is possible that pages 1–6 of the Gospel of Mary brought them into closer contact. Hartenstein thinks so, suggesting that there was a resurrection narrative at the beginning of the gospel, based on the parallel language for the actions of the Saviour and Mary:

> ⲁϥ<u>ⲁⲥⲡⲁⲍⲉ ⲙ̄ⲙⲟⲟⲩ ⲧⲏⲣⲟⲩ</u> <u>ⲉϥϫⲱ</u> ⲙ̄ⲙⲟ`ⲟ´ⲥ ϫⲉ (8,12–14)
>
> He said farewell (ⲁⲥⲡⲁⲍⲉ) to them all saying …
>
> ⲧⲟⲧⲉ ⲁⲙⲁⲣⲓϩⲁⲙ ⲧⲱⲟⲩⲛ ⲁⲥ<u>ⲁⲥⲡⲁⲍⲉ ⲙⲙⲟⲟⲩ ⲧⲏⲣⲟⲩ ⲡⲉϫⲁⲥ</u> … (9,12–14)
>
> Then Mary rose, she greeted (ⲁⲥⲡⲁⲍⲉ) them all, she said …

There is undoubtedly a parallel between these two phrases, but it is difficult to know what is intended by it. Hartenstein focuses on the word ⲧⲱⲟⲩⲛ, arguing not only that 'she stands up, which highlights the meaning of her words', but also that ⲧⲱⲟⲩⲛ has stronger implications than 'stood up'.[8] As ⲧⲱⲟⲩⲛ is used for Jesus being raised from the dead in the Sophia of Jesus Christ ($_{\text{BG}}$ 77,9–10) and the Apocryphon of James (2,20–21), she suggests that ⲧⲱⲟⲩⲛ could have been used for the Saviour's resurrection in pages 1–6: 'Mary's appearance is therefore a certain parallel.'[9]

[8] Hartenstein, *Die zweite Lehre*, 146.
[9] Hartenstein, *Die zweite Lehre*, 146.

There is no clear answer as to whether the gospel once contained a resurrection narrative, but it is possible. Textual parallels illustrate that eschatological and soteriological revelation (key themes in the Gospel of Mary) commonly took place in a post-resurrection setting, and one of the key focuses in the Gospel of Mary is that Jesus has left the disciples alone and has ascended to heaven. Therefore, the evangelist may have wanted to make the resurrection setting explicit. However, considering that by page 7 the Saviour had told the disciples 'everything' (ϩⲱⲃ ⲛⲓⲙ [7,11]), there would be little room left for an extended resurrection narrative. At best, the resurrection account would be brief. If the Gospel of Mary contained one, it may have read like the Sophia of Jesus Christ, which opens with the words, 'After he rose from the dead' (ⲙⲛ̄ⲛ̄ⲥⲁ ⲛⲧⲣⲉϥⲧⲱⲟⲩ(ⲛ) ⲉⲃⲟⲗ ϩⲛ̄ ⲛⲉⲧⲙⲟⲟⲩⲧ [$_{BG}$ 77,9–10]), or the Pistis Sophia, 'But it happened that after Jesus had risen from the dead, he spent eleven years speaking with his disciples' (ⲁⲥϣⲱⲡⲉ ⲇⲉ ⲙⲛ̄ⲛ̄ⲥⲁ ⲧⲣⲉ ⲓ̅ⲥ̅ ⲧⲱⲟⲩⲛ ⲉⲃⲟⲗ ϩⲛ̄ ⲛⲉⲧⲙⲟⲟⲩⲧ ⲁⲩⲱ ⲁϥⲣ̄·ⲙⲛ̄ⲧⲟⲩⲉ ⲛ̄ⲣⲟⲙⲡⲉ ⲉϥϣⲁϫⲉ ⲙⲛ̄ ⲛⲉϥⲙⲁⲑⲏⲧⲏⲥ (1.1 [2,1–3]).[10] The Gospel of Mary could have employed a similar incipit to stress the Saviour's resurrected status and establish the setting for the revelation.

Whether or not the gospel began like the Sophia of Jesus Christ or the Pistis Sophia, Hartenstein's suggestion leads to a more fruitful speculation: that the Gospel of Mary's setting is more closely connected to the canonical gospels than has previously been assumed. Again, the post-Easter setting is stressed as the connection lies primarily in the resurrection narratives. Mary Magdalene plays a role in every post-resurrection scene of the canonical gospels and the Gospel of Mary could be seen as a continuation of Christ's appearance to her.[11] In Matthew, Mary Magdalene along with ἡ ἄλλη

[10] Note Book Four, which is often seen as separate from 1–3, has a different opening: 'Now it happened when they crucified our Lord Jesus, he rose from the dead on the third day. His disciples gathered to him and entreated him, saying …' (ⲁⲥϣⲱⲡⲉ ϭⲉ ⲛ̄ⲧⲉⲣⲟⲩⲥⲧ̅ⲣ̅ⲟⲩ ⲙ̄ⲡⲉⲛϫⲟⲉⲓⲥ ⲓ̅ⲥ̅ ⲁϥⲧⲱⲟⲩⲛ ⲉⲃⲟⲗ ϩⲛ̄ ⲛⲉⲧⲙⲟⲟⲩⲧ ⲙ̄ⲡⲉϥⲙⲉϩϣⲟⲙ̄ⲛ̄ⲧ ⲛ̄ϩⲟⲟⲩ · ⲁⲩⲥⲱⲟⲩϩ ⲉⲣⲟϥ ⲛ̄ϭⲓ ⲛⲉϥⲙⲁⲑⲏⲧⲏⲥ ⲁⲩⲧⲱⲃ̅ϩ̅ ⲙ̄ⲙⲟϥ ⲉϥϫⲱ ⲙ̄ⲙⲟⲥ (4.136 [353,1–4]). The use of ⲧⲱⲟⲩⲛ in both Book One and Book Four of the Pistis Sophia potentially strengthens Hartenstein's proposal. Furthermore, the Gospel of Mary 9,10–12 suggests a possible reference to the crucifixion and suffering of Jesus as the disciples say that 'they' did not spare him. The 'they' refers to the 'nations' or the 'gentiles' (ϩⲉⲑⲛⲟⲥ) in contrast to the 'the Jews' as the agents of the crucifixion in Luke and the Gospel of Peter.

[11] This is based on the assumption that Mary in the Gospel of Mary is Mary Magdalene, as in Till, *Papyrus Berolinensis 8502*, 26; Anne Pasquier, *L'Évangile Selon Marie*, BCNH:T 10 (Québec: Les Presses de l'Université Laval, 1983), 23 n. 75; Michel Tardieu and Jean-Daniel Dubois, *Introduction à la littérature gnostique. I: Collections retrouvées avant 1945* (Paris: Les Éditions du Cerf, 1986), 20; Karen

Μαρία (28.1) are met by Jesus who instructs them to tell the others about his resurrection (28.10). In Luke, Mary Magdalene and the other women tell the apostles that they have seen an angel at the tomb (24.11). But it is Mark LE and John 20 that are particularly comparable. The LE of Mark opens:

> Ἀναστὰς δὲ πρωῒ πρώτῃ σαββάτου ἐφάνη πρῶτον Μαρίᾳ τῇ Μαγδαληνῇ, παρ' ἧς ἐκβεβλήκει ἑπτὰ δαιμόνια. ἐκείνη πορευθεῖσα ἀπήγγειλεν τοῖς μετ' αὐτοῦ γενομένοις πενθοῦσι καὶ κλαίουσιν· κἀκεῖνοι ἀκούσαντες ὅτι ζῇ καὶ ἐθεάθη ὑπ' αὐτῆς ἠπίστησαν (Mark 16.9–11)
>
> After he rose early on the first day of the week, he appeared first to Mary Magdalene, from whom he had cast out seven demons. She went out and told those who had been with him, while they were mourning and weeping. But when they heard that he was alive and had been seen by her, they would not believe it.

Mary Magdalene also plays a prominent role in John 20. She visits Jesus' tomb and does not find his body there. While standing outside of the tomb, she speaks to two angels and explains that she is weeping because Jesus' body is missing. Then she turns around to see Jesus,

L. King, 'The Gospel of Mary Magdalene', in *Searching the Scriptures, II: A Feminist Commentary*, ed. Elisabeth Schüssler Fiorenza (New York: Crossroad, 1994), 601; Antti Marjanen, *The Woman Jesus Loved: Mary Magdalene in the Nag Hammadi Library and Related Documents*, NHMS 40 (Leiden: Brill, 1996), 94–5; Hartenstein, *Die zweite Lehre*, 130; Karen L. King, 'Why All the Controversy? Mary in the Gospel of Mary', in *Which Mary? The Marys of Early Christian Tradition*, ed. F. Stanley Jones, SBL Symposium Series 19 (Atlanta: Society of Biblical Literature, 2002), 53–74; King, *Mary*; Dieter Lührmann, *Die apokryph gewordenen Evangelien: Studien zu Neuen Texten und zu Neuen Fragen*, NovTSup 112 (Leiden and Boston: Brill, 2004), 110–11; Esther A. de Boer, *The Gospel of Mary: Listening to the Beloved Disciple* (London and New York: T&T Clark, 2004), 16–18; Tuckett, *Mary*, 14–18. Marjanen identifies Mary as Mary Magdalene due to the spelling of her name, Antti Marjanen, 'The Mother of Jesus or the Magdalene? The Identity of Mary in the So-Called Gnostic Christian Texts', in *Which Mary?*, 31–42. Lucchesi questions this assumption, writing '*ce qui est loin d'être prouvé*', E. Lucchesi, 'Évangile selon Marie ou Évangile selon Marie-Madeleine?', *Analecta Bollandiana* 103.3–4 (1985): 366. The Magdalene assumption has again been challenged by Stephen J. Shoemaker, 'Rethinking the "Gnostic Mary": Mary of Nazareth and Mary of Magdala in Early Christian Tradition', *JECS* 9.4 (2001): 555–95. There is the possibility that Mary of the Gospel of Mary is an assimilation of various Marys from the Jesus tradition, but predominantly based on Mary Magdalene due to the text's connections with John 20.14–18.

... καὶ οὐκ ᾔδει ὅτι Ἰησοῦς ἐστιν. λέγει αὐτῇ Ἰησοῦς· γύναι, τί κλαίεις; τίνα ζητεῖς; ἐκείνη δοκοῦσα ὅτι ὁ κηπουρός ἐστιν λέγει αὐτῷ κύριε, εἰ σὺ ἐβάστασας αὐτόν, εἰπέ μοι ποῦ ἔθηκας αὐτόν, κἀγὼ αὐτὸν ἀρῶ. λέγει αὐτῇ Ἰησοῦς Μαριάμ. στραφεῖσα ἐκείνη λέγει αὐτῷ Ἑβραϊστί ραββουνι, (ὃ λέγεται διδάσκαλε) λέγει αὐτῇ Ἰησοῦς μή μου ἅπτου, οὔπω γὰρ ἀναβέβηκα πρὸς τὸν πατέρα πορεύου δὲ πρὸς τοὺς ἀδελφούς μου καὶ εἰπὲ αὐτοῖς ἀναβαίνω πρὸς τὸν πατέρα μου καὶ πατέρα ὑμῶν καὶ θεόν μου καὶ θεὸν ὑμῶν. Ἔρχεται Μαριὰμ ἡ Μαγδαληνὴ ἀγγέλλουσα τοῖς μαθηταῖς ὅτι ἑώρακα τὸν κύριον, καὶ ταῦτα εἶπεν αὐτῇ (John 20.14–18)

... but she did not know that it was Jesus. Jesus said to her, 'Woman, why are you crying? Whom do you seek?' Thinking he was the gardener, she said, 'Sir, if you have carried him away, tell me where you have put him, and I will take him away.' Jesus said to her, 'Mary.' Having turned around, she said to him in Aramaic, 'Rabbouni!' (which means 'Teacher'). Jesus said to her, 'Do not touch me, for I have not yet ascended to the Father. But go to my brothers and tell them, I am ascending to my Father and your Father, to my God and your God.' Mary Magdalene went to the disciples bringing the news: 'I have seen the Lord!' And she told them that he had said these things to her.

Mark LE shows four particular similarities with the Gospel of Mary: (1) Jesus appears first to Mary Magdalene alone; (2) Mary tells the other disciples what she has seen; (3) the two verbs πενθοῦσι καὶ κλαίουσιν appear superfluous; however, we find the same form in the Gospel of Mary: 'but they were grieved, they wept much' (ⲛⲧⲟⲟⲩ ⲇⲉ ⲛⲉⲩⲣ̄ⲗⲩⲡⲉⲓ ⲁⲩⲣⲓⲙⲉ ⲙ̄ⲡϣⲁ [9,5–6]) and (4) the other disciples doubt her words.[12] For John 20 the first two points are the same: Jesus appears first to Mary alone, and Mary tells the other disciples what she has seen. Mary's words in John ἑώρακα τὸν κύριον (20.18) are almost verbatim to the Gospel of Mary's 'I saw the Lord' (ⲁⲓⲛⲁⲩ ⲉⲡⲝ̄ⲥ̄ [10,10–11]); however, the Gospel of Mary adds 'in a

[12] The theme of 'doubt' is in all of the Synoptics. In Luke, the Eleven and others do not believe the women's testimony: καὶ ἐφάνησαν ἐνώπιον αὐτῶν ὡσεὶ λῆρος τὰ ῥήματα ταῦτα, καὶ ἠπίστουν αὐταῖς (24.11). Assuming that 24.12 is part of the original text, it is only Peter that finds their story plausible (24.12). The doubting in Matthew relates to the appearance of Jesus (28.17); in contrast, the male disciples must believe the women's testimony as they go to Galilee on their instruction (28.8–10, 16).

vision' (ϩⲛ ⲟⲩϩⲟⲣⲟⲙⲁ [10,11]).[13] What is most striking, however, is that the Johannine Jesus tells Mary about his ascension (20.17), and in the Gospel of Mary, Mary's vision is of an ascending soul. The entire premise of her revelation in the Gospel of Mary appears to be based on John 20.14–18.[14]

The connections between the canonical resurrection narratives and the Gospel of Mary are not difficult to see. The Gospel of Mary evangelist looked to fill in the gaps of what happened after the resurrection. In what sense or form did Jesus appear to Mary? What did he say to her? Why did the male disciples doubt her? In order to situate the answers provided, the Gospel of Mary may have included a brief resurrection account at the beginning of the text.

The Location

Perkins posits that revelation dialogues generally begin with a location: a mountain, Jerusalem and/or the Temple.[15] For the Gospel of Mary, the Temple can be ruled out almost immediately – the only Temple-based dialogue text that Perkins references is the Apocalypse of Peter (Coptic), which is not particularly generically comparable to the Gospel of Mary as it does not present Jesus as responding to questions from his disciples.[16]

[13] The Johannine motif of Mary's weeping (20.11, 13, 15) has been connected with her weeping in the Gospel of Mary (18,1). See e.g. Tuckett, *Mary*, 17–18; however, that connection is tentative.

[14] Pasquier, Petersen and Tuckett, among others, argue that John 20 is in the background of the Gospel of Mary, Pasquier, *Marie*, 71; Silke Petersen, *Zerstört die Werke der Weiblichkeit! Maria Magdalena, Salome und andere Jüngerinnen Jesu in christlich-gnostischen Schriften*, NHMS 48 (Leiden: Brill, 1999), 135; Tuckett, *Mary*, 170. D'Angelo suggests that 'there is a closer continuity between Mary of the fourth gospel and Mary of the Gospel of Mary than is usually recognized. Both depict Mary as prophet and originator of the mission', Mary Rose D'Angelo, '"I Have Seen the Lord": Mary Magdalen as Visionary, Early Christian Prophecy, and the Context of John 20:14–18,' in *Mariam, the Magdalen, and the Mother*, ed. Deirdre Good (Bloomington, IN: Indiana University Press, 2005), 112.

[15] Perkins, *Gnostic Dialogue*, 42, 48. There is also the option of Jesus appearing inside a room as in Mark LE and John 20. Mark has the eleven disciples sitting at a table (16.14) when Jesus appears and John places the disciples behind locked doors (John 20.19, 26). The appearance of Jesus in the Apocryphon of James could also be inside, as the disciples are sitting together writing the Saviour's teachings in books. However, James and Peter are then separated to an unknown location to receive the superior revelation. The Johannine connection is strong, but a mountain is more likely for the reasons given above.

[16] The Apocalypse of Peter (Coptic) (NHC 7,3) is a dialogue between Christ and Peter, the night before Jesus' death. Peter has a vision of the crucifixion but asks what he is seeing and who it is that the authorities are arresting – clearly the passion is not in his memory (dialogue gospels, on the whole, presuppose the Easter story).

A mountain is a much stronger contender for the location of the Gospel of Mary. Post-resurrection scenes that take place on a mountain are so common that some scholars suggest the mountain location is *typical* for Christian 'gnostic' resurrection appearances.[17] However, mountain locations are hardly reserved for 'gnostic' texts – the earliest account of this tradition is in Matt 28:

> Οἱ δὲ ἕνδεκα μαθηταὶ ἐπορεύθησαν εἰς τὴν Γαλιλαίαν εἰς τὸ ὄρος οὗ ἐτάξατο αὐτοῖς ὁ Ἰησοῦς, καὶ ἰδόντες αὐτὸν προσεκύνησαν, οἱ δὲ ἐδίστασαν (28.16–17)
>
> And the eleven disciples journeyed into Galilee to the mountain that Jesus had directed them, and on seeing him they worshipped him; but some doubted.

The Matthean mountain signifies the high points of Jesus' career, including the great commission. Donaldson argues that the commission location ties together the previous mountain locations of temptation (4.8), teaching (5.1; 8.1), feeding (15.29), transfiguration (17.1–9) and the olivet discourse (24.3).[18] It is thus not surprising to find it as an intertextual motif in early Christian literature. A mountain also features as the location of the synoptic transfiguration scene, which is referenced in 2 Pet 1.18 explicitly as ἐν τῷ ἁγίῳ ὄρει.

Mountains in dialogue gospels are sites of teaching, revelation and commission, and they can be in Jerusalem or Galilee. In the Apocryphon of John, John turns from the Temple to the mountain, which King interprets as 'a spatial setting that metaphorically suggests one must turn away from worship of the lower false gods and from the things of the world in order to comprehend the truth'.[19]

Luttikhuizen understands the revelation to be taking place simultaneously with the passion, Gerard P. Luttikhuizen, 'The Suffering Jesus and the Invulnerable Christ in the Gnostic Apocalypse of Peter', in *The Apocalypse of Peter*, ed. Jan N. Bremmer and István Czachesz, Studies on the Early Christian Apocrypha 7 (Leuven: Peeters, 2003), 190. The text is a dialogue, but it is not a question-and-answer interchange.

[17] Evans regards the typical location for 'gnostic' resurrection appearances to be the Mount of Olives. However, he notes that, 'the appearances of the Risen Christ can occur in different locations, such as the desert (Ap. John II, 1:19), a walk (Thom. Cont. II, 138:3), or even on a boat dock (Acts Pet. 12 Apost. VI, 1:33–2:1)', Craig A. Evans, 'Jesus in Gnostic Literature', *Biblica* 62.3 (1981): 408. Also, Francis T. Fallon, 'Gnostic Apocalypses', ed. John J. Collins, *Apocalypse: The Morphology of a Genre*, *Semeia* 14 (1979), 125; Tuckett, *Mary*, 36.

[18] Terence L. Donaldson, *Jesus on the Mountain: A Study in Matthean Theology*, JSNTSup 8 (Sheffield: JSOT, 1985).

[19] Karen L. King, *The Secret Revelation of John* (Cambridge, MA and London: Harvard University Press, 2006), 154.

The Epistle of Peter to Philip, the Apocalypse of Peter, the First Apocalypse of James and the Sophia of Jesus Christ are all set on a named mountain. The first appearance in the Epistle of Peter to Philip has the disciples on 'the mountain which is (the) place of Olives' (ⲡⲧⲟⲟⲩ ⲉⲧⲉ ϣⲁⲩⲙⲟⲩⲧⲉ ⲉⲣⲟϥ ϫⲉ ⲡⲁⲛⲓϫⲟⲉⲓⲧ̇), significant to the evangelist as it recalls the time 'when he [Jesus] was in the body' (ϩⲟⲧⲁⲛ ⲉϥϩⲛ ⲥⲱⲙⲁ [$_{\text{NHC}}$ 133,13–17]). The Apocalypse of Peter likewise has Jesus 'sitting on the Mount of Olives', engaging in dialogue with the disciples (1.1), and in the Pistis Sophia, the appearance of Jesus in Book One is on the Mount of Olives (1.2 [4,13]). Presumably these texts refer to the Mount of Olives near Jerusalem (as in Matt 21.1), although the Sophia of Jesus Christ relocates it to Galilee ($_{\text{BG}}$ 79, 6–9). In the First Apocalypse of James, James awaits Jesus' return on 'the mountain which is called Gaugēlan' (ⲡⲧⲟⲟⲩ ⲉⲧⲉ ϣⲁⲩⲙⲟⲩⲧⲉ ⲉⲣⲟϥ ϫⲉ ⲅⲁⲩⲅⲏⲗⲁⲛ [$_{\text{NHC}}$ 30,19–20]), where the risen Jesus appears to him.

The appearance of Christ in the Sophia of Jesus Christ is also particularly noteworthy for the Gospel of Mary. As was proposed, the short opening 'After he rose from the dead' may be comparable to the Gospel of Mary's beginning. Also, the group explicitly includes women. The location is specified:

> ⲙⲛⲛ̄ⲥⲁ ⲛⲧⲣⲉϥⲧⲱⲟⲩ̄ ⲉⲃⲟⲗ ϩⲛ̄ ⲛⲉⲧⲙⲟⲟⲩⲧ ⲛ̄ⲧⲉⲣⲟⲩⲉⲓ ⲛ̄ϭⲓ ⲡⲉϥⲙⲛ̄ⲧⲥⲛⲟⲟⲩⲥ ⲙ̄ⲙⲁⲑⲏⲧⲏⲥ ⲙⲛ̄ ⲥⲁϣϥⲉ ⲛ̄ⲥϩⲓ̈ⲙⲉ ⲉⲧⲉ ⲛⲉⲩⲙⲁⲑⲏⲧⲉⲩⲉ ⲛⲁϥ ⲉϩⲣⲁⲓ̈ ⲉⲧⲅⲁⲗⲓⲗⲁⲓⲁ ϩⲙ ⲡⲧⲟⲟⲩ ⲉⲧⲉ ϣⲁⲩⲙⲟⲩⲧⲉ ⲉⲣⲟϥ ϫⲉ ⲙⲁ(ⲛ)ⲧⲏ ϩⲓ ⲣⲁϣⲉ ($_{\text{BG}}$ 77,9–78,2)
>
> After he rose from the dead, his twelve disciples and seven women who were his disciples came to Galilee onto the mountain which is called Divination and Joy.[20]

'Divination and Joy' is differentiated from the mountain 'which is called (the) place of Olives, in Galilee' (ⲉⲧⲉϣⲁⲩⲙⲟⲩⲧⲉ ⲉⲣⲟϥ ϫⲉ ⲡⲁ ⲛ{ⲧ}ϫⲟⲉⲓⲧ ⲡⲉ ϩⲛ̄ ⲧⲅⲁⲗⲓⲗⲁⲓⲁ [$_{\text{BG}}$ 79,7–9]), where he taught them about the perfect flesh. In Book Four of the Pistis Sophia, Jesus and his disciples are on a mountain in Galilee (4.141 [369,8]). Presumably, these Galilean mountains are based on Matthew 28.

There are several other reasons to suggest that the location of the Gospel of Mary is a mountain. Firstly, the Saviour's final instructions are closely connected to the Matthean commission. As the location

[20] The name of the mountain ⲙⲁⲛⲧⲏ ϩⲓ ⲣⲁϣⲉ may be from μαντεία or could be ⲙⲁ ⲛ ⲧⲏ (place of harvest), Marvin Meyer and Madeleine Scopello, 'The Wisdom of Jesus Christ', in *The Nag Hammadi Scriptures: The International Edition* (New York: Harper Collins, 2007), 287 n. 3.

of the commission is significant, it is possible that the author of the Gospel of Mary shared this tradition. Second, the mountain is a place of announcing apostolic authority. Mark and Luke have Jesus choose the Twelve on a mountain (Mark 3.13–19; Luke 6.12–16), and the Markan version also anticipates the commission (Mark 3.14). Apostolic authority is a particular concern in the Gospel of Mary as the disciples debate whether Mary is to be trusted to teach the authentic words of Jesus. Mountain locations may reflect a new, or superior, choosing of key apostles. Third, in Matthew, the eschatological discourse is set on the Mount of Olives, demonstrating that it is an appropriate location to impart eschatological revelation. In the Gospel of Mary a mountain is the most likely location for the appearance of the risen Christ, his commission to preach, and his revelation of eschatological realities.

The Disciples

With the location on a mountain in mind, one would naturally ask who was there and what were they doing. The end of page 6 will almost certainly have read a disciple's name and ⲡⲉϫⲉ (insert name) ⲛⲁϥ ϫⲉ. Considering the format of other dialogues, disciples usually take it in turns to ask questions, and so, as Peter asks the following question, it may be suggested that it is another disciple who asks about the destruction of matter. Levi and Andrew are most likely among the named group of disciples in the dialogue. Mary may have played a role, as she does in the Dialogue of the Saviour, the Gospel of Thomas, the Sophia of Jesus Christ and the Pistis Sophia; however, it is also likely that, as she rises when the Saviour departs (in a paraclete-type role), earlier in the text she is in the background. In comparable dialogues, other named disciples asking Jesus questions are Philip, Matthew, Thomas, Mary and Bartholomew (Sophia of Jesus Christ); Matthew, Mary and Judas (Dialogue of the Saviour); and Peter, Thomas, Philip and Judas (Johannine Farewell Discourse). Small groups of disciples were common, and so it is possible that in the Gospel of Mary it is just Peter, Andrew and Levi in conversation with the Lord. It is possible that a larger group of disciples were onlookers as we find in the Sophia of Jesus Christ, in which the Saviour appears to twelve disciples and seven women, as quoted above, but only five questioners are named.[21]

[21] This may account for the use of 'all': Jesus says farewell to them 'all' (ⲧⲏⲣⲟⲩ [8,13]), and Mary greets them 'all' (ⲧⲏⲣⲟⲩ [9,13]). 'All' is used in the Sophia of Jesus

There are also commonalities between the concerns of the disciples in gospel dialogues. Luttikhuizen argues that: 'A characteristic feature of Gnostic revelation dialogues is the account of the perplexities and the troubling questions of the recipients prior to the appearance of the heavenly revealer.'[22] Again, we meet the Sophia of Jesus Christ, in which shortly before the appearance of the Saviour, the disciples are pondering the greater questions:[23]

> ⲉⲩⲁⲡⲟⲣⲓ ⲟ̅ⲩ̅ ⲉⲧⲃⲉ ⲑⲩⲡⲟⲥⲧⲁⲥⲓⲥ ⲙ̄ⲡⲧⲏⲣϥ ⲙⲛ̄ ⲧⲟⲓⲕⲟⲛⲟⲙⲓⲁ ⲙⲛ ⲧⲉⲡⲣⲟⲛⲟⲓⲁ ⲉⲧⲟⲩⲁⲁⲃ ⲙⲛ̄ ⲧⲁⲣⲉⲧⲏ ⲛ̄ⲛ̄ⲉⲝⲟⲩⲥⲓⲁ ⲉⲧⲃⲉ ϩⲱⲃ ⲛⲓⲙ ⲉⲧⲉⲣⲉⲡⲥⲱⲧⲏⲣ ⲉⲓⲣⲉ ⲙ̄ⲙⲁⲩ ⲛⲙ̄ⲙⲁⲩ ⲙ̄ⲙⲩⲥⲧⲏⲣⲓⲟⲛ ⲛ̄ⲧⲟⲓⲕⲟⲛⲟⲙⲓⲁ ⲉⲧⲟⲩⲁⲁⲃ (BG 78,2–11)
>
> They were puzzled about the underlying reality of all things, and the arrangement (of the cosmos), and the holy providence, and the power of the authorities, (and) about everything that the Saviour was doing with them in the mystery of the holy arrangement.

The disciples are ready to ask the Saviour their unanswered questions, and in the Gospel of Mary Peter says that the Saviour has told them all things (7,10–11). It may be best to assume that the disciples played a similar role to those in the Sophia of Jesus Christ. In the rest of the text, the disciples are not anonymous characters without personality; they are active interpreters of the Saviour's words, and so it fits that they would be hoping to question Jesus before he leaves them.

The Appearance of the Saviour

With Christ in a resurrected form, there are fewer restrictions on how he may have appeared. As we saw in Chapter 2, in Mark 16.12 Jesus appears ἐν ἑτέρᾳ μορφῇ, which is probably related to his unrecognizability in Luke 24.16 and John 20.15. In Luke 24.16 as

Christ (BG 79,13), the Epistle of Peter to Philip (NHC 140,17) and the Apocryphon of James (1,24; 2,8; 2,27) to refer to the larger group of disciples. Furthermore, we find disciples or apostles asking questions collectively: e.g. the Sophia of Jesus Christ (BG 102,7–14; 112,19–24), the Dialogue of the Saviour (126,5–8; 139,13–15). This is also possible in the Gospel of Mary.

[22] Gerard P. Luttikhuizen, 'Evaluation of the Teaching of Jesus in Christian Gnostic Revelation Dialogues', *NovT* 30.2 (1988): 158. He cites Zostrianos, the Sophia of Jesus Christ, the Apocryphon of John, the Epistle of Peter to Philip and the Gospel of Mary as examples. Luttikhuizen builds on Perkins' suggestion that, before the appearance of the revealer-figure, the disciples are generally being persecuted, preaching or writing/discussing Jesus' words, Perkins, *Gnostic Dialogue*, 42.

[23] This may be in reference to debating Jesus' words, as in Perkins' typology.

in the Gospel of Judas 33,18–21, Jesus appears in a different form in order to conceal his true identity.[24] Other dialogue gospels, however, have Jesus appear in a different form to make him hyper-recognizable – the Sophia of Jesus Christ includes a luminous appearance, the Apocryphon of John narrates a polymorphic christophany, and the Epistula Apostolorum depicts an entirely fleshly resurrected Christ.

The Saviour in the Gospel of Mary manifesting himself in a different form would be in keeping with the extant gospel. Within the text itself, Jesus' terse exit – 'he departed' (ⲁϥⲃⲱⲕ [9,5]) – leaves open a number of interpretations.[25] Also, Mary sees the Lord in a vision (9,10–12),[26] and a vision means that the appearance of the revealer is not bound by the conventions of flesh. The reference to Mary not wavering when she sees the Lord in a vision (10,14–15) may signify an unexpected form.[27] A new form, in both the vision and the opening dialogue, would highlight Jesus as resurrected Saviour, who brings open speech and soteriological revelation. Although this remains plausible at best, there are intra-textual reasons and compelling parallels from cognate contemporary texts.

The Missing Dialogue

One thing we can say with some level of certainty is that the Saviour had been engaged in dialogue for some time. Peter states, 'Since you have [to]ld us everything, say one other (thing) to us' (ϩⲱⲥ ⲁⲕⲧ̣ⲁ̣ⲙⲟⲛ ⲉϩⲱⲃ ⲛⲓⲙ ϫⲱ ⲙ̄ⲡⲓⲕⲉⲟ̣ⲩⲁ̣ ⲉⲣⲟⲛ [7,10–12]). As Jesus told Peter and his companions *everything* (despite him asking for another thing here and later asking Mary for further revelation [10,4–9]), we can expect a number of questions and answers before the beginning of page 7.[28]

[24] Although, as noted in Chapter 2, the disciples not recognizing Jesus in Luke is not necessarily because Jesus has appeared in a different form.

[25] See Hartenstein, *Die zweite Lehre*, 145.

[26] The vision appears to have occurred on the same day that Mary tells Jesus about the vision, but the evangelist provides no time frame in the extant text. The vision could be pre- or post-resurrection, and Hartenstein has persuaded King that it refers to a kind of transfiguration scene, Hartenstein, *Die zweite Lehre*, 130, 153; King, *Mary*, 175. However, the strong connections to John 20 suggest a post-resurrection setting.

[27] It may also signify the mere fact that Mary thought that Jesus was dead.

[28] Questions are generally shorter than the Saviour's reply and would not have occupied more than a few lines. The Saviour's answer takes up the first nine lines of page 7, with the hearing formula at the end. The Saviour's direct reply to Peter's two-line question is seven lines long (7,13–20) with an extension of the reply to another hearing formula (8,11). Sometimes, an answer can become a monologue. On average, there are twenty-three lines per page of the Coptic Gospel of Mary, leaving 138 lines

Continuing with the comparative approach, the *kind* of questions may be deduced. At the extant beginning of the Gospel of Mary, the questions are ‘will [ma]tter be dest[r]oyed or not?’ (ⲑ̣[ⲩ]ⲗ̣ⲏ ϭⲉ ⲛⲁ ⲟⲩⲱ̣[ϭ]ⲡ̣ ϫⲛ ⲙ̣ⲙⲟⲛ [7,1–2]) and ‘What is the sin of the world?’ (ⲟⲩ ⲡⲉ ⲡⲛⲟⲃⲉ ⲙⲡⲕⲟⲥⲙⲟ̣ⲥ̣ [7,12]). The questions are concerned with the fate of the cosmos and the state of humanity. These two questions represent a certain *type* of interest. For lack of a better phrase, these are concerns of the ‘bigger picture’. It could be said that they are ‘cosmocentric’ rather than christocentric. Other dialogue gospels share the focus on ‘cosmocentricism’: in the Dialogue of the Saviour, Judas asks what existed before creation (127,19–21), and the disciples of the Sophia of Jesus Christ are looking for the arrangement of the cosmos ($_{\text{BG}}$ 80,1–3). Others, such as the Apocryphon of James and the Johannine Farewell Discourse, are framed in a more christocentric way, with questions regarding Jesus, his Father and how the disciples relate to them, as discussed briefly in our comparison of the Johannine Farewell Discourse and the Apocryphon of James in Chapter 2. A number of dialogue gospels are also concerned with Jesus’ departure, and the questions and issues discussed are framed within the realization that the disciples’ time with the Saviour is almost over. As we have seen, this is the focus of the Johannine Farewell Discourse, the Apocryphon of James and, in parts, the First Apocalypse of James.

In the Gospel of Mary, a major concern is how to live in the absence of Jesus – how will the disciples preach and how will they be saved. The dialogue between Jesus and the disciples is not the complete revelation and leaves the disciples in distress. The text continues with Mary revealing the salvation of the soul. Presumably the dialogue with Christ foreshadows the revelation of the soul’s ascent, especially in light of the parallelism between matter dissolving and the soul ascending, both returning to their origins, as will be discussed in Chapters 4 and 5. The questions from the disciples at the beginning of the gospel may have been both christocentric and cosmocentric, and in many places these two are not easily distinguished.

As stated at the beginning, these suggestions are not meant to act as a reconstruction of the text. Intra-textual exegesis of the Gospel

for pages 1–6. The only fully extant question is three lines in length, and it would seem that the previous question was around two. The Saviour’s answers take up between seven lines (for the first) and seventeen lines (for the second). If we permit three lines per question and ten lines per answer, that would leave space for nine questions and answers, and for a short appearance narrative. Of course, this is highly speculative, but it gives a suggestion of what the first pages once contained.

of Mary, as well as looking at the text within its genre, allows for speculations about the missing content at the gospel's beginning. For example, the Gospel of Mary's focus on eschatological teaching and mission might point to a mountain setting, and Mary's role as a replacement for Jesus might suggest that she has not featured earlier in this text.

3.2 The Saviour's Farewell Discourse

Immediately prior to Jesus' departure, he gives a short, hortatory monologue, which we will call his farewell discourse (FD).[29] This monologue contains a dense quantity of material shared with the canonical gospels.[30] The concentration of direct canonical 'allusions' in this short speech is one of the text's most curious features. Whether the allusions demonstrate literary dependence has been contested. In 1982, Tuckett argued that the author had access to (at least) the post-redactional apocalyptic discourses of the synoptic gospels, concluding that '[t]here is virtually no evidence for the use of pre-synoptic sources'[31] – a theory he has maintained ever since.[32] King rejects this hypothesis, arguing that Tuckett made the usual but incorrect assumption that the Gospel of Mary was influenced by the canonical gospels.[33] King argues for five factors that would potentially suggest literary dependence: (1) citation, (2) ordering of material, (3) narrative context, (4) citation formula and (5) specific language. Applying these factors to the Gospel of Mary, she contends that '[i]t does not show a consistent pattern of similarity to any one source or set of sources known to us, whether in word for word citation, ordering of materials, context, or theological emphasis'.[34] Whether the Gospel of Mary knew these canonical texts in the form we have today might be an insoluble question, but it does seem that the Gospel of Mary had knowledge of traditions within the canonical gospels (and Pauline epistles), and that it was

[29] The FD is quite separate from the preceding dialogue. Jesus' greeting highlights their division. See Hartenstein, *Die zweite Lehre*, 143.

[30] All of the Gospel of Mary exegetes agree that here 'there is a significant clustering of echoes or allusions to the canonical gospels', see Tuckett, *Mary*, 57.

[31] Christopher M. Tuckett, 'Synoptic Tradition in Some Nag Hammadi and Related Texts', *VC* 36.2 (1982): 180, 184.

[32] Tuckett, *Mary*, esp. 55–75.

[33] King, *Mary*, 93.

[34] King, *Mary*, 114. Tuckett and King are the two main contenders in this debate. Perkins provides the brief suggestion that Mary knew a sayings collection, Perkins, *Gnostic Dialogue*, 134–5.

composed later than these texts. Questions of dependence are not at the forefront of this study, and it is not possible to make any absolute claims. We will look for intertextual connections, which may or may not presuppose dependence. Overall, it does seem that the Gospel of Mary will have had knowledge, at some level, of the gospels and Pauline texts that were to become canonical (and especially parts of John), and each intertextual link within the Gospel of Mary offers a new interpretation of the canonical language, grounded in the message of the later gospel.

The FD can be divided into three sections: the double-peace farewell, instructions for the individual and instructions for the benefit of the community. Each section demonstrates new interpretations and formulations of well-known Jesus sayings. By exploring these interpretations, it is possible to further situate the evangelist's message in the context of emerging Christianity.

The Double-Peace Farewell

The first expression is a 'double-peace saying':

> ⲟⲩⲉⲓⲣⲏⲛⲏ ⲛⲏⲧⲛ̄ ⲧⲁⲉⲓⲣⲏⲛⲏ ϫⲡⲟⲥ ⲛⲏⲧⲛ̄ (8,14–15)
>
> Peace to you. My peace, acquire in you.

The peace greeting is common in early Christian literature, often in the context of a greeting from the resurrected Christ appearing to his disciples.[35] In the Gospel of Mary, however, ⲟⲩⲉⲓⲣⲏⲛⲏ ⲛⲏⲧⲛ̄ is meant as a farewell rather than a greeting.

The closest parallel to the farewell double-peace saying is John 14.27: 'Peace I leave with you. My peace I give to you' (Εἰρήνην ἀφίημι ὑμῖν, εἰρήνην τὴν ἐμὴν δίδωμι ὑμῖν). The twofold structure of the saying with the repeated dative ὑμῖν and a possessive in the second clause (εἰρήνην τὴν ἐμὴν) mirrors precisely the structure of the saying in the Gospel of Mary. Furthermore, in both gospels, the

[35] John 20.19, 21, 26; Luke 24.36; SophJesChr $_{NHC}$ 91,21–22; and EpPetPhil $_{NHC}$ 140,15–20 all share the post-resurrection setting. Due to these correlations, King suggests that the author of the Gospel of Mary may have expected her readers to understand the peace saying to be set within this post-resurrection framework, King, *Mary*, 99. Hartenstein wonders whether Jesus is here repeating his greeting at the start of the gospel, Hartenstein, *Die zweite Lehre*, 144. However, this can only be speculative. On the frequent occurrence of the peace saying, particularly in contexts of war, relationships, Stoicism, death and eschatological hope, see Keener, *Gospel of John*, 1:982. Fallon regards the peace greeting as a modification of a self-identification, common in gnostic apocalypses, Fallon, 'Gnostic Apocalypses', 129.

phrase commences a farewell with Jesus imparting instructions to be enacted in his absence, despite one being set pre-crucifixion and the other post-resurrection.

The purpose of the saying is also different in the Johannine Farewell Discourse and the Gospel of Mary FD. In the Gospel of Mary, the peace is based on the disciples actively receiving it. This point is best expressed in the second clause of the Gospel of Mary 8,15: ‘my peace, *acquire* in you’ (ⲧⲁⲉⲓⲣⲏⲛⲏ ϫⲡⲟⲥ ⲛⲏⲧⲛ̄). ϫⲡⲟ⸗ is also used in Levi’s instructions to put on the Perfect Man: ‘let us be ashamed and put on the Perfect Man and *acquire* him for ourselves’ (ⲙⲁⲣⲛ̄ϣⲓⲛⲉ ⲛ̄ⲧⲛ̄ϯ ϩⲓ̈ⲱⲱⲛ ⲙⲡⲣⲱⲙⲉ ⲛⲧⲉⲗⲓⲟⲥ ⲛ̣ⲧⲛ̣̄ϫⲡⲟ̣ϥ ⲛ̣ⲁ̣ⲛ̣ [18,15–17]). To acquire the Perfect Man requires action. In contrast, the Sahidic John reads, ‘Peace I *leave* to you. It is my peace that I *give* to you’ (ϯⲕⲱ ⲛⲏⲧⲛ ⲛⲟⲩⲉⲓⲣⲏⲛⲏ ⲧⲁⲉⲓⲣⲏⲛⲏ ⲉⲧⲉ ⲧⲉ ϯϯ ⲙⲙⲟⲥ ⲛⲏⲧⲛ [14.27]). The verb ⲕⲱ equates to the Greek ἀφίημι and ϯ to δίδωμι. In the Johannine saying, Jesus is the active participant and the disciples the passive recipients of the leaving/giving. In the Gospel of Mary, the disciples must take action.

The reason for this may be related to the paraclete, whose coming in John will follow the departure of Jesus.[36] John could allow the disciples to be passive recipients due to the promised arrival of an external agent. The Gospel of Mary’s eschatological teaching, on the other hand, omits a future expectation of a divine spirit (and also the parousia); Mary steps into a paraclete-type role, comforting and teaching the others, and reminding them of the words of Jesus. The individual soul must make its own way to heaven, following Jesus by remembering his teachings. There is no external help yet to come – the disciples must figure it out for themselves.[37] It is not

[36] Brown states that the peace is based on the promise of the paraclete ‘to be actualized on Easter night … It is the peace of being freed from sin and united to God, the only complete fulfilment of all our wants. This peace cannot be disturbed by Jesus’ departure to the Father; for that return, his glorification, effects peace’, Raymond E. Brown, *The Gospel and Epistles of John: A Concise Commentary* (Collegeville, MN: Liturgical Press, 1988), 78. Not everyone agrees with Brown’s reading of John’s paraclete, see George Johnston, *The Spirit-Paraclete in the Gospel of John*, SNTSMS 12 (Cambridge: Cambridge University Press, 1970), esp. 123–5.

[37] Cf. King’s suggestion that the interiorizing of the peace is the startling twist that the Gospel of Mary offers, King, *Mary*, 99. She argues that the fundamental purpose of the Gospel of Mary is to instruct the disciples to turn inwards and thus the gospel ‘emphasizes the interiority of the peace in a way that is missing in the other [gospel] accounts’ (99). However, if the evangelist sought to emphasize the interiority of peace, it is peculiar that she was not more explicit. The Coptic ⲛⲏⲧⲛ̄ means nothing more than ‘to you’ in ‘peace to you’ and ‘receive my peace to you’. It cannot be compared to ‘the Son of Man exists *within you*’ (ⲡϣⲏⲣⲉ ⲙⲡⲣⲱⲙⲉ ⲉϥϣⲟⲡ *ⲙⲡⲉⲧⲛ̄ϩⲟⲩⲛ* [8,19]). There is no reason to read the ‘peace’ as particularly interiorized.

Jesus leaving or giving the peace, as in John; it is the disciples actively receiving it. Throughout the gospel, they must be prepared to be active participants in the Saviour's message.

Instructions to the Individual Disciples

The next section of the FD is aimed at the individual disciple, and this can be split into three parts: first, a warning against those who attempt to deceive them; second, the knowledge of where to find the Son of Man; and third, the instruction to follow, seek and find him. This section has numerous intertextual links with the synoptic eschatological discourses, but to avoid overlap with the following chapter, they will only be briefly discussed here.

> ⲁⲣⲉϩ ⲙⲡⲣ̄ⲧⲣⲉⲗⲁⲁⲩ ⲣ̄ⲡⲗⲁⲛⲁ ⲙⲙⲱⲧⲛ̄ ⲉϥϫⲱ ⲙⲙⲟⲥ ϫⲉ ⲉⲓⲥ ϩⲏⲡⲉ ⲙⲡⲉⲓ̈ⲥⲁ ⲏ ⲉⲓⲥ ϩⲏⲡⲉ ⲙ̄ⲡⲉⲉⲓⲙⲁ ⲡϣⲏⲣⲉ ⲅⲁⲣ ⲙⲡⲣⲱⲙⲉ ⲉϥϣⲟⲡ ⲙⲡⲉⲧⲛ̄ϩⲟⲩⲛ ⲟⲩⲉϩⲧⲏⲩⲧⲛ̄ ⲛ̄ⲥⲱϥ ⲛⲉⲧϣⲓⲛⲉ ⲛ̄ⲥⲱϥ ⲥⲉⲛⲁϭⲛ̄ⲧϥ (8,15–21)
>
> Beware, do not allow anyone to lead you astray saying, 'Look in this direction, or look in this place.' For the Son of Man exists within you. Follow him. Those who seek him will find him.

The warning against being deceived is a theme of the synoptic eschatological discourses, for example:

> βλέπετε μή τις ὑμᾶς πλανήσῃ· πολλοὶ γὰρ ἐλεύσονται ἐπὶ τῷ ὀνόματί μου λέγοντες, Ἐγώ εἰμι ὁ Χριστός, καὶ πολλοὺς πλανήσουσιν (Matt 24.4–5; cf. Mark 13.5–6 // Luke 21.8)
>
> Beware that no one leads you astray. For many will come in my name saying, 'I am the Messiah', and they will lead many astray.

The parallels within the synoptic gospels are relatively similar: the warning is always in the context of those who profess false teachings and often those who claim to be the messiah are in view.[38] The Gospel of Mary's warning, on the other hand, is aimed at those who claim that the Son of Man is not within. This makes the language in

[38] A point of contrast is that Matthew's deceivers claim to be ὁ Χριστός (Matt 24.4) as opposed to Mark and Luke which just have Ἐγώ εἰμι (Mark 13.6 // Luke 21.8).

the Gospel of Mary closer to another occurrence of the warning in Mark and Matthew:

> τότε ἐάν τις ὑμῖν εἴπῃ, Ἰδοὺ ὧδε ὁ Χριστός, ἤ ὧδε, μὴ πιστεύσητε … ἐὰν οὖν εἴπωσιν ὑμῖν, Ἰδοὺ ἐν τῇ ἐρήμῳ ἐστίν, μὴ ἐξέλθητε: Ἰδοὺ ἐν τοῖς ταμείοις, μὴ πιστεύσητε: ὥσπερ γὰρ ἡ ἀστραπὴ ἐξέρχεται ἀπὸ ἀνατολῶν καὶ φαίνεται ἕως δυσμῶν, οὕτως ἔσται ἡ παρουσία τοῦ υἱοῦ τοῦ ἀνθρώπου (Matt 24.23, 26–27; cf. Mark 13.21, 26)
>
> Then if anyone says to you, 'Look, here is the Messiah or there he is', do not believe it … So, if they say to you, 'Look he is in the wilderness', do not go out. If they say, 'Look, he is in the inner rooms', do not believe it. For as the lightning comes from the east and flashes as far as the west, so will be the coming of the Son of Man.

The proximity of the warning and the explanation of the Son of Man in Matthew/Mark is undeniably close to the Gospel of Mary.[39] However, the way in which these two gospels employ the warning clash. In Matthew, the warning directly refutes those who say the Messiah/Son of Man is anywhere in particular; rather, he will come as the lightning flashes. His coming is a future spectacle that will be manifest to everyone. In the Gospel of Mary, the warning is used to counter this exact idea: the Son of Man is already present, internal and, therefore, limited to disciples who follow him. The two evangelists move in opposite directions from a similar warning statement.

The third part of the instruction to the individual, to follow–seek–find, demonstrates further reformulation of traditional Jesus sayings. The command to follow reflects the numerous instances in gospel literature where Jesus meets a future disciple and says Ἀκολούθει μοι. In the canonical gospels, this command is often enacted by the literal following of Jesus across Galilee and Judea[40] or refers to the conditions of discipleship (e.g. Matt 16.24 + pars). Tuckett argues that in the Gospel of Mary:

> To 'follow the Son of Man' has been divorced from any relation to Christian discipleship in the sense of following in the way of the cross; rather, it has been radically internalized

[39] Tuckett argues that '[i]t is uncertain how precise one should make any comparison here', and, in any case, the phrase in the Gospel of Mary is closer to Luke 17.23 'in being unspecific about the nature or identity of any false figures', Tuckett, *Mary*, 58–9.

[40] For example, Matt 8.22, 9.9, 19.21; Mark 1.17, 2.14, 10.21; Luke 5.27, 9.59, 18.22; John 1.43.

> and 'spiritualized' in terms of a 'Gnostic' self-understanding and set of ideas and presuppositions.[41]

The Gospel of Mary, however, does not focus solely on turning inwards: internal spiritual achievement is a *prerequisite* for the external activity of preaching the gospel and also for the soul's eschatological journey to heaven. Pasquier interprets the instruction to follow in the Gospel of Mary as to take as a model.[42] Indeed, there are several examples of imitation throughout the gospel: Mary imitates Jesus in his words and actions (9,10–24); Mary also imitates the soul in her silence (17,8); and Levi imitates both the words of Saviour's farewell discourse and Mary's actions (18,5–19,2). Furthermore, the disciples' souls are to imitate Jesus' heavenly journey. The Gospel of Mary uses the command to 'follow' in a similar way to the Apocryphon of James, in which it is found in an eschatological–soteriological context: 'I have commanded you to follow me, and I have taught you what to say before the archons' (ⲁϩⲓ̈ϩⲱⲛ ⲁⲧⲟⲟⲧⲕ̄· ⲁⲧⲣⲉⲕⲟⲩⲁϩⲕ̄ ⲛⲥⲱⲉⲓ ⲁⲩⲱ ⲁϩⲓ̈ⲧⲥⲉⲃⲉ ⲉⲓⲉⲧⲕ ⲁⲃⲁⲗ ⲁⲑⲩⲡⲟⲑⲉⲥⲓⲥ ⲛ̄ⲛⲁϩⲣⲛ̄ ⲛ̄ⲛⲁⲣⲭⲱⲛ [8,33–36]). Here, the disciples are instructed to *follow* the Lord to heaven.

It is also possible, though not certain, that Tuckett is wrong in saying that the command to follow has been divorced from the sense of following in the way of the cross. In the Apocryphon of James, the heavenly archons parallel earthly persecution, also seen in the First Apocalypse of James, and the text has often been read as an invitation to martyrdom.[43] Therefore, the invitation to follow reflects Jesus' words to Peter in John 21.19 (Ἀκολούθει μοι). Just before Jesus' death, he told Peter that he could not follow him now but that he would be able to afterward (13.36), despite Peter's protest that he would lay down his life for him (13.37). After Jesus' resurrection, Peter becomes the shepherd who must lay down his life for his flock (10.11 + 21.18–19). It is possible that the command to follow in the Gospel of Mary has a martyrdom connotation. Once Jesus departs, the disciples are anxious about undertaking his command to preach, asking, 'If they did not spare him, how will they spare us?' (ⲉϣϫⲉ ⲡⲉⲧⲙ̄ⲙⲁⲩ ⲙ̄ⲡⲟⲩϯⲥⲟ ⲉⲣⲟϥ ⲛⲁϣ ⲛ̄ϩⲉ ⲁⲛⲟⲛ ⲉⲩⲛⲁϯⲥⲟ ⲉⲣⲟⲛ [9,10–12]). Mary comforts the disciples, explaining that Jesus' grace will protect them (9,16–18). She does not say what from. Perhaps to follow the

[41] Tuckett, *Mary*, 156.

[42] Pasquier, *Marie*, 62.

[43] David Brakke, 'Parables and Plain Speech in the Fourth Gospel and the Apocryphon of James', *JECS* 7.2 (1999): 205; Jacques van der Vliet, 'Spirit and Prophecy in the Epistula Iacobi Apocrypha (NHC I,2)', *VC* 44.1 (1990): 25–53.

Son of Man in the Gospel of Mary is to follow Jesus ascending into heaven, via the cross. Martyrdom may not be explicitly encouraged in the Gospel of Mary, but that does not disqualify it as an option.

The seek/find command is also common in early Christian gospels (e.g. GThom 2, 38, 59, 92; BookThom 140,42–141,2; cf. Matt 7.7 // Luke 11.9) and may have circulated as a freestanding saying.[44] The author of the Gospel of Mary uses it here in the same christological way as to 'follow'.[45] Those who seek Jesus within will find him, and this will ultimately lead the disciple to her eschatological 'rest'. However, seeking and finding the Son of Man within is also prerequisite for the penultimate instruction of the farewell discourse: to preach the gospel.

Preach the Gospel but Do Not Be Like the Lawgiver

In the final section of the FD, Jesus exhorts the disciples to act for the benefit of the wider community.[46] The first part is a commission to preach; the second is an injunction against laying down extra rules.

The first instruction, 'Go then and preach the gospel of the kingdom' (ⲃⲱⲕ ϭⲉ ⲛ̄ⲧⲉⲧⲛ̄ⲧⲁϣⲉⲟⲉⲓϣ ⲙⲡⲉⲩⲁⲅⲅⲉⲗⲓⲟⲛ ⲛ̄ⲧⲙⲛⲧⲉⲣⲟ [8,21–22]), leads to the gospel's finale when the disciples (or Levi alone if reading PRyl.GM) depart to preach.[47] The command is clearly an important motif in early Christian texts and is comparable to Matt 28.19, as discussed in Chapter 2. The Gospel of Mary differs from Matthew in that we see the disciples' reaction to the commission:

> ⲁⲩⲣⲓⲙⲉ ⲙ̄ⲡϣⲁ ⲉⲩϫⲱ ⲙⲙⲟⲥ ϫⲉ ⲛⲛⲁϣ ⲛ̄ϩⲉ ⲉⲛⲛⲁⲃⲱⲕ ϣⲁ ⲛϩⲉⲑⲛⲟⲥ ⲛ̄ⲧⲛ̄ⲧⲁϣⲉⲟⲉⲓϣ ⲛ̄ⲡⲉⲩⲁⲅⲅⲉⲗⲓⲟⲛ ⲛⲧⲙⲛ̄ⲧⲉⲣⲟ ⲙⲡϣ`ⲏ'ⲣⲉ ⲙⲡⲣⲱⲙⲉ ⲉϣϫⲉ ⲡⲉⲧⲙ̄ⲙⲁⲩ ⲙ̄ⲡⲟⲩϯⲥⲟ ⲉⲣⲟϥ ⲛⲁϣ ⲛ̄ϩⲉ ⲁⲛⲟⲛ ⲉⲩⲛⲁϯⲥⲟ ⲉⲣⲟⲛ (9,6–12)

[44] See Francis Watson, *Gospel Writing: A Canonical Perspective* (Grand Rapids, MI and Cambridge: Eerdmans, 2013), 356–70.

[45] King contends that readers who were familiar with both the Gospel of Mary and alternative seeking and finding commands 'would not have understood them in terms of borrowing or influence, but as differing, even conflicting meanings of Jesus' command', King, *Mary*, 106.

[46] This goes against twentieth-century assumptions that so-called 'gnostic' texts focus on self-knowledge with little concern for others due to their world-negating or anti-social attitude. For discussion of this point, see Lance Jenott and Elaine Pagels, 'Antony's Letters and Nag Hammadi Codex I: Sources of Religious Conflict in Fourth-Century Egypt', *JECS* 18.4 (2010): 557–89; Michel Robert Desjardins, *Sin in Valentinianism*, SBLDS 108 (Atlanta: Scholars Press, 1990).

[47] De Boer believes that 'the main purpose of the Gospel of Mary is to encourage the disciples to go out and preach the gospel', de Boer, *Gospel of Mary*, 56–7.

> They wept much, saying, 'How shall we go to the nations and preach the gospel of the kingdom of the Son of Man? If they did not spare him, how will they spare us?'

In the Gospel of Mary, the mission anxiety is directed towards preaching to the 'nations', which has led Pasquier and Lührmann to see a direct connection with Matthew's use of ἔθνος both in the eschatological discourse (24.14) and the great commission (μαθητεύσατε πάντα τὰ ἔθνη [28.19]). They both see the Gospel of Mary's use of ἔθνος as *polemical* against Matthew. Pasquier focuses on Matthew's olivet discourse, which further connects to the Gospel of Mary through the unusual shared phrase 'the gospel of the kingdom':

> καὶ κηρυχθήσεται τοῦτο τὸ εὐαγγέλιον τῆς βασιλείας ἐν ὅλῃ τῇ οἰκουμένῃ εἰς μαρτύριον πᾶσιν τοῖς ἔθνεσιν, καὶ τότε ἥξει τὸ τέλος (Matt 24.14)
>
> And this gospel of the kingdom will be proclaimed throughout the world, as a testimony to all the nations, and then the end will come.

She argues that Matt 24 and the Gospel of Mary FD share three elements, but these three elements are formulated in opposite sequence:

> Matthew: Preach the gospel of the kingdom to all nations (24.14) → warning against error (24.23–26) → coming of the Son of Man (24.27).
>
> Gospel of Mary: Warning against error (8,15–18) → Son of Man within (8,18–19) → preach the gospel of the kingdom (8,21–22).

For Matthew, the preaching of the gospel leads to the coming of the Son of Man; in the Gospel of Mary, finding the Son of Man within is a condition of preaching the gospel.[48]

Lührmann, on the other hand, focuses on the Matthean resurrection scene, and specifically the instructions in 28.18–20, and the final instruction of the FD in the Gospel of Mary:

> ⲙⲡⲣ̄ⲕⲁ ⲗⲁⲩ ⲛ̄ϩⲟⲣⲟⲥ ⲉϩⲣⲁï ⲡⲁⲣⲁ ⲡⲉⲛⲧⲁïⲧⲟϣϥ̄ ⲛⲏⲧⲛ̄ ⲟⲩⲇⲉ ⲙ̄ⲡⲣ̄ϯ ⲛⲟⲙⲟⲥ ⲛ̄ⲑⲉ ⲙⲡⲛⲟⲙⲟⲑⲉⲧⲏⲥ ⲙⲏⲡⲟⲧⲉ ⲛ̄ⲥⲉⲁⲙⲁϩⲧⲉ ⲙ̄ⲙⲱⲧⲛ̄ ⲛϩⲏⲧϥ (8,22–9,4)

[48] Pasquier, *Marie*, 62. See also King, *Mary*, 108.

> Do not lay down any rules beyond what I have appointed for you, nor give a law like the Lawgiver in case you be dominated by it.

The admonition is further stressed by its repetition at the end of the gospel:

> ⲕ̣ⲁ̣ⲧⲁ ⲑ̣ⲉ ⲛ̄ⲧ̣ⲁϥ ϩⲱⲛ ⲉⲧⲟⲟⲧⲛ̄ ⲛ̄ⲧⲛ̄ⲧⲁϣⲉⲟⲉⲓϣ ⲙⲡⲉⲩⲁⲅⲅⲗⲉⲓⲟⲛ ⲉⲛⲕⲱ ⲁⲛ ⲉϩⲣⲁï ⲛⲕⲉϩⲟⲣⲟⲥ ⲟⲩⲇⲉ ⲕⲉⲛⲟⲙⲟⲥ̣ ⲡⲁⲣⲁ ⲡⲉⲛⲧⲁⲡⲥ̅ⲱ̅ⲣ̅ (18,17–21)
>
> … as he commanded us and preach the gospel, not laying down other rules or another la[w] beyond what the Saviour told us.

The stress on the importance of what Jesus has commanded them is shared with the Matthean commission:

> διδάσκοντες αὐτοὺς τηρεῖν πάντα ὅσα ἐνετειλάμην ὑμῖν (Matt 28.20)
>
> … teaching them to obey everything that I have commanded you.

Lührmann argues that the references to making new laws in the Gospel of Mary are a polemic against Matthew, in which Jesus appears as a lawgiver and instructs the disciples to obey his laws.[49] Lührmann goes as far as to question whether the Gospel of Mary takes up the tradition of Levi becoming Matthew and asks whether the real Matthew is here depicted as Levi, rejecting the gospel under his name.[50] The eschatology of the Gospel of Mary and of Matthew appear to be at odds, but the depiction of Jesus is not. Matthew's instruction regarding the laws is more positive than the Gospel of Mary's – it is what the disciples should do as opposed to what they should not do. But both are about following Jesus' teachings; namely, the stress on the importance of what Jesus has commanded them is something that they have in common.

In the Gospel of Mary, the ⲡⲁⲣⲁ clause in both passages above shows that the prohibition is aimed at rules/law *beyond* the

[49] Lührmann, *Die apokryph gewordenen Evangelien*, 45–7.

[50] 'So wäre der wahre Matthäus, dargestellt als Levi, derjenige, der mit dem Evangelium unter seinem falschen Namen nichts zu tun haben will', Lührmann, *Die apokryph gewordenen Evangelien*, 47. *Contra* Hartenstein, *Die zweite Lehre*, 131; Tuckett, *Mary*, 21–2.

Saviour's.[51] What constitutes these other rules and laws is a matter of disagreement: de Boer assumes that Peter and Andrew are following different laws than Mary about gender and prophets;[52] Schaberg sees the Gospel of Mary as comparing Peter's behaviour to 'that of heretical Christians or more likely that of the Powers ... There are indeed rules or laws under the surface of what Peter has said, rules that "dominate" him';[53] Pagels assumes that this was written to combat the silencing of women, as seen in 1 Corinthians 14.33–35;[54] and King offers a setting of intra-Christian debate.[55]

The warning in the Gospel of Mary is aimed both at the creation of new rules and not following the Saviour's command. The imposition of new rules was clearly an issue in early Christian communities. As an example, the *Didache* proposes strict rules for fasting. The ὑποκριταί fast on Monday and Thursday, but the readers of the *Didache* should distinguish themselves from the hypocrites by fasting on Wednesday and Friday (8.1).[56] These rules clearly extend beyond Jesus' teachings and were being debated among early Christians. Ptolemy refutes those who practise fasting that has been prescribed for a particular day (*Ep. Flora* 33.5.13), and this could well be the kind of situation that the Gospel of Mary is warning against.

However, most interpreters agree that ὁ νομοθέτης is used to refer to Moses in the Gospel of Mary.[57] Although the Gospel of Mary

[51] Cf. PRyl.GM 22, discussed below.

[52] de Boer, *Gospel of Mary*, 206. The laws refer to women's inability to experience a direct relationship with God.

[53] Jane Schaberg, *The Resurrection of Mary Magdalene: Legends, Apocrypha, and the Christian Testament* (London and New York: Bloomsbury, 2004), 177; King, *Mary*, 53–6. The rules that Schaberg refers to are those of female oppression.

[54] In conversation with King, see King, *Mary*, 56 n. 9. Tuckett argues that as 1 Cor 14.34–35 is probably a post-Pauline gloss, and as a result, the author of the Gospel of Mary would have been unaware of it, Tuckett, *Mary*, 159 n. 84. Nevertheless, the author of the Gospel of Mary would have been aware of the sort of argument that shaped 1 Cor 14.33–35.

[55] King, *Mary*, 54.

[56] See Kurt Niederwimmer, *The Didache: A Commentary*, ed. Harold W. Attridge, trans. Linda M. Maloney, Hermeneia (Minneapolis, MN: Fortress Press, 1998), 132.

[57] Lampe gives five options for ὁ νομοθέτης: God, Christ, Moses, Paul or church leaders, G. W. H. Lampe, ed., *Patristic Greek Lexicon* (London: Oxford University Press, 1961), 919b. On the 'Lawgiver' being Moses in the Gospel of Mary, see King, *Mary*, 53; Pasquier, *Marie*, 64; Michel Tardieu, *Écrits gnostiques: Codex de Berlin* (Paris: Les Éditions du Cerf, 1984), 229. Tuckett writes that it unclear whether the Lawgiver in the Gospel of Mary is Moses himself or the demiurge of the Hebrew Bible, Tuckett, *Mary*, 158. *Contra* Hartenstein who argues that the Lawgiver is Jesus as he refers to laws that he has appointed. She understands Jesus to say that his instructions are not meant to be supplemented or abolished, and if the disciples were to act like the Lawgiver, it may dominate them. The disciples must not act like Jesus. See Hartenstein, *Die zweite Lehre*, 145.

does not appear particularly interested in Moses or the Jewish law, its placement alongside the Apocryphon of John in the Berlin Codex may account for the use of νομοθέτης language. The Apocryphon of John regards Moses' account of the history of humankind, as told in Genesis, as incorrect. Teaching laws outside of God's, with Moses as the νομοθέτης, is a concern for Ptolemy, who teaches Flora that the law is defective. Ptolemy argues that the Lawgiver (ὁ νομοθέτης) cannot be the perfect God as the law still needs to be fulfilled by the Saviour,[58] and the Lawgiver cannot be the devil as the law abolishes injustice. In the first instance, the Lawgiver is the demiurge or the 'God of Justice' (3.6–7, 7.5).[59] The law is subdivided into three commandments that are good (the decalogue), unjust (an eye for an eye) and symbolic (rituals) (33.5). However, the law in the Pentateuch had multiple authors, and some of its commandments were established by human beings (4.1). Ptolemy argues that Moses created laws outside of God's and is thus himself a Lawgiver:

> Διαλεγόμενός που ὁ σωτὴρ πρὸς τοὺς περὶ τοῦ ἀποστασίου συζητοῦντας αὐτῷ, ὅ δὴ ἀποστάσιον ἐξεῖναι νενομοθέτητο. ἔφη αὐτοῖς ὅτι Μωυσῆς πρὸς τὴν σκληροκαρδίαν ὑμῶν ἐπέτρεψεν τὸ ἀπολύειν τὴν γυναῖκα αὐτοῦ. ἀπ' ἀρχῆς γὰρ οὐ γέγονεν οὕτως. Θεὸς γάρ, φησί, συνέζευξε ταύτην τὴν συζυγίαν, καὶ ὅ συνέζευξεν ὁ κύριος, ἄνθρωπος, ἔφη, μὴ χωριζέτω. Ἐνταῦθα ἕτερον μὲν < τὸν > τοῦ θεοῦ δείκνυσι νόμον, τὸν κωλύοντα χωρίζεσθαι γυναῖκα ἀπὸ ἀνδρὸς αὐτῆς, ἕτερον δὲ τὸν τοῦ Μωυσέως, τὸν διὰ τὴν σκληροκαρδίαν ἐπιτρέποντα χωρίζεσθαι τοῦτο τὸ ζεῦγος. Καὶ δὴ ḳατὰ τοῦτο ἐναντία τῷ θεῷ νομοθετεῖ ὁ Μωυσῆς · ἐναντίον γάρ ἐστι < τὸ διαζευγνύναι > (4.4–6)
>
> When the Saviour was talking with those who were arguing with him about divorce – and it has been ordained (νενομοθέτητο) that divorce is permitted – he said to them: 'For of your hardness of heart Moses allowed divorce of one's wife. Now, from the beginning it was not so.' For God, he says, has joined together this union, and 'what the Lord joined together, let no man dissolve'. Here he shows that (the) law of God is one thing, forbidding a woman to

[58] As Thomassen writes, 'the Saviour came to complete, abrogate, or change the Law by giving it a new and spiritual meaning', Einar Thomassen, *The Spiritual Seed: The Church of the Valentinians*, NHMS 60 (Leiden and Boston: Brill, 2006), 123.

[59] For a summary of the point I make concerning this text, see Francis T. Fallon, 'The Law in Philo and Ptolemy: A Note on the Letter to Flora', *VC* 30.1 (1976): esp. 45–7.

> be divorced from her husband, while the law of Moses is another, permitting the dissolving of the union because of hard-heartedness. So Moses laid down (νομοθετεῖ) a law contrary to that of God, for separating is contrary to not separating.[60]

Ptolemy has a relatively neutral view of the demiurge and Moses as Lawgivers. He writes that Moses only created laws outside of God's as a lesser of two evils.

The Gospel of Mary has a much more negative view of creating laws that deviate from the Saviour's commands than Ptolemy does of Moses creating laws outside of his God's. Although the Gospel of Mary does not necessarily have to be referring to the Jewish law, the gospel shares Ptolemy's view that only the Saviour's law is perfect.[61] The Gospel of Mary uses the traditional νομοθέτης language but uses it to refer to community rules, possibly including visions and female authority. There is evidence later in the gospel that Peter and Andrew have become dominated by these new rules as they declare Mary's revelation as heresy.

Through the reformulation of traditional Jesus sayings, the FD generates a new interpretation of the resurrected Christ. At points, his message is different from other gospel literature but at other points, it is recognizably the same. The Saviour in the FD teaches the message of the Gospel of Mary: the disciples must play an active role, are warned against an apocalyptic Son of Man, invited to achieve spiritual enlightenment as a prerequisite for preaching the gospel, and banned from creating new laws for the community.

3.3 Mary's Intervention

Mary is characterized as a visionary, a teacher and, to some extent, a paraclete. The evangelist underpins her exalted status as the Saviour calls her 'blessed' (ⲛⲁïⲁⲧⲉ [10,14]) and Peter says, 'Sister, we know that the Saviour loved you more than the other women' (ⲧⲥⲱⲛⲉ

[60] Greek text taken from G. Quispel, *Ptolémée. Lettre à Flora: Texte, Traduction et Introduction* (Paris: Les Éditions du Cerf, 1949), 52. English text (adapted) from Bentley Layton, 'Ptolemy's Epistle to Flora', in *The Gnostic Scriptures: A New Translation with Annotations and Introductions* (Garden City: Doubleday, 1987), 306–15.

[61] *Contra* Tuckett who suggests that it is easier to 'see here part of the general polemic employed by some Gnostics against the "orthodox" that the latter are too dependent on, and use too much, the Jewish Law and its demands', Tuckett, *Mary*, 160.

ⲧⲛ̄ⲥⲟⲟⲩⲛ ϫⲉ ⲛⲉⲣⲉⲡⲥ̄ⲱ̄ⲣ̄ ⲟⲩⲁϣⲉ̣ ⲛϩⲟⲩⲟ ⲡⲁⲣⲁ ⲡⲕⲉⲥⲉⲉⲡⲉ ⲛ̄ⲥϩⲓ̈ⲙⲉ [10,1–3]).[62] In many ways she is recognizably the Mary Magdalene of other gospel literature, but she has been developed and interpreted in new ways. Her exalted status brings to mind her role as disciple, visionary and dialogue participant in John 20, the Gospel of Thomas, the Sophia of Jesus Christ, the Pistis Sophia and the Dialogue of the Saviour. In the Gospel of Thomas and the Sophia of Jesus Christ, she asks about discipleship and knowledge (GThom 21; SophJesChr $_{\text{NHC}}$ 98,9–11, 114,8–12). In the Dialogue of the Saviour she is one of the three disciples to gain special knowledge and instruction. In the Pistis Sophia she is able to quote Isaiah, Psalms, Jesus and Paul,[63] and similarly in the Dialogue of the Saviour, she quotes Jesus (139,8–11). She is called 'a woman who knew all things' (ⲥϩⲓⲙⲉ ⲉⲁⲥⲉⲓⲙⲉ ⲉⲡⲧⲏⲣϥ̄ [DialSav 139,12–13]).[64]

In the Gospel of Mary, Mary's status changes slightly between the Coptic and Greek versions, especially with regard to her relationship with the male disciples – they are only small changes, but enough to make a difference. This is what we will explore here.

Mary and the Men

We find the first substantial difference in the depiction of the disciples' relationships in the Greek and Coptic MSS at the point when Mary arises:

> ⲧⲟⲧⲉ ⲁⲙⲁⲣⲓϩⲁⲙ ⲧⲱⲟⲩⲛ ⲁⲥⲁⲡⲁⲍⲉ ⲙⲙⲟⲟⲩ ⲧⲏⲣⲟⲩ (9,12–14)
>
> Then Mary rose, she greeted them all …
>
> [τοτε αναστασα Μαριαμμη και ασπαζομενη α]υτους κατεφιλησε̣ [αυτους] … (POxy.GM 8–9)

[62] The issue of Mary's gender has been studied extensively and will not be discussed here. For my thoughts on the matter, see Sarah Parkhouse, 'The Fetishization of Female Exempla: Mary, Thecla, Perpetua and Felicitas', *NTS* 63.4 (2017): 567–87.

[63] 1.18 [26,21–27.19]; 1.60 [119,5–12]; 1.62 [123,11–14]; 3.113 [293,18–294,1]. In the Pistis Sophia, she is also called 'blessed among all women on earth' (1.19 [28,21–22]) and 'blessed by all generations' (1.34 [56,11–13]). Because of these titles, Shoemaker argues that this Mary is Jesus' mother, Shoemaker, 'Rethinking the "Gnostic Mary"', 572–3. Brock, however, examines all of the unidentified Marys in the Pistis Sophia and argues that they are all Mary Magdalene, Brock, *Mary Magdalene, The First Apostle*, 47. Marjanen and de Boer agree with this identification, Marjanen, *The Woman Jesus Loved*, 173–4; de Boer, *Gospel of Mary*, 18.

[64] Mary also has an active role in the Epistula Apostolorum, the Gospel of Philip and the Gospel of Peter, among others.

[Then Mary arising and greeting th]em, kissed [them] …

The Greek verbs ἀσπαζομένη (reconstructed) and κατεφίλησε correspond to the single verb ⲁⲥⲡⲁⲍⲉ in Coptic. It is debated whether POxy.GM ever read ἀσπαζομένη and κατεφίλησε. Lührmann and Tuckett suggest that two verbs match the spacing of the missing part of the MS;[65] however, Parsons disagrees, suggesting that the line would have read: τότε ἀναστᾶσα Μαριάμμη αὐτοὺς κατεφίλησε with ⲁⲥⲡⲁⲍⲉ replacing κατεφίλησε in the Coptic translation.[66] Whether the Greek MS read ἀσπαζομένη is unimportant, the significance is in the translation, assimilation, replacement or deletion of καταφιλέω in the Coptic MS.

It is unlikely that κατεφίλησε has simply been *translated* as ⲁⲥⲡⲁⲍⲉ. In the Sahidic New Testament καταφιλέω is always translated as ϯⲡⲓ,[67] suggesting that the translator of the Gospel of Mary would not naturally have chosen ⲁⲥⲡⲁⲍⲉ for καταφιλέω.[68] Till and Mohri propose that the two verbs were *assimilated*: the word ἀσπαζομένη may have included a kiss of greeting, and so ⲁⲥⲡⲁⲍⲉ is simply an abbreviation of the longer ἀσπαζομένη and κατεφίλησε.[69] However, Tuckett rightly questions why then POxy.GM would have used both verbs, since this would indicate that 'the "kissing" is something additional to a more general "greeting"'.[70]

[65] Lührmann, *Die apokryph gewordenen Evangelien*, 109; Tuckett, *Mary*, 110.

[66] P. J. Parsons, '3525: Gospel of Mary', in *The Oxyrhynchus Papyri*, Graeco-Roman Memoirs 70, Vol. 50 (London: Egypt Exploration Society, 1983), 13–14.

[67] For example, a son kissing a father (Luke 15.20), the kissing of Jesus' feet (Luke 7.38, 45), and Judas' kiss (Matt 26.48–49; Mark 14.45).

[68] Further confusion arises from the English translation of the Gospel of Philip. Exegetes and translators generally regard ⲁⲥⲡⲁⲍⲉ as kiss, with Jesus kissing his companion (ⲕⲟⲓⲛⲱⲛⲟⲥ) Mary Magdalene on her … (63,32–36). The sentence ends with a lacuna but is usually reconstructed as mouth (ⲧⲁⲡⲣⲟ). For example: R. McL. Wilson, *The Gospel of Philip: Translated from the Coptic Text, with an Introduction and Commentary* (London: A. R. Mowbray & Co, 1962); Petersen, *Zerstört die Werke*, 145–7; Paul Foster, 'The Gospel of Philip', in *The Non-Canonical Gospels*, ed. Paul Foster (London and New York: T&T Clark, 2008), 75; Karen L. King, 'The Place of the Gospel of Philip in the Context of Early Christian Claims about Jesus' Marital Status', *NTS* 59.4 (2013): 578. The translation 'kiss' is based on the ⲧⲉⲥ- (her) and the assumption that the first word in the lacuna that follows was probably ⲧⲁⲡⲣⲟ 'mouth'. This would be an uncommon use of the word ⲁⲥⲡⲁⲍⲉ.

[69] Till, *Papyrus Berolinensis 8502*, 338; Erika Mohri, *Maria Magdalena: Frauenbilder in Evangelientexten des 1. bis 3. Jahrhunderts*, Marburger theologische Studien 63 (Marburg: Elwert, 2000), 262.

[70] Tuckett, *Mary*, 121. He does not note this, but the kiss is a form of greeting: 'Greet each other with a holy kiss' (ⲁⲥⲡⲁⲍⲉ ⲚⲚⲉⲧⲚⲉⲣⲏⲩ ϩⲚⲟⲩⲡⲓ ⲉⲥⲟⲩⲁⲁⲃ [Rom 16.16; 1 Cor 16.20; 2 Cor 13.12]).

It seems, then, that the Coptic translator/scribe is purposefully *replacing* or *deleting* κατεφίλησε. The question is: why? King, in her earlier work on the Gospel of Mary, suggests that the reference to kissing was excluded from the Coptic text as 'the practice of exchanging chaste kisses had come into disrepute in the later Egyptian Christian circles which produced the Coptic version'.[71] Although she does not cite him, Clement supports King's claim as he worries about the holy kiss being turned into a shameless act (*Paed.* 3.11.81). The concern over sexual indecorum is a plausible reason; however, in the New Testament καταφιλέω never suggests a sexual relationship, and it is improbable that this is the primary concern here.

Rather than sexual indecency alone, the issue is also likely to be theological indecency. In an extensive study of kissing Christians, Penn shows that the kiss was used as a symbol of Christian unity and community. Christians could only kiss fellow Christians and were prohibited from exchanging a kiss with potential heretics.[72] This is likely to be in the background of the Gospel of Mary; the Coptic scribe/translator would not accept Mary kissing Peter and Andrew as they do not belong to the same community. Andrew essentially declares her a heretic when he says, 'I myself do not believe that the Saviour said such things, for surely these are alien teachings' (ⲁⲛⲟⲕ ⲙⲉⲛ ϯⲣ̄ⲡⲓⲥⲧⲉⲩⲉ ⲁⲛ ϫ̣ⲉ ⲁⲡⲥ̄ⲱ̄ⲣ̄ ϫⲉ ⲛⲁϊ ⲉϣϫⲉ ⲛⲓⲥⲃⲟⲟⲩⲉ ⲅⲁⲣ ϩⲛ̄ⲕⲉⲙⲉⲉⲩⲉ ⲛⲉ [17,13–15]).[73] The omission of κατεφίλησε heightens the sense of disunity within the group of disciples.

The idea of disunity is found throughout the Coptic text, especially in relation to the Greek fragments. Another example is in Mary's words:

> ⲁϥⲥⲃ̄ⲧⲱⲧⲛ̄ ⲁϥⲁⲁⲛ ⲛ̄ⲣⲱⲙⲉ (9,19–20)
>
> he has prepared us; he has made us Men[74]
>
> σ̣υ̣νηρ̣τηκ̣εν ημας και ανο̅[υ̅ς̅ πεποιηκεν] (POxy.GM 12)
>
> he has united us and [has made us M]en

[71] King, 'Gospel of Mary Magdalene', 630 n. 4.

[72] Michael Philip Penn, *Kissing Christians: Ritual and Community in the Late Ancient Church*, Divinations: Rereading Late Ancient Religion (Philadelphia, PA: University of Pennsylvania Press, 2005).

[73] See the discussion of ϩⲛⲕⲉⲙⲉⲉⲩⲉ later in this chapter.

[74] The words ⲣⲱⲙⲉ and ἄνθρωπος are gender inclusive and should be translated as 'human'. However, the phrase 'the Son of Man' is so familiar in the study of the New Testament and Early Christianity that I have decided to translate ⲣⲱⲙⲉ as 'Man' at 8,18 and correspondingly 'Men' 9,20 and 'Perfect Man' 18,16.

In POxy.GM, συναρτάω has the sense of the disciples being joined or 'knit together' as one.[75] It is possible that it refers to elements of the individual being joined together into a Perfect Man, but it can also be read as the group of Christians being joined together into a holy community (cf. Eph 4.16, ἐξ οὗ πᾶν τὸ σῶμα συναρμολογούμενον καὶ συμβιβαζόμενον …). In contrast, ⲥⲟⲃⲧⲉ ('prepared') in the Coptic has no sense of group identity and pertains instead to the individual. Although these differences are slight, they are not negligible.

In both the Greek and Coptic versions, the male disciples recognize Mary's superior knowledge and close relationship with the Saviour before she reveals it. It is Peter who requests that she tells them what she knows; however, the words again differ slightly between BG and POxy.GM:

> ϫⲱ ⲛⲁⲛ ⲛ̄ⲛ̄ϣⲁϫⲉ ⲙ̄ⲡⲥ̅ⲱ̅ⲣ̅ ⲉⲧⲉⲉⲓⲣⲉ ⲙⲡⲉⲩⲙⲉⲉⲩⲉ ⲛⲁï ⲉⲧⲉⲥⲟⲟⲩⲛ ⲙ̄ⲙⲟⲟⲩ ⲛ̄ⲛⲁⲛⲟⲛ ⲁⲛ ⲟⲩⲇⲉ ⲙⲡⲛ̄ⲥⲟⲧⲙ`ⲟ′ⲩ ⲁⲥⲟⲩⲱϣⲃ̄ ⲛϭⲓ ⲙⲁⲣⲓϩⲁⲙ ⲡⲉϫⲁⲥ ϫⲉ ⲡⲉⲑⲏⲡ ⲉⲣⲱⲧⲛ̄ ϯⲛⲁⲧⲁⲙⲁ ⲧⲏⲩⲧⲛ̄ ⲉⲣⲟϥ (10,4–9)
>
> 'Tell us the words of the Saviour that you remember, those that you know and we do not, nor have we heard them.' Mary answered and said, 'What is hidden from you, I will proclaim to you.'
>
> ειπον ουν ημειν ọ[σους συ γινωσκεις λογο]ụς του σωτηρος [ους] ηṃẹịς ουκ ηκουσαμẹṿ ụπ̣ẹ̣[λαβε Μαριαμμη λεγουσα οσα υμ]ạς λανθανει και απομνημονευω ạṿạ[γγελω υμιν] (POxy. GM 16–18)
>
> 'Tell us [those words that you know] of the Saviour [which] we have not heard.' [Mary answered, saying, 'What is] unknown to you and I remember, I will pr[oclaim to you.']

In both recensions, Peter is perfectly willing to acknowledge that the Saviour gave a private revelation to Mary. We might expect an element of bravado from Peter, unwilling to accept that a woman could possess hidden knowledge; however, the text shows no hint of any … yet. However, the reason that the teaching is unknown to the male disciples has stronger negative connotations in the Coptic. ϩⲏⲡ suggests that

[75] The sense of cohesion that συναρτάω implies can be seen through its use in Hippocrates: ἡ ἄνω γνάθος … συνήρτηται τῇ κεφαλῇ καὶ οὐ διήρθρωται ('the upper jaw is joined to the head and is not easily broken'). Another example is συνηρτημέναι [ἀρεταὶ] τοῖς πάθεσι ('[virtues] are joined to the passions'; Aristotle). For these examples and more, see Liddell, Scott, and Jones, eds. *A Greek-English Lexicon*, 9th ed. (Oxford, 1940 [1843]), 1699.

the words of the Saviour were *hidden* from the disciples. Tuckett does not regard this variation as significant;[76] however, according to King, '[i]n the Coptic version, Mary really rubs it in: she says that she has the teaching that has been *hidden* from them … because the Savior singled her out'.[77] Although ϩⲏⲡ can be translated from λανθάνω, it is more commonly used for κρύπτω in the Sahidic NT, and so it is more likely to have a sense of concealment than simply escaping notice.[78] There appears to be a Coptic scribe/translator at work highlighting the unworthiness of Peter and his companions in comparison with Mary.

'*Verkörperung*' or Paraclete?

The language used to depict Mary's relationship with the Saviour is different in the Greek and Coptic:

> ϩⲱⲥⲧⲉ ⲛ̄ⲧⲁⲡⲥ̄ⲱ̄ⲣ̄ ϣⲁϫⲉ ⲛⲙ̄ⲙⲁⲥ ϣⲁ ⲡⲉⲉⲓⲙⲁ (17,8–9)
>
> as the Saviour had spoken *with her* to this point.
>
> ως του σωτηρος μεχρι ω̣δε ειρηκοτος (PRyl.GM 21,4–5)
>
> as the Saviour had spoken to this point.

Lührmann regards these versions as radically different due to the Coptic addition of ⲛⲙ̄ⲙⲁⲥ, showing that the Saviour and Mary spoke *with each other*. He argues that the Greek, conversely, implies that the Saviour had been speaking in and through her, making Mary a '*Verkörperung*' ('embodiment') of the Saviour.[79] Tuckett questions this proposal:

> [W]hether … Mary is a 'Verkörperung' ('embodiment') of the Saviour is not so certain. Whilst there is no question that, in a number of important respects, Mary takes on the role of the Saviour, nevertheless here Mary can be seen as simply the vehicle through whom the words of the Saviour are transmitted to others via the report of her dream. It may then be going a little too far to suggest that the Coptic text has 'reduced' Mary's significance.[80]

[76] Tuckett, *Mary*, 123.
[77] King, *Mary*, 84.
[78] M. Wilmet, *Concordance du Nouveau Testament sahidique, II. Les mots autochtones, 3*, CSCO 185 (Louvain: Secrétariat du CorpusSCO, 1959), 1462a.
[79] Lührmann, *Die apokryph gewordenen Evangelien*, 187. Also, Mohri, *Maria Magdalena*, 263.
[80] Tuckett, *Mary*, 186–7.

At no point does the gospel indicate that Mary has *become* the Saviour: she is in dialogue with him, imitates him and, in some respects, replaces him. In all likelihood, this textual variation is an addition to aid the narrative rather than demonstrating any theological significance.

Mary does not become Jesus, but she does replace him. Mary rises as Jesus departs. As Mary stands and speaks to the other disciples, her voice is elided with that of the Saviour, and she takes a position analogous to him. She becomes their consoler, comforter and encourager, allaying their fears about mission and turning their minds towards the Good (9,12–22). For these reasons, Petersen suggests that Mary fulfils the role of the Johannine paraclete:

> Mary fulfils the role that is announced for the Paraclete in John: She comforts and encourages the disciples, and she reminds them of Jesus' words. She proclaims to the disciples not her own ideas, but what she has heard from Jesus. And through her intercession, they become aware of what is to come, namely the taught ascension of the soul. The teaching of the ascension of the soul definitely could be designated the 'whole truth' for the Gospel of Mary; Mary here relays a central matter of gnostic theology.[81]

Indeed, there are many similarities between the paraclete in the Johannine Farewell Discourse and Mary in the Gospel of Mary:

The paraclete will come as Jesus departs (15.26; 16.7, 8, 13)	Mary rises as the Saviour departs (9,5–12)
The disciples can recognize the paraclete (14.17)	True disciples, such as Levi, recognize Mary's status (18,10–15)
The world neither sees nor recognizes the paraclete (14.17)	Peter and Andrew do not recognize or accept Mary's authority (17,11–17)
The paraclete will teach the disciples everything (14.26) and the things to come (16.13)	Mary teaches the disciples what they do not know; and of the things to come (10,7–17,9)
will glorify Jesus (16.14)	Mary glorifies the Saviour (9,18–19)
will bear witness on Jesus' behalf (15.26)	Mary bears witness once the Saviour has departed (9,12–20)
will remind the disciples of all that Jesus told them (14.26)	Mary reminds the disciples that which the Saviour told her (10,4–9)
and will speak only what he hears and nothing on his own (16.13)	Mary only speaks what she has heard and nothing on her own (17,7–9)

[81] Petersen, *Zerstört die Werke*, 141. Schaberg simply says that Mary is 'much like the paraclete', Schaberg, *The Resurrection of Mary Magdalene*, 172.

I want to draw attention to three points in particular. In John, the paraclete will come as Jesus departs. In the Gospel of Mary, the use of ⲧⲱⲟⲩⲛ (arose) in describing Mary's 'entrance' suggests that she only comes to the fore after Jesus departs. In both texts, the two revealers are in tandem. The second point, that Mary *reminds* the disciples of the Saviour's words, is clear through the short dialogue between her and Peter (although slightly different in the Greek and Coptic versions, as discussed above). John insists that the paraclete teaches nothing new but does not simply recall the past. As Brown writes, 'the Paraclete played an interpretative role – making what Jesus had said and done relevant and meaningful to succeeding generations'.[82] Mary recalls only what the Saviour said to her and makes it relevant for the disciples after his departure, although they do not all agree with it. The third point, that Mary only tells the others what she has heard from the Saviour, is so strongly demonstrated that she remains 'silent *because* (or *as*) the Saviour had spoken with her to this point' (ⲁⲥⲕⲁⲣⲱⲥ ϩⲱⲥⲧⲉ ⲛ̄ⲧⲁⲡⲥⲱⲣ̄ ϣⲁϫⲉ ⲛⲙ̄ⲙⲁⲥ ϣⲁ ⲡⲉⲉⲓⲙⲁ [17,8–9]).

Furthermore, in John the paraclete is said to 'declare to you the things that are to come' (τὰ ἐρχόμενα ἀναγγελεῖ ὑμῖν [16.13]). Mary's teaches them something that will take place: the ascent of the soul. With this connection in mind, there is a new possible reconstruction of a verb in POxy.GM. Tuckett follows Parsons in reconstructing ἀπαγγέλω in [οσα υμ]ας λανθανει καιι απομνημονευω απα[γγελω υμιν] (POxy.GM 18).[83] But he notes that the first three letters are 'very uncertain'.[84] The verb ἀναγγέλω ('to announce, make manifest, unveil') is used for the paraclete in John 16.13, as well as in apocalyptic literature in the sense of unveiling the truth of a vision.[85] It is therefore plausible that this is the verb in POxy.GM.[86]

It is not to be argued that Mary is the *equivalent* of the Johannine paraclete. There are, of course, differences between the two. Tuckett dismisses the connection outright, writing:

> [T]he roles of the two figures in the respective texts, and the relationship of each figure to Jesus, differ significantly. Thus

[82] Raymond E. Brown, 'The Paraclete in the Fourth Gospel', *NTS* 13.2 (1967): 129.

[83] Parsons, '3525: Gospel of Mary'; Tuckett, *Mary*, 108.

[84] Tuckett, *Mary*, 111.

[85] For example, Dan 5.12,15; 9.23; 10.21; 11.2 Theod; cf. Isa 46.10. It is also used instead of ἀπαγγέλω in some MSS of John 16.25: 'The hour is coming when I will no longer speak to you in riddles, but will tell [ἀναγγέλω] you plainly of the Father.'

[86] See Brown, 'The Paraclete in the Fourth Gospel', 121. Furthermore, Crum has ἀναγγέλλειν for ⲧⲁⲙⲟ, W. E Crum, *A Coptic Dictionary* (Oxford: The Clarendon Press, 1939), 413b.

> the reminding function of the Paraclete seems to relate more to a recalling of things already known (cf. John 14.26), not mediating new teaching (as Mary does in her vision and to which Andrew and Peter object). So too there is no idea of Jesus 'sending' Mary 'from the Father' as the Paraclete will be 'sent' by Jesus (John 15.26). Conversely, there is no mention in John of a relationship of love between Jesus and the Paraclete.[87]

These are valid objections.[88] Indeed, there are further objections to be made against equating Mary to the Johannine Paraclete; for example, Mary does not seem hostile to the world nor does she put the world on trial.[89] Also, in John, the Paraclete 'represents Jesus and has no independent existence of his own … he is Jesus' Doppelgänger or double, his alter ego'.[90] This is not true of Mary. And she is not the spirit of truth (although she declares truths) nor the Holy Spirit (although she is blessed).

But the idea of the paraclete was not always understood strictly in the Johannine sense – it was being reinterpreted by other Christian authors, and this might be what we see in the Gospel of Mary. The Valentinians embraced the idea of the παράκλητος, usually identifying it with Christ,[91] and the term paraclete is used in the Apocryphon of James, probably referring to Jesus: 'Woe to you who lack a paraclete' (ⲟⲩⲁⲉⲓ ⲛⲏⲧⲛ̄ ⲱ ⲛⲉⲧϣⲁⲁⲧ· ⲛ̄ⲛⲟⲩⲡⲁⲣⲁⲕⲗⲏⲧⲟⲥ· [11,11–13]). Mani declared himself a new incarnation of the paraclete, and the Montanists, likewise, held the notion that Montanus himself was the paraclete or the 'spirit of God'. In the First Apocalypse of James, once Jesus departs (for the first time), James is called a 'comfort' (ⲥⲟⲗⲥⲓⲗ̄ [$_{CT}$ 17,13]) and described as a 'second teacher' (ⲡⲙⲉϩⲥⲁϩ̄ ⲥⲛⲉⲩ [$_{CT}$ 17,14–15]), with his own disciples. 'Comfort' and paraclete are closely related.[92] For the Gospel of Mary, if we interpret

[87] Tuckett, *Mary*, 192 n. 210.

[88] However, it is quite possible that in the missing pages Jesus sent Mary to the brothers to teach them about the ascent of the soul. The narratival connections to John 20 have been noted, and in John 20.17, Jesus sends Mary to her brothers to tell them that Jesus is ascending.

[89] As Brown states for the Johannine paraclete, Brown, 'The Paraclete in the Fourth Gospel', 114.

[90] Ashton, *Understanding the Fourth Gospel*, 442.

[91] *Exc. Theod.* 23.1–12; *Adv. Haer.* 1.4.3.

[92] Davies argued that the primary function of the term παράκλητος is 'comforter' based on its LXX background of παρακαλεῖν, a verb that John never uses. See J. G. Davies, 'The Primary Meaning of Παράκλητος', *JTS* 4.1 (1953): 35–8. *Contra* Brown

'paraclete' as a 'comforter' who reminds the disciples of the Saviour's teachings after his departure, Mary fits this role perfectly. She is not the same as the Johannine paraclete, but she does embody features ascribed to it.

3.4 The Breach and Its Healing

In the Gospel of Mary, the four disciples play specific roles: Mary is a teacher, visionary and comforter; Andrew is the champion of, for lack of a better word, 'conventional' teachings; Peter defends male authority and open revelation; and Levi supports Mary and reminds them all of the Saviour's words. It could be said that the four characters exist on three levels, with Peter and Andrew representing lower, unenlightened followers of Jesus, Mary as having achieved a higher spiritual understanding, and Levi as something halfway. He understands that they should listen to Mary and be focused on the Saviour, but he does not possess the knowledge that Mary does.[93]

The Gospel of Mary tells a dramatic story. The disciples do not simply follow the teachings of the Saviour; instead they fall out over them. The Saviour's departure is followed by accusations of lying, female insubordination, weeping and reprimand. Mary's teaching and role is not accepted by Peter and Andrew, and Peter's criticism of Mary is not accepted by Levi. The three primary objections of Peter and Andrew are novel and/or strange teachings, secret teachings and female authority, and these will be discussed here in turn.

Strange Teachings

As Mary falls silent, Andrew and Peter jump to attack her on the basis of the unfamiliarity of the revelation:

> ⲁϥⲟⲩⲱϣⲃ̄ ⲇⲉ ⲛ̄ϭⲓ ⲁⲛⲇⲣⲉⲁⲥ ⲡⲉϫⲁϥ ⲛ̄ⲛⲉⲥⲛⲏⲩ ϫⲉ ⲁϫⲓ ⲡⲉⲧⲉⲧⲛ̄ϫⲱ ⲙⲙⲟϥ ϩⲁ ⲡⲣⲁ ⲛ̄ⲛⲉⲛⲧⲁⲥϫ[ⲟ]ⲟ̣ⲩ ⲁⲛⲟⲕ ⲙⲉⲛ ϯⲣ̄ⲡⲓⲥⲧⲉⲩⲉ ⲁⲛ ϫ̣ⲉ ⲁⲡ̄ⲥ̄ⲱ̄ⲣ̄ ϫⲉ ⲛⲁⲓ̈ ⲉϣϫⲉ ⲛⲓⲥⲃⲟⲟⲩⲉ ⲅⲁⲣ ϩⲛ̄ⲕⲉⲙⲉⲉⲩⲉ ⲛⲉ ⲁϥⲟⲩⲱϣⲃ̄ ⲛϭⲓ ⲡⲉⲧⲣⲟⲥ ⲡⲉϫⲁϥ ϩⲁ ⲡⲣⲁ ⲛⲛⲉⲉⲓϩⲃⲏⲩⲉ ⲛⲧⲉⲉⲓⲙⲓⲛⲉ (17,10–17)
>
> Then Andrew answered and said to the brothers, 'Say whatever you say about what she said. I myself do not believe

who writes, '[W]hile "Comforter" is not an adequate translation, it does throw light on a facet of the Paraclete's role', Brown, 'The Paraclete in the Fourth Gospel', 118.

[93] This has possible allusions to the tripartite division of humanity in the Valentinian system, but this would require a much longer study.

> that the Saviour said such things, for surely these are alien teachings.' Peter answered, he spoke about such matters.

ϩⲛⲕⲉⲙⲉⲉⲩⲉ literally means 'in other thoughts', but 'alien' or 'heterodox' are better translations. In PRyl.GM the word is [ετε]ρογνωμονειν (21,9–10), and the ἑτερο- prefix signifies *hetero*doxy.[94] ἑτερο- in 1 Tim 1.3 (ἵνα παραγγείλῃς τισὶν μὴ ἑτεροδιδασκαλεῖν) corresponds to -ⲕⲉ- (ⲛ̄ϩⲟⲉ̈ⲓⲛⲉ ⲉⲧⲙ̄ϯⲕⲉⲥⲃⲱ), and so the ⲕⲉ in the Gospel of Mary represents 'false', not just 'other'. The first challenge to Mary is based on what was said, rather than who said it. Mary's revelation was her vision of the Lord in which he taught her about the ascent of the soul, among other things. (There are four missing pages.) This individual eschatological journey is distinct from the cosmic eschatology that the Saviour revealed in the dialogue of page seven and unknown to Jesus traditions that were to become canonical. Mary is essentially preaching a *different gospel* than the one they are familiar with, and one that they claim is false.

Andrew's objection to this revelation is also found in the Pistis Sophia, in which Andrew cannot accept the teaching of the ascent of the soul. Andrew says:

> ⲡⲁϫⲟⲉⲓⲥ ⲉⲓⲣ(ⲛ)ϣⲡⲏⲣⲉ ⲁⲩⲱ ⲉⲓ̈ⲑⲁⲩⲙⲁⲍⲉ ⲉⲙⲁϣⲟ · ϫⲉ ⲛ̄ⲣⲱⲙⲉ ⲉⲧϩ̄ⲛ̄ ⲡⲕⲟⲥⲙⲟⲥ ⲉⲧϩ̄ⲛ̄ ⲡⲥⲱⲙⲁ ⲛ̄ⲧⲉⲓ̈ϩⲩⲗⲏ ⲡⲱⲥ ⲉⲩϣⲁⲛⲉⲓ'ⲉⲃⲟⲗ ϩⲙ̄ ⲡⲉⲓ̈ⲕⲟⲥⲙⲟⲥ ⲥⲉⲛⲁⲟⲩⲱ̅ⲧ̅ⲃ̅ ⲛ̄ⲛⲉⲓ̈ⲥⲧⲉⲣⲉⲱⲙⲁ ⲙ̅ⲛ̅ ⲛⲉⲓ̈ⲁⲣⲭⲱⲛ ⲧⲏⲣⲟⲩ … ⲡⲉⲓ̈ϩⲱⲃ ⲟⲩⲛ ⲡⲁϫⲟⲉⲓⲥ ϥⲙⲟⲕϩ ⲛ̄ⲛⲁϩⲣⲁⲓ̈ (2.100 [248,4–8, 13–14])
>
> My Lord, I am astonished and marvel greatly that when humankind who are in the world and in the body of this matter come forth (from) this world; they will surpass these firmaments and all these archons … This fact now, my Lord, is difficult for me.

Jesus' reaction is one of annoyance, asking how long he must suffer the ignorance of his disciples. After Jesus repeats the teaching, Andrew understands, and the other disciples ask the Lord to forgive Andrew's ignorance – which he grants. The fact that Andrew comes to understanding in the Pistis Sophia may give us a clue as to the end of the Gospel of Mary.

In the Gospel of Mary, Peter and Andrew are further able to challenge Mary's teaching about the soul due to the visionary nature of the revelation. She might just be making it up. Along with prophecy,

[94] The prefix is used in words that denote teaching false doctrines, for example, ἑτεροδιδασκαλία and ἑτεροδοξέω; see Lampe, *Patristic Greek Lexicon*, 552b.

ecstasy and dreams, visions were part of the ongoing philosophical debate concerning authority.[95] There were acceptable modes of prophesying associated with rationality – otherwise, it was considered madness.[96] Visions were not always thought of as true teaching, and conversely, they had the potential to question the value of apostolic authority as they revealed new truths. Mary is well aware of what she is accused of, answering: 'My brother Peter, what do you think then? Do you think that I have thought of these (things) myself in my heart, or that I am lying about the Saviour?' (ⲡⲁⲥⲟⲛ ⲡⲉⲧⲣⲉ ϩⲓ̈ⲉ ⲉⲕⲙⲉⲉⲩⲉ ⲉⲟⲩ ⲉⲕⲙⲉⲉⲩⲉ ϫⲉ ⲛ̄ⲧⲁⲓ̈ ⲙⲉⲉⲩⲉ ⲉⲣⲟⲟⲩ ⲙⲁⲩⲁⲁⲧ ϩⲙ̄ ⲡⲁϩⲏⲧ ⲏ ⲉⲉⲓϫⲓ ϭⲟⲗ ⲉⲡⲥ̄ⲱ̄ⲣ̄ [18,2–5]). She basically asks whether Peter thinks she is mad or bad.

The gospel shows Mary as a true prophet. The Saviour himself praises Mary's stability (ⲛⲧⲉⲕⲓⲙ ⲁⲛ [10,14]), which shows her advanced spiritual ability in the face of the divine. Often in early Christian literature, appearances of the divine resulted in fear and the recipients falling or wavering;[97] however, the condition of stability was seen as part of the unchanging spiritual realm to which Mary belongs.[98] After revealing her vision, Levi recognizes that the Saviour thought her to be worthy (18,11).

Andrew and Peter's challenge may suggest that the gospel was written in a milieu that understood its marginality in relation to those who followed 'conventional' teachings. Many scholars place the gospel in this context, arguing that the debate between Mary and Peter signifies a larger debate between 'orthodox' and 'gnostic' Christianity.[99] The phrase ϩⲛ̄ⲕⲉⲙⲉⲉⲩⲉ demonstrates the evangelist's

[95] King argues that in early Christianity, in the majority of cases, female leadership was based on a woman's prophetic abilities. See Karen L. King, 'Prophetic Power and Women's Authority: The Case of the Gospel of Mary (Magdalene)', in *Women Preachers and Prophets Through Two Millennia of Christianity*, ed. Beverly Mayne Kienzle and Pamela J. Walker (Berkeley and LA: University of California Press, 1998), 21–41.

[96] See Laura Salah Nasrallah, *An Ecstasy of Folly: Prophecy and Authority in Early Christianity*, HTS 52 (Cambridge, MA: Harvard University Press, 2003); Christine Trevett, 'Prophets, Economics, and the Rites of Man', in *Revelation, Literature, and Community in Late Antiquity*, ed. Philippa Townsend and Moulie Vidas (Tübingen: Mohr Siebeck, 2011), 43–64.

[97] For example, at the transfiguration, the voice from the cloud causes the disciples to be overcome with fear and fall facedown (Matt 17.6); and in Rev 1.17, John falls at the feet of the one like the Son of Man, playing dead. Somewhat similarly, but perhaps out of shame rather than fear, the disciples fall on their faces when finally realizing that the 'ghost' is not a ghost but the risen Christ in the Epistula Apostolorum 12.2.

[98] See Michael A. Williams, *The Immovable Race: A Gnostic Designation and the Theme of Stability in Late Antiquity*, NHMS 29 (Leiden: Brill, 1985); King, *Mary*, 63.

[99] Elaine Pagels, *The Gnostic Gospels* (New York: Random House, 1979), 12–14; Perkins, *Gnostic Dialogue*, 133; King, 'Gospel of Mary Magdalene', 83–92;

self-awareness that this gospel proposes a different interpretation of Jesus' teachings, whilst engaging with ongoing questions of true and false revelation.[100]

Secret Teachings

Peter's objection is not just against the strangeness of the teachings, but also Mary's gender and the secrecy of the revelation.

> ⲁϥϫⲛⲟⲩⲟⲩ ⲉⲧⲃⲉ ⲡⲥⲱⲣ ϫⲉ ⲙⲏⲧⲓ ⲁϥϣⲁϫⲉ ⲙⲛ̄ ⲟⲩⲥϩⲓ̈ⲙⲉ ⲛϫⲓⲟⲩⲉ ⲉⲣⲟⲛ ϩⲛ <ⲟⲩ>ⲟⲩⲱⲛϩ ⲉⲃⲟⲗ ⲁⲛ ⲉⲛⲛ̣ⲁ̣ⲕⲧⲟⲛ ϩⲱⲱⲛ ⲛ̄ⲧⲛ̄ⲥⲱⲧⲙ̄ ⲧⲏ̣ⲣ̣ⲛ̄ ⲛⲥⲱⲥ ⲛ̄ⲧⲁ̣ϥⲥⲟⲧⲡⲥ ⲛϩⲟⲩⲟ ⲉⲣ̣ⲟⲛ (17,17–22)
>
> He asked them about the Saviour, 'Did he speak with a woman secretly (and) not openly to us? Are we all to turn and listen to her? Did he choose her over us?'

Peter's questioning of Mary's status as a woman is certainly an issue in the text – her gender is mentioned three times[101] and relates to Peter's objection in the Gospel of Thomas 114 and the Pistis Sophia.[102] However, as the majority of scholarship on the Gospel of Mary addresses the gender issue, we will focus on the accusation of secrecy. The nature of the objection is stressed through the repetition of 'secretly' (ⲛϫⲓⲟⲩⲉ) and 'not publicly' (ⲟⲩⲱⲛϩ ⲉⲃⲟⲗ ⲁⲛ) and should be read in light of Mary's earlier words: 'What is hidden from you, I will proclaim to you' (ⲡⲉⲑⲏⲡ ⲉⲣⲱⲧⲛ̄ ϯⲛⲁⲧⲁⲙⲁ ⲧⲏⲩⲧⲛ̄ ⲉⲣⲟϥ [10,8–9]), where ϩⲏⲡ was used instead of λανθάνει (POxy.GM), heightening antipathy between the disciples.[103]

Hartenstein, *Die zweite Lehre*, 135; Tuckett, *Mary*, 201. Schaberg argues that 'Magdalene Christianity offers an alternative and a challenge to Petrine Christianity, which has never been able to silence it', Schaberg, *The Resurrection of Mary Magdalene*, 19.

[100] As the concept of what was acceptable in the mainstream church hardened towards the end of the second century, this may suggest that material was composed/edited into this form no earlier than the second half of the second century. Although the date of composition is not a focus of this work, it may be worth noting.

[101] As well as the quote above, Peter acknowledges that the Saviour loved Mary 'more than the other women' (ⲡⲁⲣⲁ ⲡⲕⲉⲥⲉⲉⲡⲉ ⲛ̄ⲥϩⲓ̈ⲙⲉ [10,3]), and Levi refers to Peter contesting 'the woman' (18,9).

[102] In the Gospel of Thomas 114, Peter says that Mary should be removed from the group of disciples 'because women are not worthy of life' (ⲛ̄ϩⲓⲟⲙⲉ ⲙ̄ⲡϣⲁ ⲁⲛ ⲙ̄ⲡⲱⲛϩ). In the Pistis Sophia, Peter protests against Mary talking all the time: 'We are not able to suffer this woman' (ⲧ̄ⲛ̄ⲛⲁϣ·ⲁⲛⲉⲭⲉ ⲁⲛ ⲛ̄ⲧⲉⲓ̈ⲥϩⲓⲙⲉ [1.36 (58,12)]), and Mary later complains that she is afraid of Peter because he threatens her and hates 'our gender' (ⲡⲉⲛⲅⲉⲛⲟⲥ [2.72 (162,16–18)]).

[103] Pasquier notes that Peter's opposition in the Gospel of Mary follows 'le scénario classique de certains évangiles apocryphes et indiquerait deux modes d'enseignement

Contention between open and secret knowledge is seen throughout the body of early Christian literature. In Graeco-Roman antiquity, it was common practice that certain things were disclosed only to those who had reached a higher level of understanding, and we have seen this through the 'mystery' language in Paul and the Synoptics. The idea of secrecy was utilized polemically in later authors: Irenaeus claims that the Valentinians considered themselves to be the recipients of hidden wisdom and so only revealed their beliefs to insiders (*Adv. Haer.* 3.15.2),[104] and Celsus made the same claim against all Christians (*c. Cels.* 1.1.7).[105]

It is debatable to what extent Mary's teaching is secret. Although she hears it alone to start with, she does relay it to the other disciples. It is unlike the undisclosed revelation of the Gospel of Thomas 13, in which Jesus takes Thomas aside to tell him 'three words' (ⲛ̄ϣⲟⲙⲧ ⲛ̄ϣⲁϫⲉ), but Thomas is unable to repeat these words to the other disciples.[106] Likewise, in the First Apocalypse of James, Jesus' revelation to James is to be revealed only to select people for several generations, when it will be disclosed to everyone (NHC 36,13–37,22). The Gospel of Mary scenario is closer to John 20 in that Jesus speaks to Mary alone, but instructs her to tell her brothers that he is ascending (20.17).

Peter the Adversary

After Peter's attack on Mary, she weeps and asks why he accuses her of lying. Before Peter has a chance to respond, Levi steps in, rebuking Peter and defending Mary:

> ⲁϥⲟⲩⲱϣⲃ̄ ⲛ̄ϭⲓ ⲗⲉⲩⲉⲓ ⲡⲉϫⲁϥ ⲙⲡⲉⲧⲣⲟ`ⲥ´ ϫⲉ ⲡⲉⲧⲣⲉ ϫⲓⲛ ⲉⲛⲉϩ ⲕϣⲟⲡ ⲛⲣⲉϥⲛⲟⲩϭⲥ ϯⲛⲁⲩ ⲉⲣⲟⲕ ⲧⲉⲛⲟⲩ ⲉⲕⲣ̄ⲅⲩⲙⲛⲁⲍⲉ ⲉϩⲛ ⲧⲉⲥϩⲓ̈ⲙⲉ ⲛ̄ⲑⲉ ⲛ̄ⲛⲓⲁⲛⲧⲓⲕⲉⲓⲙⲉⲛⲟⲥ ⲉϣϫⲉ ⲁⲡⲥⲱⲧⲏⲣ ⲇⲉ ⲁⲁⲥ ⲛⲁⲝⲓⲟⲥ ⲛ̄ⲧⲕ ⲛⲓⲙ ⲇⲉ ϩⲱⲱⲕ ⲉⲛⲟϫⲥ ⲉⲃⲟⲗ (18,5–12)
>
> Levi answered, he said to Peter, 'Peter, you are always wrathful! I see you now disputing with the woman like the

connus'. Peter's problem lies in the fact that '[l]a révélation secrète est un privilège. Elle manifeste l'élection', Pasquier, *Marie*, 98–9.

104 See also Elaine Pagels, *The Gnostic Paul: Gnostic Exegesis of the Pauline Letters* (Philadelphia, PA: Fortress Press, 1975), 57–8.

105 Also, *c. Cels.* 1.9, 12.

106 On this see Mark Goodacre, *Thomas and the Gospels: The Case for Thomas's Familiarity with the Synoptics* (Grand Rapids: Eerdmans, 2012), 177–9. He writes that the Gospel of Thomas 'encourages the initiate to go beyond the public writings in [the] other gospels, and to trump them with its own private revelation', 179.

adversaries. If the Saviour made her worthy, who are you to reject her?'

Πετρε ἀ[ει] σο[ι] το οργιλον· παρακειται και αρτι ουτως συνζητει[ς] τη γυναικι ως αντικειμενος αυτη (PRyl.GM 22,2–4)

Peter, wrath is always with yo[u], and so now you are disputing with the woman like an adversary to her.

Here we see another variation between the Greek and Coptic MSS that again heightens the antagonism between the disciples. The Greek Levi says to Peter 'wrath is always with you' (το οργιλον παρακειται [22,2]), but the Coptic Levi calls him 'wrathful' (ⲛⲣⲉϥⲛⲟⲩϭⲥ [18,7–8]). Although the meanings are similar, the Coptic puts Peter in line with an evil cosmic power that the soul must overcome called 'the Wisdom [of the] Wrathful One' (ⲧⲥⲟⲫⲓⲁ [ⲛ̄]ⲣⲉϥⲛⲟⲩϭⲥ [16,11–12]).[107]

The gulf between Mary and the male disciples is further reinforced by Levi in the Coptic reading:

ⲡⲁⲛⲧⲱ`ⲥ´ ⲉⲣⲉⲡⲥⲱⲧⲏⲣ ⲥⲟⲟⲩⲛ ⲙ̄ⲙⲟⲥ ⲁⲥⲫⲁⲗⲱⲥ ⲉⲧⲃⲉ ⲡⲁï ⲁϥⲟⲩⲟϣⲥ̄ ⲛ̄ϩⲟⲩⲟ ⲉⲣⲟⲛ (18,13–15)

Surely the Saviour knew her infallibly, and therefore he loved her *more than us*.

παντως γαρ εκεινος ειδως αυτην ασφ[αλ]ω[ς] ηγαπησεν (PRyl. GM 22,6–8)

For surely he, knowing her i[n]fallib[ly], loved (her).

Although both versions confess that the Saviour loved Mary, the Coptic emphasizes her exalted status by adding 'more than us' (ⲛ̄ϩⲟⲩⲟ ⲉⲣⲟⲛ).[108] The comparative widens the gap between Mary and the male disciples and fits with the harsher language used by the Coptic Levi to Peter, discussed in the last example. The Coptic Mary's exalted status is always at the expense of Peter. In the Greek manuscripts, the disciples are on a more level playing field.

[107] *Contra* Tuckett and Hartenstein who regard any polemic against Peter as mild, if present at all, Tuckett, *Mary*, e.g. 197, 203; Hartenstein, *Die zweite Lehre*, 133–4. Hartenstein refers to Peter and Levi as having a common basis in both accepting the Saviour as authoritative. Tuckett regards το οργιλον παρακειται//ⲛⲣⲉϥⲛⲟⲩϭⲥ as 'less an accusation *against* Peter as an indirect apology *for* Peter, excusing his behaviour: Peter's accusation is simply due to his impetuosity, and may not reflect his more measured thought', 202 (italics original).

[108] It has been debated whether the comparative was original. Marjanen suggests a Greek original that read along the lines of ἠγάπησεν μᾶλλον αὐτὴν ἢ ἡμᾶς. The scribe

The Last Words of Levi

Levi's speech becomes the final spoken words in the gospel. As Mary presumably continues to weep silently, Levi reminds them all of the Saviour's instructions.[109]

> ⲙⲁⲗⲗⲟⲛ ⲙⲁⲣⲛ̄ϣⲓⲡⲉ ⲛ̄ⲧⲛ̄ϯ ϩⲓ̈ⲱⲱⲛ ⲙⲡⲣⲱⲙⲉ ⲛⲧⲉⲗⲓⲟⲥ ⲛ̣ⲧⲛ̣̄ϫⲡⲟ̣ϥ ⲛ̣ⲁ̣ⲛ̣ ⲕ̣ⲁ̣ⲧⲁ ⲑ̣ⲉ ⲛ̄ⲧ̣ⲁϥϩⲱⲛ ⲉⲧⲟⲟⲧⲛ̄ ⲛ̄ⲧⲛ̄ⲧⲁϣⲉⲟⲉⲓϣ ⲙⲡⲉⲩⲁⲅⲅⲉⲗⲓⲟⲛ ⲉⲛⲕⲱ ⲁⲛ ⲉϩⲣⲁⲓ̈ ⲛⲕⲉϩⲟⲣⲟⲥ ⲟⲩⲇⲉ ⲕⲉⲛⲟⲙⲟⲥ̣ ⲡⲁⲣⲁ ⲡⲉⲛⲧⲁⲡⲥ̅ⲱ̅ⲣ̅ ϫⲟⲟϥ (18,15–21)
>
> Rather, let us be ashamed and put on the Perfect Man and acquire him for ourselves as he commanded us and preach the gospel, not laying down other rules or another la[w] beyond what the Saviour told us.
>
> μαλλ[ο]ν αι̣σχυ[ν]θ̣ω̣[με]ν και ενδυσαμενο̣[ι] τον τ̣[ελειο]ν α̅ν̅ο̅ν̅ εκεινο το προστα<χ>θ[εν η]μειν π[ο]ι̣ησωμεν κηρυσ{ε}σ̣[ειν το] ευαγγ[ε]λ̣ιον μηδεν ο[ρ]ι̣ζον τ̣[ες μ]ηδε νομ̣οθε̣τ[ο]υντ̣ες ως ειπ̣[εν ο] σ̣ωτηρ (PRyl.GM 22,8–14)
>
> Rath[e]r, l[et] us be as[h]amed and having put on the P[erfect] Man; let [u]s do what was comm[an]ded of us, to pre[ach the] gos[p]el, la[yi]ng down nothing [n]or law-making, as [the] Saviour sai[d].

Here Levi is paraphrasing what Jesus said in his farewell discourse: (1) put on the Perfect Man and (2) acquire him = (1) Son of Man is within and (2) follow, seek and find him. Secondly, preaching the gospel and not laying down any rules unmistakeably reflect the Saviour's FD. Furthermore, Levi emphasizes that he is referring to

of PRyl.GM missed a few words between two instances of μᾶλλον (one in Marjanen's reconstructed clause and the μᾶλλον following ἠγάπησεν in PRyl.GM), Marjanen, *The Woman Jesus Loved*, 116. Tuckett agrees, as (1) 'why would a later scribe add such a harsh comment?', and (2) the comparative phrase 'provides a striking, if somewhat ironic, twist by Levi to Peter's earlier words that Mary was loved by the Saviour more than the other women', Tuckett, *Mary*, 129.

[109] Tuckett emphasizes this point: 'Further, it may or may not be significant that, in the sequel, the main response to Peter's (and derivatively Andrew's) charges against Mary does not come from Mary herself but from Levi (though Mary does make an initial response at 18.2–5). At one level, of course, Mary is simply adopting the role expected of a woman at the time in being silent. Yet this is somewhat at odds with the earlier part of the gospel where Mary has been far from passive or silent! All this may suggest, though, at least negatively, that Mary's "character" is not quite as perfect as some have suggested: she too can display the weaknesses which the other disciples showed earlier. However positive the picture of Mary in the gospel is in general terms, there are also features that are not quite so positive!', Tuckett, *Mary*, 189–90.

Jesus' earlier words by saying 'as he commanded us' (ⲕ̣ⲁⲧⲁ ⲑ̣ⲉ ⲛ̄ⲧ̣ⲁϥ ϩⲱⲛ ⲉⲧⲟⲟⲧⲛ̄ [18,17]) and 'beyond what the Saviour told us' (ⲡⲁⲣⲁ ⲡⲉⲛⲧⲁⲡ̄ⲥ̄ⲱ̄ⲣ̄ ϫⲟⲟϥ [18,21]).[110]

The Ambiguous Finale

The conclusion of the narrative is perhaps the extant Gospel of Mary's greatest mystery. The variation between the Greek and Coptic MSS alters the whole gospel. Although the Rylands MS is fragmentary, it is unlikely that it read anything different from:

> [ταυ]τα ειπ̣ων ο Λε̣υ̣[εις μεν απελθων] ηρ̣χεν κη̣[ρυσσειν] (PRyl. GM 22,14–16)
>
> When he had said [the]se things Levi dep[arted] and he began to pr[each.]

Despite the lacunae, the extant singular verb ἤρχεν matches ὁ Λευείς, and so it is safe to assume that Levi alone departs and preaches. The Coptic, on the other hand, reads:

> [ⲛ̄ⲧⲉⲣⲉ ± 8]ⲁ̈ï ⲁⲩⲱ ⲁⲩⲣ̄ⲁⲣⲭⲉⲓ ⲛ̄ⲃⲱⲕ [ⲉⲧⲣⲉⲩⲧ]ⲁⲙⲟ ⲛ̄ⲥⲉⲧⲁϣⲉⲟⲉⲓϣ (18,21–19,2)
>
> [When ± 8], and *they* began to depart [to tea]ch and preach.

The plural ⲁⲩⲣ̄ⲁⲣⲭⲉⲓ ('they began') agrees with ⲛ̄ⲥⲉⲧⲁϣⲉⲟⲉⲓϣ ('and they to preach') and so the plural is unquestionable. However, it is unclear who 'they' are. Do Peter and Andrew follow Levi in listening to Mary and putting on the Perfect Man, and then proclaim the gospel? Or are Peter and Andrew left behind as Mary and Levi go out to preach? As has been argued, the Coptic text strengthens

[110] King, Lührmann and Tuckett suggest that the use of ὡς in Greek and ⲡⲁⲣⲁ in Coptic changes the meaning of the text. In the Coptic, the disciples must not lay down any rules *beyond* what the Saviour said, whereas the Greek reads *as* the Saviour said. King and Lührmann see the Coptic as softening the command, King, 'Gospel of Mary Magdalene', 617; Lührmann, *Die apokryph gewordenen Evangelien*, 119. Tuckett suggests that the Coptic is a 'somewhat over-literalistic, secondary attempt to tie Levi's words together with Jesus', Tuckett, *Mary*, 131. But in his FD, Jesus tells the disciples not to lay down rules '*beyond* what I appointed to you' (ⲡⲁⲣⲁ ⲡⲉⲛⲧⲁïⲧⲟϣϥ̄ ⲛⲏⲧⲛ̄ [9,1–2]) *and* not to give a law '*like* the Lawgiver' (ⲛ̄ⲑⲉ ⲙⲡⲛⲟⲙⲟⲑⲉⲧⲏⲥ [9,3]). Therefore, either 'beyond' or 'as' can refer back to the Saviour's speech. I see the difference between the meanings in the Greek and Coptic versions of Levi's instruction as relatively insignificant (both refer back to Jesus) and unlikely to be the result of active interpretation by a translator/scribe.

animosity between the disciples, but does it here imply a reconciliation or rule it out altogether?

The Gospel of Mary interpreters are undecided which way to read it. Marjanen suggests that, due to the tense tone of Levi's final speech, the Coptic is a 'cumbersome correction' of the Greek intended to include Mary alone.[111] Tuckett writes of being left in a 'textual limbo' over whether the breach is healed.[112] If Levi and Mary do not get through to Peter and Andrew, the purpose of the gospel is transformed. A lack of reconciliation would ensure that, despite friendship prior to Mary's revelation, there is continued polemic against other Christians. Those Christians that Peter and Andrew represent will not accept the higher teachings of the heavenly soul. It would also warn against certain, possibly Petrine traditions, that deny private revelation and belittle female authority.

The Greek text certainly undermines Mary's authority – she does not teach. Perkins doubts whether Mary ever received the Saviour's command to preach:

> Although the narrative elements in *Gospel of Mary* depict her as the first to attain gnosis, she is not a recipient of the commission to preach the gospel to the nations. *Gospel of Mary* evidently understands the narrative accounts in which the risen Jesus sends his followers out to preach to refer only to the male disciples.[113]

Tuckett also raises this question:

> [T]he exhortation to preach is given earlier in the gospel to the male disciples, before Mary appears on the scene (8.21–2, before 9.12). Thus it is by no means clear that Mary is ever envisaged as an active preacher of the gospel at all.[114]

The idea that Mary was not an intended recipient of the commission, as well as being implied by the ending of the Rylands fragment, is supported by her paraclete-type role. Mary rises as Jesus departs,

[111] Marjanen, *The Woman Jesus Loved*, 119.

[112] Tuckett, *Mary*, 193.

[113] Pheme Perkins, *Gnosticism and the New Testament* (Minneapolis, MN: Fortress Press, 1993), 183.

[114] He continues: 'Mary is thus not necessarily presented as the archetypal, or ideal, preacher of the gospel. Rather, she is presented more as the reliable guarantor of (at least part of) the *content* of the gospel, as the recipient of the revelation, which perhaps *others* (Levi and perhaps other male followers) go and preach,' Tuckett, *Mary*, 198 (italics original). Tuckett wonders whether the text is similar to Mark's shorter ending, with the women being silent in fear (194 n. 216).

and it is because of Jesus' departure that Mary rises. Therefore, although she may have been in the group of disciples for Jesus' dialogue, she does not play an active role, and the commission was not aimed at her.

The possibility that 'they' in the Coptic text did not include Mary is supported by Mary's own words to her brothers. When they weep over the idea of mission-related persecution, Mary says:

> ⲙⲡⲣ̅ⲣⲓⲙⲉ ⲁⲩⲱ ⲙⲡ̅ⲣ̅ⲣ̅ⲗⲩⲡⲉⲓ ⲟⲩⲇⲉ ⲙ̅ⲡ̅ⲣ̅ⲣ̅ ϩⲏ̣ⲧ ⲥⲛⲁⲩ ⲧⲉϥⲭⲁⲣⲓⲥ ⲅⲁⲣ ⲛⲁϣⲱⲡⲉ ⲛⲙ̅ⲙⲏⲧⲛ̅ ⲧⲏⲣ<ⲧ>ⲛ̣ ⲁⲩⲱ ⲛⲥⲣ̅ⲥⲕⲉⲡⲁⲍⲉ ⲙⲙⲱⲧⲛ̅ ⲙⲁⲗⲗⲟⲛ ⲇⲉ ⲙⲁⲣⲛ̅ⲥⲙⲟⲩ ⲉⲧⲉϥⲙⲛ̅ⲧⲛⲟϭ ϫⲉ ⲁϥⲥⲃ̅ⲧⲱⲧⲛ̅ ⲁϥⲁⲁⲛ ⲛ̅ⲣⲱⲙⲉ (9,14–20)[115]
>
> Do not weep, and do not grieve, and do not doubt! For his grace will be with you all and will protect you. Rather let us give thanks for his greatness, for he has prepared us; he has made us Men.

Mary does not say that Jesus' grace will be with *us* and protect *us*. Yet the first person plural is acceptable when she refers to giving thanks and to making the disciples (perfect) Men.[116] Mary, despite her gender, can become a Perfect Man (in fact, she already has), but she may not be a member of the preaching mission. This passage need not mean much on its own, but the Pistis Sophia provides a similar impression of these gender politics. In the Pistis Sophia, Mary plays an active role (perhaps the most active of all the disciples), relentlessly questioning Jesus to the point that he tells her she must allow the others to ask questions too (4.146 [377,16–17]). She is continually called blessed. But at one point she says:

> ⲡⲁϫⲟⲉⲓⲥ · ⲙ̅ⲡ̅ⲣ̅ϭ̅ⲱ̅ⲛ̅ⲧ̅ ⲉⲣⲟⲓ̈ ⲉⲓ̈ϣⲓⲛⲉ ⲙ̅ⲙⲟⲕ ⲉⲃⲟⲗ ϫⲉ ⲁⲓ̈ⲉⲛⲱⲭⲗⲉⲓ ⲛⲁⲕ ⲛ̅ⲟⲩⲙⲏⲏϣⲉ ⲛ̅ⲥⲟⲡ · ⲧⲉⲛⲟⲩ ϭⲉ ⲡⲁϫⲟⲉⲓⲥ ⲙ̅ⲡ̅ⲣ̅ϭ̅ⲱ̅ⲛ̅ⲧ̅ ⲉⲣⲟⲓ̈ ⲉⲓ̈ϣⲓⲛⲉ ⲛ̅ⲥⲁ ϩⲱⲃ ⲛⲓⲙ ϩⲛ̅ ⲟⲩⲱⲣ̅ϫ̅ ⲙ̅ⲛ̅ ⲟⲩⲁⲥⲫⲁⲗⲓⲁ ϫⲉ ⲉⲣⲉ ⲛⲁⲥⲛⲏⲩ ⲕⲏⲣⲩⲥⲥⲉ ⲙ̅ⲙⲟⲟⲩ ϩ̅ⲙ̅ ⲡⲅⲉⲛⲟⲥ ⲛ̅ⲧⲉ ⲧⲙ̅ⲛ̅ⲧ̅ⲣⲱⲙⲉ (2.88 [201,10–14])
>
> My Lord, be not angry with me that I question you because I have troubled you many times. Now my Lord, be not angry with me that I question all things with assurance and certainty, because *my brothers* preach them among the nations of humankind.

[115] For the reading ⲧⲏⲣ<ⲧ>ⲛ̣, see Appendix B.
[116] POxy.GM is not helpful here as these lines are so fragmentary.

In Chapter 2, we saw examples from the Epistula Apostolorum and the Epistle of Peter to Philip in which male disciples persistently question the Lord so as to be equipped for mission. In the Pistis Sophia, Mary persistently questions the Lord because *her brothers* preach. She does not say because 'we' preach. There is no explanation of this, which perhaps suggests that it is just a given that women do not preach.

Levi preaching alone in PRyl.GM means that Peter and Andrew do not. Tuckett argues that the Greek Gospel of Mary does not imply polemic against Peter: '[T]he Greek text simply implies that, at this point, Levi goes out to preach: it may imply that, at this time, Peter does not – but that in no way excludes the possibility that Peter goes out to preach later!'[117] This seems unlikely. If Peter was to preach, having listened to Levi and accepted Mary's authority, the text would probably state it. In the Greek text, the final point about Peter likens him to the ἀντικείμενος/ἀντικειμένοι – this surely points to polemic.

It seems more likely, then, that the Coptic text, by continually portraying heightened antagonism between Peter/Andrew and Mary/Levi, allows for a greater reconciliation between the two groups (a reconciliation that would not be as potent had the disciples been less averse to each other, as in the Greek MSS). Just as Andrew in the Pistis Sophia comes to realize that the ascent of the soul is correct doctrine, the Coptic Peter and Andrew most likely accept Levi's instructions in the Gospel of Mary – especially as they are just rehashing the Saviour's words. Whether Mary preaches or not is unclear, but, in light of the Pistis Sophia, possibly not.

3.5 Conclusion

The Gospel of Mary cannot easily be divided into dialogue and narrative frame; the two eschatological dialogues are integrally connected to the narrative that surrounds it. And much of this narrative frame encompasses its own dialogues. Within the 'narrative frame', I have included the Saviour's farewell discourse, Mary's paraclete moment, her downfall at the hands of Peter and Andrew, the final instructions from Levi, and the disciple(s) leaving to preach. I have also suggested that a narrative setting opened the gospel. Most of these sections include dialogue between the disciples themselves, whether it be comforting conversation or argument.

[117] Tuckett, *Mary*, 194.

The narrative frame tells us a lot about the message of the Gospel of Mary. It most likely began with an explicit post-resurrection setting, and the opening dialogue is set on the eve of Jesus' final departure. The disciples are going to be left alone; their Saviour is leaving them forever. In the farewell discourse, Jesus prepares them for this, giving them instructions for the individual and for the community.

Jesus' departure then brings Mary to the forefront, in a Johannine paraclete-type role. She comforts the male disciples and teaches them about their salvation. I have argued that the way she is portrayed in relation to the male disciples has different nuances in the Greek and Coptic versions of the gospel. The Coptic signifies a greater sense of antagonism between Mary and Peter/Andrew: in the Greek, Jesus has knitted his disciples into one community, whereas in the Coptic, Mary does not kiss her heretical brothers. The breach between them is dramatized after Mary's account of the ascending soul, in both Greek and Coptic, with accusations of heresy, secrecy and ill will. It may be resolved when Levi reminds them of Jesus' instructions before he departed, and this may or may not bring reconciliation to the group.

The surrounding narrative sets the scene for the two main dialogues: the Saviour and his disciples and Mary's account of her vision of the Lord. Both are eschatological in nature, the first concerned with cosmic eschatology, and the second with personal salvation.

4

THE COSMOS AND ITS UNDOING

The Cosmic Eschatology of the Gospel of Mary

At the beginning of the extant gospel, a disciple asks the Saviour whether matter will be destroyed. The Saviour replies that every nature, form and creature, created from matter, will be dissolved to its root. As discussed briefly in Chapter 1, the texts within the dialogue gospel genre have divergent views on cosmic eschatology. Although some dialogue gospels do not appear to be particularly interested in the end of the world, the idea lies in the background that the cosmos is perishable (Sophia of Jesus Christ, Gospel of Judas) and/or that all things will return to their origins (Apocryphon of John). Others conceive of apocalyptic signs, the parousia and judgement at the end of age (Apocalypse of Peter, Epistula Apostolorum). In the Pistis Sophia, cosmic and individual eschatology converge, as all souls will ascend to the heavens at the end of the age, when the cosmos dissolves. On the whole, the destruction or dissolution of the world is secondary to human salvation in dialogue gospels, but they still reflect the fact that the end of the world is a significant theme in early Christianity.[1] On this topic, the Gospel of Mary finds significant dialogue partners in the Gospel of Thomas and the canonical gospels.

In this chapter, I will attempt to show that the cosmology of the Gospel of Mary is simpler and more christocentric than has been assumed by past exegetes. The heavens and the earth are formed from matter. This material cosmos will be restored to its origins, or its constituent parts, through dissolution. The text is broken and convoluted, and it is not clear what will be dissolved, why it will be dissolved, or how it will be dissolved. These questions will be addressed in two stages. Firstly, the cosmological question of how matter is understood in relation to forms and creatures, which in turn asks how to understand the Gospel of Mary's vocabulary of 'nature', 'passion',

[1] For the argument that the 'end of the world' is significant in early Christian eschatology, see Edward Adams, *The Stars Will Fall from Heaven: Cosmic Catastrophe in the New Testament and Its World*, LNTS 347 (London and New York: T&T Clark, 2007).

'sin' and 'death'. Secondly, the question of how to understand the role of Christ in relation to 'the Good' and the Son of Man. It will be shown how the Gospel of Mary's cosmic eschatology fits within the wider Christian landscape, arguing that matter is the raw material of the cosmos, which will be dissolved at the hand of Christ.

4.1 The Cosmos and the Dissolution of the Cosmos

Matter as the Raw Material of the Cosmos

The extant gospel begins with an eschatological question and reply, followed by a short discourse on sin (7,9–16) and then a further explanation regarding cosmic eschatology:

(Q1) ϩ̣[ⲩ]ⲗ̣ⲏ ϭⲉ ⲛⲁⲟⲩⲱ̣[ϭ]ⲡ̣ ϫⲛ ⲙ̣ⲙⲟⲛ (7,1–2)
then will m[a]tter be dest[r]oyed or not?

(A1) ⲫⲩⲥⲓⲥ ⲛⲓⲙ ⲡⲗⲁⲥⲙⲁ ⲛⲓⲙ ⲕⲧⲓⲥⲓⲥ ⲛⲓⲙ ⲉⲩϣⲟⲡ ϩⲛ̄ ⲛⲉⲩⲉⲣⲏⲩ {ⲙ}ⲛⲙ̄ⲙⲁⲩ ⲁⲩⲱ ⲟⲛ ⲉⲩⲛⲁⲃⲱⲗ ⲉⲃⲟⲗ ⲉⲧⲟⲩⲛⲟⲩⲛⲉ ⲙ̄ⲙⲓⲛ ⲙⲙⲟⲟⲩ ϫⲉ ⲧⲉⲫⲩⲥⲓⲥ ⲛⲑⲩⲗⲏ ⲉⲥⲃⲱⲗ ⲉⲃⲟⲗ ⲉⲛ̣ⲁ ⲧⲉⲥⲫⲩⲥⲓⲥ ⲟⲩⲁⲁⲥ (7,3–8)
Every nature, every form, every creature exist in (and) with each other and will be dissolved again to their own root; for the nature of matter is to dissolve to the elements (of) its nature alone.

(A2) ⲉⲧⲃⲉ ⲡⲁï ⲁϥⲉⲓ ⲛ̄ϭⲓ ⲡⲁⲅⲁⲑ̣ⲟ̣(ⲛ) ϩⲛ ⲧⲉⲧⲙ̄ⲙⲏⲧⲉ ϣⲁ ⲛⲁ ⲫⲩⲥⲓⲥ ⲛⲓⲙ ⲉϥⲛⲁⲕⲁⲑⲓⲥⲧⲁ ⲙⲙⲟⲥ ⲉϩⲟ̣ⲩ(ⲛ) ⲉⲧⲉⲥⲛⲟⲩⲛⲉ (7,17–20)
This is why the Good came into your midst to the things of every nature, so as to restore it inward to its root.

Q1 contains the end of a question regarding the fate of 'matter'.[2] We do not know who asked the question, what it followed or what the context was – although, as discussed in the previous chapter, it is likely to be the penultimate question from a list of many, posed by one or more of the disciples looking for clear information from the

[2] Martin argues against the translation of ὕλη as 'matter' due to the varying meanings in ancient philosophies that depart from our modern one. See Dale Martin, *The Corinthian Body* (New Haven, CT and London: Yale University Press, 1995), 6–10. For the Gospel of Mary, this is made even more complicated as we are dealing with the Coptic article and noun ϩⲩⲗⲏ, which is also heavily reconstructed at 7,1. However, as ⲑⲩⲗⲏ appears again in A1 we can assume that it is the same term in Q1. Although I will translate this term as 'matter', we must be aware that our modern definition of the term is not the same as in the ancient world.

Saviour following his resurrection. Q1 is followed by a reply directly from the Saviour (A1) regarding the current make-up and future dissolution of nature, form and creature. The Saviour explains that nature, form and creature are currently constructed from matter, but matter will be dissolved to its own root. A2 follows a teaching on the nature of sin (called adultery) and reinforces A1 regarding the dissolution of matter. However, A2 takes A1 further: A1 appears to be concerned with the natural dissolution of created matter, but A2 explains that the dissolution is dependent upon the 'Good'.

To understand the text's eschatology, we must first make sense of its cosmology.[3] The primary question is: what will be dissolved? There are several caveats to bear in mind when working with the first pages of the Berlin Codex, such as the previous missing text, reconstructed words such as ⲁ̣[ⲡ]ⲉ̣ (8,2), the possibility that the meaning behind the Graeco-Coptic vocabulary such as ⲫⲩⲥⲓⲥ, ⲡⲁⲑⲟⲥ and ϩⲩⲗⲏ is not the same as that of their Greek forerunners,[4] and that the text probably contains ideas that the author considered self-evident, particularly those that we might regard as Platonic or Stoic. By the second century, philosophical schools of thought frequently borrowed from each other,[5] and Stoic terms and ideas in particular were used without knowledge of their provenance.[6] Nonetheless,

[3] We might propose that a cosmogonic narrative was included in the preceding dialogue in the Gospel of Mary; however, this would be based on little substantial evidence. Tuckett mentions that the origin of the universe was of concern to other 'gnostic' writers; Tuckett, *Mary*, 138–9. However, the cosmogonies of dialogue gospels are varied, and so it is difficult to apply them to the Gospel of Mary.

[4] Although here φύσις, πάθος, and ὕλη may be on safe ground as these terms are so commonly used that the meanings remained largely the same through the language transmission.

[5] For modern readers, the extant cosmological motifs, including the intentions, principles and nuances, do not fit into any established typology, and we must be vigilant against the scholarly tendency to start labelling ideas 'Platonic' or 'Stoic' at every opportunity. Platonism and Stoicism did influence early Christianity, however; see the following two collections of essays: Tuomas Rasimus, Troels Engberg-Pedersen, and Ismo Dunderberg, eds., *Stoicism in Early Christianity* (Grand Rapids, MI: Baker Academic, 2010); Kevin Corrigan and Tuomas Rasimus, eds., *Gnosticism, Platonism and the Late Ancient World: Essays in Honour of John D. Turner*, NHMS 82 (Leiden and Boston: Brill, 2013). It must also be mentioned that, just because a text has a Graeco-Roman background, that does not exclude overlap with Jewish thought. For example, Adams highlights similar ideas between Jewish, Epicurean and Stoic eschatological views, Adams, *Stars Will Fall from Heaven*, 127–9. In terms of eschatology and the afterlife, however, there is no typical 'Jewish' view, but a plurality of beliefs existed side by side; see Outi Lehtipuu, *The Afterlife Imagery in Luke's Story of the Rich Man and Lazarus*, NovTSup 123 (Leiden and Boston: Brill, 2007), 119–54.

[6] See John M. Dillon, *The Middle Platonists, 80 B.C. to A.D. 220*, Revised (New York: Cornell University Press, 1996), xiv–xv.

as we shall see, the Gospel of Mary shares much in common with certain Platonic concepts, interpreted christologically.

With this in mind, we must attempt to answer what it is that Jesus says will be dissolved. In his first answer (A1), he tells his disciples that nature, form, creature and matter will be dissolved, but he does not explain what these constructs mean or how they relate to each other. It is probably presupposed that the language of nature, form and creature is to be understood as the material things, moulded from matter. Matter as the raw material from which God forms the cosmos is common to early Christian and philosophical thinking. Platonists, Stoics, and Jewish and early Christian interpreters of Genesis hold disparate versions of the theory that a divine or celestial force formed passive matter into created order. Genesis 1.2 LXX speaks of an invisible and unformed earth (ἡ δὲ γῆ ἦν ἀόρατος καὶ ἀκατασκεύαστος), subsequently shaped by God.[7] Plato understands matter as the quality-less material from which the cosmos is created by a 'demiurge' or divine craftsman (*Tim.* 51a),[8] and the Stoics see matter as an unqualified substance (τὴν ἄποιον οὐσίαν) that is acted upon by God (Diogenes Laertius, *Vit. Phil.* 7.134).

These concepts permeated the minds of early Christian thinkers (and not just those that profess a demiurge-creator).[9] Justin understood God to have created all things 'from formless matter' (ἐξ ἀμόρφου ὕλης [*1 Apol.* 10]), and Tatian wrote that 'the whole construction and creation of the world has derived from matter (ἐξ ὕλης) and that matter has itself been produced by God … so that everything has a common origin' (*Or. Graec.* 12.22–29). Theophilus understood God as creating amorphous matter and then giving it form (*ad Autol.* 2.4.10), whereas Irenaeus' God creates and shapes matter in a single act (*Adv. Haer.* 2.28.7). It is likely that Valentinus regarded God as creating the world from pre-existent matter,[10] and,

[7] Ἀκατασκεύαστος, as 'an antonym of the verb κατασκεύαζω (to construct), implies an unconstructed state and is thus an apt description of the earth before God speaks its elements into existence', Susan Brayford, *Genesis*, Septuagint Commentary Series (Leiden and Boston: Brill, 2007), 207.

[8] Plato does not actually speak of 'formless matter' but of the formless state of creation. Matter is the mother and receptacle of Form: 'an invisible, formless receptacle of everything' (*Tim.* 51a).

[9] By 'demiurge' I mean a lesser deity than the highest God. The term can also refer to the highest God, as in *1 Clem.* 20.11 and Justin, *1 Apol.* 8.2; see Lampe, *Patristic Greek Lexicon*, 342b.

[10] This is based on Dunderberg's argument that the heterodox Christian in Methodius' *On Free Will* represents the doctrine of Valentinus (which differed considerably from later Valentinians), as the author of the *Dialogue on the True Faith in God* claimed. See Ismo Dunderberg, *Beyond Gnosticism: Myth, Lifestyle, and Society in the School of Valentinus* (New York: Columbia University Press, 2008), esp. 67–74.

according to Irenaeus, Valentinus' followers taught that the demiurge created psychic and hylic things by bringing order to chaotic matter that the Saviour created from Wisdom's emotions (*Adv. Haer.* 1.4.5; 1.5.2). The Jesus of the Pistis Sophia tells Andrew about the angels, archangels, God, archons and other cosmic bodies, and discloses: 'You are all (existing) with one another out of one dough and one matter and one substance. And you are all out of the same mixture' (ⲛ̄ⲧⲉⲧⲛ̄ϩⲉⲛⲉⲃⲟⲗ ⲧⲏⲣⲧⲛ̄ ϩⲛ̄ ⲛⲉⲧⲛ̄ⲉⲣⲏⲩ ϩⲙ̄ ⲡⲓⲟⲩⲱϣⲙ̄ ⲛ̄ⲟⲩⲱⲧ ⲙⲛ̄ ϯϩⲩⲗⲏ ⲛ̄ⲟⲩⲱⲧ · ⲙⲛ̄ ϯⲟⲩⲥⲓⲁ ⲛ̄ⲟⲩⲱⲧ: ⲁⲩⲱ ⲛ̄ⲧⲉⲧⲛ̄ϩⲉⲛⲉⲃⲟⲗ ϩⲙ̄ ⲡⲓⲕⲉⲣⲁⲥⲙⲟⲥ ⲛ̄ⲟⲩⲱⲧ ⲧⲏⲣⲧⲛ̄ [2.100 (249,1–4)]).[11] For all their differences, these writers are united in the belief that creation came into being by the imposition of form on unformed matter.[12]

The Gospel of Mary's terminology of nature, form and creature is preceded in Paul, who can use κτίσις for all of creation (e.g. Rom 8.18–23) and πλάσμα to mean 'the thing formed' (Rom 9.20).[13] In the Patristic era, φύσις came to take on a multitude of meanings, including the substance of created things.[14] The Gospel of Mary's notion that matter had been shaped into every nature, creature and form (also referred to as the earthly and heavenly things [15,19–16,1]) was evidently shared among contemporary Christian thinkers.

It is this moulded matter that forms the 'cosmos' or 'world' (ⲕⲟⲥⲙⲟⲥ), and it is the 'world' from which the personified soul becomes free during her eschatological heavenly ascent. During the soul's journey, she says:

> \`ϩ̣ⲛ̄′ ⲟ̣ⲩ[ⲕⲟⲥⲙ]ⲟⲥ ⲛ̄ⲧⲁⲩⲃⲟⲗⲧ′ ⲉⲃⲟⲗ ϩⲛ̄ⲛ ⲟⲩⲕⲟⲥⲙⲟⲥ [ⲁⲩ]ⲱ ϩⲛ̄ ⲟⲩⲧⲩⲡⲟⲥ ⲉⲃⲟⲗ ϩⲛ ⲟⲩⲧⲩⲡⲟⲥ ⲉⲧⲙ̄ⲡⲥⲁ ⲛⲧⲡⲉ (16,21–17,3)
>
> In a [wor]ld I was dissolved from a world, [an]d in a type from a type which is above.

[11] Dough, matter and substance appear to be synonyms in the Pistis Sophia, as nature, form and creature are in the Gospel of Mary.

[12] On the origins of the concept of *creatio ex nihilo*, see Gerhard May, *Creatio ex Nihilo: The Doctrine of 'Creation out of Nothing' in Early Christian Thought*, trans. A. S. Worrall (London and New York: T&T Clark, 2004). May writes, 'throughout the second century and the early part of the third the doctrine of the pre-existence of matter was firmly held by philosophically educated Christians', 147. These include Marcion, Athenagoras, Hermogenes and Clement of Alexandria.

[13] For Paul's use of κτίσις, see Edward Adams, *Constructing the World: A Study in Paul's Cosmological Language*, Studies of the New Testament and Its World (Edinburgh: T&T Clark, 2000), esp. 19–20.

[14] Φύσις is often used in a creation context and can refer to incorporeal creation, such as heavenly creatures, or creation generally, or the constitution of things, Lampe, *Patristic Greek Lexicon*, 1496a–1497a.

The Graeco-Coptic term ⲕⲟⲥⲙⲟⲥ is another use of vocabulary found in the doctrines of philosophical schools and Paul. However, the Gospel of Mary's conception of the 'world' diverges from the main tenets of the major philosophical schools. The Presocratics believed that it was not created (as in Heraclitus fr. 30); Plato imagined that it would never be destroyed (*Tim.* 41a–b); the Epicureans believed it would naturally dissolve (*Letter to Pythocles* 88); and the Stoics did not conceive of God and κόσμος as wholly separate entities.[15] The point at which the Gospel of Mary's worldview does converge with the philosophers is that the κόσμος, in its best state, is characterized by order and unity (a shared assumption in the great variety of Greek and Hellenistic cosmological speculation[16]). The Gospel of Mary's cosmos must be dissolved due to the 'disturbance' (ⲧⲁⲣⲁⲭⲏ) that has occurred in the whole 'body' (ⲥⲱⲙⲁ) (8,5–6) – the word often used in Plato for the 'world'. But for the Gospel of Mary, it is due to the *disturbance* that the *created* world will be *dissolved* through the agency of *Christ* (who is a quite separate entity from the world).[17]

The Gospel of Mary's understanding of the term ⲕⲟⲥⲙⲟⲥ comes closer to Paul. In Paul, κόσμος has 'a spectrum of usage from strongly negative at the one end (for the world in its distance from and hostility to God), to highly positive at the other (for the world as God's good creation)', but his 'predominant style of usage is negative'.[18] Paul's negative sense, as found for example in Rom 5.12, is comparable to the use in the Gospel of Mary, which appears to understand the 'world' as a place of sin and death, corrupted by passion. It is from this ⲕⲟⲥⲙⲟⲥ, constructed from matter, that the soul will be freed.

[15] For discussion of the use of κόσμος in these schools, including these references, see Adams, *Constructing the World*, 44–58. For God and the κόσμος in Stoicism in particular, God is seen as the soul of the κόσμος and so in some cases they are considered to be indistinguishable, see Ricardo Salles, ed., *God and Cosmos in Stoicism* (Oxford: Oxford University Press, 2009).

[16] See Adams, *Constructing the World*, 64–5.

[17] There is no need to read a demiurgical creator into the gospel, and if one was intended, the soul might have met it during her heavenly journey. (Paul meets the demiurge in the seventh heaven in the Coptic Apocalypse of Paul 22,23–23,28.) De Boer argues against the possibility of a demiurge in the Gospel of Mary, writing that 'the world is not created by an inferior Demiurge, but is created by God himself through his Nature', de Boer, *Gospel of Mary*, 202. Tuckett, on the other hand, contends that a version of the Sophia and Yaldabaoth myth 'may be among the presuppositions which it [the Gospel of Mary] assumes as a given and from which it then goes on to draw out other implications', Tuckett, *Mary*, 53.

[18] Adams, *Constructing the World*, 241.

The soul is freed not just from the 'world' but from the 'body', and the ⲕⲟⲥⲙⲟⲥ is representative of the individual ⲥⲱⲙⲁ, which will be discussed shortly. The body, made of matter, will dissolve too, when the body is no longer necessary, and the soul ascends to the heavenly realm. As Genesis says, 'you [will] return to the earth from which you were taken; for earth you are, and into the earth you will be taken' (ἀποστρέψαι σε εἰς τὴν γῆν, ἐξ ἧς ἐλήμφθης· ὅτι γῆ εἶ καὶ εἰς γῆν ἀπελεύσῃ [3.19 LXX]).

The Dissolution is Restoration

How, then, does the 'restoration' of every nature in A2 relate to the 'dissolution' of material creation in A1? Pasquier, King and Tuckett feel the pull of dualism at this point, assuming an opposition that differentiates between 'every nature' that will 'dissolve' (ⲃⲱⲗ ⲉⲃⲟⲗ) in A1, and 'every nature' that will be 'restored' (ⲕⲁⲑⲓⲥⲧⲁ) in A2. Due to the phrase 'the nature of matter' (ⲧⲉⲫⲩⲥⲓⲥ ⲛⲑⲩⲗⲏ), they understand the first 'nature' (to be dissolved) as belonging to the lower material realm and the second 'nature' (to be restored) as part of the superior, spiritual realm. Pasquier sees the second 'nature' as 'the antithesis of the first',[19] and Tuckett agrees, writing that 'confusingly the Coptic text uses the same word ⲫⲩⲥⲓⲥ ("nature") for both'.[20] King does not make this point quite so explicitly but alludes to it, stating that 'the "root" of perishable matter is contrasted with the proper "root" of a person's true spiritual nature which the Good will establish'.[21] The material nature is dissolved and so destroyed, whereas the heavenly nature is restored to its root.[22]

However, reading the *two uses* of the terms 'nature' and 'root' as representing *two natures* and *two roots* is also confusing – and unnecessary. De Boer argues that the two uses of 'nature' can mean the same thing, proposing a Stoic reading (in the sense that Stoic philosophy can help clarify the text's meaning, not that the text is

[19] Pasquier, 'L'eschatologie dans l'Évangile selon Marie', 393.

[20] Tuckett, *Mary*, 142.

[21] King, *Mary*, 51 (see also 45–46, 50). Also, Till, *Papyrus Berolinensis 8502*, 27; Tardieu, *Écrits Gnostiques*, 226.

[22] The addition of ⲛ̄ⲙⲓⲛ ⲙⲙⲟⲟⲩ ('their own', 7,6) might support their point, but both uses of ⲛⲟⲩⲛⲉ ('root') have a singular possessive article, and so the 'united' root of the 'heavenly nature' to which Pasquier appeals is unconvincing, Pasquier, 'L'eschatologie dans l'Évangile selon Marie', 391–2; cf. de Boer, 'A Stoic Reading of the Gospel of Mary: The Meaning of 'Matter' and 'Nature' in the Gospel of Mary 7.1–8.11', in *Stoicism in Early Christianity*, ed. Tuomas Rasimus, Troels Engberg-Pedersen and Ismo Dunderberg (Grand Rapids, MI: Baker Academic, 2010), 203.

Stoic), arguing that matter and nature are intertwined rather than contrasted. She argues that 'ϕγcιc ΝΙΜ in GosMar 7.3–4 as well as in 7.18–19 refers to all natural phenomena (all Nature) as an appearance of the Divine'.[23] This interpretation is much closer to my own – that matter is the raw material acted upon by God (which the Stoics would call 'nature').[24]

For the Gospel of Mary, it is easier and clearer to understand the repeated terms 'every nature' and 'root' in A1 and A2 as referring to the same thing and thus the same action. 'Every nature' (A2) is simply a terse way of referring to 'Every nature, every form, every creature', which exist together as the created heavens and earth. Nature, form and creature are not different from matter: they are created from matter. And at the eschaton, creation will be dissolved – unformed, unbound and returned to its original constituent state, called here its 'root' (ΝΟΥΝΕ). This does not mean that there is no heavenly realm; we will meet the soul's journey home in the next chapter. But it is clear that A2 is not referring to the restoration of the soul, as Andrew and Peter deny ever having heard a teaching like this. And so, both ϕγcιc ΝΙΜ in 7,3–4 and 7,18–19 refer to creation that will be dissolved and thus restored to its origins (roots). The eschatology is also protological. The dissolution is the restoration.

The concept of the dissolution of the cosmos places the Gospel of Mary firmly among other works of early Christian literature.[25] In the Book of Thomas, we read: '(There is) little time until what is visible will dissolve' (ⲚⲞⲨⲔⲞⲨⲒ̈ ⲚⲞⲨⲞⲈⲒϢ ϢⲀⲚⲦⲈϤⲂⲰⲖ ⲈⲂⲞⲖ Ⲛ̄ϬⲒ ⲠⲈⲦⲞⲨⲞⲚϨ ⲈⲂⲞⲖ [141,14–15]). And 2 Peter speaks of the day:

> ἐν ᾗ οἱ οὐρανοὶ ῥοιζηδὸν παρελεύσονται, στοιχεῖα δὲ καυσούμενα λυθήσεται, καὶ γῆ καὶ τὰ ἐν αὐτῇ ἔργα *κατακαήσεται*[26] (2 Pet 3.10)

[23] de Boer, *Gospel of Mary*, 37. Pasquier also notes that the language is dependent on Stoicism, Pasquier, 'L'eschatologie dans l'Évangile selon Marie', 392.

[24] 'In Stoic philosophy, matter is formed by Nature into a harmonious cosmos', de Boer, *Gospel of Mary*, 37.

[25] Ehrman contrasts the eschatology in the Gospel of Mary with the proto-orthodox 'apocalyptic' view in which 'matter will not be destroyed but redeemed when God reasserts his will over the good creation that he made', Bart D. Ehrman, *Peter, Paul, and Mary Magdalene: The Followers of Jesus in History and Legend* (New York: Oxford University Press, 2006), 240.

[26] Κατακαήσεται is a variant but well attested reading, which makes sense in this context whether or not it was the original reading. For the variants (and support of the usual εὑρεθήσεται, as in NA[28]), see Al Wolters, 'Worldview and Textual Criticism in 2 Peter 3:10', *Westminster Theological Journal* 49 (1987): 405–13.

> in which the heavens will pass away with a loud noise, and the elements will be dissolved with fire, and the earth and everything that is done on it will be burned up.

Dissolution of the heavens and the earth (or the visible things) is also a feature of the Synoptics and the Gospel of Thomas. The synoptic language of dissolution is connected to the renewal of all things (Matt 19.28), and the Gospel of Mary gives no indication of a renewal; yet the Gospel of Mary shares an almost identical phrase with the olivet discourse: 'Heaven and earth will pass away' (ὁ οὐρανὸς καὶ ἡ γῆ παρελεύσεται [Matt 24.35 + pars]), and 'all things are dissolving, both the things of the earth and the things of the heav[en]' (ⲉⲩⲃⲱⲗ ⲉⲃⲟⲗ ⲙⲡⲧⲏⲣϥ ⲉⲓⲧⲉ ⲛⲁ ⲡⲕⲁϩ ⲉⲓⲧⲉ ⲛⲁ ⲧⲡ[ⲉ] [15,20–16,1]). This idea appears also in the Gospel of Thomas 11 and 111:

> ⲡⲉϫⲉ ⲓ̅ⲥ̅ ϫⲉ ⲧⲉⲉⲓⲡⲉ ⲛⲁⲣ̄ⲡⲁⲣⲁⲅⲉ ⲁⲩⲱ ⲧⲉⲧⲛ̄ⲧⲡⲉ ⲙ̄ⲙⲟⲥ ⲛⲁⲣ̄ⲡⲁⲣⲁⲅⲉ (GThom 11.1)
>
> Jesus said, 'This heaven will pass away, and the one above it will pass away.'
>
> ⲡⲉϫⲉ ⲓ̅ⲥ̅ ϫⲉ ⲙ̄ⲡⲏⲩⲉ ⲛⲁϭⲱⲗ ⲁⲩⲱ ⲡⲕⲁϩ ⲙ̄ⲡⲉⲧⲛ̄ⲙ̄ⲧⲟ ⲉⲃⲟⲗ ⲁⲩⲱ ⲡⲉⲧⲟⲛϩ ⲉⲃⲟⲗ ϩⲛ̄ ⲡⲉⲧⲟⲛϩ ϥⲛⲁⲛⲁⲩ ⲁⲛ ⲉⲙⲟⲩ (GThom 111.1)
>
> Jesus said, 'The heavens and the earth will roll up in your presence, and he who lives from the Living One will not see death.'

However, the Gospel of Thomas diverges from the Synoptics as its eschatology is cast in protological terms. If we interpret logion 18, which tells us that the 'end' (ϩⲁⲏ) is found in the place of the 'beginning' (ⲁⲣⲭⲏ), in terms of cosmic eschatology, then a protological understanding of the cosmos dissolving to its origins comes to light.[27] We find this also in the Gospel of Mary through the use of the term 'root'.

Protological eschatology does not have to be an oxymoron. It denotes an ending in which things return to their beginnings. Davies argues that salvation in the Gospel of Thomas is found in

[27] In the Gospel of Thomas 18, the disciples ask about 'our end', and the end probably refers to both the cosmic end and the individual end. Gathercole favours the former, DeConick the latter, Simon Gathercole, *The Gospel of Thomas: Introduction and Commentary*, TENT 11 (Leiden and Boston: Brill, 2014), 286–8; April D. DeConick, *The Original Gospel of Thomas in Translation: With a Commentary and New English Translation of the Complete Gospel*, LNTS 287 (London: T&T Clark, 2006), 102.

the original condition of Gen 1.1–2.4, and that humanity should 'restore themselves to the condition of the image of God' and live 'with the rest and immortality proper to the seventh day of creation'.[28] The Gospel of Mary appears to see the original condition as the pre-created state, rather than the pre-fall state as in the Gospel of Thomas, and so it shares more in common with the Apocryphon of John, which reads: 'It is because of you that all things have come into being, and it is to you that all things will return' (ⲉⲧⲃⲏⲧⲕ ⲁⲡⲧⲏⲣϥ ϣⲱⲡⲉ ⲁⲩⲱ ⲉⲣⲉⲡⲧⲏⲣϥ ⲛⲁⲛⲁⲩϩϥ ⲉⲣⲟⲕ [$_{\text{NHC2}}$ 9,7–8]). In the Gospel of Mary, the material cosmos (also called 'all things' [15,20]) will return to the 'root' from which things were created. The broader concept of eschatological dissolution is shared with the Book of Thomas, 2 Peter and the Synoptics, but in the Gospel of Mary it is narrowed into a protological understanding of restoration to an original or past state, as in the Gospel of Thomas and the Apocryphon of John.

The Birth of Passion

The Gospel of Mary sees the need for dissolution as due to a corruption of the cosmos. The world itself is not the original cause of the problem; rather, the world made of matter has been contaminated through the production of passion:

> [ⲁⲑ]ⲩⲗ̣ⲏ̣ ⲭ̣[ⲡ]ⲉ̣ ⲟⲩⲡⲁⲑⲟⲥ ⲉⲙⲛ̄ⲧⲁϥ ⲙⲙⲁⲩ ⲙ̄ⲡⲉⲓⲛⲉ ⲉⲁϥⲉⲓ ⲉⲃⲟⲗ ϩⲛ ⲟⲩⲡⲁⲣⲁⲫⲩⲥⲓⲥ ⲧⲟⲧⲉ ϣⲁⲣⲉⲟⲩⲧⲁⲣⲁⲭⲏ ϣⲱⲡⲉ ϩ̣ⲙ̄ ⲡⲥⲱⲙⲁ ⲧⲏⲣϥ (8,2–10)
>
> [Mat]ter [produc]ed a passion without likeness, which came forth unnaturally. Then a disturbance occurs in the whole body.

While a link between matter and passion is commonplace, the way that it is articulated in the Gospel of Mary appears to point to a myth of origin. Matter's production of passion was unnatural.[29] The language about passion being produced without likeness (ⲉⲓⲛⲉ) was

[28] Stevan Davies, 'The Christology and Protology of the "Gospel of Thomas"', *JBL* 111.4 (1992): 664.

[29] An alternative translation is provided by de Boer: 'Matter [brought forth] passion that, since it proceeds from an opposite nature, has no form. From then on confusion exists in the whole body,' de Boer, *Gospel of Mary*, 41. She imagines that 'a combination of matter and an opposite nature [ⲟⲩⲡⲁⲣⲁⲫⲩⲥⲓⲥ] are responsible' for producing passion, resulting in an unstable cosmos (47). The disciples must thus be freed from 'ⲟⲩⲡⲁⲣⲁⲫⲩⲥⲓⲥ'. Rather than reading ⲟⲩⲡⲁⲣⲁⲫⲩⲥⲓⲥ as a noun, however, we should read the clause adverbially – it is not 'an opposite nature' that the disciples must be freed from, but passions produced unnaturally.

a recognized, albeit complicated, way to depict corrupt creation.[30] In the Apocryphon of John, Sophia wants to bring forth a likeness (ⲉⲓⲛⲉ) of herself (NHC2 9,28–29), but because she does not have the consent of the spirit nor her partner, her offspring is not made in her likeness (10,7–14), and it becomes the evil creator deity.[31] However, the Gospel of Mary appears to have a more neutral view of the material world than the Apocryphon of John, and there is no indication of a Sophia myth or Yaldabaoth, and so the reference here may simply point to the fact that the material world became corrupt and now needs be dissolved. There is no evidence in the Gospel of Mary of an extreme cosmological dualism that regards the created cosmos as inherently evil or as the flawed product of a wicked and ignorant demiurge.[32] It is passion, not matter, that is not made in the likeness of the divine, and thus creates chaos within the otherwise-ordered cosmos.

The negative opinion of passion rather than matter itself makes more sense in the context. In early Christian thought, passions were vices to be controlled. To be under the influence of passions was to suffer. Paul recognizes that living under the influence of fleshly passions and desires is to be living without life (Gal 5.24); and the Paul of Colossians links πάθος to sexual immorality, impurity, desire and evil (Col 3.5, cf. Rom 1.26–27). Along with Paul, the Stoic concept that all passions are vices[33] influenced Clement of Alexandria who read the fight 'not against flesh and blood' in Ephesians 6.12 as

[30] For other interpretations not referenced here, including Clement, Philo, Irenaeus and the Valentinians, see Benjamin H. Dunning, 'What Sort of Thing Is This Luminous Woman? Thinking Sexual Difference in On the Origin of the World', *JECS* 16.1 (2009): 65–73. Clement understands that all of humankind are in the image of God, but not all are in the likeness, as being in the likeness is sharing in the redemption of Christ (being 'Christ-like'), see Eric Osborn, *Clement of Alexandria* (Cambridge and New York: Cambridge University Press, 2005), 233–6.

[31] Alternatively, in the Apocryphon of John, 'image' refers to the image of the divine (understood in light of Gen 1.26) whereas 'likeness' refers to the 'flawed mimicry of Yaldabaoth's realm'. When the archons want to create Adam, they say: 'Let us create a human being according to the image of God and according to our likeness' (ⲛ̄ⲧⲛ̄ⲧⲁⲙⲓⲟ ⲛ̄ⲟⲩⲣⲱⲙⲉ ⲕⲁⲧⲁ ⲑⲓⲕⲱⲛ ⲙ̄ⲡⲛⲟⲩⲧⲉ ⲁⲩⲱ ⲕⲁⲧⲁ ⲡⲛ̄ⲉⲓⲛⲉ [NHC2 15,2–3]). See King, *Secret Revelation of John*, esp. 100. Tuckett writes, 'the reference to the "offspring" of matter "not having a form"' in the Gospel of Mary 'may be a cryptic reference to the production by Wisdom of the demiurge Ialdabaoth', Tuckett, *Mary*, 145. However, the extant Gospel of Mary shows no knowledge of the Sophia myth, and a difference between image and likeness could be asserted apart from this myth.

[32] King writes: 'The Savior argues that the material world is destined to dissolve back into its original root-nature; he does not say that it is evil and will be destroyed,' King, *Mary*, 46.

[33] Stobaeus parallels the Gospel of Mary to an extent, stating that passion is παρὰ φύσιν (Stobaeus 2.88.8), A. A. Long and D. N. Sedley, *The Hellenistic*

a fight against the passions (ἐμπαθῶν παθῶν) (*Strom.* 7.3.20.16–17).[34] For the Gospel of Mary, it seems as though to be in the material world is to be under the influence of passions and so the two concepts are inextricably connected.

A Life under Sin and Death

Passion causes sin and death. After the question about the dissolution of matter (A1), there is another question and answer regarding sin:

> ⲟⲩ ⲡⲉ ⲡⲛⲟⲃⲉ ⲙⲡⲕⲟⲥⲙⲟ̣ⲥ̣ ⲡⲉϫⲉ ⲡ̅ⲥ̅ⲱ̅ⲣ̅ ϫⲉ ⲙⲛ̄ ⲛⲟⲃⲉ ϣⲟⲡ ⲁⲗⲗⲁ ⲛ̄ⲧⲱⲧⲛ̄ ⲡⲉϯⲣⲉ ⲙ̄ⲡⲛⲟⲃⲉ ⲉⲧ̣ⲉⲧⲛ̄ⲉⲓⲣⲉ ⲛ̄ⲛⲉϯⲛⲉ ⲛ̄ⲧⲫⲩⲥⲓⲥ ⲛⲧⲙⲛ̄ⲧⲛⲟⲉⲓⲕ ⲉⲧ<ⲟⲩ>ⲙⲟⲩⲧⲉ ⲉⲣⲟⲥ ϫⲉ ⲡⲛⲟ̣ⲃⲉ (7,12–17)
>
> 'What is the sin of the world?' The Saviour said, 'Sin does not exist, but you make sin when you do the things that are like the nature of adultery, which is called sin.'

Jesus continues, stating that it is because of this that the Good came to dissolve matter (A2), followed by: 'This is why you are si[c]k and you die, for [. . . . .] of the one who [. . . . . . who]ever understands, let him understand' (ⲉⲧⲃⲉ ⲡⲁⲓ ⲧⲉⲧⲛ̄ϣⲱ[ⲛ]ⲉ ⲁⲩⲱ ⲧⲉⲧⲙ̄ⲙⲟⲩ ϫⲉ ⲧ[. . . . .] ⲙ̄ⲡⲉⲧⲁⲣ̣̄. ⲡ̣ⲁ̣[. . . . . . ⲡ]ⲉ̣ⲧ̣[ⲣ̣̄]ⲛⲟ̈ⲓ ⲙⲁⲣⲉϥⲣ̄ⲛⲟⲉⲓ [7,21–8,2]). A number of letters are damaged beyond reconstruction, but sin is clearly linked with sickness and death.

It has been suggested that Peter's question is an echo of John 1.29, 'the sin of the world' (τὴν ἁμαρτίαν τοῦ κόσμου).[35] In John, the Baptist is talking about Jesus coming to take away sin. In the Gospel of Mary, Peter is asking about the nature of sin. The fact that Jesus appears to deny the existence of sin leads King to see this dialogue within the context of intra-Christian debate, and to argue that it is 'another attempt to counter a Christology that was deemed unacceptable … [S]ince sin does not exist, atonement is unnecessary'.[36] But sin does exist, and it is the reason that the cosmos must be dissolved. Sin does not exist without passion, but passion has

Philosophers: Translations of the Principal Sources with Philosophical Commentary Vol. 1. (Cambridge: Cambridge University Press, 1987), 411. Quoted in Tuckett, *Mary*, 144.

[34] 'Passionlessness dominates much of Clement's writing', Osborn, *Clement of Alexandria*, 239.

[35] Tuckett, *Mary*, 141; King, *Mary*, 127; de Boer, *Gospel of Mary*, 23.

[36] King, *Mary*, 127.

been born from matter, and to succumb to this passion is to act in the way of adultery. Humanity can break free from sinful actions through passion; sin does not exist independently of human participation in it. Essentially, one must stop fraternizing with 'passions' and instead find Christ within.

The erring soul is described in terms of adultery in other early Christian literature, such as the Exegesis on the Soul. In the Exegesis on the Soul, when the personified soul enters the body, she is riddled with a life of promiscuity, and the author casts her in the role of a prostitute and sex slave. She is trapped in this lifestyle, unable to resist the adulterers who deceive, use and leave her. Their pull is too strong, and even when she turns away from those adulterers, she runs to others (ⲡⲁⲗⲓⲛ ⲉⲥϣⲁ(ⲛ)ⲕⲧⲉ ⲡⲉⲥϩⲟ ⲉⲃⲟⲗ ⲛ̄ⲛⲉⲉⲓⲙⲟⲓⲭⲟⲥ ϣⲁⲥⲡⲱⲧ ⲉϩⲟⲩⲛ ⲉϩⲛ̄ⲕⲟⲟⲩⲉ ([128,8–9]). The Exegesis on the Soul uses biblical passages to explain its understanding of the soul on earth; for example, the text cites Ezekiel, with regard to being a prostitute for the sons of Egypt (16.26 LXX), representing the domain of the flesh, including food, wine, oil, clothing and 'other external nonsense' (ⲧⲕⲉϕⲗⲟⲓⲁⲣⲓⲁ [130,26]) that the soul thinks that she needs. Adultery in the Exegesis on the Soul is to crave material things: the message is deeply ascetic. The Exegesis on the Soul represents a trajectory of Christian thought in which renunciation is key, using the language of adultery in a related but different way to the Gospel of Mary. In the Gospel of Mary, adultery and sin are linked to passions and the material cosmos or body, construed in a way that comes closer to Paul.

The link between passions, sin and death, and the potential to overcome them through Christ, is a point at which the Gospel of Mary's theology seems closely related to Pauline thought. As Paul writes in Rom 7.5, 'While we were living in the flesh, our sinful passions, aroused by the law, were at work in our members to bear fruit for death' (ὅτε γὰρ ἦμεν ἐν τῇ σαρκί, τὰ παθήματα τῶν ἁμαρτιῶν τὰ διὰ τοῦ νόμου ἐνηργεῖτο ἐν τοῖς μέλεσιν ἡμῶν εἰς τὸ καρποφορῆσαι τῷ θανάτῳ). This fleshly and sinful existence can be overcome by having Christ within: 'For if Christ is in you, though the body is dead because of sin, the spirit is life because of righteousness' (εἰ δὲ Χριστὸς ἐν ὑμῖν, τὸ μὲν σῶμα νεκρὸν διὰ ἁμαρτίαν, τὸ δὲ πνεῦμα ζωὴ διὰ δικαιοσύνην [Rom 8.10]). This discourse is paralleled in Galatians, where Paul juxtaposes the desire of the flesh with the spirit (5.17), linking flesh with the law (5.18), death and passions: 'And those who belong to Christ Jesus have crucified the flesh with its passions and desires' (οἱ δὲ τοῦ Χριστοῦ Ἰησοῦ τὴν σάρκα ἐσταύρωσαν σὺν τοῖς παθήμασιν καὶ ταῖς ἐπιθυμίαις [5.24]). In these examples, Paul understands passions as sin (associated with sexuality and adultery, as in Rom 1.26–27), leading to death. In the Gospel of Mary, passions and sin affect the soul, but can be countered by following Christ and having him within (8,18–20).

The Pauline connections to the Gospel of Mary are understood in a different way by Pasquier who uses Rom 7 to understand sin in relation to the law. As Jesus says in his farewell discourse, disciples must not make laws or they may be dominated by them (8,22–9,4). In Pasquier's exegesis, domination under the law in Rom 7.3–4 is compared with adultery and enslavement to passion (cf. Gospel of Mary 7,14–16); being free from the law equates to joining another (Rom 7.3–4), which in the Gospel of Mary represents finding the Son of Man within and freeing oneself of the material world (GMary 8,18–20); and in Rom 7.6 this freedom indicates the new existence and the overcoming of the dominance of death (GMary 9,2–4). Furthermore, in the absence of the law, sin no longer exists (GMary 7,13–14; Rom 7.8).[37] But in the Gospel of Mary, the question of sin is surrounded by the discourse on the dissolution of matter, not the law. It is followed by the explanation that passion is contrary to human nature, and so it should be read in this context[38] – it is still comparable to Paul, but with a different emphasis.[39] Although making rules and laws is prohibited in the Gospel of Mary, it is not necessarily connected to sin.

In the Gospel of Mary, the construction of the cosmos, its dissolution and the reasons for it all share elements with other early Christian texts, including the Pauline corpus, the Synoptics, the Gospel of Thomas and the Apocryphon of John. Matter is the raw material of the cosmos, which encompasses the lower heavens and the earth. The cosmos must be dissolved due to the disturbance that has arisen from the unnatural production of passion. These passions affect the soul and cause sin and death. The dissolution is not a catastrophic destruction of the world nor a creation of a new world, but the restoration into its pre-formed state.

[37] Pasquier, *Marie*, 14–17.

[38] *Contra* Tuckett: 'the question, with the reference to the sin "of the world", is artificial. It does not arise out of the immediately preceding discourse, but is simply a literary device to enable the teaching of Jesus to progress to the next stage', Tuckett, *Mary*, 141.

[39] See King, *Mary*, esp. 121–4.

4.2 The Role of Christ

Despite the fundamental differences between synoptic eschatology and the Gospel of Mary's protologically orientated dissolution of matter, these gospels have in common the idea that Christ is at the centre of the eschaton. In the Gospel of Mary, A1 appears to refer to a process of natural, inevitable dissolution of created matter (as in the Gospel of Thomas 11 and 111, quoted above), but A2 explains that the dissolution is dependent on 'the Good'.

The Good and the Parousia

Pasquier sees an entropy idea in the Gospel of Mary, stating that 'in the end, by a movement of self-destruction, the material [*hylique*] nature will dissolve in its roots'.[40] But the ⲉⲧⲃⲉ ⲡⲁϊ in A2 shows that the dissolution-restoration of matter may not be *self*-destruction, but rather subject to an external agent. To repeat:

> ⲉⲧⲃⲉ ⲡⲁϊ ⲁϥⲉⲓ ⲛ̄ϭⲓ ⲡⲁⲅⲁⲑⲟ̣(ⲛ) ϩⲛ ⲧⲉⲧⲙ̄ⲙⲏⲧⲉ ϣⲁ ⲛⲁ ⲫⲩⲥⲓⲥ ⲛⲓⲙ ⲉϥⲛⲁⲕⲁⲑⲓⲥⲧⲁ ⲙⲙⲟⲥ ⲉϩⲟ̣ⲩ(ⲛ) ⲉⲧⲉⲥⲛⲟⲩⲛⲉ (7,17–20)
>
> This is why the Good came into your midst to the things of every nature, so as to restore it inward to its root.

'The Good' most likely refers to the Saviour, just as he is later called 'the Blessed One' (ⲡⲙⲁⲕⲁⲣⲓⲟⲥ, 8,12).[41] The Gospel of Mary's

[40] Pasquier, 'L'eschatologie dans l'Évangile selon Marie', 401. Gathercole argues for an entropy idea in the Gospel of Thomas 11 and 111, likening it to Epicurean philosophy in which things passively dissolve into their elements, Simon Gathercole, '"The Heavens and Earth Will Be Rolled up": The Eschatology of the Gospel of Thomas', in *Eschatologie – Eschatology. The Sixth Durham-Tübingen Research Symposium: Eschatology in Old Testament, Ancient Judaism and Early Christianity (Tübingen, September, 2009)*, ed. Hans-Joachim Eckstein, Christof Landmesser, and Hermann Lichtenberger (Tübingen: Mohr Siebeck, 2011), 298. However, this necessitates reading the Gospel of Thomas 10 as separate from saying 11. In the Gospel of Thomas 11, quoted earlier, Jesus says that the heavens will pass away, with no indication of an external agent. However, in the Gospel of Thomas 10 Jesus said: 'I have cast fire upon the world, and behold I am guarding it until it burns' (ⲁⲉⲓⲛⲟⲩϫⲉ ⲛ̄ⲟⲩⲕⲱϩ̄ⲧ ⲉϫⲛ̄ ⲡⲕⲟⲥⲙⲟⲥ ⲁⲩⲱ ⲉⲓⲥϩⲏⲏⲧⲉ ϯⲁⲣⲉϩ ⲉⲣⲟϥ ϣⲁⲛⲧⲉϥϫⲉⲣⲟ). This may indicate that Jesus has inaugurated the dissolution of the heavens.

[41] Marjanen contends that the neuter form necessitates that the referent cannot be a person; however, it can relate to the Saviour's teaching, Marjanen, *The Woman Jesus Loved*, 108. King refers ἀγαθόν to some abstract 'Good' or transcendent God, King, *Mary*, 38, 51. Pasquier argues that it is a reference to the Saviour, Pasquier, 'L'eschatologie dans l'Évangile selon Marie', 393–4. But she does not connect it to the dissolution of matter. Tuckett writes, ⲡⲁⲅⲁⲑⲟ(ⲛ) is 'almost certainly [a reference] to the Saviour himself and/or his teaching', Tuckett, *Mary*, 142. Support for the reading as the Good being Jesus is found in the Book of Thomas and the Gospel of Thomas.

eschatology is then christologically orientated, seeing the Saviour as the instigator of the end of the created order, reading that it is 'because of' (ⲉⲧⲃⲉ ⲡⲁ̈ⲓ) passion and sin that the Saviour (i.e. 'the Good') 'came into your midst' (A2).[42] He is the lamb that takes away the 'sin of the world' (although the sacrificial element is not explicitly present) by dissolving-restoring the material cosmos to its 'root'.

The Good has already come (ⲁϥⲉⲓ), and in the Gospel of Mary there is explicit criticism of the idea of his return. In early Christian literature, 'Son of Man' language is often found within the context of apocalyptic eschatology rooted in parousia theology, but in the Gospel of Mary the title is used within Jesus' farewell discourse and in polemic against those who profess him to be a future being:

> ⲁⲣⲉϩ ⲙⲡⲣ̄ⲧⲣⲉⲗⲁⲁⲩ ⲣ̄ⲡⲗⲁⲛⲁ ⲙⲙⲱⲧⲛ̄ ⲉϥϫⲱ ⲙⲙⲟⲥ ϫⲉ ⲉⲓⲥ ϩⲏⲧⲉ ⲙⲡⲉ̈ⲓⲥⲁ ⲏ ⲉⲓⲥ ϩⲏⲡⲉ ⲙ̄ⲡⲉⲉⲓⲙⲁ ⲡϣⲏⲣⲉ ⲅⲁⲣ ⲙⲡⲣⲱⲙⲉ ⲉϥϣⲟⲡ ⲙⲡⲉⲧⲛ̄ϩⲟⲩⲛ ⲟⲩⲉϩⲧⲏⲩⲧⲛ̄ ⲛ̄ⲥⲱϥ ⲛⲉⲧϣⲓⲛⲉ ⲛ̄ⲥⲱϥ ⲥⲉⲛⲁϭⲛ̄ⲧϥ (8,15–21)
>
> Beware, do not allow anyone to lead you astray saying, 'Look in this direction, or look in this place.' For the Son of Man exists within you. Follow him. Those who seek him will find him.

This saying is intertextually connected with Matt 24.23–27 (// Mark 13.21–26), which warns against believing those that profess the Χριστός to be in the wilderness, among other things, for (γάρ) the Son of Man is coming as the lightning flashes. Whether or not this exact parallel is intentional, the language used in the Gospel

In the Book of Thomas, we read 'you will receive rest from the good one' (ⲧⲉⲧⲛⲁϫⲓ [ⲛ̄ⲟ]ⲩⲁⲛⲁⲡⲁⲩⲥⲓⲥ ⲛ̄ⲧⲟⲟⲧϥ ⲙ̄ⲡⲁⲅ̣ⲁⲑⲟⲥ), and in the Gospel of Thomas 28 Jesus says: 'I stood in the midst of the world' (ⲁⲉⲓⲱϩⲉ ⲉⲣⲁⲧ ϩⲛ̄ ⲧⲙⲏⲧⲉ ⲙ̄ⲡⲕⲟⲥⲙⲟⲥ).

[42] This presumably refers to the whole Christ event: incarnation, death and resurrection. No translator or exegete, to my knowledge, has ever interpreted A2 as the words of the narrator rather than the speech of the Saviour. If this sentence is the narrator's, then the Saviour does not have to be referring to himself, which might appear slightly odd – though not unheard of for Jesus. As the words of the narrator, A2 is emphasizing, through repetition, the Saviour's words concerning dissolution (A1). The textual reasons for understanding these words as belonging to the narrator include the words that follow this sentence: 'Then he continued and said, "This is why you are [sic]k and you die"' (ⲉⲧⲓ ⲁϥⲟⲩⲱϩ ⲉⲧⲟⲧ̣ϥ ⲡⲉϫⲁϥ ϫⲉ ⲉⲧⲃⲉ ⲡⲁⲓ ⲧⲉⲧⲛ̄ϣⲱ̣[ⲛ]ⲉ ⲁⲩⲱ ⲧⲉⲧⲙ̄ⲙⲟⲩ [7,21–22]), which must refer to sin. If the Saviour had not ended his speech at the discussion of sin, it would read that the Good is the cause of sickness and death. My reading of Jesus' speech is more natural: 'you make sin when you do the things that are like the nature of adultery, which is called sin … This is why you are si[c]k and die'.

of Mary explicitly positions the text in contradiction of an eschatological expectation of Jesus' coming.[43]

The evangelist's primary interest in the Son of Man saying is to encourage her readers to find him within themselves. The internalization of the divine is comparable to what we find in Luke 17.20–23 and the Gospel of Thomas 3 and 113:

> Ἐπερωτηθεὶς δὲ ὑπὸ τῶν Φαρισαίων πότε ἔρχεται ἡ βασιλεία τοῦ θεοῦ ἀπεκρίθη αὐτοῖς καὶ εἶπεν, Οὐκ ἔρχεται ἡ βασιλεία τοῦ θεοῦ μετὰ παρατηρήσεως, οὐδὲ ἐροῦσιν, Ἰδοὺ ὧδε: ἤ, Ἐκεῖ: ἰδοὺ γὰρ ἡ βασιλεία τοῦ θεοῦ ἐντὸς ὑμῶν ἐστιν … καὶ ἐροῦσιν ὑμῖν, Ἰδοὺ ἐκεῖ: [ἤ,] Ἰδοὺ ὧδε: μὴ ἀπέλθητε μηδὲ διώξητε (Luke 17.20–21, 23)[44]
>
> Once Jesus was asked by the Pharisees when the kingdom of God was coming, and he answered, 'The kingdom of God is not coming with things that can be observed nor will they say, "Look here or there." For, in fact, the kingdom of God is within you[45] … They will say to you, "Look there or look here." Do not go; do not set off in pursuit'.'
>
> ⲡⲉϫⲉ ⲓ̅ⲥ̅ ϫⲉ ⲉⲩϣⲁϫⲟⲟⲥ ⲛⲏⲧⲛ̄ ⲛ̄ϭⲓ ⲛⲉⲧⲥⲱⲕ ϩⲏⲧⲧⲏⲩⲧⲛ̄ ϫⲉ ⲉⲓⲥϩⲏⲏⲧⲉ ⲉⲧⲙⲛ̄ⲧⲉⲣⲟ ϩⲛ̄ ⲧⲡⲉ ⲉⲉⲓⲉ ⲛ̄ϩⲁⲗⲏⲧ ⲛⲁⲣ̄ ϣⲟⲣⲡ ⲉⲣⲱⲧⲛ̄ ⲛ̄ⲧⲉ ⲧⲡⲉ ⲉⲩϣⲁⲛϫⲟⲟⲥ ⲛⲏⲧⲛ̄ ϫⲉ ⲥϩⲛ̄ ⲑⲁⲗⲁⲥⲥⲁ ⲉⲉⲓⲉ ⲛ̄ⲧⲃⲧ ⲛⲁⲣ̄

[43] Tuckett writes of 'effectively a *denial* of any eschatological expectation', Tuckett, *Mary*, 153.

[44] Tuckett deems Luke 17.23 as 'all but verbatim' in the Gospel of Mary, Tuckett, *Mary*, 152. He writes: 'The *Gospel of Mary* is closer to the Lukan version in being unspecific about the nature or identity of any false figures: thus Mark and Matthew both have Jesus warn about people saying "Look, here is the Christ", where Luke has the simpler "Look here, look there" … Specific talk about the "Son of Man" here in the *Gospel of Mary* would be more readily explicable as having been influenced by the Gospel of Luke if the previous parallel is also seen as related to the wording of Luke 17.23 … Luke 17.21 (which is at least as open to an interpretation about the presence of the kingdom) comes just before, and the reference here to "Son of Man" could be engendered by the references to the day of the Son of Man in the same context in Luke 17.22, 24, 26', 59–60.

[45] Ἐντὸς ὑμῶν has been subject to a number of translations: 'in your midst', 'among you' and 'within you'. For modern interpreters who take ἐντὸς ὑμῶν to mean 'inside you', see George Raymond Beasley-Murray, *Jesus and the Kingdom of God* (Grand Rapids, MI: Eerdmans, 1986), 101; Darrell L. Bock, *Luke 2: 9:51–24:53*, BECNT (Grand Rapids, MI: Baker Books, 1996), 1415; François Bovon, *Luke 2: A Commentary on the Gospel of Luke 9:51–19:27*, ed. Helmut Koester, trans. Donald S. Deer, Hermeneia (Minneapolis, MN: Fortress Press, 2013), 516. Goodacre considers the 'oddity' of this phrase in Luke to point towards a direct link with the Gospel of Thomas, Goodacre, *Thomas and the Gospels*, 35–6.

ϣορπ ερωτⲚ̄ ⲁⲗⲗⲁ ⲧⲙⲚ̄ⲧⲉⲣⲟ ⲥⲙ̄ⲡⲉⲧⲚ̄ϩⲟⲩⲛ ⲁⲩⲱ ⲥⲙ̄ⲡⲉⲧⲚ̄ⲃⲁⲗ (GThom 3)

Jesus said, 'If your leaders say to you, "Look the kingdom is in the sky," then the birds of the sky will precede you. If they say to you, "It is in the sea," then the fish will precede you. Rather, the kingdom is within you, and it is outside you.'[46]

ⲡⲉϫⲁⲩ ⲛⲁϥ Ⲛ̄ϭⲓ ⲛⲉϥⲙⲁⲑⲏⲧⲏⲥ ϫⲉ ⲧⲙⲚ̄ⲧⲉⲣⲟ ⲉⲥⲚ̄ⲛⲏⲩ Ⲛ̄ⲁϣ Ⲛ̄ϩⲟⲟⲩ ⲉⲥⲚ̄ⲛⲏⲩ ⲁⲛ ϩⲚ̄ ⲟⲩϭⲱϣⲧ ⲉⲃⲟⲗ ⲉⲩⲛⲁϫⲟⲟⲥ ⲁⲛ ϫⲉ ⲉⲓⲥϩⲏⲏⲧⲉ ⲙ̄ⲡⲓⲥⲁ ⲏ ⲉⲓⲥϩⲏⲏⲧⲉ ⲧⲏ ⲁⲗⲗⲁ ⲧⲙⲚ̄ⲧⲉⲣⲟ ⲙ̄ⲡⲉⲓⲱⲧ ⲉⲥⲡⲟⲣϣ ⲉⲃⲟⲗ ϩⲓϫⲙ̄ ⲡⲕⲁϩ ⲁⲩⲱ ⲣ̄ⲣⲱⲙⲉ ⲛⲁⲩ ⲁⲛ ⲉⲣⲟⲥ (GThom 113)

His disciples said to him, 'On what day will the kingdom come?' 'It will not come by watching (for) it. It will not be said, "Look here" and "look there"; rather, the kingdom of the Father is spread out upon the earth, and people do not see it.'

Luke's ἡ βασιλεία τοῦ θεοῦ and the Gospel of Thomas' ⲧⲙⲚ̄ⲧⲉⲣⲟ is likely to be equivalent to the Gospel of Mary's 'the kingdom of the Son of Man' (ⲛⲧⲙⲚ̄ⲧⲉⲣⲟ ⲙⲡϣⲏⲣⲉ ⲙⲡⲣⲱⲙⲉ [9,9–10]), and so these three texts recognize the kingdom to be (at least partly) within. Luke and the Gospel of Thomas 3 allow both to be possible and may not stand in contradiction of a parousia theology. The Gospel of Thomas 113, on the other hand, is actively against the future expectation.[47] The kingdom is not 'within' the disciples, but it is present. Schröter regards the Gospel of Mary as standing with the Gospel of Thomas 113 in correcting the future expectation.[48]

[46] The Greek of the Gospel of Thomas 3 appears to have a modifier: Gathercole reconstructs ἡ βασ[ιλεία τῶν οὐρανῶν] as it is a better fit than 'kingdom of God', Gathercole, *Gospel of Thomas*, 208.

[47] Gathercole writes that the kingdom in the Gospel of Thomas 113 is not in a specific place, and the 'consummation of the kingdom was still expected', Gathercole, *Gospel of Thomas*, 604. However, he writes on logion 3 that the Gospel of Thomas is 'against the *localisation* of the kingdom of God in some particular heavenly or earthly sphere … the kingdom, then, is simultaneously all around as well as within', 209–11. Hogeterp argues for an already/not yet eschatology in the Gospel of Thomas, Albert L. A. Hogeterp, 'The Gospel of Thomas and the Historical Jesus: The Case of Eschatology', in *The Wisdom of Egypt: Jewish, Early Christian and Gnostic Essays in Honour of Gerard P. Luttikhuizen*, ed. A. Hilhorst and G. H. van Kooten, AGJU 59 (Leiden: Brill, 2007), 394. DeConick suggests that the internal kingdom is a later development, writing that between 100 and 120 Christians transformed the 'imminent Kingdom into the immanent kingdom', DeConick, *Original Gospel of Thomas*, 7.

[48] Jens Schröter, 'Zur Menschensohnvorstellung im Evangelium nach Maria', in *Ägypten und Nubien in spätantiker und christlicher Zeit. Akten des 6. Internationalen*

On the whole, the Gospel of Thomas places greater emphasis on the present reality of the kingdom;[49] and, as Gathercole writes, this 'bring[s] out what is already there in some other Jesus traditions, such as Luke 4:21 and Luke 17:20–21'.[50] However, according to Popkes, the Gospel of Thomas takes the realized eschatology a step beyond Luke, implying a confrontation with emerging Christian parousia traditions. He notes logion 51 in particular:

> ⲡⲉϫⲁⲩ ⲛⲁϥ'ⲛ̄ϭⲓ ⲛⲉϥⲙⲁⲑⲏⲧⲏⲥ ϫⲉ ⲁϣ ⲛ̄ϩⲟⲟⲩ ⲉⲧⲁⲛⲁⲡⲁⲩⲥⲓⲥ ⲛ̄ⲛⲉⲧⲙⲟⲟⲩⲧ ⲛⲁϣⲱⲡⲉ ⲁⲩⲱ ⲁϣ ⲛ̄ϩⲟⲟⲩ ⲉⲡⲕⲟⲥⲙⲟⲥ ⲃ̄ⲃⲣ̄ⲣⲉ ⲛⲏⲩ ⲡⲉϫⲁϥ ⲛⲁⲩ ϫⲉ ⲧⲏ ⲉⲧⲉⲧⲛ̄ϭⲱϣⲧ' ⲉⲃⲟⲗ ϩⲏⲧⲥ̄ ⲁⲥⲉⲓ ⲁⲗⲗⲁ ⲛ̄ⲧⲱⲧⲛ̄ ⲧⲉⲧⲛ̄ⲥⲟⲟⲩⲛ ⲁⲛ ⲙ̄ⲙⲟⲥ (GThom 51)
>
> His disciples said to him, 'When will the rest for the dead take place, and when will the new world come?' He said to them, 'What you are looking forward to has come, but you do not recognize it.'

Popkes argues that by placing a traditional expectation in the mouths of the disciples and with Jesus refuting them, 'the expectation of a future "new world" is thus rejected. The argumentative developments of this logion thereby appear to imply a dispute with an opposing early Christian understanding of the parousia and resurrection'.[51]

The use of 'Son of Man' language in the Gospel of Mary corresponds to the hostility towards a parousia theology that Popkes sees in the Gospel of Thomas. But for the Gospel of Mary, it is not as simple as an explicit *denial* of a parousia figure – the Good acts in the way that the parousia does (to dissolve the world).[52] If the Good has come to dissolve the cosmos, then the one to inaugurate the eschaton is not a future Christ coming on the clouds, but the Jesus that the disciples are conversing with. (Whether the Good is understood as the incarnated or resurrected Jesus is not specified.) Although the internalizing of the Son of Man is present in the Gospel of

Koptologenkongresses Münster, 20.–26. Juli 1996. Band 2 Schrifttum, Sprache und Gedankenwelt, ed. Stephen Emmel et al. (Wiesbaden: Reichert Verlag, 1999), 182.

49 See esp. Hogeterp, 'Gospel of Thomas and the Historical Jesus', 396.

50 Gathercole, 'Eschatology of the Gospel of Thomas', 284.

51 Enno Edzard Popkes, 'Von der Eschatologie zur Protologie: Transformationen apokalyptischer Motive im koptischen Thomasevangelium', in *Apokalyptik als Herausforderung neutestamentlicher Theologie*, ed. Michael Becker and Markus Öhler, WUNT II 214 (Tübingen: Mohr Siebeck, 2006), 217–18.

52 In New Testament studies, 'parousia' is understood as the return of Christ at the end of the world, but it also means 'presence' and is taken in a number of ways in the Patristic world; see Lampe, *Patristic Greek Lexicon*, 1043b–1044a.

Mary (associated with 'gnosticism' but also found in Clement and Origen[53]), this is not exclusively the case – the external Christ has come to restore matter (and the soul), but this is not predicated on his coming again.[54]

The Son of Man Within

As the Son of Man will not be coming again in the Gospel of Mary, the question that follows is: how are we to understand the Son of Man in this gospel? Just as the canonical Son of Man has been subject to much debate, there is a lack of consensus regarding how we should interpret it in the Gospel of Mary.[55] Pasquier, Marjanen, King and Hartenstein contend that the Gospel of Mary's Son of Man is the archetypal human or the spiritual essence of humanity located within the self, and thus the name is never used to refer to Christ.[56] Pasquier specifically contrasts this with the apocalyptic Son of Man of the canonical gospels,[57] and Marjanen and King state that it is a 'clear Gnostic reinterpretation'.[58] Conversely, Perkins argues that the Gospel of Mary's Son of Man image stems from Philonic and 'gnostic' Genesis exegesis, rather than a reinterpretation of the canonical sayings. She sees the concept of the Son of Man in the canonical gospels as so different from the heavenly

[53] The internalizing of the parousia in 'gnosticism' is argued by Malcolm L. Peel, 'Gnostic Eschatology and the New Testament', *NovT* 12.2 (1970): 141–65. For Clement and Origen, see Jeffrey S. Siker, 'The Parousia of Jesus in Second- and Third-Century Christianity', in *The Return of Jesus in Early Christianity*, ed. John T. Carroll (Peabody, MA: Hendrickson, 2000), 147–67.

[54] On the importance of a Second Coming in the New Testament see A. L. Moore, *The Parousia in the New Testament*, NovTSup 13 (Leiden: Brill, 1966). It also features heavily in the Epistula Apostolorum and the Apocalypse of Peter, as seen in Chapter 1.

[55] A good starting point for this debate concerning biblical material is Delbert Burkett, *The Son of Man Debate: A History and Evaluation* (Cambridge: Cambridge University Press, 1999).

[56] Pasquier, 'L'eschatologie dans l'Évangile selon Marie', 61–2; Marjanen, *The Woman Jesus Loved*, 108; King, *Mary*, 102; Hartenstein, *Die zweite Lehre*, 129 n. 9, 144. Pasquier bases this interpretation on Eugnostos and the Sophia of Jesus Christ in which the Son of Man is an aeon identified with Christ. Also, Tuckett: 'the Son of Man is all but a cipher for the true humanity which is attainable by all who recognize their origins and their true destiny', Tuckett, *Mary*, 63 n. 22.

[57] Pasquier, *Marie*, 62.

[58] King, 'Gospel of Mary Magdalene', 606; Marjanen, *The Woman Jesus Loved*, 108.

Man-Son of Man image in 'gnostic' writings that it 'cannot be the source for its appearance in gnostic texts'.[59] Schröter, on the other hand, argues that the Gospel of Mary is pushing in a Johannine direction: The Son of Man in John 3.13 has come from heaven (a parousia has taken place). Through participation in him, he enables the disciple to gain eternal life.[60] De Boer takes the similarity between John and the Gospel of Mary further, reading κἀγὼ ἐν αὐτοῖς in John 17.26 as showing that the exalted Son of Man can live 'within his disciples'.[61]

In the Gospel of Mary, finding the Son of Man within corresponds to putting on the Perfect Man (ⲛ̄ⲧⲛ̄ϯϩⲓⲱⲱⲛ ⲙ̄ⲡⲣⲱⲙⲉ ⲛ̄ⲧⲉⲗⲓⲟⲥ [18,15–16]; ενδυσαμενο[ι̣] τον τ̣[ελειο]ν ανον [PRyl 21,9–10]), which Levi instructs the others to do at the end of the gospel.[62] These are clearly christological titles, related also to Mary's praise of the Lord for making the disciples 'Men' (ⲛ̄ⲣⲱⲙⲉ [9,20]; ανο[υς] [POxy 12]).[63] The Son of Man in the Gospel of Mary then takes up the Johannine idea that the Son of Man is present and can dwell within, but pushes this in a (deutero-) Pauline direction as the Perfect Man (Col 1.28; Eph 4.13) can be 'put on' (ϯ ϩⲓⲱⲱⲛ [Rom 13.14; Gal 3.27]). The Perfect Man is Christ, and the 'making us into Men' refers to making us into Christs (hence the nomen sacrum[64]).

[59] Perkins, 'Gnostic Christologies', 593. Presumably this includes the Gospel of Mary's use of Son of Man language, as Perkins classifies the Gospel of Mary as 'gnostic', as seen in Chapter 1.

[60] Schröter, 'Zur Menschensohnvorstellung', 178–88.

[61] de Boer, *Gospel of Mary*, 28.

[62] Levi's final instructions mirror the Saviour's farewell discourse (Son of Man/ Perfect Man → preach the gospel → no other laws [8,18–9,4; 18,15–21]), and so Levi's putting on the Perfect Man is a clear echo of the Saviour's Son of Man within. Most interpreters agree with this parallel, e.g. Pasquier, *Marie*, 100; Marjanen, *The Woman Jesus Loved*, 118; Hartenstein, *Die zweite Lehre*, 129, 151; King, *Mary*, 60–1; Tuckett, *Mary*, 192. The Greek ἐνδυσάμενοι indicates that they have already put on the Perfect Man, just as in the Coptic Mary says that the Saviour has already made them Men (9,20).

[63] The Gospel of Philip, as an example, shows that these titles were used for Christ; see Hugo Lundhaug, *Images of Rebirth: Cognitive Poetics and Transformational Soteriology in the Gospel of Philip and the Exegesis on the Soul*, NHMS 73 (Leiden and Boston: Brill, 2010), 170.

[64] Cf. Tuckett comments on the 'surprising' occurrence of ἄνθρωπος as a nomen sacrum, stating that it 'is used here in a highly charged sense, referring to the true or "real" humanity', Tuckett, *Mary*, 82. Cf. Christopher Tuckett, '"Nomina Sacra": Yes and No?', in *Biblical Canons*, ed. J. M. Auwers and H. J. de Jonge (Leuven: Peeters, 2003), 431–58.

The idea of putting on the Perfect Man-Christ is explicit in the Gospel of Philip:

> ⲛ̄ⲧⲁⲣⲉⲡⲉⲭ̅ⲥ̅ ⲉⲓ ⲡⲧⲉⲗⲓⲟⲥ ⲣ̄ⲣⲱⲙⲉ ⲁϥⲉⲓⲛⲉ ⲛ̄ⲟⲩⲟⲉⲓⲕ ⲉⲃⲟⲗ ϩⲛ̄ⲧⲡⲉ ϣⲓⲛⲁ ⲉⲣⲉⲡⲣⲱⲙⲉ ⲛⲁⲣ̄ⲧⲣⲉⲫⲉⲥⲑⲁⲓ ϩⲛ̄ⲧⲧⲣⲟⲫⲏ ⲙ̄ⲡⲣⲱⲙⲉ (GPhil 55,11–14)
>
> When Christ came, the Perfect Man, he brought bread from heaven so that man would be nourished with the food of Man.

The tractate later states that Jesus Christ is 'a Blessed One' (ⲟⲩⲙⲁⲕⲁⲣⲓⲟⲥ) for the very reason that he is 'a Perfect Man' (ⲟⲩⲧⲉⲗⲉⲓⲟⲥ ⲣ̄ⲣⲱⲙⲉ) (80,1–4). This language further parallels the Perfect Man in the Gospel of Mary (in which he is also called the Blessed One [8,12]) with Jesus. And in the Gospel of Philip, it is through becoming children of the Perfect Man (ⲛ̄ϣⲏⲣⲉ ⲙ̄ⲡⲧⲉⲗⲉⲓⲟⲥ ⲣ̄ⲣⲱⲙⲉ) that one can avoid death (58,20–22). This can be done through the ritual act of drinking the eucharistic cup:

> ϩⲟⲧⲁ(ⲛ) ⲉⲛϣⲁⲛⲥⲱ ⲙ̄ⲡⲁⲉⲓ ⲧⲛⲁϫⲓ ⲛⲁⲛ ⲙ̄ⲡⲧⲉⲗⲉⲓⲟⲥ ⲣ̄ⲣⲱⲙⲉ ⲡⲙⲟⲟⲩ ⲉⲧⲟⲛϩ ⲟⲩⲥⲱⲙⲁ
>
> ⲡⲉ ϣϣⲉ ⲉⲧⲣⲛ̄ϯϩⲓⲱⲱⲛ ⲙ̄ⲡⲣⲱⲙⲉ ⲉⲧⲟⲛϩ (75,19–22)
>
> Whenever we drink this, we will receive the Perfect Man. The living water is a body.
>
> It is necessary for us to put on the Living Man.

The Living Man and the Perfect Man can only be equated. As Lundhaug writes, 'becoming a perfect man is a primary goal for the Christian and must be understood in terms of the overall goal of becoming a Christ'.[65] In the Gospel of Mary, Mary states that Jesus has made the disciples into 'Men' – presumably having the same connotations as drinking the eucharistic cup in the Gospel of Philip.[66]

[65] Lundhaug, *Images of Rebirth*, 247.

[66] DeConick sees a eucharistic background to the Gospel of Mary, April D. DeConick, *Holy Misogyny: Why the Sex and Gender Conflicts in the Early Church Still Matter* (New York and London: Continuum, 2011), 140–1. A baptismal background is more likely in view of the language of 'putting on' Christ (Gal 3.27). Furthermore, Rom 6.3–4, Eph 2.1–6 and Col 3.1–4 understand baptism as the experience of undergoing death and attaining eternal life, and in the next chapter I will propose that the Gospel of Mary has an element of realized salvation.

The Gospel of Mary also mentions the Son of Man with reference to the gospel of his kingdom: 'How shall we go to the nations and preach the gospel of the kingdom of the Son of Man?' (ⲛⲛⲁϣ ⲛ̄ϩⲉ ⲉⲛⲛⲁⲃⲱⲕ ϣⲁ ⲛϩⲉⲑⲛⲟⲥ ⲛ̄ⲧⲛ̄ⲧⲁϣⲉⲟⲉⲓϣ ⲛ̄ⲡⲉⲩⲁⲅⲅⲉⲗⲓⲟⲛ ⲛⲧⲙⲛ̄ⲧⲉⲣⲟ ⲙⲡϣⲏⲣⲉ ⲙⲡⲣⲱⲙⲉ [9,7–10]). As the Son of Man is Christ, there is not a great deal of difference between Christ within and his kingdom. The Son of Man within is the internal kingdom, as we find in Luke and the Gospel of Thomas. Luke 17.20–21, the Gospel of Thomas 3 and the Gospel of Thomas 113 follow the same structure as the Gospel of Mary (and Matt 24.26–27), with the warning that some will profess the Messiah/Son of Man/Kingdom (of God) to be in a certain place followed by the revelation of the real location, and these passages also stand alongside the Gospel of Mary's soteriological message by allowing the kingdom to be (at least) partly realized.

4.3 Conclusion

The cosmic eschatology of the Gospel of Mary should be read protologically and christologically. Christ has come to restore the material cosmos to its pre-moulded configuration. In this chapter, I have shown that matter has been moulded into every nature, form and creature (the created heavens and earth). But matter unnaturally created passions – a malevolent presence that affects the soul, causing sin and death, and the reason that the cosmos must be dissolved into its 'root'. The destruction-restoration takes place at the hand of Christ: sin and death are the reason that 'the Good' (Jesus) has come into the world. The Good is linked also with the 'Son of Man' that resides within humanity. Both are Jesus. The christological element in the Gospel of Mary does not stand poles apart from other gospel literature but lies on the same trajectory as Luke and the Gospel of Thomas, but with Pauline underpinnings. It does not reject the identification of the Son of Man with Jesus himself, although it does reject an eschatological expectation of his future coming. The Gospel of Mary does not deny the synoptic idea of a cosmic eschaton, but radically reinterprets it. There is no expectation of a future external figure, nor need there be one: with Christ's coming, the end time has broken in. The Son of Man is within; the Good dissolves the cosmos; and Christ is both. He has come (ⲁϥⲉⲓ) and will restore (ⲉϥⲛⲁⲕⲁⲑⲓⲥⲧⲁ) the cosmos to its original state. He also facilitates the ascent of the Christian soul to heaven, to which we will now turn.

5

THE JOURNEY OF THE SOUL

The Individual Eschatology of the Gospel of Mary

In the second eschatological revelation in the Gospel of Mary, Mary reveals the possibility of human salvation, telling her brothers about Jesus' ascension (cf. John 20.17) and how to follow him. She recalls a narrative of the journey of a personified soul through four powers (ⲉⲝⲟⲩⲥⲓⲁ) that challenge her on her way to 'rest'. The ascent of the soul is connected to the dissolution of matter – both return to their origins, instigated by the incarnation, resurrection or ascension of Christ.[1]

In the ancient world, individual salvation was a more pressing issue than cosmic dissolution. As seen in Chapter 1, *all* dialogue gospels are concerned with the fate of the human, less with the end of the world. In the extant Gospel of Mary, the teaching on the individual soul is more extensive than the few words on the dissolution of matter (although this may not have been the case in the full text). It begins with Mary's vision and ends with Mary's silence as mirroring the soul as she reaches her eschatological destination. However, individual eschatology is woven throughout the gospel and is especially prominent in the idea of finding the Son of Man/Perfect Man within, as discussed in the last chapter.

The journey of the soul in the Gospel of Mary illustrates the text's multifaceted cultural background; prominent resemblances are found in Platonic texts and the 'Orphic' gold tablets. This chapter

[1] It has been proposed in earlier, more source-critical scholarship that the ascent of the soul was interpolated into the existing narrative of the Gospel of Mary. However, Peter's and Andrew's objections to Mary's teaching demonstrate the author's/editor's awareness of the 'strangeness' of the teaching to the point that it actually fits the entire narrative perfectly. On the disunity of the Gospel of Mary, see Till, *Papyrus Berolinensis 8502*, 26; Henri-Charles Puech and Beate Blatz, 'The Gospel of Mary', in *New Testament Apocrypha*, ed. Wilhelm Schneemelcher, trans. R. McL. Wilson, 2nd ed., Vol. 1 (Louisville, KY and London: Westminster John Knox Press, 2003), 344; R. McL. Wilson, 'The New Testament in the Gnostic Gospel of Mary', *NTS* 3.3 (1957): 240; Pasquier, *Marie*, 7–10.

takes these into account, while still building on the work of the previous chapters by situating the Gospel of Mary within an early Christian context. Mary receives private revelation from Jesus, as in John 20; the descent and ascent of the soul recalls the descent-ascent of the Jesus who creates a way for the disciples to follow; the soul must ascend through a Pauline cosmos of powers and principalities; and at the end the soul finds 'rest' and restoration, common eschatological motifs in Christian discourse.

5.1 The Vision

In the middle of the Coptic Gospel of Mary, pages 11–13 are missing. Just before the lacuna, Peter asked Mary to disclose what she remembers about the Saviour, and the final passage on page 10 is the beginning of Mary's report:

> ⲁⲩⲱ ⲁⲥⲁⲣⲭⲉⲓ ⲛ̄ϫⲱ ⲛⲁⲩ ⲛ̄ⲛⲉ̈ⲓϣⲁϫⲉ ϫⲉ ⲁ{ï}ⲛⲟⲕ ⲡⲉϫⲁⲥ ⲁⲓⲛⲁⲩ ⲉⲡϫ̄ⲥ̄ ϩⲛ ⲟⲩϩⲟⲣⲟⲙⲁ ⲁⲩⲱ ⲁⲉⲓϫⲟⲟⲥ ⲛⲁϥ ϫⲉ ⲡϫ̄ⲥ̄ ⲁ̈ⲓⲛⲁⲩ ⲉⲣⲟⲕ ⲙ̄ⲡⲟⲟⲩ ϩⲛ ⲟⲩϩⲟⲣⲟⲙⲁ ⲁϥⲟⲩⲱϣⲃ ⲡⲉϫⲁϥ ⲛⲁ̈ⲓ ϫⲉ ⲛⲁ̈ⲓⲁⲧⲉ ϫⲉ ⲛ̄ⲧⲉⲕⲓⲙ ⲁⲛ ⲉⲣⲉⲛⲁⲩ ⲉⲣⲟⲉⲓ ⲡⲙⲁ ⲅⲁⲣ ⲉⲧⲉⲣⲉⲡⲛⲟⲩⲥ ⲙ̄ⲙⲁⲩ ⲉϥⲙⲙⲁⲩ ⲛϭⲓ ⲡⲉϩⲟ ⲡⲉϫⲁ̈ⲓ ⲛⲁϥ ϫⲉ ⲡϫ̄ⲥ̄ ⲧ̣ⲉ̣ⲛ̣ⲟⲩ ⲡ̣ⲉⲧⲛⲁⲩ ⲉⲫⲟⲣⲟⲙⲁ ⲉϥⲛ̣ⲁ̣ⲩ ⲉ̣ⲣ̣ⲟ̣ϥ <ϩⲙ̄> ⲧ̣ⲉ̣ⲯⲩⲭⲏ <ⲏ̣> ⲡⲉⲡ̄ⲛ̄ⲁ̄ ⲁϥⲟⲩⲱϣⲃ̄ ⲛ̄ϭⲓ ⲡ̄ⲥ̄ⲱ̄ⲣ̄ ⲡⲉϫⲁϥ ϫⲉ ⲉϥⲛⲁⲩ ⲁⲛ ϩⲛ̄ ⲧⲉⲯⲩⲭⲏ ⲟⲩⲇⲉ ϩⲙ ⲡⲉⲡ̄ⲛ̄ⲁ̄ ⲁⲗⲗⲁ ⲡⲛⲟⲩⲥ ⲉⲧϣ̣[ⲟⲡ] ϩⲛ ⲧⲉⲩⲙⲏⲧⲉ ⲙⲡⲉⲩⲥ̣ⲛⲁⲩ ⲛ̣̄ⲧⲟ̣[ϥ ⲡⲉⲧ]ⲛⲁⲩ ⲉⲫⲟⲣⲟⲙⲁ ⲁⲩ[ⲱ] ⲛ̄ⲧⲟϥ ⲡ̣[ⲉⲧ … (10,9–22)
>
> And she began to say to them these words: 'I', she said, 'I saw the Lord in a vision and I said to him, "Lord, I saw you today in a vision." He answered and said to me, "Blessed (are) you, for you did not waver as you saw me. For where the mind is, there is the treasure." I said to him, "Lord, now the one who sees the vision, does he see it through the soul or the spirit?" The Saviour answered and said, "He sees not through the soul nor through the spirit, but the mind, which is between the two. [It is that which] sees the vision, an[d] it is that [which …"'

Mary provides no context for the vision – *when* she sees it or *where* she sees it. Instead, the focus is on *how* she sees it.[2] It is possible that *when* and *where* are answered through the intertextual connection with

[2] The time reference 'today' (ⲙ̄ⲡⲟⲟⲩ) is ambiguous. As discussed earlier, Hartenstein and King think that it could be a reference to a transfiguration-type scene, Hartenstein, *Die zweite Lehre*, 130, 153. King writes that this 'solves the problem of the perfect tense with the present ("I *saw* you in a vision *today*"), and the oddness of discussing the

John 20, in view of the corresponding vocabulary and characters. In John, the risen Lord appears to Mary Magdalene outside the tomb in which he was laid (20.14). At first Mary does not recognize him and asks if he knows where Jesus' body has been taken (20.15). When Jesus speaks to her, she realizes that he is her teacher (20.16). Jesus tells her not to touch him but instructs her to tell his brothers that he is ascending to their Father (20.17).

Mary's words in the Gospel of Mary 'I saw the Lord in a vision' are closely connected to Mary's words in John 'I have seen the Lord' ('Εώρακα τὸν κύριον [20.18]) – the words she announces to the 'brothers' on Jesus' command. In both gospels, Mary will tell the other disciples what Jesus said to her privately – she will tell them about a heavenly ascension.[3] Furthermore, Jesus is here called 'Lord' (as opposed to Saviour elsewhere), mirroring the Johannine nomenclature.[4] The difference is that in the Gospel of Mary, Mary sees the Lord in a 'vision' (ϩοροⲙⲁ), which is often interpreted as something unusual, something seen in a dream or the mind's eye and something that can be contested. As Tuckett writes: 'The scene here in the *Gospel of Mary* may then be an elaboration of the account in John's gospel, though with the parameters significantly shifted so that it is now in a *vision* that Mary has "seen the Lord".'[5] But a vision is necessary for the soteriological teaching that the Lord will reveal to her – the ascending soul can only be seen through the mind, and it can perhaps be argued that through the power of a vision Mary herself can reach the heavenly state of silence and 'rest'.

The *how* question hints at a developed anthropology, with soul, spirit and mind having clear but distinct functions. The question about how one sees a vision reflects the question that Paul cannot answer in 2 Cor 12:

> οἶδα ἄνθρωπον ἐν Χριστῷ πρὸ ἐτῶν δεκατεσσάρων, εἴτε ἐν σώματι οὐκ οἶδα, εἴτε ἐκτὸς τοῦ σώματος οὐκ οἶδα, ὁ θεὸς οἶδεν, ἁρπαγέντα τὸν τοιοῦτον ἕως τρίτου οὐρανοῦ. καὶ οἶδα τὸν τοιοῦτον ἄνθρωπον, εἴτε ἐν σώματι εἴτε χωρὶς τοῦ σώματος οὐκ οἶδα, ὁ θεὸς οἶδεν ὅτι ἡρπάγη εἰς τὸν παράδεισον καὶ ἤκουσεν ἄρρητα ῥήματα ἃ οὐκ ἐξὸν ἀνθρώπῳ λαλῆσαι (2 Cor 12.2–4)

visionary experience within the vision itself', King, *Mary*, 175. But the connections to John 20 are too important to render this solely a transfiguration setting.

[3] See D'Angelo, 'I Have Seen the Lord', 95–122.

[4] See Petersen, *Zerstört die Werke*, 135.

[5] Emphasis original. Tuckett, *Mary*, 170.

> I know a person in Christ who, fourteen years ago, was caught up to the third heaven, whether in the body or out of the body I do not know – God knows. And I know that such a person – whether in the body or out of the body I do not know, God knows – was caught up into Paradise and heard inexpressible words that no person is permitted to speak.

In 2 Cor 12, the question of whether the vision[6] was in or out of the body is just one example of the ongoing distinction between different types of ascent.[7] Other dialogue gospels also engage with the question of different types of vision. In the Dialogue of the Saviour, Jesus refers to the great vision of 'that which is eternal' (ⲉⲡⲉⲧϣⲟⲟⲡ ϣⲁⲉⲛⲉϩ [137,10]). The disciples want to see it, and Jesus asks whether they would like to do so through a 'transient vision or an eternal (vision)' ([ⲟ]ⲩϩⲟⲣⲁⲥⲓⲥ ⲉⲥⲛⲁⲟⲩⲱⲥϥ ⲁⲛ̄ ⲟⲩϩⲟ[ⲣⲁⲥ]ⲓ̣ⲥ ⲛ̄ϣⲁⲉⲛⲉϩ [137,14–16]). Koester and Pagels argue that these differentiated types of vision belong to different stages of the Christian experience: the disciples have already received the transient vision, partly through baptism and initiation, whereas the eternal vision is reserved for the eschatological future.[8]

In the Gospel of Mary, Mary wants to know how she sees the vision, and Jesus likens the 'mind' to 'treasure'.[9] With regard to the mind seeing the vision, we also find this in the Ascension of Isaiah, which twice states that it is Isaiah's *mind* that is taken up during the vision (6.10, 11); in the Coptic Apocalypse of Paul it is the mind (ⲛⲟⲩⲥ) that must awaken to see the vision (19,10–14);[10] and in the

[6] Paul states that he writes of ὀπτασίας καὶ ἀποκαλύψεις κυρίου (v.1). Most commentators read κυρίου as a subjective genitive: the Lord is the source not the content of the revelation. See William Baird, 'Visions, Revelation, and Ministry: Reflections on 2 Cor 12:1–5 and Gal 1:11–17', *JBL* 104.4 (1985): 659. This makes sense as the content of the revelation cannot be spoken about.

[7] Collins makes an interesting point: 'The reader of Paul's letter, however, might have been aware that the Jewish tradition was more familiar with in-body experience, whereas the Hellenistic tradition was more familiar with out-of-body experiences,' Raymond F. Collins, *Second Corinthians*, Paideia (Grand Rapids, MI: Baker Academic, 2013), 237.

[8] S. L. Emmel, Helmut Koester, and Elaine Pagels, *Nag Hammadi Codex III,5: The Dialogue of the Savior* (Leiden: Brill, 1984), 14.

[9] On the inversion of the synoptic saying ('where your treasure is, there will your heart be also'; Matt 6.21 // Luke 12.34), see Pasquier, *Marie*, 72–3; Tuckett, *Mary*, 171–2.

[10] Despite this connection between the Coptic Apocalypse of Paul and the Ascension of Isaiah, Himmelfarb shows how the experience of the visionary differs dramatically in the two texts, Martha Himmelfarb, 'The Experience of the Visionary and Genre in the Ascension of Isaiah 6–11 and the Apocalypse of Paul', *Semeia* 36 (1986): 97–112.

Authoritative Teaching, the soul's bridegroom 'applied the word to her [the soul's] eyes as a medicine to make her *see with her mind* and perceive her kinsmen and learn about her root' (ⲁϥϯ ⲙ̄ⲡⲗⲟⲅⲟⲥ ⲉⲛⲉⲥⲃⲁⲗ ⲛ̄ⲑⲉ ⲛ̄ⲟⲩⲡⲁϩⲣⲉ ⲉⲧⲣⲉⲥⲛⲁⲩ ⲉⲃⲟⲗ ϩⲙ̄ ⲡⲉⲥⲛⲟⲩⲥ ⲛ̄ⲥⲣ̄ⲛⲟⲉⲓ ⲛ̄ⲛⲉⲥⲥⲩⲅⲅⲉⲛⲏⲥ · ⲛ̄ⲥϫⲓ ⲥⲟⲟⲩⲛ ⲉⲧⲉⲥⲛⲟⲩⲛⲉ [22,26–30]). The function of the mind in the Authoritative Teaching is comparable to the Gospel of Mary as it is through the mind that the soul will learn about her root. The Authoritative Teaching also has the mind-treasure link, stating that the soul's treasure (ⲁϩⲟ) is in the same place as her mind (ⲛⲟⲩⲥ) (28,24–26). Treasure comes in the ability to perceive one's origins. In each of these texts, it is possible that the mind is understood as the most accessible human faculty, and without the mind there would be no knowledge of the eschatological destination.

The mind between the soul and the spirit in the Gospel of Mary is unusual (often, the trio is soul, spirit and body).[11] Pasquier places spirit in the superior position as, unlike the soul, it is unaffected by the passions. Still, she writes, the spirit 'needs to be awakened'.[12] She argues that the soul and the spirit in the Gospel of Mary will be reunited, as they are in the Apocryphon of James, which reads that the spirit raises the soul, and the soul cannot be saved without the spirit (11,38–12,5). In the Gospel of Mary, however, there is no real indication that the spirit needs to be awakened, nor that it already resides in the heavens. The extant text preserves the conclusion of the soul's journey, and there is no mention of the spirit. Instead, the soul finds silence and 'rest'.

It is impossible to know what once followed the end of page 10, but it is possible that an explanation of the mind and the spirit was given. Hartenstein proposes that page 11 began with another line about the mind, but further questions from Mary would cause a change in topic.[13] The topics, however, have probably already been introduced in Mary's question about what sees the vision. Half of page 14 must have been the dialogue between the soul and the first power. The top of that page may have been an explanation of the journey of the soul. This leaves pages 11 to 13 to explain the mind and the spirit. It is also possible that the soul's origins were explained, as the extant text shows that the soul has descended from her heavenly home.

[11] The Dialogue of the Saviour appears to favour the soul, mind and spirit trio, but it is too fragmentary to aid interpretation of the Gospel of Mary.

[12] Pasquier, *Marie*, 75.

[13] Hartenstein, *Die zweite Lehre*, 128.

5.2 Jesus and the Soul: Descent and Ascent

Whose Soul?

The identity of the soul in the Gospel of Mary is not entirely clear. With journeys into heaven, it is often difficult to determine whether the protagonist is a living visionary or a deceased spirit – and, likewise, whether the point lies in the ascent itself or in the topography of the celestial realms.[14] Tuckett argues that the soul is the Saviour's, since, '[i]f it were Mary's soul, there would be the problem of the fact that, at the time of her report, she has not yet died and her soul detached from her body'.[15] Yet as Mary mirrors the soul in her silence, she undeniably shares a connection with the soul.[16] Pasquier, alternatively, sees the ascent as symbolic of a transcendent, religious experience.[17]

As discussed in Chapter 3, the Gospel of Mary shares narratival connections with John 20: Jesus appears to Mary alone and she later recalls her meeting to the male disciples in which she says ἑώρακα τὸν κύριον (20.18), akin to her announcement in the Gospel of Mary (10,10–11). The connection between John 20.18 and the Gospel of Mary is often noted, but at the peril of missing the connection to John 20.17:

> λέγει αὐτῇ Ἰησοῦς, Μή μου ἅπτου, οὔπω γὰρ ἀναβέβηκα πρὸς τὸν πατέρα: πορεύου δὲ πρὸς τοὺς ἀδελφούς μου καὶ εἰπὲ αὐτοῖς, Ἀναβαίνω πρὸς τὸν πατέρα μου καὶ πατέρα ὑμῶν καὶ θεόν μου καὶ θεὸν ὑμῶν
>
> Jesus said to her, 'Do not touch me, because I have not yet ascended to the Father. But go to my brothers and say to them, I am ascending to my Father and your Father, to my God and your God.'

In the Gospel of Mary, Mary tells her 'brothers' (ⲥⲛⲏⲩ [9,14]) about an ascension.[18] The 'rest' to which the personified soul ascends surely

[14] See e.g. C. Colpe, 'Die "Himmelsreise der Seele" ausserhalb und innerhalb der Gnosis', in *Le origini dello gnosticismo, Colloquia di Messina 13–18 aprile 1966*, ed. U. Bianchi (Leiden: Brill, 1967), 429–47.

[15] Tuckett, *Mary*, 174. On this topic, Hartenstein simply asks, 'spricht Jesus von seiner Seele oder von Marias oder gibt es noch ganz andere Möglichkeiten?', Hartenstein, *Die zweite Lehre*, 128 n. 7.

[16] King writes, 'Mary become[s] silent, modeling in her behavior the perfect rest of the soul set free', King, *Mary*, 79.

[17] Pasquier, *Marie*, 22.

[18] Curiously, although Tuckett argues that the soul in the Gospel of Mary belongs to the Saviour, he nowhere refers to John 20.17.

is the heavens in which the Father of Jesus resides. The ascending soul of the Gospel of Mary is then to be connected to the ascension of the Johannine Jesus, about which he told Mary Magdalene outside the tomb, and she then told his brothers.

The story of the soul's journey in the Gospel of Mary is not simply a narrative of Christ's ascent.[19] There are clearly consequences for the disciples. Mary mirrors the soul in her silence, and Mary shares in the soul's eschatological 'rest'. In the Johannine Farewell Discourse, Jesus declares himself 'the way, the truth and the life' (ἡ ὁδὸς καὶ ἡ ἀλήθεια καὶ ἡ ζωή [14.6]); he lays down the path for the disciples to gain access to heaven. Similarly, in the Dialogue of the Saviour, Jesus states that: 'But when I came, I opened the way; I taught them about the passage that the elect and solitary will pass through' (ⲁⲗⲗⲁ ⲛ̄ⲧⲉⲣⲓⲉⲓ ⲁⲉⲓⲟⲩⲱⲛ ⲉⲧⲉϩⲓⲏ ⲁⲉⲓⲧⲥⲁⲃⲟⲟⲩ ⲉⲧⲇⲓⲁⲃⲁⲥⲓⲥ ⲉⲧⲉⲩⲛⲁϫⲱⲃⲉ ⲙ̄ⲙ̣[ⲟⲥ] ⲛ̄ϭⲓ ⲛ̄ⲥⲱⲧ`ⲡ´ ⲙⲛ̄ ⲛ̄ⲙⲟⲛⲟⲭⲟⲥ [120,23–26]). The point in the Gospel of Mary too is to follow Jesus into heaven. As well as being a story about Jesus' ascension, it is an invitation to follow him, and it thus acts also as a didactic story. The dialogue prepares the disciples for their heavenly ascent.

Christ's Descent

The soul not only ascends but has descended from the heavenly realm. After we meet the soul following the four-page hiatus, she is immediately confronted by the second power named Desire, who says:

> ⲙ̄ⲡⲓⲛⲁⲩ ⲉⲣⲟ ⲉⲣⲉⲃⲏⲕ ⲉⲡⲓⲧⲛ̄ ⲧⲉⲛⲟⲩ ⲇⲉ ϯⲛⲁⲩ ⲉⲣⲟ ⲉⲣⲉⲃⲏⲕ ⲉⲧⲡⲉ (15,2–4)
>
> I did not see you descending, but now I see you ascending.

Desire mistakenly believes that the soul belongs to the realm below (15,4–5), but the soul corrects her:

> ⲁ̈ⲓ̈ⲛⲁⲩ ⲉⲣⲟ ⲙ̄ⲡⲉⲛⲁⲩ ⲉⲣⲟ̈ⲓ̈ ⲟⲩⲇⲉ ⲙⲡⲉⲉⲓⲙⲉ ⲉⲣⲟⲉⲓ ⲛⲉⲉⲓϣⲟⲟⲡ ⲛⲉ ⲛ̄ϩⲃ̄ⲥⲱ ⲁⲩⲱ ⲙⲡⲉⲥⲟⲩⲱⲛⲧ (15,6–8)

[19] John 20.17 can be read in an alternative way. Jesus tells Mary to tell her brothers ἀναβαίνω – but is she to tell them that Jesus ('I') is ascending or that 'I am ascending', referring to herself? I have chosen to translate it the traditional way (as opposed to inserting speech marks: 'say to them: "I am ascending"') so that Mary is to tell Jesus' brothers that *he* is ascending, but in the case of the Gospel of Mary it can be read both ways, and it is possible that the Gospel of Mary is exploiting this ambiguity.

> I saw you. You did not see me, nor did you know me. I was to you garments, and you did not recognize me.

Evidently, the soul has descended to earth and has not been recognized on her way down. The obvious connection is to the Johannine Logos, who existed before the world but now dwells in the world in flesh, although the world does not recognize him (John 1.10, 11, 14).[20] This idea appears in a number of dialogue gospels and is most likely in the background of the Gospel of Mary.

In the Apocryphon of John and the Epistle of Peter to Philip, the Saviour descends from above and puts on a mortal, fleshly body. In the Apocryphon of John, Jesus reveals that he entered 'the middle of the prison … which is the prison of the body' (ⲧⲙⲏⲧⲉ ⲙ̄ⲡⲉϣⲧⲉⲕⲟ … ⲉⲧⲉ ⲡⲁï ⲡⲉ ⲡⲉϣⲧⲉⲕⲟ ⲙⲡⲥⲱⲙⲁ [$_{\text{NHC2}}$ 30,18–19; 31,3–4]). And thus, Jesus was hidden from the powers of this world, 'and they did not recognize me' (ⲁⲩⲱ ⲙ̄ⲡⲟⲩⲥⲟⲩⲱⲛⲧ [30,21]). This idea is also found in the Epistle of Peter to Philip, in which Christ was sent to the cosmos below to awaken the fallen light-seed in humanity. Meyer writes, '[f]or the sake of this descent the redeemer apparently put on a body as a disguise, and went unrecognized by the cosmic powers'.[21] Similarities between the Epistle of Peter to Philip and John 1 include the phrase 'sent down in the body' (ⲧⲛⲛⲟⲟⲩⲧ ⲉϩⲣⲁï ϩⲙ ⲡⲥⲱⲙⲁ [EpPetPhil $_{\text{NHC}}$ 136,17]) and 'became flesh' (σὰρξ ἐγένετο [John 1.14]), the nonrecognition of the Saviour (EpPetPhil 136,20–21; John 1.10) and coming to one's own (EpPetPhil 136,23; John 1.11).[22]

The Epistula Apostolorum and the Ascension of Isaiah contain expanded versions of Christ's descent, involving not only becoming flesh, but several transformations throughout his journey in order that the heavenly powers (angels in these cases) should not recognize him. In the Epistula Apostolorum, Jesus descends from the Father of all things, putting on the Father's wisdom and power, travels incognito through the various heavens and earth, and then becomes flesh in Mary's womb. During his descent, Jesus transforms

[20] The Ephesian author also understood Christ to have descended 'to the lower parts of earth' (τὰ κατώτερα [μέρη] τῆς γῆς; [Eph 4.9]), referring presumably to the incarnation. See Charles H. Talbert, *Ephesians and Colossians*, Paideia (Grand Rapids, MI: Baker Academic, 2007), 112.

[21] Marvin W. Meyer, *The Letter of Peter to Philip*, SBLDS 53 (Chico, CA: Scholars Press, 1981), 130.

[22] On these parallels and more, see Klaus Koschorke, 'Eine gnostische Paraphrase des johanneischen Prologs: zur Interpretation von "Epistula Petri ad Philippum" (NHC VIII, 2) 136,16–137,4', *VC* 33.4 (1979): 383–92. Meyer argues that only some of Koschorke's parallels are convincing, Meyer, *Letter of Peter to Philip*, 132–3.

himself into the angelic form specific to each of the seven heavens; the angels Michael, Gabriel, Uriel and Raphael follow him to 'the fifth firmament, for they were thinking in their hearts that I was one of them' (ⲁⲡⲙⲁϩϯⲟⲩ ⲛ̄ⲥⲧⲉⲣⲉⲱⲙⲁ ⲉⲩⲙⲉⲩⲉ ⲅⲁⲣ ⲁⲃⲁⲗ ϩ̣ⲛ̄ ⲡⲟⲩϩⲏⲧ ϫⲉ̣ ⲁⲛⲁⲕ ⲟⲩⲉ ⲁⲃⲁⲗ ⲛ̄ϩ̣ⲏⲧⲟⲩ [13.4]).[23] The Ascension of Isaiah is comparable: Christ changes his form as he descends through the seven heavens, the firmament and to earth. The purpose is to disguise himself: 'none of the angels of that world shall know that you [are] Lord with me [the Father] of the seven heavens and their angels' (10.11). When Christ becomes flesh, 'he suckled at the breast like an infant, as was customary, that he might not be recognized' (11.17).

Although the unrecognized descending soul of the Gospel of Mary is not explicitly said to be Jesus, it is highly likely that a descent-ascent christology lies behind the text. Christ descends to earth to restore all things to their origins – he inaugurates the dissolution of matter and paves the way for souls to journey to heaven, as in comparable literature. For the First Apocalypse of James, Jesus' ascent through the hostile powers makes the ascent of James and other disciples possible, as by ascending through the archons, 'I shall reveal to them that he [the children of the Pre-Existent Father] cannot be seized' (ⲛ̄ⲧⲁⲟⲩⲱ̣ⲛϩ̄ ⲙ̄ⲡⲁⲓ̈ ⲛⲁⲩ ⲉⲃⲟⲗ ϫⲉ ⲟⲩⲁⲧⲉⲙⲁϩⲧⲉ ⲙ̄ⲙⲟϥ [$_{\text{NHC}}$ 30,2–4]).[24] A comparable idea is found in the Epistle of Peter to Philip, in which Jesus is sent down in the body to give those who belong to him authority to enter the inheritance of his Fatherhood ($_{\text{NHC}}$ 136,16–28). In the passage that follows, Christ tells the apostles how to defeat the archons above (137,15–30) and that they must become illuminators (ⲫⲱⲥⲧⲏⲣ, 137,8) – the same word used for Christ (133,27; 139,15). Christ teaches the apostles how to become like him. In the Ascension of Isaiah, Christ descends, and the ascending Christ takes the souls of the righteous with him (9.16–18).

Christ's ascent may be challenged, however, and in the First Apocalypse of James he acknowledges that he too must confront the archons. James asks,

> ϩⲣⲁⲃⲃⲓ ⲛ̄ⲁϣ ⲛ̄ϩⲉ ϯⲛⲁⲕⲁⲧⲁⲛⲧⲁ ⲉϩⲣⲁⲓ̈ ⲉⲡⲉⲧ ϣⲟⲟⲡ ⲉⲣⲉⲛⲉⲓ̈ϭⲟⲙ ⲧⲏⲣⲟⲩ ⲙⲛ̄ ⲛⲉⲉⲓ ⲥⲧⲣⲁⲧⲓⲁ ⲉⲩϩⲏⲕ ⲟⲩⲃⲏⲉⲓ· ⲡⲉϫⲁϥ ⲛⲁⲓ̈ ϫⲉ ⲉⲣⲉ

[23] Hartenstein argues that the similarities between the descent in the Epistula Apostolorum, the Gospel of Mary and the Pistis Sophia 8 suggest that the Epistula Apostolorum is clearly influenced by 'gnostic' language and ideas, Hartenstein, *Die zweite Lehre*, 106.

[24] See Sarah Parkhouse, 'Identity, Death and Ascension in the Gospel of John and the First Apocalypse of James', forthcoming.

> ⲛⲉⲉ̈ϭⲟⲙ ϩⲏⲕ ⲟⲩⲃⲏⲕ ⲟⲩⲁⲁⲕ ⲁⲛ· ⲁⲗⲗⲁ ⲉⲩϩⲏⲕ ⲟⲩⲃⲉ ϭⲉ· ⲉⲣⲉ ⲛⲉⲉ̈ϭⲟⲙ ϩⲏⲕ ⲟⲩⲃⲏⲉⲓ … ϯⲉ ⲛ̄ϭⲁⲃϩⲏⲧ ϩⲁⲑⲏ ⲙ̄ⲡⲉⲩⲃⲱⲗⲕ̄ (NHC 27,14–21; 28,3–4).
>
> 'Rabbi, how shall I reach the One who Is when all these powers and hosts are armed against me?' He said to me, 'These powers are not armed against you only but against another: it is against me that they are armed … I am fearful before their anger.'

Christ's victory is assured, however: 'If they seize him, then he will seize each of them' (ⲉⲩϣⲁⲛⲁⲙⲁϩⲧⲉ ⲙ̄ⲙⲟϥ· ⲧⲟⲧⲉ ϣⲁϥⲁⲙⲁϩⲧⲉ ⲉ̂ⲓⲁⲛ̄ ⲟⲩⲟⲛ ⲛⲓⲙ [NHC 30,4–6]). Similarly, in the Gospel of Mary the anonymous soul who overcomes the powers is, in the first instance, the soul of Jesus, who prepares the way for those who will follow.

In all these diverse texts, we find the idea that Christ became human so that humans could become Christlike. Jesus descended from the heavens in order to ascend and pave the way for believers to follow him. As Christ will ascend, defeating the cosmic powers that stand in his way, the individual human soul can do likewise. The ascent of the soul is orientated towards Christ.

The Soul's Descent

If the individual soul, like Mary's, can follow Christ to heaven, then she too must overcome the interrogations of the archons. As we shall see in the next section, there is a standard formula in which the powers ask the soul where she is from and where she is going, and the standard retort from the soul is that she is from 'above'. This answer indicates that the heavenly 'rest' that the soul attains was her original state before being embodied, and that, like Christ, she too descended. The rationale of the descent of the soul in the Gospel of Mary is not clear. It may have been explained in the missing pages; alternatively, the descent may simply have been accepted without explanation. The Exegesis on the Soul and the Authoritative Teaching are two texts that are focused on how the embodied soul must defeat bodily lusts and passions, and both texts accept that the soul has 'fallen' into the body but never explain why. The soul's descent into flesh in the Gospel of Mary most likely builds on the multitude of traditions that profess that (some) humans possess a divine soul.[25]

[25] Dillon shows that 'within the Platonism of the first few centuries AD [we have] a fairly wide spectrum of doctrines concerning the descent of the soul into the body',

Within the extant text, we find a particular affinity to the Platonic notion of the soul's descent from rest to motion.[26] In the Gospel of Mary, the powers attempt to destabilize the soul, but she gains 'rest' (ἀνάπαυσις) and 'silence' (ⲕⲁⲣⲱϥ; σιγή) at the culmination of her ascent (17,5–7 // PRyl.GM 21,2). Plato's souls always move (*Phaedr.* 245c-246a), but stability can be achieved by the souls who 'stand on the outer surface of heaven' which is devoid of disorder and disturbance (*Phaedr.* 245c–247c).[27] In the *Timaeus*, becoming stable is concurrent with overcoming the passions. Before the souls are placed in bodies, they are stable and restful; once they are bound to flesh, they are moved with passions:

> When, from necessity, they are implanted in bodies, and there is the to and fro movement of their bodies (καὶ τὸ μὲν προσίοι, τὸ δ' ἀπίοι τοῦ σώματος αὐτῶν), then the first necessity which would befall them is the innate sense perception common to all, which comes from violent passions (ἐκ βιαίων παθημάτων); second, desire (ἔρωτα) mixed with pleasure and grief; and added to these, fear and anger and whatever (passions) naturally go with these, along with whatever (passions) are their opposites. (*Tim.* 42a–b)[28]

It is at the beginning of the 'to and fro' movement, the movement of the soul entering into the body, that the souls will experience the power of the passions. In the Gospel of Mary, it is in the body that a 'disturbance' happens, caused by the passions that mirror the cosmic powers that the soul must overcome (8,2–6).

Such Platonic ideas and language are employed also in the Apocryphon of John, in which Sophia begins 'to move to and fro' (ϣⲉⲉⲓ [$_{\text{NHC2}}$ 13,13]; ⲉⲡⲓⲫⲉ̣ⲣ̣[ⲉ] [$_{\text{BG}}$ 45,1][29]) in distress on realizing her

John Dillon, 'The Descent of the Soul in Middle Platonic and Gnostic Theory', in *The Rediscovery of Gnosticism: Proceedings of the International Conference on Gnosticism at Yale, March 28–31, 1978*, ed. Bentley Layton, Vol. 1, Studies in the History of Religion 41 (Leiden: Brill, 1980), 363. He argues that Christian belief in the descent of the soul is likely to be the manifestation of the divine in the world (359).

[26] This is not to say that the soul presented in the Gospel of Mary is entirely Platonic. There is no indication that the soul of the Gospel of Mary is composed of three parts, one rational and two non-rational, as we find in Platonic texts such as the *Phaedrus, Republic* and *Timaeus*.

[27] See Williams, *Immovable Race*, esp. 114.

[28] Also quoted in Williams in relation to the Apocryphon of John, *Immovable Race*, 114–15.

[29] ⲉⲡⲓⲫⲉⲣⲉ is the Graeco-Coptic word from ἐπιφέρεσθαι and is only in the BG recension. ϣⲉⲉⲓ has the sense of wandering to and fro, Crum, *A Coptic Dictionary*, 547a.

error as Yaldabaoth boasts that he is the only God.[30] In the text, John asks what moving 'to and fro' means, to which Jesus replies that it is not the spirit of God being borne along (ἐπιφέρεσθαι) over the waters, as Moses said (Gen 1.2 LXX), but Sophia travelling back and forth in angst, not daring to return home ($_{BG}$ 45,6–19). Pleše argues that Sophia's movement refers to her yielding to the violent movement of the passions of shame, weeping and repenting.[31] This stands in contrast to the aeon of the highest Father, which exists in a state of tranquillity 'at rest in silence' (ⲉϥⲙ̄ⲧⲟⲛ ⲙ̄ⲙⲟϥ ϩⲛ ⲟⲩⲕⲁⲣⲱϥ [$_{BG}$ 26,7–8]). Williams writes that the verb ἐπιφέρεσθαι 'has become a peg on which to hang the contrast between the stability of the aeonic realm and the instability of the chaotic realm of darkness'.[32] Humanity is saved when it overcomes its entrapment in the realm of movement and reaches the realm of tranquillity. (Sophia too is made stable, and her outpouring of passion ceases when the spirit responds to her prayer [$_{BG}$ 46,15–47,14].) The language of 'rest' and silence is also used in the Gospel of Mary for the desired state of the human soul (ⲁⲛⲁⲡⲁⲩⲥⲓⲥ is synonymous with ⲙ̄ⲧⲟⲛ) as it escapes from the earthly sphere of disturbance, passion and motion.

In the Gospel of Mary, during the soul's descent, Desire did not recognize her because she was clothed. As in the christologically orientated descent narratives discussed above, her clothing is her disguise, and the descent culminates in her incarnation: the clothing, called here ϩⲃ̄ⲥⲱ (garment), is most likely flesh.[33] The use of the word ϩⲃ̄ⲥⲱ, rather than ϣⲧⲉⲕⲟ (prison [e.g. ApJohn $_{NHC2}$ 30,18–19]) or ⲙ̄ϩⲁⲟⲩ (tomb [e.g. ApJohn $_{BG}$ 55,10]), may suggest that the body is not a *tomb* or a *prison* for the soul, as in some Platonic texts (e.g. *Phaed.* 82e) as well as several other ancient thought patterns.[34]

[30] Williams suggests that *Tim.* 42a–b, quoted above, directly influenced the account of Sophia in the Apocryphon of John, Williams, *Immovable Race*, 114.

[31] Pleše, *Poetics of the Gnostic Universe*, 124. Pleše sees here an amalgamation of Stoic and Platonic ideas: 'Sophia's movement of repentance combines two seemingly incompatible alternatives – it represents a particular state of mind stirred by the rational acknowledgment of evil as well as an irrational affection resulting from the soul's union with the flowing and ebbing tide of the bodily substrate.'

[32] Williams, *Immovable Race*, 113.

[33] Tuckett, *Mary*, 181; King, *Mary*, 70. This is unlike the Epistula Apostolorum and the Ascension of Isaiah, in which Christ transforms himself into the form of angels.

[34] In the *Chaldean Oracles*, the physical world is both a tomb and a jail which the soul must escape, ridding itself of the ὄχημα (vehicle) or χιτών (garment) that it acquired during the descent through the planetary spheres; see Brian P. Copenhaver, *Hermetica: The Greek Corpus Hermeticum and the Latin Asclepius in a New English Translation with Notes and Introduction* (Cambridge: Cambridge University Press, 1992), xxv. Also, we find this in Josephus' description of Essene belief: 'They believe that the bodies are corruptible and their matter impermanent, but that the souls

ϩⲃ̄ⲥⲱ can be a more neutral term, as is illustrated by the Sentences of Sextus: 'The garment of your soul [is] the body, so keep it holy since it is without sin' (ⲧϩⲃ̄ⲥⲱ ⲛ̄ⲧⲉⲕⲯⲩⲭⲏ [ⲧⲉ] ⲡⲥⲱⲙⲁ · ⲁⲣⲏϩⲉ ϭⲉ ⲉⲣⲟϥ ⲉϥ[ⲟⲩ]ⲁⲁⲃ · ⲉϥⲟ ⲛ̄ⲁⲧⲛⲟⲃⲉ [30,12–14]). In the Gospel of Mary, 'garment' may be closer to the idea of the body, also seen in Plato, as a woven fabric that holds the soul within itself as a means to protect it (to an extent); eventually, it unravels, and the 'soul is then released in a natural way' (*Tim.* 73b, 74a, 81d). A similar idea is found in 'Orphism' (as reported by Aristotle), in which the body is an undemanding but brief enclosure for the soul, called a garment.[35] A less negative view of the body corresponds with the more neutral view of matter, proposed in the previous chapter. It is not the body, made of matter, which is the fundamental problem; it is the passions that it finds difficult to overcome.

5.3 Powers and Passwords

The Heavens and the Gatekeepers

During the ascent, the soul meets four powers: the first is most likely to be named Darkness (to correspond with the first power of Wrath);[36] the second is named Desire (ⲧⲉⲡⲓⲑⲩⲙⲓⲁ); the third, Ignorance (ⲧⲙⲛⲧⲁⲧⲥⲟⲟⲩⲛ); and the fourth, the seven forms of Wrath (ⲧⲟⲣⲅⲏ). In the extant text, Darkness, Desire and Wrath act as cosmic gatekeepers that challenge the soul and attempt to prevent her from progressing to the next level.

Levels of heavens and their gatekeepers are another common motif in antiquity.[37] We often find three or seven heavens; the Gospel of Mary's four guardians for four realms with 'rest' above is unusual, especially when combined with the collective seven guardians in

persevere. Coming from the finest ether, the souls become entangled in the bodies, as in prison, drawn down by some natural spell. When once they leave the bonds of the flesh, just as if released from a long slavery, then they rejoice and are lifted high in the air' (*War* 2.8.11).

[35] *On the Generation of Animals* B1 734a16, see Radcliffe G. Edmonds III, *Redefining Ancient Orphism: A Study in Greek Religion* (Cambridge: Cambridge University Press, 2013), 278–9.

[36] The first power is not met in the extant text. As Desire and Ignorance correspond to the second and third of the seven forms of Wrath (16,4–13), the first form, Darkness, is most likely the name of the first power.

[37] See esp. Simon Gathercole, 'Quis et Unde? Heavenly Obstacles in Gos. Thom. 50 and Related Literature', in *Paradise in Antiquity: Jewish and Christian Views*, ed. Markus Bockmuehl and Guy G. Stroumsa (Cambridge: Cambridge University Press, 2010), 82–101.

the final power of Wrath.[38] On the other hand, seven heavens are extremely common.[39] In the Ascension of Isaiah, Christ and his Father reside in the seventh heaven, and Christ descends through the heavens and the lower firmament. The Hypostasis of the Archons has seven heavens controlled by Sabaoth, the son of Yaldabaoth. In the Coptic Apocalypse of Paul, Paul must have the appropriate sign to pass through the Old Man (the demiurge) at the seventh heaven; in the Apocryphon of John, the archons number seven.[40] For the Gospel of Mary, Tardieu, Pasquier and King argue that the seven powers of Wrath correspond to the astrological spheres that control fate.[41]

The narrative of seven rulers questioning the soul is paralleled in On the Origin of the World:

> ⲡⲥⲁϣϥ̄ ⲇⲉ ⲛ̄ⲁⲣⲭⲱⲛ ⲛ̄ⲧⲁⲣⲟⲩⲉⲓ ⲁⲩⲛⲁⲩ ⲉⲣⲟϥ ⲁⲩϣⲧⲟⲣⲧⲣ̄ ⲉⲙⲁⲧⲉ ⲁⲩϯ ⲡⲉⲩⲟⲩⲟⲉⲓ ⲉϩⲟⲩⲛ ⲉⲣⲟϥ ⲁⲩⲉⲙⲁϩⲧⲉ ⲙ̄ⲙⲟϥ ⲁⲩⲱ ⲡⲉϫⲁϥ ⲙ̄ⲡⲛⲓϥⲉ ⲉⲧⲛ̄ϩⲏⲧϥ̄ ϫⲉ ⲛ̄ⲧⲟⲕ ⲛⲓⲙ ⲁⲩⲱ ⲛ̄ⲧⲟⲕ ⲉⲓ ⲉⲃⲟⲗ ⲧⲱⲛ ⲉⲛⲓⲙⲁ ⲁϥⲟⲩⲱϣⲃ̄ ⲡⲉϫⲁϥ ϫⲉ ⲛ̄ⲧⲁⲉⲓⲉⲓ ⲉⲃⲟⲗ ϩⲓⲧⲛ̄ ⲧⲇⲩⲛⲁⲙⲓⲥ ⲙ̄ⲡⲣⲱⲙⲉ ⲉⲧⲃⲉ ⲡⲧⲁⲕⲟ ⲙ̄ⲡⲉⲧⲛ̄ⲉⲣⲅⲟⲛ (115,17–23)
>
> Then when the seven rulers came, they saw him and were greatly disturbed. They went up to him and seized him. And the chief ruler said to the breath within him, 'Who are you? And where did you come from?' It answered and said, 'I have come from the power of Man for the destruction of your work.'

Here, the soul is the life-force that Sophia has sent to introduce life into Adam's newly created body. It is neither Jesus nor a soul

[38] There may be a Platonic background here: the four categories of living creatures that inhabit the cosmos (*Tim.* 39e-40a) combined with the seven wandering stars.

[39] See esp. Adela Yarbro Collins, *Cosmology and Eschatology in Jewish and Christian Apocalypticism*, Supplements to the Journal for the Study of Judaism 50, ed. John J. Collins (Leiden and New York: Brill, 1996), 47–52.

[40] This number may derive from the 'young gods' (planets) in the *Timaeus*, as argued by King, *Secret Revelation of John*, 111; Nicola Denzey Lewis, *Cosmology and Fate in Gnosticism and Graeco-Roman Antiquity: Under Pitiless Skies*, NHMS 81 (Leiden and Boston: Brill, 2013), 114. However, Pétrement regards Jewish days of the week to be a possibility, Simone Pétrement, *A Separate God: The Origins and Teachings of Gnosticism*, trans. Carol Harrison (San Francisco, CA: Harper & Row, 1984), 65. Welburn cannot accept this: 'no significant correlations result from taking the order of the weekdays as that of the Archons', see A. J. Welburn, 'The Identity of the Archons in the "Apocryphon Johannis"', *VC* 32.4 (1978): 242. Collins repeatedly refers to Babylonian parallels – particularly for the literature that does not explicitly refer to planets, John Collins, *Cosmology and Eschatology in Jewish and Christian Apocalypticism*, 21–46.

[41] Tardieu, *Écrits Gnostiques*, 290–2; Pasquier, *Marie*, 80–6; King, *Mary*, 71.

following Jesus, and the challenge from the archons comes at the soul's incarnation, not at its departure from the body.[42]

The gatekeepers indicate an (indirect) influence from the Pauline corpus, which envisages a cosmos dominated by hostile cosmic beings. As we discussed in Chapter 2, a key passage is Eph 6.12 in which the author talks of struggling against cosmic powers (πρὸς τὰς ἐξουσίας, πρὸς τοὺς κοσμοκράτορας τοῦ σκότους τούτου) and evil spiritual forces in heavenly places (τὰ πνευματικὰ τῆς πονηρίας ἐν τοῖς ἐπουρανίοις). Several early Christian thinkers shared the belief that demonic powers governed the world; for example, Tatian tells his addressees that humanity is under the influence of demons and that they should take up arms against them and conquer them by repudiating matter (*ad. Graec.* 16).[43] In the background here is, once again, Plato, who argues in the *Phaedo* that the soul is not in harmony with the body – it is 'something much too divine to rank as an attunement' (94e) – and rather works against it, sometimes 'conversing with the desires and passions and fears (ταῖς ἐπιθυμίαις καὶ ὀργαῖς καὶ φόβοις) as though it were quite separate and distinct from them' (94d). The righteous soul conversing with the inner forces of the desires and passions is entirely at home in Plato, but some Christian thinkers saw them as mirrored in the heavenly sphere. In the Gospel of Mary, the wise soul can converse with and conquer the passions and fears who act as gatekeepers on her heavenly journey, by imitating Christ's ascension.

The Key to Open the Gate

Whenever there are gatekeepers, there are ways in which to pass through their gates. In early Christian texts, the cosmic traveller generally has to make a verbal proclamation in response to the gatekeepers'

[42] Tuckett links the names of the seven forms of Wrath in the Gospel of Mary with the seven archons in the Apocryphon of John and the feminine names of the archons in On the Origin of the World, Tuckett, *Mary*, 176. Although the lists are comparable, their similarities should not be overstated. The names of the powers in the Gospel of Mary are likely to derive from traditions of vice lists that were notoriously fluid in antiquity, see Philip L. Tite, *Valentinian Ethics and Paraenetic Discourse: Determining the Social Function of Moral Exhortation in Valentinian Christianity*, NHMS 67 (Leiden and Boston: Brill, 2009), 164–75.

[43] Gathercole states that brief allusions to this motif are common, citing the Sentences of Sextus 40, the Apocryphon of James 8,27–36, Treatise on the Resurrection 45,38–39 and Acts of Thomas 148, 167, Gathercole, 'Quis et Unde?', 83 n. 5. For monastic literature, see David Brakke, *Talking Back: A Monastic Handbook for Combating Demons*, Cistercian Studies Series 229 (Collegeville, MN: Liturgical Press, 2009), 1–40.

questions in order to unlock the gates. In the Ascension of Isaiah, Christ himself needs to provide 'passwords' to descend through most of the lower heavens (10.24–30). (The 'angels of the air' seem to forget to ask him for a password as they are too busy fighting each other [10.31].) Christians, following Jesus, were learning this procedure: Origen quotes Celsus as referring to those who have 'wretchedly learnt by heart the names of the [seven] door-keepers' (*c. Cels*. 7.40, cf. 6.30) and the Dialogue of the Saviour, the Gospel of Thomas 50 and the First Apocalypse of James demonstrate that these passwords or verbal declarations were being taught. The disciples could learn how to pass through the archons, modelled on Jesus' own ascension.

The Dialogue of the Saviour explicitly shows that these verbal pronouncements were *taught* by Jesus:

ϯⲛⲁⲧⲥⲁⲃⲱⲧⲛ̄ ϩⲟⲧⲁⲛ ⲉϥϣⲁⲛϣⲱⲡⲉ ⲛ̄ϭⲓ ⲡⲉⲟⲩⲟⲉⲓϣ ⲙ̄ⲡⲃⲱⲗ ⲉⲃⲟⲗ ⲧϣⲟⲣⲡ˙ ⲛ̄ϭⲟⲙ ⲙ̄ⲡⲕⲁⲕⲉ ⲛⲁ > ⲧⲱⲙⲛ̄ⲧ ⲉⲣⲱⲧⲛ̄ · ⲙ̄ⲡⲣ̄ⲣ̄ϩⲟⲧⲉ ⲛ̄ⲧⲉⲧⲛ̄ϫⲟⲟⲥ ϫⲉ ⲉⲓⲥ ⲡⲉⲟⲩⲟ > ⲉⲓϣ ⲁϥϣⲱⲡⲉ · ⲁⲗⲗⲁ ⲉϣⲁⲧⲉⲧⲛ̄ⲛⲁⲩ̣ ⲉⲩϭⲉⲣⲱⲃ ⲛ̄ⲟⲩⲱⲧ˙ ⲉ … (121,1–8)

I will *teach* you. When the time of the dissolution arrives, the first power of darkness will come upon you. Do not be afraid and say, 'Behold. The time has come.' But seeing a single staff …

Unfortunately, lacunae render a large part of the next eight lines and the following leaf illegible. It is impossible to deduce how far these instructions continue or what Jesus taught Mary, Matthew and Judas.

In the Gospel of Thomas and the First Apocalypse of James, pronouncements take the form of declaring one's origins. As one saying in the Gospel of Thomas reads:

ⲡⲉϫⲉ ⲓ̅ⲥ̅ ϫⲉ ⲉⲩϣⲁⲛϫⲟⲟⲥ ⲛⲏⲧⲛ̄ ϫⲉ ⲛ̄ⲧⲁⲧⲉⲧⲛ̄ϣⲱⲡⲉ ⲉⲃⲟⲗ ⲧⲱⲛ ϫⲟⲟⲥ ⲛⲁⲩ ϫⲉ ⲛ̄ⲧⲁⲛⲉⲓ ⲉⲃⲟⲗ ϩⲙ̄ ⲡⲟⲩⲟⲉⲓⲛ ⲡⲙⲁ ⲉⲛⲧⲁ ⲡⲟⲩⲟⲉⲓⲛ ϣⲱⲡⲉ ⲙ̣̄ⲙ̣ⲁ̣ⲩ ⲉⲃⲟⲗ ϩⲓⲧⲟⲟⲧϥ ⲟⲩⲁⲁⲧϥ ⲁϥⲱϩⲉ ⲉⲣⲁⲧϥ ⲁ̣ⲩⲱ ⲁϥⲟⲩⲱⲛϩ ⲉ̣[ⲃ]ⲟⲗ ϩ̣ⲛ̄ ⲧⲟⲩϩⲓⲕⲱⲛ ⲉⲩϣⲁϫⲟⲟⲥ ⲛⲏⲧⲛ̄ ϫⲉ ⲛ̄ⲧⲱⲧⲛ̄ ⲡⲉ ϫⲟⲟⲥ ϫⲉ ⲁⲛⲟⲛ ⲛⲉϥϣⲏⲣⲉ ⲁⲩⲱ ⲁⲛⲟⲛ ⲛ̄ⲥⲱⲧⲡ ⲙ̄ⲡⲉⲓⲱⲧ ⲉⲧⲟⲛϩ ⲉⲩϣⲁⲛϫⲛⲉ ⲧⲏⲩⲧⲛ̄ ϫⲉ ⲟⲩ ⲡⲉ ⲡⲙⲁⲉⲓⲛ ⲙ̄ⲡⲉⲧⲛ̄ⲉⲓⲱⲧ ⲉⲧϩⲛ̄ ⲧⲏⲩⲧⲛ̄ ϫⲟⲟⲥ ⲉⲣⲟⲟⲩ ϫⲉ ⲟⲩⲕⲓⲙ ⲡⲉ ⲙⲛ̄ ⲟⲩⲁⲛⲁⲡⲁⲩⲥⲓⲥ (GThom 50)

Jesus says: 'If they say to you, "Where do you come from?" say to them, "We have come from the light; the place where the light has come into being by itself has establish[ed itself] and has appeared in their image." If they say to you, "Is

> it you?" say, "We are his children, and we are the elect of the living Father." If they ask you, "What is the sign of your Father among you?" say to them, "It is movement and rest."'

What is actually being referred to here is unclear.[44] It has been read as taking place in a secular environment[45] – as a dialogue between the soul and powers in preparation for mystical experience,[46] or as Jesus preparing the disciples for their post-mortem heavenly ascent.[47] The last option not only parallels the eschatological context of the Dialogue of the Saviour and the Gospel of Mary, but also is complemented by the previous saying. There Jesus says, 'Blessed are the solitary and elect, for you will find the kingdom. For you are from it, and you will return there again' (ϩⲉⲛⲙⲁⲕⲁⲣⲓⲟⲥ ⲛⲉ ⲛⲙⲟⲛⲁⲭⲟⲥ ⲁⲩⲱ ⲉⲧⲥⲟⲧⲡ ϫⲉ ⲧⲉⲧⲛⲁϩⲉ ⲁⲧⲙⲛ̄ⲧⲉⲣⲟ ϫⲉ ⲛ̄ⲧⲱⲧⲛ̄ ϩⲛ̄ⲉⲃⲟⲗ ⲛ̄ϩⲏⲧⲥ̄ ⲡⲁⲗⲓⲛ ⲉⲧⲉⲧⲛⲁⲃⲱⲕ ⲉⲙⲁⲩ [GThom 49]). In the First Apocalypse of James and the Gospel of Mary, the dialogue with the powers precedes the disciple returning to their heavenly home, and so it is possible that the Gospel of Thomas 50 is the same.

The First Apocalypse of James has a very clear passage where Jesus is instructing James what to say to the otherworldly guardians, called toll-collectors:

> ⲉϣⲱⲡⲉ ϭⲉ ⲉⲕϣⲁⲛⲉ̂ⲓ ⲉⲧⲟⲟⲧⲟⲩ · ⲟⲩⲛ̄ ⲟⲩⲁ ⲉⲃⲟⲗ ⲛ̄ϩⲏⲧⲟⲩ ⲛⲁϫⲟⲟⲥ ⲛⲁⲕ · ⲉⲩⲣⲉϥⲁⲣⲉϩ ⲛ̄ⲧⲁⲩ ⲡⲉϫⲉ ⲛ̄ⲧⲕ̄ ⲛⲓⲙ ⲏ̄ ⲛ̄ⲧⲕ̄ ⲟⲩⲉⲃⲟⲗ ⲧⲱⲛ · ⲉⲕⲉϫⲟⲟⲥ ⲛⲁϥ ϫⲉ ⲁⲛⲁⲕ ⲟⲩϣⲏⲣⲉ ⲁⲩⲱ ⲁⲛⲟⲕ ⲟⲩⲉⲃⲟⲗ ϩⲙ̄ ⲡⲓⲱⲧ ($_{\text{NHC}}$ 33,11–18)
>
> When you come into their power, one of them who is their guard will say to you, 'Who are you, or where are you from?' You are to say to him, 'I am a son, and I am from the Father.'
>
> ⲉϥⲛⲁϫⲟⲟⲥ ⲛⲁⲕ ⲟⲛ ϫⲉ ⲉⲕⲛⲁⲃⲱⲕ ⲉⲧⲱⲛ · ⲉⲕⲉϫⲟⲟⲥ ⲛⲁϥ ϫⲉ ⲉⲡⲙⲁ ⲉⲧⲁï̂ⲉⲓ ⲉⲃⲟⲗ ⲙ̄ⲙⲁⲩ ⲉ̈ⲓⲛⲁⲃⲱⲕ ⲟⲛ ⲉⲙⲁⲩ ($_{\text{NHC}}$ 34,15–17)

[44] The combination of motion and rest is also difficult to interpret: DeConick turns to the Corpus Hermeticum to interpret it as God's immobility, April D. DeConick, *Seek to See Him: Ascent and Vision Mysticism in the Gospel of Thomas*, VCSup 33 (Leiden: Brill, 1996), 93–5. Gathercole sees the combination as a divine unity, Gathercole, *Gospel of Thomas*, 410.

[45] See Gathercole, *Gospel of Thomas*, 406–7.

[46] DeConick, *Seek to See Him*, 43–99.

[47] Gathercole, *Gospel of Thomas*, 407; Gathercole, 'Quis et Unde?'.

> When he again says to you, 'Where will you go?', you are to say to him, 'To the place from which I have come, there shall I return.'[48]

James will be saved by declaring that he is returning home.

Similar questions are posed to the soul in the Gospel of Mary:

> [ⲁⲥ]ⲣ̣̄ⲉϩⲉⲧⲁⲍⲉ ⲛ̄ⲧⲉⲯⲩⲭⲏ ⲉⲥϫ[ⲱ ⲙ̄]ⲙⲟⲥ ϫⲉ ⲉⲣⲉⲃⲏⲕ ⲉⲧⲱⲛ (15,13–14)
>
> [She] questioned the soul, sa[yi]ng 'Where are you going?'
>
> ⲛⲁï ⲛⲉ ⲧⲥⲁϣϥⲉ ⲛ̄ⲛ̣ⲉ̣[ϩ]ⲟⲩⲥⲓⲁ ⲛⲧⲉ ⲧⲟⲣⲅⲏ ⲉⲩϣⲓⲛⲉ ⲛ̄ⲧⲉⲯⲩⲭⲏ ϫⲉ ⲉⲣⲉⲛⲏⲩ ϫⲓⲛ ⲧⲱⲛ ⲧϩⲁ̣ⲧⲃⲣⲱⲙⲉ ⲏ ⲉⲣⲉⲃⲏⲕ ⲉⲧⲱⲛ ⲧⲟⲩⲁ̣ⲥϥⲙⲁ (16,12–16)
>
> These are the seven p[o]wers of Wrath. They ask the soul, 'Where do you come from Human-Slayer? Or where do you go Space-Destroyer?'

The 'who are you' and 'where are you from/going' questions are widespread, being found across cultures and times.[49] But in a Christian context, they may relate directly to Jesus. Looking at the First Apocalypse of James, Haxby regards the instructions as 'reflect[ing] a complex and creative reading of John', particularly John 7–8.[50] As Jesus teaches in the Temple, a debate breaks out regarding whether he is the Messiah.[51] The questions and answers are orientated around who Jesus is and where he is from/going.

> ἀλλὰ τοῦτον οἴδαμεν πόθεν ἐστίν· ὁ δὲ χριστὸς ὅταν ἔρχηται οὐδεὶς γινώσκει πόθεν ἐστίν (John 7.27)
>
> Yet we know where this man is from, but when the Messiah comes, no one will know where he is from.

[48] The CT version is similar.

[49] Examples include the Egyptian 'Book of the Dead' (chap. 122) and the Jaiminiya Brahmana (46–50) from India. For these and more examples, see Alberto Bernabé and Ana Isabel Jiménez San Cristóbal, *Instructions for the Netherworld: The Orphic Gold Tablets*, Religions in the Graeco-Roman World 162 (Leiden and Boston: Brill, 2008), 207–26.

[50] Mikael Haxby, 'The First Apocalypse of James: Martyrdom and Sexual Difference' (PhD Thesis, Harvard, 2013), 67–71.

[51] As 7.53–8.11 is not part of the original text, 8.12 presumably continues in the Temple; cf. v. 59.

> κἀμὲ οἴδατε καὶ οἴδατε πόθεν εἰμί· καὶ ἀπ᾽ ἐμαυτοῦ οὐκ ἐλήλυθα, ἀλλ᾽ ἔστιν ἀληθινὸς ὁ πέμψας με, ὃν ὑμεῖς οὐκ οἴδατε· ἐγὼ οἶδα αὐτόν, ὅτι παρ᾽ αὐτοῦ εἰμι κἀκεῖνός με ἀπέστειλεν (7.28–29)
>
> You know me, and you know where I am from. I have not come of my own accord, but the one who sent me is true, and you do not know him. I know him because I am from him, and he sent me.
>
> ἔτι χρόνον μικρὸν μεθ᾽ ὑμῶν εἰμι καὶ ὑπάγω πρὸς τὸν πέμψαντά με (7.33)
>
> I will be with you a little longer, and then I am going to him who sent me.
>
> Εἶπον οὖν αὐτῷ οἱ Φαρισαῖοι· σὺ περὶ σεαυτοῦ μαρτυρεῖς· ἡ μαρτυρία σου οὐκ ἔστιν ἀληθής. ἀπεκρίθη Ἰησοῦς καὶ εἶπεν αὐτοῖς· κἂν ἐγὼ μαρτυρῶ περὶ ἐμαυτοῦ, ἀληθής ἐστιν ἡ μαρτυρία μου, ὅτι οἶδα πόθεν ἦλθον καὶ ποῦ ὑπάγω· ὑμεῖς δὲ οὐκ οἴδατε πόθεν ἔρχομαι ἢ ποῦ ὑπάγω (8.13–14)
>
> Then the Pharisees said to him, 'You are testifying on your own behalf; your testimony is not valid.' Jesus answered, 'My testimony is valid because I know where I have come from and where I am going, but you do not know where I come from or where I am going.'
>
> ὑμεῖς ἐκ τῶν κάτω ἐστέ, ἐγὼ ἐκ τῶν ἄνω εἰμί· ὑμεῖς ἐκ τούτου τοῦ κόσμου ἐστέ, ἐγὼ οὐκ εἰμὶ ἐκ τοῦ κόσμου τούτου (8.23)
>
> You are from below; I am from above. You are of this world; I am not of this world.

The debate over origins and destination in John 7–8 mirrors the dialogue that James must expect with the soul-collecting archons in the First Apocalypse of James. Haxby argues:

> The questions which are asked of Jesus in *John*, and which the 'guard' and 'toll collectors' pose in *1ApocJas*, concern the same issues of origin and destination. The answers are the same: just as Jesus came from God the Father, so James has come from the Father. Just as Jesus is returning to the Father, so James is going to the place from which he came.[52]

[52] Haxby, 'First Apocalypse of James', 69.

Jesus' self-knowledge in John 7–8, which authenticates his authority, is reformulated in the First Apocalypse of James as the knowledge that James must acquire about himself: 'The Christology of *John* comes to be knowledge about the self in *1ApocJas*.'[53] And this knowledge is the path to true martyrdom and James' return to 'the place from which I have come' (ⲡⲙⲁ ⲛ̄ⲧⲁⲉⲓⲉⲓ ⲙ̄ⲙⲟϥ [$_{CT}$ 21,18]).[54]

The knowledge of one's origins as the verbal key to pass through otherworldly gatekeepers predates Christianity by centuries; we find it on the gold 'Orphic' tablets, on which the deceased must remember what path to take and what to say to the guardians as they journey into Hades.[55] These are grave tablets dating from the end of the fifth century BCE to the second century CE and have been 'found throughout the margins of the Greek world, from Thessaly to southern Italy and Crete'.[56] They functioned as mnemonic devices to aid the deceased in remembering what to say as they entered into the afterlife. By nature of being a mnemonic device, and small tablets, they do not offer continuous narratives about the afterlife, but Graf and Johnston argue that in the tablets 'we should expect to find brief allusions to bigger stories and ritual sequences with which their possessors were familiar'.[57] They are of interest due to the dialogue

[53] Haxby, 'First Apocalypse of James', 70.

[54] Edwards, similar to Haxby, sees the narrative of the ascent of the soul in the First Apocalypse of James as serving two purposes within the text: 'The first purpose is to act as a recapitulation and expansion on the earlier cosmology. More importantly, however, is the fact that this part of the narrative serves to impart instructions to the dying person on successfully navigating in the afterlife. In this context we might go so far as to assert that these instructions are intended for the believers about to be martyred,' Robert Michael Edwards, 'The Rhetoric of Authority: The Nature of Revelation in the First Apocalypse of James', in *La littérature des Questions et Réponses dans l'Antiquité profane et chrétienne: De l'enseignement à l'exégèse*, ed. Marie-Pierre Bussières, Instrumenta Patristica et Mediaevalia 64 (Turnhout: Brepols Publishers, 2013), 68–9.

[55] For a redefinition of 'Orphic' and 'Orphism' (much like the redefinition of 'gnosticism'), see Edmonds, *Redefining Ancient Orphism*. The relationship between Orphism and 'gnosticism' is 'an old conundrum of the history of religions'; see Einar Thomassen, 'Gnostics and Orphics', in *Myths, Martyrs, and Modernity: Studies in the History of Religions in Honour of Jan N. Bremmer*, ed. Jitse Dijkstra, Justin Kroesen, and Yme Kuiper, Studies in the History of Religions 127 (Leiden and Boston: Brill, 2010), 468.

[56] Radcliffe G. Edmonds III, *Myths of the Underworld Journey: Plato, Aristophanes, and the 'Orphic Gold Tablets'* (Cambridge: Cambridge University Press, 2004), 29.

[57] Fritz Graf and Sarah Iles Johnston, *Ritual Texts for the Afterlife: Orpheus and the Bacchic Gold Tablets* (London and New York: Routledge, 2007), 95.

between the 'guards' and the deceased, who must declare that they are from a heavenly race:

> You will find to the left of the house of Hades a spring
> and standing by it a white cypress.
> Do not even approach this spring!
> You will find another, from the Lake of Memory,
> cold water pouring forth; there are guards before it.
> Say, 'I am a child of Earth and starry Sky,
> but my race is heavenly. You yourselves know this.
> I am parched with thirst and am dying; but quickly grant me
> cold water flowing from the Lake of Memory.'
> And they themselves will grant you to drink from the sacred spring.
> And thereafter you will rule among the other heroes.
> This is the work of Memory. When you are about to die
> to die … write this
> enwrapped … darkness.[58]

This tablet is one of the earliest, dated to the fourth century BCE, approximately six or seven centuries before the Gospel of Mary (and the First Apocalypse of James and the Gospel of Thomas). In addition to other tablets from the same period that follow a similar format, there are several examples from the second to first century BCE that include the question 'Who are you? Where are you from?' (τίς δ' ἐΖί; πῶ δ' ἐΖί), to which the person must answer that they are a son or daughter of the Earth and starry Sky.[59] In contrast to the example above, in these tablets there is no declaration that they are from a heavenly race or the like.[60] Tablets that include a reference to the heavenly race begin with the strongly adversative αὐτάρ, which Edmonds suggests points to 'a more dualistic outlook that privileges the starry sky of Heaven over the material world of the Earth'. This is opposed to 'the original claim to be the child of both Earth and Heaven [that] implies not dualism but primeval unity'.[61]

[58] Translation from Graf and Johnston, *Ritual Texts for the Afterlife*, 6–7.

[59] For example, Eleutherna 1, 2, 3, 4 and 5; Mylopotamos; Rethymnon 2; and Pharsalos; see Graf and Johnston, *Ritual Texts for the Afterlife*, 20–35. Note: 'in the local alphabet, Z stands for the sharp double -σσ' (20).

[60] The exception to this is tablet 29, from a grave of an unknown location in Thessaly, mid-fourth century BCE, which reads, 'Who are you? Where are you from? I am son of the Earth and starry Sky. But my race is heavenly' (τίς δ' ἐσί; πῶ δ'ἐσί; Γᾶς υἱός εἰμι καὶ Οὐρανοῦ ἀστερόεντος· αὐτὰρ ἐμοὶ γένος οὐράνιον); see Graf and Johnston, *Ritual Texts for the Afterlife*, 40–1.

[61] Edmonds III, *Myths of the Underworld Journey*, 79.

The dialogue gospels that instruct the soul how to combat its opponents do not share many of the motifs that we find on the Orphic tablets, such as the crossroads, cypress tree and spring.[62] Furthermore, the idea that the dead were thirsty (which Edmonds argues is a universal human idea[63]) is common on the tablets: the dead must refrain from drinking the first body of water that s/he comes across. (In this case, drinking from the spring of forgetfulness – they must hold out for the spring of memory.) In the Christian narratives, instead of conquering thirst, it is passions that must be conquered. Both thirst and passions represent bodily desires and needs, and in both cases, failing memory also has the capacity to hamper progress.

A commonality between Orphic tablets and the First Apocalypse of James is the instruction that, in order to gain access to the superior afterlife, one must *remember*. On several of the Orphic tablets, the dead must resist the water of forgetfulness and drink only from the spring of memory. Forgetfulness is seen as a quality of the disembodied. In the First Apocalypse of James, however, forgetfulness hits when one becomes embodied. James praises Jesus for not being subject to the folly of forgetfulness in a somewhat poetic adoration:

> ϩ̄ⲣ̄ⲁ̄ⲃⲃⲉⲓ ⲁⲕⲉⲓ ⲅⲁ̣ⲣ̣ [ϩⲛ̄] ⲟⲩⲥⲟⲟⲩⲛⲉ ⲉϫⲡⲓⲟ ⲛ̄ⲧⲟⲩⲙⲛ̄ⲧⲁⲧⲥⲟⲟⲩⲛⲉ ⲁⲩⲱ ⲛ̄ⲧⲁⲕⲉⲓ ϩⲛ̄ ⲟⲩⲣ̄ⲡⲙⲉⲟⲩⲉ ⲉϫⲡⲓⲟ ⲛ̄ⲧⲉⲩⲃ̄ϣⲉ} ⲁⲗⲗⲁ ⲛ̄ϯϥⲓ ⲣⲟⲟⲩϣ ⲁⲛ ϩ̄ⲁ̄ⲣⲟⲕ ⲁⲕⲉⲓ ⲅⲁⲣ ⲉⲧⲙⲛ̄ⲧⲁⲧⲥⲟⲟⲩⲛⲉ ⲁ̣ⲩⲱ̣ [ⲙ̄]ⲡⲕⲧⲱⲗⲙ̄ ⲗⲁⲟⲩⲉ ϩⲣ̣̄ⲏ̣ⲓ̣̈ ⲛ̣̄ϩⲏⲧⲥ̣ ⲁⲕⲉⲓ ⲉⲧⲃ̄ϣⲉ ⲁⲩⲱ ⲡⲣ̄ⲡⲙⲉⲟⲩⲉ ⲛ̄ϩⲏⲧⲕ̄ ⲁⲕⲙⲟϣⲉ ϩⲙ ⲡⲟⲙⲉ ⲙ̄ⲡⲕⲧⲱⲗⲙ̄ ($_{CT}$ 14,21–15,7)[64]

> Rabbi, for you have come [with] knowledge to rebuke their ignorance. And you have come with remembrance to rebuke their forgetfulness. But I am not worried about you. You have come to ignorance, and you have not been defiled at all by it. You have come to forgetfulness, and remembrance was in you. You have walked in mud but have not become dirty.

[62] Thomassen writes that there are three points of comparison between Orphism and 'gnosticism' (namely the First Apocalypse of James and *Adv. Haer.* 1.21.5): '1) a similar scenario of [cosmic] interrogation; 2) a declaration made by the deceased about her divine origin and nature; and 3) the reference to a previous ritual of initiation which has assured the dead person of her divine nature, made her immortal and provided her with the knowledge needed to overcome the obstacles faced after death and to produce the right answers to the questions asked,' Thomassen, 'Gnostics and Orphics', 467–8.

[63] Edmonds III, *Myths of the Underworld Journey*, 47.

[64] The NHC version is similar but more fragmentary.

James continues by comparing himself with Jesus, but where Jesus succeeds, James fails: by becoming incarnate, his memory fades. The theme of forgetting one's origins when embodied is shared with the Apocryphon of John, in which the body acts as a chain of forgetfulness (NHC2 21,9–12), alongside the first humans being made to drink 'water of forgetfulness' (ⲟⲩⲙⲟⲟⲩ ⲛ̄ⲃϣⲉ [NHC2 25,7]) so that they would not know where their origins lay. The Exegesis on the Soul and the Authoritative Teaching also urge the soul to *remember* where she originated.

The soul's ascent in the Gospel of Mary frees her from 'the chain of forgetfulness' (ⲧⲙⲣ̄ⲣⲉ ⲛⲧⲃ̄ϣⲉ [17,3]) – presumably meaning the embodied state of forgetfulness that we see in the First Apocalypse of James and the Apocryphon of John. The male disciples have forgotten their true origins, and that is why Mary can say '[what is] unknown to you and I remember, I will pr[oclaim to you]' ([οσα υμ]α̣ς λανθανει (=ϩⲏⲡ) και απομνημονευω α̣ν̣α̣[γγελω υμιν] [POxy.GM 18]). It is not simply that the male disciples are absentminded through their own ineptness; they are entangled in the material realm of forgetfulness.

5.4 The Soul's Victory

Human-Slayer and Space-Destroyer

As the soul ascends, she meets the third power named Ignorance, who asks the usual question of where the soul is going. The soul does not answer, but asserts her dominance over the cosmos below:

> [ⲁⲥ]ⲣ̣̄ⲉⲝⲉⲧⲁⲍⲉ ⲛ̄ⲧⲉⲯⲩⲭⲏ ⲉⲥϫ[ⲱ ⲙ̄]ⲙⲟⲥ ϫⲉ ⲉⲣⲉⲃⲏⲕ ⲉⲧⲱⲛ ϩⲛ̣ [ⲟ]ⲩⲡ̣ⲟ̣ⲛ̣ⲏⲣⲓⲁ ⲁⲩⲁⲙⲁϩⲧⲉ ⲙ̄ⲙⲟ ⲁⲩ[ⲁ]ⲙ̣ⲁ̣ϩ̣ⲧⲉ ⲇⲉ ⲙ̄ⲙⲟ ⲙ̄ⲡⲣ̄ⲕⲣⲓⲛⲉ ⲁⲩ[ⲱ] ⲡⲉϫⲉ ⲧⲉⲯⲩⲭⲏ ϫⲉ ⲁϩⲣⲟ ⲉⲣⲉⲕⲣ̣ⲓ̣ⲛ̣ⲉ̣ ⲙ̄ⲙⲟⲓ̈ ⲉⲙⲡⲓⲕⲣⲓⲛⲉ ⲁⲩⲉⲙⲁϩⲧⲉ ⲙ̄ⲙⲟⲓ̈ ⲉⲙⲡⲓⲁⲙⲁϩⲧⲉ ⲙⲡⲟⲩⲥ̣ⲟ̣ⲩⲱⲛⲧ ⲁⲛⲟⲕ ⲇⲉ ⲁⲓ̈ⲥⲟⲩⲱⲛⲟⲩ ⲉⲩⲃⲱⲗ ⲉⲃⲟⲗ ⲙⲡⲧⲏⲣϥ ⲉⲓⲧⲉ ⲛⲁ ⲡ̣ⲕ̣ⲁ̣ϩ̣ ⲉⲓⲧⲉ ⲛⲁ ⲧⲡ[ⲉ] ⲛ̣̄ⲧⲉⲣⲉⲧⲉⲯⲩⲭⲏ ⲟⲩⲱⲥϥ̄ ⲛ̄ⲧⲙⲉϩϣⲟⲙⲛⲧⲉ ⲛ̄ⲛⲉⲝⲟⲩⲥⲓⲁ ⲁⲥⲃⲱⲕ ⲉⲡⲥⲁ ⲛⲧⲡⲉ ⲁⲩⲱ ⲁⲥⲛⲁⲩ ⲉⲧⲙⲁϩϥⲧⲟⲉ ⲛ̄ⲛⲉⲝⲟⲩⲥⲓⲁ (15,12–16,4)
>
> [She] questioned the soul, sa[yi]ng, 'Where are you going? In [w]ickedness, they bound you. Indeed, they b[o]und you. Do not judge.' An[d] the soul said, 'Why do you judge me? I did not judge. They bound me; I did not bind. They did not recognize me, but I recognized them. All things are dissolving, both the things of the earth and the things of the heav[en].'

> When the soul had destroyed the third of the powers, she went upwards and saw the fourth of the powers.

As in the exchange with Desire, the soul exploits the claims made by Ignorance, claiming that she did not judge or bind and that it was the cosmic powers (and their corresponding passions) that bound her. She recognized their true identity, but they did not recognize hers.[65] What exactly the soul means by judgement is difficult to understand. King and Tuckett regard this passage as reflecting the Saviour's teachings on sin: without sin, there is no judgement or condemnation.[66] However, in John, Jesus' knowledge of where he has come from and where he is going is directly linked to his statement that he judges no one (John 8.14). Much like the First Apocalypse of James, the Gospel of Mary's narrative of the ascending soul can be linked to Jesus' declarations of heavenly identity in John 7–8, further affirming that the soul of the Gospel of Mary does belong to the Johannine Jesus.

Conquering Ignorance allows the soul to proceed to the fourth power, embodying 'the seven p[o]wers of Wrath' (ⲧⲥⲁϣϥⲉ ⲛ̄ⲛ̣ⲉ̣[ⲝ]ⲟⲩⲥⲓⲁ ⲛⲧⲉ ⲧⲟⲣⲅⲏ [16,12–13]). These powers also question the soul, asking, 'Where do you come from Human-Slayer? Or where do you go Space-Destroyer?' (ⲉⲣⲉⲛⲏⲩ ϫⲓⲛ ⲧⲱⲛ ⲧϩⲁⲧ̣ⲃⲣⲱⲙⲉ ⲏ ⲉⲣⲉⲃⲏⲕ ⲉⲧⲱⲛ ⲧⲟⲩⲁ̣ⲥϥⲙⲁ [16,14–15]). At this point, the soul does not see this as a challenge; rather, she declares that she is already free:

> ⲁⲥⲟⲩⲱϣⲃ̄ ⲛ̄ϭⲓ ⲧⲉⲯⲩⲭⲏ ⲡⲉϫⲁⲥ ϫⲉ ⲡⲉⲧⲉⲙⲁϩⲧⲉ ⲙ̄ⲙⲟⲓ̈ ⲁⲩⲕⲟⲛⲥϥ̄ ⲁⲩⲱ ⲡⲉⲧⲕⲧⲟ ⲙ̄ⲙⲟⲓ̈ ⲁⲩⲟⲩⲟⲥϥ<ϥ> ⲁⲩⲱ ⲧⲁⲉⲡⲓⲑⲩⲙⲓⲁ ⲁⲥϫⲱⲕ ⲉⲃⲟⲗ ⲁⲩⲱ ⲧⲙⲛⲧⲁⲧⲥⲟⲟⲩ(ⲛ) ⲁⲥⲙⲟⲩ `ϩ̣ⲛ̄′ ⲟ̣ⲩ[ⲕⲟⲥⲙ]ⲟⲥ ⲛ̄ⲧⲁⲩⲃⲟⲗⲧ′ ⲉⲃⲟⲗ ϩⲛ̄ⲛ ⲟⲩⲕⲟⲥⲙⲟⲥ [ⲁⲩ]ⲱ ϩⲛ̄ ⲟⲩⲧⲩⲡⲟⲥ ⲉⲃⲟⲗ ϩⲛ ⲟⲩⲧⲩⲡⲟⲥ ⲉⲧⲙ̄ⲡⲥⲁ ⲛⲧⲡⲉ ⲁⲩⲱ ⲧⲙⲣ̄ⲣⲉ ⲛⲧⲃ̄ϣⲉ ⲉⲧϣⲟⲟⲡ ⲡⲣⲟⲥ ⲟⲩⲟⲓ̈ϣ ϫⲓⲛ ⲙ̄ⲡⲓⲛⲁⲩ ⲉⲉⲓⲛⲁϫⲓ ⲛⲧⲁⲛⲁⲡⲁⲩⲥⲓⲥ ⲙⲡⲉⲭⲣⲟⲛⲟⲥ ⲙⲡⲕⲁⲓⲣⲟⲥ ⲙⲡ`ⲁⲓ′ⲱⲛ ϩⲛ̄ ⲛⲟⲩⲕⲁⲣⲱϥ (16,16–17,7)

> The soul answered and said, 'That which bound me has been slain, and that which surrounds me has been destroyed. And my desire deceased, and ignorance died. In a [wor]ld I was dissolved from a world, [an]d in a type from a type which is above, and the chain of the forgetfulness which exists only

[65] There is a translation difficulty here as the third-person prefixes ⲁⲩ- and ⲙⲡⲟⲩ- may be translated in the active or the passive sense. Either way, the soul was bound and not recognized.

[66] King, *Mary*, 71; Tuckett, *Mary*, 183.

> for a while. From this time on, I will receive rest from the time of the season of the age, in silence.'

The soul explains where she has been – bound in the material world, dominated by passions, and living in a state of forgetfulness – and where she is going – to receive 'rest'. At the same time, she replies to the charges of 'Human-Slayer', as eliminating the body corrupted by passion, and 'Space-Destroyer', as overcoming the cosmic archons and recognizing the state of the dissolving, impermanent cosmos. The syntax of the final sentence is not clear here: Wilson and MacRae translate 'rest of the time',[67] but Pasquier suggests rest *from* the time.[68] Pasquier's suggestion works well here as temporality can be used as a means of oppression, as in the Apocryphon of John, in which humans are 'bound by means of measure and times and moments' (ⲥⲱⲛϩ ϩⲛ ⲟⲩϣⲓ ⲙⲛ̄ ϩⲛ̄ⲥⲏⲩ ⲙⲛ̄ ϩⲛ̄ⲟⲩⲟⲉⲓϣ [$_{\mathrm{BG}}$ 72,4–6]), related to fate. By translating this 'rest from the time', the immutable heaven is understood as existing beyond temporal and spatial limits.

Human recognition of the dissolving cosmos, and overcoming it, is also found in the Gospel of Thomas. As we saw in the last chapter, logion 3 and 113 pronounce a realized eschatology in that the kingdom is already present (like the Gospel of Mary's Son of Man); and logion 11 and 111 reflect the idea that the heaven and earth will pass away. Logion 111 is particularly comparable to the Gospel of Mary:

> ⲡⲉϫⲉ ⲓ̅ⲥ̅ ϫⲉ ⲙ̄ⲡⲏⲩⲉ ⲛⲁϭⲱⲗ ⲁⲩⲱ ⲡⲕⲁϩ ⲙ̄ⲡⲉⲧⲛ̄ⲙ̄ⲧⲟ ⲉⲃⲟⲗ ⲁⲩⲱ ⲡⲉⲧⲟⲛϩ ⲉⲃⲟⲗ ϩⲛ̄ ⲡⲉⲧⲟⲛϩ ϥⲛⲁⲛⲁⲩ ⲁⲛ ⲉⲙⲟⲩ (GThom 111.1)
>
> Jesus said, 'The heavens and the earth will roll up in your presence, and the one who lives from the Living One will not see death.'

Davies reads the Gospel of Thomas 3 and 113 in light of 11 and 111 and argues that 'when a man of light discovers the kingdom within, he is superior to the world previously and ordinarily apprehended, a world which for him has now passed away'.[69] Gathercole, likewise, contends that the cosmic collapse of 11 and 111 is a 'relatively quiet matter' and is insignificant to the Thomasine disciple who, having

[67] R. McL. Wilson and George W. MacRae, 'The Gospel According to Mary: BG, 1:7,1–19,5', in *Nag Hammadi Codices V,2–5 and VI with Papyrus Berlinensis 8502,1 and 4.*, ed. D. M. Parrott, NHS 11 (Leiden: Brill, 1979), 567.

[68] Pasquier, *Marie*, 95–6.

[69] Davies, 'Christology and Protology', 672.

undergone a challenge from hostile archons (GThom 50), will live forever.[70] It is the living one who understands this message who 'will not taste death' (ϥⲛⲁϫⲓ ϯⲡⲉ ⲁⲛ ⲙ̄ⲡⲙⲟⲩ [GThom 1]). Like the Thomasine disciple, the soul of the Gospel of Mary understands that she is separate from, and superior to, the dissolving cosmos. As she ascends, she eliminates material passions and understands the nature of the material heavens and earth.

Rest and Restoration

The terms 'rest' and 'silence' describe the ultimate destiny for the soul after her ascent. The two terms are connected, as seen in the description of the divine realm in the Apocryphon of John, quoted earlier: 'at rest in silence' (ⲉϥⲙ̄ⲧⲟⲛ ⲙ̄ⲙⲟϥ ϩⲛ ⲟⲩⲕⲁⲣⲱϥ [BG 26,7–8]). Silence is simply a state of 'rest'.[71]

The motif of 'rest' as the post-mortem goal of the human is fairly common in early Christian literature, including Matt 11.29 ('you will find rest for your souls' [εὑρήσετε ἀνάπαυσιν ταῖς ψυχαῖς ὑμῶν]) and Heb 4.1–11, in which the righteous are invited to enter into God's 'rest' (κατάπαυσις).[72] It is found in a number of dialogue gospels, including the Epistula Apostolorum (12.3; 19.14; 26.5), the Epistle of Peter to Philip (NHC 137,10), the Dialogue of the Saviour (120,5–8) and the Book of Thomas (145,8–16). In the same way, 'rest' in the Gospel of Mary is the final resting place of the soul; it is the post-mortem fate of the individual but can be partly realized in the present. Mary falls silent as the soul does – she has attained the state of 'rest', as will be discussed in the next section.

In the Gospel of Mary, the 'rest' is protological. As the soul returns to the place from which she came, ἀνάπαυσις is related to the idea of ἀποκατάστασις, understood as the return of all creation,

[70] Gathercole, 'Eschatology of the Gospel of Thomas', 294–5.

[71] King: 'It is in silence that one ultimately encounters God', Karen L. King, 'Hearing, Seeing, and Knowing God: Allogenes and the Gospel of Mary', in *Early Christian Voices in Texts, Traditions, and Symbols: Essays in Honor of François Bovon*, ed. David H. Warren, Ann Graham Brock and David W. Pao (Boston and Leiden: Brill, 2003), 325.

[72] On the multiple parallels, see C. Schneider, 'Anapausis', *Reallexikon für Antike und Christentum* I (1950): 414–18. For the eschatological interpretation of Matt 11.28–30, see W. D. Davies and Dale C. Allison, *Matthew 8–18*, Vol. 2, ICC (London and New York: T&T Clark, 1991), 288–9. On the various interpretations of 'rest' in Hebrews, see Harold W. Attridge, '"Let Us Strive to Enter That Rest": The Logic of Hebrews 4:1–11', *HTR* 73.1–2 (1980): 279.

or at least rational beings, to the Good, or to God.[73] For Philo, ἀποκατάστασις is in reference to the restoration of the *soul* (τελείαν ἀποκατάστασιν ψυχῆς [*Her.* 293]) from sins and passions (πάθη).[74] Clement, influenced by Philo, also depicts the perfection of the 'gnostic' soul, which dwells in the divine, as an apokatastasis or restitution to the highest place of rest (εἰς τὸν κορυφαῖον ἀποκαταστήσῃ τῆς ἀναπαύσεως τόπον [*Strom.* 7.10.57.1–4]). There, it will see God 'face-to-face'. But for Clement the restoration of the soul is not entirely protological: thanks to Christ's coming, the end is better than the beginning.[75]

Realized or Post-Mortem Salvation?

The disciple, for the Gospel of Mary, does not need to be deceased to attain 'rest' – or partial 'rest', at least. The interrogations from the powers act, on one level, as a narrative of the post-mortem journey of the soul, but they also can be seen as the embodied soul's ongoing battle with impulses and passions.

Although the story of the soul in the Gospel of Mary is primarily Mary's report of what Jesus has told her, Mary, the living and embodied disciple, does not appear to be under the influence of the powers named Ignorance, Wrath and Desire. She receives private revelation from the Lord; she is 'blessed' (ⲛⲁⲓ̈ⲁⲧⲉ) as she does not waver at the vision of the Saviour (10,14–15); she comforts the male disciples, turning their minds towards the Good (9,12–22); and the Saviour not only 'loved her more than the other women' (ⲟⲩⲁϣⲉ̣ ⲛϩⲟⲩⲟ ⲡⲁⲣⲁ ⲡⲕⲉⲥⲉⲉⲡⲉ ⲛ̄ⲥϩⲓ̈ⲙⲉ [10,1–3]), but also, as Levi tells Peter and Andrew, the Saviour 'loved her more than us' (ⲟⲩⲟϣⲥ̄ ⲛ̄ϩⲟⲩⲟ ⲉⲣⲟⲛ [18,14–15]). The beloved disciple and comforter who teaches the others about salvation is put in contrast to the 'wrathful' (ⲛⲣⲉϥⲛⲟⲩϭⲥ) Peter, who is likened to the adversaries (18,7–10). As the soul reaches silence at the end of her journey, Mary falls silent at the end of her recollection. The Coptic MS inserts a scribal break here, showing that Mary's silence should be read alongside the soul's

[73] See Ilaria Ramelli, *The Christian Doctrine of Apokatastasis: A Critical Assessment from the New Testament to Eriugena*, VCSup 120 (Leiden: Brill, 2013), 1. Origen is usually credited with being the founder of this doctrine in Christianity, but Ramelli shows that he had several antecedents.

[74] See Ramelli, *Christian Doctrine of Apokatastasis*, 6–7. For Philo, apokatastasis can also refer to the restoration of the soul to health after the abandonment of evil.

[75] Ramelli, *Christian Doctrine of Apokatastasis*, 119–36, esp. 135–6.

and Jesus', rather than as part of the subsequent argument between the disciples.[76]

It is often noted that, in Jewish and Christian literature, the ascent of the soul can be post-mortem or while embodied.[77] Embodied journeys might be ecstatic or moralistic, through which one overcomes passions and ignorance. In terms of eschatological salvation, these journeys can be characterized in terms of future or realized eschatology. But these do not have to be mutually exclusive – salvation can be a process. Salvation in the Gospel of Mary may have been realized in two stages: the knowledge gained in the body alongside moral progress of overcoming passions and the journey of the soul after death. Pagels and Koester see this idea in the Dialogue of the Saviour, noting a realized/future 'paradox' throughout the text. The opening projects a realized eschatology:

> ⲎⲆⲎ ⲁⲡⲉⲟⲩⲟⲉⲓϣ ϣⲱⲡⲉ ⲚⲈⲤⲚⲎⲞⲨ ⲆⲈⲔⲀⲀⲤ ⲈⲚⲁⲔⲰ Ⲛ̄ⲤⲰⲚ Ⲙ̄ⲠⲈⲚϨⲒⲤⲈ Ⲛ̄ⲦⲚ̄ⲁϩⲉ ⲉⲣⲁⲧⲚ̄ ϩⲚ̄ ⲧⲁⲛⲁⲡⲁⲩⲥⲓⲥ ⲡⲉⲧⲛⲁⲱϩⲉ ⲅⲁⲣ ⲉⲣⲁⲧϥ̄ ϩⲚ̄ ⲧⲁⲛⲁⲡⲁⲩⲥⲓⲥ ϥⲛⲁⲘ̄ⲦⲞⲚ Ⲙ̄ⲘⲞϥ Ⲛ̄ϣⲁⲉⲚⲈϩ (120,3–6)
>
> Already the time has come, brothers, for us to abandon our labour and stand in rest, for whoever stands in rest will rest forever.

This is shortly followed by an implication of future eschatology, 'when the time of dissolution comes' (ϩⲟⲧⲁⲛ ⲉϥϣⲁⲛϣⲱⲡⲉ Ⲛ̄ϭⲓ ⲡⲉⲟⲩⲟⲉⲓϣ Ⲙ̄ⲡⲃⲱⲗ ⲉⲃⲟⲗ [122,2–3]), and Jesus instructs his disciples that the power of fear will come upon them. The little that remains of the account of cosmic powers battling the soul in the very fragmentary text appears to be similar to the Gospel of Mary. The Dialogue of the Saviour, however, contains an explicit reference to baptism (134,5–8) and a vision of the Eternal existent (134,24–138,1) that Pagels and Koester understand to inform the whole tractate: '[W]e find *Dial. Sav.* dealing with the tension between what the disciples have received "already" through baptism, initiation and visions, and what they anticipate as "not yet"'.[78] DeConick, on the other hand,

[76] Hartenstein understands Mary's silence as indicating that 'Maria wird also als eine dargestellt, die ein hohes Maß an Vollkommenheit erreicht hat', Hartenstein, *Die zweite Lehre*, 149.

[77] See e.g. Jan N. Bremmer, 'Descents to Hell and Ascents to Heaven in Apocalyptic Literature', in *The Oxford Handbook of Apocalyptic Literature*, ed. John J. Collins (Oxford and New York: Oxford University Press, 2014), 350–2.

[78] Emmel et al., *Nag Hammadi Codex III,5*, 14. They find parallels in the Epistle of Peter to Philip, Ephesians, Hebrews, 1 Peter and the Gospel of Philip.

regards the Dialogue of the Saviour as *anticipating* death, ascent and immortalization; baptism does not guarantee such ascent (or foretaste of salvation), but knowledge of one's origins is what is necessary.[79] In the Gospel of Mary, it appears that Mary, while knowing the soul's origins, has achieved a (semi-)state of eschatological salvation and has fulfilled the teachings of the gospel: she has found the Son of Man within and put on the Perfect Man.

Evidently there is an aspect of a realized salvation or eschatology in the Gospel of Mary akin to the Johannine 'eternal life' and the Ephesian idea of already being seated in heaven (Eph 2.6). For John, the crucial event is the coming of Jesus, and one abides in a figurative death until one believes. John's eternal life can begin in the present body; the evangelist has Jesus tell his readers that believers have already passed from death to life (5.24–25). The language of resurrection figures in the present ('For as the Father raises the dead and gives them life, so also the Son gives life to whom he will' [ὥσπερ γὰρ ὁ πατὴρ ἐγείρει τοὺς νεκροὺς καὶ ζῳοποιεῖ, οὕτως καὶ ὁ υἱὸς οὓς θέλει ζῳοποιεῖ, 5.21]), yet they will not be raised until the 'last day' (ἐσχάτῃ ἡμέρᾳ [6.40]). At Lazarus' tomb, Martha echoes this sentiment ('I know that he will rise again in the resurrection at the last day' [οἶδα ὅτι ἀναστήσεται ἐν τῇ ἀναστάσει ἐν τῇ ἐσχάτῃ ἡμέρᾳ, 11.24]), but Jesus corrects her assumption, declaring himself the resurrection and the life (11.25).[80] As Lazarus is raised, it is evident that the 'last day' has already come. Neither the Gospel of Mary nor John emphasize the coming of Christ as a future eschatological event.[81] Rather, the individual eschatology focuses on the 'realized' element: the Saviour's coming has the ability to bring eternal life, or 'rest', in the present time.

The Pauline influence is evident here too, as (pseudo-)Paul exhorts his readers to fight the cosmic powers (Eph 6.12), while also

[79] April D. DeConick, 'The "Dialogue of the Savior" and the Mystical Sayings of Jesus', *VC* 50.2 (1996): esp. 183.

[80] This is not to deny the Johannine tension between future and realized eschatology: John 5.28–29 clearly suggests that there will be an eschatological resurrection in the future. As Ashton writes, John 'has not altogether abandoned the belief that there will be a *future* judgement as well … [yet for] the most part John effectively *de-eschatologizes* judgement by making it the immediate consequence of an option for or against Christ in the lifetime of each individual', Ashton, *Understanding the Fourth Gospel*, 406, 409. Dodd argues that the evangelist is deliberately juxtaposing two contrasting eschatologies, Dodd, *Interpretation of the Fourth Gospel*, 320–8.

[81] The exception to this in John is 14.3: 'And if I go and prepare a place for you, I will come again and will take you to myself, so that where I am, there you may be also' (καὶ ἐὰν πορευθῶ καὶ ἑτοιμάσω τόπον ὑμῖν, πάλιν ἔρχομαι καὶ παραλήμψομαι ὑμᾶς πρὸς ἐμαυτόν, ἵνα ὅπου εἰμὶ ἐγὼ καὶ ὑμεῖς ἦτε).

declaring that, although they were once 'children of wrath' (τέκνα ὀργῆς) living in the 'passions of the flesh' (ἐπιθυμίαις τῆς σαρκός, 2.3), they can now participate in heaven whilst living on earth. As Talbert writes, believers 'live in two dimensions'.[82] The language as well as the concepts of battling the cosmic ἐξουσίαι (ⲉⳅⲟⲩⲥⲓⲁ), linked with ἐπιθυμία (ⲉⲡⲓⲑⲩⲙⲓⲁ), σάρξ (ⲥⲁⲣⳅ) and ὀργή (ⲟⲣⲅⲏ), mirror those we have seen in the Gospel of Mary. Mary, having defeated the Powers, lives in both the earth and the heavens and has achieved 'rest', which in effect is eternal life.

Yet in spite of Mary's embodied state of 'rest', for salvation in the fullest sense, the soul requires freedom from the body. The dialogue with Wrath points to a post-mortem, post-body ascent in which the soul is declared a Human-slayer (16,15). The soul was once bound in the body-garment, influenced by passions, but she does not belong there. Her destiny is a passion-free existence in her heavenly home. Salvation, then, must occur in two phases: belief/knowledge/passion-free (leading to a possibly initiatory ascent) and post-mortem ascent. The Gospel of Mary conceives the event of eschatological salvation as beginning with belief/knowledge, to be furthered at the moment of death, and as culminating in following Jesus into post-mortem 'rest'.

5.5 Conclusion

In our discussion of the narrative frame of the Gospel of Mary, we saw a parallelism between Jesus and Mary. This parallelism continues in this chapter, in which Mary represents the Christian soul following Christ into heaven. The individual salvation in the gospel is predicated entirely on Christ's own ascension, and Mary tells her brothers about his ascension, as she is instructed to do in John 20.17. By doing so, she also teaches them how to gain their own eschatological 'rest'. Like Christ, the soul in the Gospel of Mary descends from her heavenly home through a cosmos full of archons and enters a body. Once embodied, she must fight disturbance, passion and forgetfulness, overcoming bodily desires and remembering her heavenly origin. Then she can ascend through the heavens, each with its guardian that will attempt to stop her, but she must tell them that she is free from their influence. And she can do so under the instruction of Jesus, just as Jesus has done during his own descent and ascent. It is then that she is free from the dissolving cosmos and gains 'rest'.

[82] Talbert, *Ephesians and Colossians*, 60.

Although Peter and Andrew profess that they have never heard revelation of this kind, we see it throughout the early Christian world and its wider context. The Ascension of Isaiah and the Epistula Apostolorum narrate Jesus descending through the archons in disguise; Plato tells us that restful souls have descended into a body in which they have been thrown into movement through the passions. In the Gospel of Thomas 50 and the First Apocalypse of James, Jesus instructs the disciples to remember their divine origins and to declare this to the cosmic archons during their heavenly ascent. The disciple will then find 'rest', which is a common motif for post-mortem salvation in Matthew, Hebrews, the Book of Thomas, the Epistula Apostolorum and elsewhere.

The individual eschatology of the Gospel of Mary finds parallels not only with the gospel's narrative frame, in which Mary and Jesus are constructed in tandem, but also with the cosmic eschatology as both matter and the soul return to their origins through Christ.[83] The Saviour in the Gospel of Mary has come to dissolve the cosmos to its root. He also lives within the disciples, like the Johannine Jesus and the Pauline Christ, and by seeking, finding and following him, the disciple can also be free from passion. The soul can follow Jesus through the planetary spheres of Pauline cosmology to find 'rest', akin to the Johannine eternal life. As in John, the disciple can reach this state of eschatological salvation in the present Christian experience, although full eschatological salvation will be met after death. The disciple's salvation is neither dependent on, nor concerned with, the dissolving heavens and earth – the soul recognizes this but overcomes it. Both the individual and cosmic eschatology is conditional upon Jesus, but neither is conditional upon the other.

[83] For more on the relationship between the dissolution of the cosmos and the ascent of the soul in the Gospel of Mary, see Sarah Parkhouse, 'Matter and the Soul: The Bipartite Eschatology of the Gospel of Mary', in *Connecting Gospels*, ed. Francis Watson and Sarah Parkhouse (Oxford: Oxford University Press, 2018), 216–32.

CONCLUSION

After Jesus' death, his followers were writing gospels in which he speaks with those who were his disciples in Galilee, revealing new teachings or explaining those that needed clarification. In these dialogue gospels, Jesus might speak to Mary or Peter or James alone, or the Twelve or some of the Twelve, or another combination of disciples known to us from the canonical gospels, and he tells them about their salvation. In most cases, he then leaves the disciples on their own, to follow his commands, preach the gospel to the nations, or keep the gospel hidden for a time.

The dialogue gospels are a subset of gospel literature. The wider 'gospel' genre comprises a range of texts in which we find a wealth of interpretations of the character Jesus and his revelation. Each gospel, whether canonical or non-canonical, offers a new narrative of ancient Christianity and a new interpretation of its foundational figure. It is on this basis that canonical gospels and dialogue gospels find a common ground and can be brought into conversation. These two overlapping collections of gospel literature, which cross at the point of the Johannine Farewell Discourse, are intrinsically interrelated: their content reflects similar concepts and concerns, centred around the salvific figure of Christ.

Matthew, Mark, Luke and John converge at the point of form, which differentiates the dialogue gospels from these biographies.[1] But canonical gospels are not just biographies, and the dialogue gospels are not just dialogues. (The Epistula Apostolorum and the Epistle of Peter to Philip, for example, are also letters.) John may be primarily a biography, but it contains a farewell discourse, in which dialogue is found. John 13.31–17.1 shares its structure with many other dialogue gospels, depicting Jesus in conversation with selected

[1] In acceptance of the argument that canonical gospels are biographies put forward by Richard A. Burridge, *What Are the Gospels? A Comparison with Graeco-Roman Biography*, SNTSMS 70 (Cambridge: Cambridge University Press, 1992).

disciples imparting his final revelations, answering their questions, with shorter or longer answers, some verging on the point of a monologue, and also with snippets of narrative. There are many points of convergence between canonical gospels and dialogue gospels, and reading them together as belonging within the field of early Christian gospels produces fruitful results for our understanding of the textual world of early Christianity.

That is not to say that gospel literature itself should be segregated from its wider literary context. Throughout this work, I have attempted to read dialogue gospels alongside canonical gospels *and* Pauline letters *and* early Christian thinkers *and* related literature, while showing that they are grappling with similar themes, issues and questions. They do not think the same way on every matter, and even issues that shape our whole understanding of theology will see great divergence (e.g. creation and resurrection). Yet despite these divergences, they converge at the single fundamental, theological issue: the saving role of Christ. And from this beginning point, connections are many and various, and these connections show that dialogue gospels do not stand on the margins of the Christian world but firmly within it.[2]

Looking back …

In this work, I started with a broad discussion about dialogue gospels as a whole, asking how and why we define a genre, and then compared them to selected texts that we find in the New Testament. This included snippets of dialogue gospels and broad, sweeping overviews. In order to develop points about shared and contrasting features within the dialogue gospel genre, its key themes and intertextual relationship with New Testament texts, I homed in on one example – the Gospel of Mary. Part I informed Part II; it provided a basis for the Gospel of Mary's literary context. However, here

[2] An issue that has not been dealt with is the *scriptural* status of the Johannine Farewell Discourse and the contested status of the Apocalypse of Peter, which was provisionally included within the Muratorian Canon (ll. 71–72), cited as Scripture by Clement, belonged to 'the inspired writings' of Methodius, and was 'disputed' alongside Jude and the catholic epistles by Eusebius. On the reception of the Apocalypse of Peter by these authors and more, see A. Jakab, 'The Reception of the Apocalypse of Peter in Ancient Christianity', in *The Apocalypse of Peter*, ed. Jan N. Bremmer and István Czachesz, Studies on Early Christian Apocrypha 7 (Leuven: Peeters, 2003), 174–86. I have tried to disassociate these texts from scriptural/semi-scriptural/heresy biases as much as possible and to read them in their own right, but mentioning that some of them were embraced by 'orthodox' thinkers in the ancient world demonstrates that the genre as a whole was not marginalized.

in the conclusion I will work backwards to see how Part II can develop Part I.

Part II's focus on the Gospel of Mary ended with two chapters on the gospel's eschatology and began with a discussion of the narrative frame. The final chapter, the analysis of the ascent of the soul, highlighted the Gospel of Mary's connections to John and the First Apocalypse of James – it is in the first instance Jesus' own ascension, which he instructed Mary to disclose to his brothers in John 20.17, that is narrated in the Gospel of Mary. However, in the second instance it is a didactic story for the disciple's salvation: through Jesus' ascension he has paved a way for the ascent of the disciple's soul, as in the First Apocalypse of James, and here we find instruction on how to follow him. The soul must declare to heavenly powers that it is from 'above' and is returning home. This narrative is connected with the Gospel of Thomas 50, in which Jesus speaks of an uncontextualized dialogue in which the disciple must declare that s/he is from the light and the living Father. Further connections to the dialogue in the Gospel of Mary can be found in Plato and 'Orphism', and placing these various traditions side by side highlighted how the individual eschatology of the Gospel of Mary has a christological basis. The basic message of the gospel is not dissimilar to what we find in John: Jesus is Saviour – he has ascended – his disciples can follow. The descending-ascending soul in the Gospel of Mary takes on features ascribed to Jesus in John's Gospel, and the context takes over the narrative frame of John 20.14–18. The soul's ascension can be post-mortem, when the soul frees itself from the bodily passions, or realized, as exemplified by the model disciple Mary.

The Gospel of Mary's cosmic eschatology was the subject of Chapter 4. Like the individual eschatology, this was interpreted christologically and placed within a wider Christian context. It was argued that the Gospel of Mary shares the common Christian belief that matter is the raw material of the cosmos, shaped by God. Matter has been affected by passions, which in turn affect the individual causing sin and death. And this is why Jesus (called 'the Good') has come: to dissolve-restore the cosmos to its original constituent parts (called its 'root'). The concept of dissolution is a point at which the Gospel of Mary converges with other early Christian literature; yet it diverges from the 'traditional' expectation of a future parousia (cf. Matt 24.30–31) and actively contradicts this by stating that the Son of Man is 'within'. King and Tuckett, among others, read the Son of Man to be distinct from Christ, but my interpretation follows de

Boer and Schröter who argue that the Son of Man is Jesus, who can live within the disciples and be 'put on' (cf. John 17.26; Rom 13.14). In the Gospel of Mary, the Son of Man has descended from heaven (cf. John 3.13), which is understood both as the Good coming to inaugurate the dissolution and Christ being within. The Gospel of Mary does not reduce the eschatological idea that we find particularly in Matthew, but reinterprets it by using ideas already present in John and Paul.

The gospel's cosmic eschatology is partly connected to its individual eschatology and partly separate from it. Jesus will dissolve the material cosmos to its original constituent parts, and Jesus will enable the soul to ascend to its heavenly home. Yet despite this parallel movement, the two eschatological systems appear to have little overlap; as the soul makes her journey to heaven, she recognizes that heaven and earth are dissolving, but she is undisturbed by the process. The two teachings form a 'bipartite' eschatology, which is reflected also in the structure of the Gospel of Mary: the two teachings are quite literally in two parts. The first teaching is the conversation between the Saviour and his disciple(s), in which he teaches them about cosmic eschatology; the second is Mary's recollection of her vision of the ascending soul, in which she teaches her brothers about individual eschatology.

I have attempted to extricate the Gospel of Mary from the construct of 'gnosticism' that it is often encumbered by and relocate it in a broader category of general Christian traditions. The preference to read it alongside the Apocryphon of John must stem from their adjacent positions in the Berlin Codex rather than the texts themselves. The Apocryphon of John contains an evil and ignorant demiurge named Yaldabaoth who creates the world, and he and his cronies entrap Adam in the body out of spite. The Gospel of Mary does not have this. There are certain similarities between the two texts, such as the body being a place where humans forget their heavenly origins or 'divine spark', but that does not have to be the work of a malevolent creator. If the Gospel of Mary envisaged a chief archon that loiters over the world, the soul might be expected to meet it on her way through the heavens (cf. Apocalypse of Paul), or the reader might have been introduced to Sophia/Achamoth (cf. the First Apocalypse of James). Rather than viewing the material world as the invention and playground of the demiurge or devil, the Gospel of Mary merely states that the material cosmos has been overwhelmed with passions that sway the soul from its original state of heavenly 'rest' (cf. Clement of Alexandria, Philo), and it is these passions, named Darkness, Desire, Ignorance and Wrath, that the soul of the Gospel of Mary encounters. Passions are the soul's vices, not matter itself, although at some point these two appear to have become inextricably connected. The condition of humanity in the world stands as close to Paul as it does to the Apocryphon of John.

In this study, we have seen how the eschatological revelations of Jesus and Mary play their part within the narrative frame, but to frame the question backwards: how does the narrative frame work to serve the eschatological teachings? Although the answer is similar, this question takes a slightly different nuance and coheres with our holistic understanding of the gospel. The bipartite eschatological system is divided into two teachings: two separate dialogues with two separate revealers. But for the teachings contained in the Gospel of Mary to work, the narrative frame is essential. For Mary to recall Jesus' soul's journey, he must have *departed* and *ascended*. He must also have *appeared* to her to *reveal* the story of his ascension. But Mary could not have successfully revealed the ascent of the soul without this setting: it must be clear to the readers/hearers that it is Jesus who is ultimately the revealer and Saviour. If Mary alone revealed eschatological truth, there might be no actual truth in it. Jesus' presence as Saviour at the beginning of the text authenticates the whole gospel. Furthermore, the disciples must discuss the eschatological teachings.[3] They debate (ⲅⲩⲙⲛⲁⲍⲉ) the Saviour's words following his eschatological teaching; they contest Mary's eschatological teaching, declaring it heterodox (ϩⲛ̄ⲕⲉⲙⲉⲉⲩⲉ). The debate in the narrative frame serves to authenticate the revelation: as Levi says, Jesus loved and trusted Mary, and therefore, Peter and Andrew (and thus the readers) should do likewise. The narrative frame substantiates the eschatological revelation. Contrary to a widespread view of dialogue gospels, there is absolutely no evidence that the Gospel of Mary is a Christian narrative frame imposed on a 'gnostic' (non-Christian) dialogue – quite the opposite.

Having focused on the Gospel of Mary, drawing comparisons to other literature where appropriate, we can now reflect on its wider literary context – which takes us back to Part I. Here the focus was on dialogue gospels as a genre, asking what could be included and

[3] The reason why is unclear; presumably some sort of wider debate lies in the background. Peter's and Mary's debate in the Gospel of Thomas 114, and the Pistis Sophia (2.72 [162,16–18]), as well as Andrew's inability to accept the ascent of the soul (although it is Jesus telling him about it!) in the Pistis Sophia show that the Gospel of Mary is not in isolation in presenting these issues.

by what criteria we exclude texts from a genre. For the purpose of comparison, genre should be inclusive and open. Texts can participate in more than one genre – the Johannine Farewell Discourse, for example, belongs within a *bios* gospel, but that does not preclude its inclusion in the dialogue gospel genre. The Epistle of Peter to Philip and the Epistula Apostolorum are letters, gospels *and* dialogues. Any construction of a genre is heuristic and temporary. It is formed to serve a purpose, and it can be unformed.

With this in mind, genre allows various, even disparate, texts to be brought together for comparison, and juxtaposition allows their similarities and unique qualities to be brought to the surface. At the end of the first chapter, I provided a preliminary comparative survey of two main themes found within dialogue gospels: the Saviour and eschatology. Dialogue gospels are comparable in that each is attentive to eschatological revelation, yet the revelations themselves are divergent. Looking at how dialogue gospels portray the post-mortem fate of the individual, there are six things that might be included: (1) judgement, (2) resurrection of the flesh, (3) ascent of the disembodied soul, (4) torments/hell, (5) reincarnation and (6) 'rest'/heaven. A number of these can be combined in a single dialogue gospel: the Apocryphon of John proposes that a human can be judged, be reincarnated, find 'rest' or be damned. Judgement can happen to the soul (Book of Thomas) or to resurrected flesh (Apocalypse of Peter). The overlaps and connections in these revelations demonstrates how problematic it is to taxonomize these texts into particular theological groups. When considering dialogue gospels, rather than imposing categories, whether watertight or permeable, it is more useful to think in terms of a rhizomatic structure that displays the intricate and non-hierarchical web of early Christian thought.

To construct a dialogue gospel genre allows for this sort of comparative work, which draws out connections between texts in thematic clusters and highlights unique qualities of individual texts. Reading the Gospel of Mary alongside the Epistula Apostolorum, the ascent of Jesus' ethereal soul stands in contrast with the confirmation of the unyielding corporeality of Jesus' risen body. Yet such differences are not at the expense of the texts' similarities – both texts emphasize an ascent-descent christology through levels of heavens in which divine beings dwell. The Gospel of Mary focuses on Jesus' post-mortem ascension (15,1–17,7); the Epistula Apostolorum on Jesus' incarnational descent (13.1–14.5). As the

Gospel of Mary concentrates on leaving the flesh, the Epistula Apostolorum concentrates on entering it. But neither is at the expense of the other: the Gospel of Mary *also* implies an incarnational descent through the soul's dialogue with the powers (15,2–3), and the Epistula Apostolorum *also* includes a cinematic narration of Jesus' (albeit fleshly) ascension as a bright cloud takes him away (51.2–3). In both texts, Jesus descends in disguise from the heavenly beings – whether it is for their protection or his is where these gospels differ. In spite of these differences, the points of convergence suggest that the Epistula Apostolorum and the Gospel of Mary can sit very closely together in the extensive body of early Christian literature.

By comparing and contrasting a risen Jesus who may or may not be in 'another form' (as in Mark 16.12), the corporeality of Jesus in the Epistula Apostolorum alone is highlighted. Had we compared the Epistula Apostolorum only to John 20.24–29 or Luke 24.36–43, in which all the texts invite the disciples to touch Jesus, we may have noted their similarities, without noticing how the Epistula Apostolorum takes Jesus' corporeality further than the canonical stories. In the Epistula Apostolorum, there is *one* appearance of the risen Jesus. He appears to the women outside the tomb, and they travel together to the male disciples. The author of the Epistula Apostolorum leaves absolutely no room to allow for another appearance of Jesus – he does not and could not appear through locked doors (cf. John 20.19) or vanish (cf. Luke 24.31). The Epistula Apostolorum does not sit as closely to Luke and John as one might expect due to the traditional (proto-)'orthodox' label. Rather, the Epistula Apostolorum is taking the Lukan and Johannine issue of physicality and pushing it in one direction – the direction that became 'orthodox' but diverges from the canonical gospels.

Further thematic connections between dialogue gospels and texts that came to be included in the New Testament were drawn out in Chapter 2. In general, dialogue gospels stem from traditions found within the canonical gospels and thought-world of Paul. Certain themes were selected from each of the canonical gospels, Acts and selected Pauline epistles, and it was seen how they were developed in the dialogue gospels, either in line with their predecessors or diverging from them. In many cases, dialogue gospels and canonical texts are really rather close, with comparable interests including the risen Jesus, the worldwide apostolic mission and the disclosure (or non-disclosure) of mysteries.

Going Forward … Further Research on Dialogue Gospels

Dialogue gospels are rarely read as holistic texts. Too often our reading of them is shaped by the presupposition that they are a composite of sources cobbled together. The Sophia of Jesus Christ is seen as a narrative frame superimposed onto a 'gnostic' dialogue (Eugnostos, which precedes it in NHC 3), and the Dialogue of the Saviour is seen as sayings of Jesus moulded into a single text. The Gospel of Thomas, likewise, is a collection of sayings that are often not read in light of each other. But someone has put these texts together and made sense of them as a whole. And once we appreciate that they are a work of craftsmanship rather than some incompetent scribe haphazardly assembling various texts and traditions, then they can then be subjected to the same hermeneutical methodologies that are used for New Testament texts. All texts are inspired by previous texts: Luke used Mark and Q/Matthew, but the gospel is not primarily read as an amalgamation of other older texts.

This view of dialogue gospels leads to the general assumption that the authors used non-Christian sources and thus that the text has been 'christianized'. As I have shown in Part II, the Gospel of Mary is a unified text and is thoroughly Christian. Every part of its teachings is predicated on the saving role of Christ. Dialogue gospels are often read as 'not really Christian' or 'superficially Christian', which skews their interpretation and use. I would propose, going forward, that we apply christological readings to the teachings that we are not too sure about and see what happens. Whether we understand the 'Son of Man within' in the Gospel of Mary as Jesus or a non-christological inner being determines the way that we see the gospel in the context of early Christianity. By experimenting with this strategy, we will produce new results for dialogue gospels (and other non-canonical gospels) and their environment.

The relationships between gospel literature often centre around the question of dependency. This is the case both for canonical gospels (e.g. did Luke use Matthew?) and for whether non-canonical gospels are dependent on the canonical (e.g. did the Apocalypse of Peter know Matthew?). The interdependency of dialogue gospels has not been a feature of this work and is rarely explored elsewhere. (We have briefly touched upon Hartenstein's interesting argument that the Apocryphon of James knew and used the First Apocalypse of James, but this takes up three pages of her monograph.) Dependency within the genre itself might be an interesting new avenue of research. It is my inclination that the Pistis Sophia knew and used the Gospel of

Mary and the Gospel of Thomas (logion 114 at least). In the Pistis Sophia, Andrew cannot accept the teaching on the ascent of the soul (cf. Gospel of Mary), and Mary declares that Peter hates women (cf. the Gospel of Thomas 114). The text also uses a version of the Sophia myth, but appears to diverge from the Apocryphon of John in that Sophia does not originate from nor is restored to the divine realm. In the Pistis Sophia, she resides in the lower heavens.

Going Forward … Dialogue Gospels for New Testament Studies and Beyond

New Testament studies often examines texts outside of the New Testament, but rarely do scholarly works show much engagement with dialogue gospels. When New Testament scholarship seeks to engage with the wider context, it typically focuses only on the predecessors and contemporaries of its primary texts. Studies relating to the canonical gospels will typically feature a wide range of Jewish material, from the Hebrew Bible to Qumran to Josephus and beyond, as well as Graeco-Roman literature in various genres. Occasionally, we will see engagement with some patristic sources and perhaps a few quotations from the Gospel of Thomas, but on the whole, literature that postdates the New Testament sits on the margins. But the closest literary neighbours to New Testament texts are those Christian writings that postdate it, given the shared genres, characters and themes: gospels, epistles, acts and apocalypses, mostly attributed pseudonymously to apostolic authors or other prestigious figures. As the non-canonical works tend to be later, they thus represent 'reception' instead of 'influence', but are no less useful than pre-Christian literature in informing interpretation of New Testament texts as they often belong within similar literary contexts.

Going forward, we might see dialogue gospels within the rhizomatic network of early Christian literature, in which texts can be connected at any point in any number of ways without the need for a single text or group of texts at the top of the metaphorical pyramid. This would go hand in hand with an open understanding of genre that allows various, even disparate, texts to be brought together for comparative analysis. Yet at the same time, temporary and heuristic taxonomic constructions can be useful as they allow literary groupings to draw out both similarities and unique qualities of the texts being analysed. The genre constructed in this thesis has been that of 'dialogue gospels', but the methods employed can be applied to a wider, narrower or completely different taxonomy, such as gospel literature as an entirety, post-resurrection narratives or acts. Each of these constructions has the potential to build bridges between canonical and non-canonical literature and consequently provide us with a fuller picture of the early Christian literary landscape.

APPENDIX A

The Gospel of Mary: Coptic and Greek MSS

The Gospel of Mary exists for us today in three incomplete manuscripts. The fullest version is in the fifth-century Coptic codex *Papyrus Berolinensis 8502* (BG), but this has a six-page lacuna at the beginning and four pages missing in the middle. The extant material is pages 7–10 and 15–19, with a title on the final page. There are also two third-century Greek fragments, *Papyrus Oxyrhynchus L 3525* (POxy.GM) and *Papyrus Rylands 463* (PRyl.GM). They roughly correspond to 8,22–10,17 and 17,5–19,5 of BG, respectively. It is almost certain that the Gospel of Mary was originally penned in the Greek language at some point in the second or early third century.[1] It is probable that there were several more copies of the Gospel of Mary circulating between the third and fifth centuries. Neither POxy.GM nor PRyl.GM work as a *Vorlage* for the Coptic text, and so there must have been a text that BG was based on.[2] Till suggests that the

[1] Most scholars date the Gospel of Mary to the second century, but I think an early-third-century date is also plausible. For example, Tuckett writes, 'A clear *terminus ad quem* for the writing of the gospel is provided by the Greek fragments. The existence of two independent Greek manuscripts of the text from the early third century, along with some copying errors in them, means that the gospel must have been in existence by c.200 CE. Further, the evidence from the manuscripts, as noted above, suggests that the gospel must have existed in a number of copies. Thus the text is at latest a second-century production,' Tuckett, *Mary*, 11. A more precise date is debated. King conjectures the first half of the second century, King, 'Gospel of Mary Magdalene', 628. Pasquier argues for the second half, Pasquier, *Marie*, 3–4.

[2] Whether a minimum of three Greek MSS in circulation implies a wide readership in the ancient world is debated; King argues that, '[b]ecause it is unusual for several copies from such early dates to have survived, the attestation of the Gospel of Mary as an early Christian work is unusually strong', King, *Mary*, 11. Hurtado, on the other hand, proposes that three Greek MSS of the Gospel of Thomas 'hardly [stand] out', Larry W. Hurtado, 'The Greek Fragments of "The Gospel of Thomas" as Artefacts: Papyrological Observations on P. Oxy. 1, P.Oxy 654, and P. Oxy 655', in *Das Thomasevangelium: Entstehung – Rezeption – Theologie*, ed. Jörg Frey, Enno Edzard Popkes, and Jens Schröter (Berlin and New York: de Gruyter, 2008), 29. The Gospel of Mary is never quoted or referenced in any other extant literature.

BG version was copied from a Coptic *Vorlage* due to the BG scribe confusing the letters ϥ and ϒ.[3]

Working with the Gospel of Mary's extant manuscripts is challenging. We must deal with a hypothetical second- or third-century author, two Greek scribes in the third century, a hypothetical translator and a fifth-century scribe writing in Coptic. Often the art of textual analysis requires seeking the 'original' text, and so working with the earliest sources available, but in the case of the Gospel of Mary, they are small badly damaged fragments.[4] The fullest text is not in the original language, several centuries later than its first composition, and of an original eighteen and a half pages, only eight and a half remain.

There are several reasons to assume that the Gospel of Mary underwent some degree of change between the second- or third-century Greek and fifth-century Coptic text. In these centuries, textual transmission was not orchestrated or controlled.[5] Second- and third-century New Testament texts have 'been defined variously

[3] On an earlier edition of the Gospel of Mary in Coptic, see Till, *Papyrus Berolinensis 8502*, 12.

[4] The quest for the 'original' has started to change. Epp's excellent article on the term 'original text' and the quest to find it poses several important questions about scholarly approaches to textual criticism, Eldon Jay Epp, 'The Multivalence of the Term "Original Text" in New Testament Textual Criticism', *HTR* 92.3 (1999): 245–81. In light of these questions, certain scholars working on Nag Hammadi material have turned their attention to the fourth- or fifth-century *Coptic* manuscripts, without trying to ascertain what an original Greek might have looked like. These include: Eduard Iricinschi, 'Scribes and Readers of Nag Hammadi Codex II: Book Production and Monastic Paideia in Fourth-Century Egypt' (PhD Thesis, Princeton, 2009); Hugo Lundhaug, *Images of Rebirth*; Jenott, *Gospel of Judas*; Ulla Tervahauta, *A Story of the Soul's Journey in the Nag Hammadi Library: A Study of Authentikos Logos (NHC VI,3)*, Novum Testamentum et Orbis Antiquus 107 (Göttingen: Vandenhoeck & Ruprecht, 2015). Iricinschi suggests that: 'If writers "produce" their texts, late antique scribes could be said to "reproduce" their texts' (75), and therefore, we must read the later texts in their own right. However, the Gospel of Mary is available in earlier Greek fragments, and so reading this text is a delicate balance between understanding the gospel as a second- or third-century Greek production, and working with the extant text as a fifth-century Coptic work.

[5] As a small sample of recent work in this field: Frederick Wisse, 'The Coptic Versions of the New Testament', in *The Text of the New Testament in Contemporary Research: Essays on the Status Quaestionis*, ed. Bart D. Ehrman and Michael W. Holmes (Grand Rapids, MI: Eerdmans, 1995), 131–41; Helmut Koester, 'The Text of the Synoptic Gospels in the Second Century', in *Gospel Traditions in the Second Century: Origins, Recensions, Text, and Transmission*, ed. William L. Peterson, Christianity and Judaism in Antiquity (Notre Dame, IN: University of Notre Dame Press, 1989), 19–37; David C. Parker, *The Living Text of the Gospels* (Cambridge: Cambridge University Press, 1997).

as "uncontrolled", "unstable", "wild", and "free"',[6] and scribal modifications were often socially, theologically or ideologically motivated.[7] Translation makes this even more complicated; the conventions of the Coptic language necessitate certain changes to the meaning behind the Greek text. Shisha-Halevy points out:

> The [Coptic] translator 'improves' on the Greek, by necessity, since Coptic makes distinctions the Greek does not, and choice in the re-writing by the Coptic writer-translator must be made, by the exigencies of the Coptic system. This then often results in additional or different information being introduced into the text.[8]

It would be implausible to propose that the Gospel of Mary of the Berlin Codex had not undergone significant modification since its original composition. The scribe lived centuries later and operated in a different language. The Apocryphon of John, which follows the Gospel of Mary in the codex (but exists in another three Coptic recensions) and looks to be written by the same hand, is the result of διασκευή, a revision including modification in detail.[9] Therefore, we should expect some changes in detail also in the Gospel of Mary.

Comparing the Greek Gospel of Mary fragments to BG, the overall content appears to be very similar – but with small details amended (see Appendix C). In Chapter 3, I proposed that these changes in the Coptic MS demonstrate a situation of greater hostility between Mary and Levi on one side and Peter and Andrew on the other. In the Greek fragments, Mary is the superior disciple; but in the BG, Mary is the superior disciple *at the expense of Peter.* Such small changes between the earlier Greek fragments and the later Coptic MS may amount to a great diversity in the meaning of the gospel. Although most of the Gospel of Mary's material on eschatology (the subject of Chapters 4 and 5) are not in the extant Greek,

[6] Kim Haines-Eitzen, *Guardians of Letters: Literacy, Power, and the Transmitters of Early Christian Literature* (Oxford and New York: Oxford University Press, 2000), 106.

[7] Haines-Eitzen, *Guardians of Letters*, 124; Bart D. Ehrman, *The Orthodox Corruption of Scripture: The Effect of Early Christological Controversies on the Text of the New Testament* (Oxford and New York: Oxford University Press, 1993), esp. 280.

[8] Ariel Shisha-Halevy, 'Future, Present, Narrative Past: A Triple Note on Oxyrhynchite Tempuslehre', in *Sprache und Geist. Peter Nagel zum 65. Geburtstag*, ed. Walter Beltz, Ute Pietruschka und Jürgen Tubach (Halle: Martin-Luther-Universität Halle-Wittenberg, 2003), 250–1.

[9] Pleše refers to this technique in the composition of the Apocryphon of John, Pleše, *Poetics of the Gnostic Universe*, 4, 7–20.

the possibility that what remains to us in Coptic is not quite the same as the second- or third-century text must remain in mind.

(A) The Berlin Codex

The Berlin Codex was discovered in 1896 at a Christian burial site near Panopolis, and the legend goes that it was hidden in a wall niche, wrapped in feathers.[10] However, due to the good condition of the text, scholars contest this tale: '[I]t is thought to be unlikely that the codex can have been in such a location for any substantial length of time'.[11] The codex had a troublesome beginning in the academic world – floods, war, death – until it was published by Till in 1955, nearly sixty years after its discovery.[12] Since then, the pages have faded and certain letters in Till's 1955 (and 1972) and Pasquier's 1983 editions can no longer be read. The Coptic used is mainly Sahidic, the most readable and widespread dialect among fourth-century unilingual Copts, with elements of Subakhmimic.

BG is a miniature papyrus codex (measuring around 12.7cm long and 10.5cm wide), and the Gospel of Mary was bound alongside the Apocryphon of John, the Sophia of Jesus Christ and an epitome of the Act of Peter. As discussed at the beginning of Chapter 3, it is reasonable to assume that the Gospel of Mary begins the 152-page codex, and so it may be considered the most authoritative text – as opposed to the Nag Hammadi codices 2, 3 and 4, in which the Apocryphon of John is the first text which has 'long been cited as indications of the importance of *Ap. John* itself'.[13] The final lines of the Gospel of Mary read ⲡ̣[ⲉ]ⲩⲁⲅⲅⲉⲗⲓⲟⲛ ⲕⲁⲧⲁ ⲙⲁ̣ⲣⲓϩⲁⲙⲙ (19,3–5), and following this title the Apocryphon of John begins immediately.

(B) Papyrus Oxyrhynchus 3525

POxy.GM is a small, very fragmentary papyrus leaf, measuring just under 12cm at its highest point and 11.5cm at its widest point. There is another fragment measuring *circa* 0.6cm x 1cm, which is placed at the left-hand side of the text, around line 5. The script is only found on one side of the papyrus, indicating that it was part of a roll. The

[10] Tardieu and Dubois, *Introduction à la littérature gnostique*, 99–100; de Boer, *Gospel of Mary*, 12.

[11] Tuckett, *Mary*, 5. Also, King, *Mary*, 7.

[12] On the history of the MS and its 'mini-saga', see Tuckett, *Mary*, 5–6.

[13] Williams, *Rethinking 'Gnosticism'*, 248.

fragment contains eighteen decipherable lines of script, but none are complete.[14] Line 3 contains the first legible letters. At the widest part of the papyrus (line 15), *circa* thirty letters can be read.

The writing is a cursive script, which is uncommon for literary texts. The lines are not regular or straight (particularly the gap between lines 8 and 9 and the smaller size of the letters on line 16). Parsons (the editor of the *editio princeps*) writes: 'The script, and perhaps the roll-form, shows this to be an amateur copy.'[15] The cursive script is dated to the third century.[16] There is one nomen sacrum, ανθρωπους as $\overline{\text{ανους}}$; whereas κυριε is unusually written in full. (Κυριος was one of the earliest nomina sacra, and it is found abbreviated in all of the earliest Greek New Testament MSS.[17])

It would seem that POxy.GM was prepared for private use and by a scribe of modest literary ability. The general preference for Christian texts was the codex, and so the roll format is unusual. These two factors may suggest that this particular manuscript was used outside of a communal setting. Both POxy.GM and PRyl.GM were discovered on the rubbish heaps in Oxyrhynchus.[18]

(C) Papyrus Rylands 463

PRyl.GM is a small papyrus leaf measuring *circa* 8.8cm wide and 9.9cm long. Unlike POxy.GM, it is from a codex. The extant portion contains *circa* fifteen decipherable lines on both the recto and verso sides. The top of the fragment shows page numbers κα (21) and κβ (22). The start of 21 begins τὸ λοιπὸν corresponding with BG 17,5, and the end of 22 is the end of the Gospel of Mary. The version of the gospel of PRyl.GM may have been longer than BG as it ends on page 22, but there is also more text on the Greek pages than on the Coptic.[19]

The original form of the papyrus is thought to have been a small codex.[20] Miniature codices were most likely made for private reading,

[14] King states that the fragment has approximately twenty lines, whereas Tuckett states around twenty-one. See King, *Mary*, 11; Tuckett, *Mary*, 81.

[15] Parsons, '3525: Gospel of Mary', 12.

[16] Parsons, '3525: Gospel of Mary', 12.

[17] Philip Comfort, *Encountering the Manuscripts: An Introduction to New Testament Paleography and Textual Criticism* (Nashville: B&H Publishing, 2005), 199.

[18] For discussion on the rubbish heaps, see AnneMarie Luijendijk, 'Sacred Scriptures as Trash: Biblical Papyri from Oxyrhynchus', *VC* 64.3 (2010): 217–54.

[19] Till, *Papyrus Berolinensis 8502*, 25.

[20] Cf. POxy 1, which Hurtado deduces had a total page height of 27+ cm, Hurtado, 'Greek Fragments of "The Gospel of Thomas"'.

possibly commissioned by the collector themselves. The script is also suggestive of a private codex. At its publication, Roberts wrote: 'The text is written in a hand which, if clear and upright, is also ugly and ill-proportioned and shows considerable cursive influence.'[21] However, Tuckett has reviewed this assessment and concluded, 'it is clearly an uncial, not a cursive, hand'.[22] This may be in comparison to POxy.GM, which is barely decipherable to the untrained eye.[23]

PRyl.GM was dated by Roberts in the *editio princeps* to the early third century on palaeographic grounds.[24] The date has not subsequently been questioned. Like POxy.GM, PRyl.GM abbreviates ανθρωπον as $\overline{\text{ανον}}$. In PRyl.GM σωτήρ is not abbreviated.[25] The inside margin (to the left of the recto) is relatively intact suggesting that the leaf may havẹ fallen out of a codex rather than being torn out. The wear to the outside margin looks as though it was subject to time damage on the rubbish heaps of Oxyrhynchus.

[21] Roberts, '463: The Gospel of Mary', 20.

[22] Tuckett, *Mary*, 83.

[23] Parsons writes that the scribe of PRyl.GM is 'more professional' than the 'amateur' POxy.GM, Parsons, '3525: Gospel of Mary', 12.

[24] Roberts, '463: The Gospel of Mary', 20.

[25] Tuckett argues that this is unsurprising as σωτήρ was not abbreviated in manuscripts until the fourth century, Tuckett, *Mary*, 85.

APPENDIX B

The Gospel of Mary: Text and Translations

Textual signs for the following editions and translations:

.	Dot underneath letter indicates uncertain letters.
[ ]	Square brackets indicate a lacuna in the MS.
{ }	Braces indicate letters unnecessarily added by the scribe.
< >	Pointed brackets indicate an editorial correction of a scribal omission or error.
\` ′	High strokes indicate that the letter was written above the line by the scribe, as a correction.
cont.	The line has been continued from following section.
[[ ]]	Double square brackets indicate an erased letter in the MS.

(A) Text and Translation of Berlin Codex, 1, Gospel of Mary

The following transcription of the Coptic text of the Gospel of Mary is based on photographs of the Berlin Codex, kindly sent to me by Christopher Tuckett, as well as the critical editions of Till (1972),[1] Wilson/MacRae (1979),[2] Pasquier (1983)[3] and Tuckett (2007).[4] The translation here is my own.[5] Rather than offering the most fluent English translation possible, I have aimed to provide a relatively literal translation of the Coptic. I have provided limited textual and translation notes to highlight ambiguities in the MS and to bring to attention different possible translations of certain words.

[1] Till, *Papyrus Berolinensis 8502*.

[2] Wilson and MacRae, 'The Gospel According to Mary', 456–71.

[3] Pasquier, *Marie*, 28–47.

[4] Tuckett, *Mary*, 86–106.

[5] Other English translations include King, *Mary*, 13–18; Bass, 'Composition and Redaction', 144–51; Bart D. Ehrman and Zlatko Pleše, *The Apocryphal Gospels: Texts and Translations* (Oxford and New York: Oxford University Press, 2011), 587–600. Hartenstein offers text and translation of the narrative frame, Hartenstein, *Die zweite Lehre*, 137–42. Notes will also be to Crum, *A Coptic Dictionary*.

(1) Dialogue between the Saviour and his Disciples (7,1–8,11)

[ζ]	[7]
[.] . [8±] . . θ̣[γ]λ̣η ϭε να	then will m[a]tter
ογω̣[ϭ]π̣ ϫν μ̣μον πεϫε πc̄ω̄ρ̄ ϫε	be dest[r]oyed or not?' The Saviour said,
φγcιc νιμ πλαcμα νιμ κτιcιc	'Every nature, every form, every creature
νιμ εγϣοπ ϩν̄ νεγερηγ {μ}νμ̄	exist in (and) with each other
μαγ αγω ον εγναβωλ εβολ ε	and will be dissolved again to
τογνογνε μ̄μιν μμοογ ϫε τε	their own root; for the
φγcιc νθγλη εcβωλ εβολ εν̣α	nature of matter is to dissolve to the elements
τεcφγcιc ογααc πετε ογν μαα	(of) its nature alone. Whoever has ears
ϫε μ̄μοϥ εcωτμ̄ μαρεϥcωτμ̄	to hear let him hear.'
πεϫε πετροc ναϥ ϫε ϩωc ακτα̣	Peter said to him, 'Since you have
μον εϩωβ νιμ ϫω μπικεογα	[to]ld us everything, say one other (thing)
ερον ογ πε πνοβε μπκοcμο̣c̣	to us. What is the sin of the world?'
πεϫε πc̄ω̄ρ̄ ϫε μν̄ νοβε ϣοπ αλ	The Saviour said, 'Sin does not exist,
λα ν̄τωτν̄ πεϯρε μ̄πνοβε ε̣τε	but you make sin when you
τν̄ειρε ν̄νεϯνε ν̄τφγcιc ντμν̄τ	do the things that are like the nature of
νοεικ ετ<ογ>μογτε εροc ϫε πνο̣	adultery, which is called sin.'
βε ετβε παϊ αϥει ν̄ϭι παγαθο̣(ν)	This is why the Good came
ϩν τετν̄μητε ϣα να φγcιc	into your midst to the things of
νιμ εϥνακαθιcτα μμοc εϩο̣γ̣(ν)	every nature, so as to restore it inward
ετεcνογνε ετι αϥογωϩ ετοτ̣ϥ̣	to its root. Then he continued
πεϫαϥ ϫε ετβε παι τετν̄ϣω	and said, 'This is why you
[ν]ε αγω τετμ̄μογ ϫε τ[. . . . .]	are si[c]k and you die, for [. . . . .]
[η̄]	[8]
μ̄πεταρ̣̄. π̣α̣[. . . . . . π]ε̣τ̣[ρ̣̄]	of the one who [. . . . . . who]ever
νοϊ μαρεϥρ̄νοει [αθ]γ̣λ̣η̣ ϫ̣[π]ε̣ ογ	understands, let him understand. [Mat]ter [produc]ed a
παθοc εμν̄ταϥ μμαγ μ̄πεινε	passion without likeness,
εαϥει εβολ ϩν ογπαραφγcιc το	which came forth unnaturally.
τε ϣαρεογταραχη ϣωπε ϩ̣μ̄	Then a disturbance occurs in
πcωμα τηρϥ ετβε παϊ αϊϫοc νη	the whole body. That is why I told you
τν̄ ϫε ϣωπε ετετν̄τητ ν̄ϩητ̣	(to) be united in heart,

ⲁⲩⲱ ⲉⲧⲉⲧⲛ̄ⲟ ⲛ̄ⲛⲁⲧⲧⲱⲧ ⲉⲧⲉ	and if you are disjointed, nevertheless
ⲧⲛ̄ⲧⲏⲧ ⲙⲉⲛ ⲛ̄ⲛⲁϩⲣⲙ̄ ⲡⲓⲛⲉ ⲡⲓⲛⲉ	be united in the presence of each likeness
ⲛⲧⲉⲫⲩⲥⲓⲥ ⲡⲉⲧⲉ ⲟⲩⲛ ⲙⲁⲁϫⲉ ⲙ̄	of nature. Whoever has ears
ⲙⲟϥ ⲉⲥⲱⲧⲙ̄ ⲙⲁⲣⲉϥⲥⲱⲧⲙ̄	to hear, let him hear.'

Textual Issues

7,1. The reading of ⲑⲩⲗⲏ is unclear. ⲑⲩⲗⲏ follows Till, Wilson/MacRae, Pasquier and Tuckett. | **7,2**. ⲟⲩⲱϭⲡ: Wilson/MacRae write '[t]he traces of letters seem to fit ⲟⲩⲱϭⲡ better than ⲟⲩϫⲁⲓ "saved"'. | **7,16.** <ⲟⲩ> supplied, following Wilson/MacRae, Pasquier, Tuckett. | **7,21–22.** Till reads ϣⲱ̣[ⲡ]ⲉ 'come into being'. | **7,22–8,1.** ⲧ̣[ⲉⲧⲛⲙⲉ] ⲙ̄ⲡⲉⲧⲁⲣ̣̄ⲡ̣ⲁ̣[ⲧⲁ ⲙ̄ⲙⲱⲧⲛ ⲡ]ⲉⲧ[ⲣ̄] 'for you love that which deceives you', Till/Schenke.

Translation Issues

7,5. ⲃⲱⲗ ⲉⲃⲟⲗ: 'resolved' in Wilson/MacRae, Bass. Pasquier adds a verb in her translation to emphasize the point of returning: 'that they will return (*retourneront*) to dissolve'. Presumably 'retourneront' is based on ⲟⲛ. | **7,6.** ⲧⲟⲩⲛⲟⲩⲛⲉ is singular: 'their root'. Cf. 'roots', Wilson/MacRae, Tuckett, Bass. | **7,7.** 'to the elements of': Wilson/MacRae, write 'the context suggests roots', but 'the essence of' is possible. | **7,16–20.** No other translations read this as the comment of the narrator. | **7,18**. 'your midst': Cf. 'among you', Tuckett. | **8,7.** The intransitive rendering of ⲧⲱⲧ can be translated as 'joined', 'persuaded' or 'agreeable', Crum, *Coptic Dictionary*, 473b. However, with ⲛϩⲏⲧ, Crum limits the translation to 'content heart, persuade, satisfy', 438a. Other translations include: 'obedient', Tuckett; 'obéissants', Pasquier; 'of good courage', Wilson/MacRae, Bass. The translation 'united' fits better for the message of the Gospel of Mary, as Mary warns the others against making their hearts into two (ⲙⲡⲣ̄ⲣ̄ ϩⲏⲧ ⲥⲛⲁⲩ [9,15–16]).

(2) The Saviour's Farewell Discourse (8,11–9,5)

ⲛⲧⲁ	When
ⲣⲉϥϫⲉ ⲛⲁï ⲛϭⲓ ⲡⲙⲁⲕⲁⲣⲓⲟⲥ ⲁϥⲁⲥ	the Blessed One had said these things, he
ⲡⲁⲍⲉ ⲙ̄ⲙⲟⲟⲩ ⲧⲏⲣⲟⲩ ⲉϥϫⲱ ⲙ̄ⲙⲟ`ⲟ'ⲥ	said farewell to them all, saying,
ϫⲉ ⲟⲩⲉⲓⲣⲏⲛⲏ ⲛⲏⲧⲛ̄ ⲧⲁⲉⲓⲣⲏⲛⲏ	'Peace to you. My peace
ϫⲡⲟⲥ ⲛⲏⲧⲛ̄ ⲁⲣⲉϩ ⲙⲡⲣ̄ⲧⲣⲉⲗⲁⲁⲩ ⲣ̄	acquire in you. Beware, do not allow

	anyone to lead
ⲡⲗⲁⲛⲁ ⲙⲙⲱⲧⲛ̣̄ ⲉϥϫⲱ ⲙⲙⲟⲥ ϫⲉ	you astray saying,
ⲉⲓⲥ ϩⲏⲡⲉ ⲙⲡⲉⲓ̈ⲥⲁ ⲏ̣ ⲉⲓⲥ ϩⲏⲡⲉ ⲙ̄	"Look in this direction, or look in
ⲡⲉⲉⲓⲙⲁ ⲡϣⲏⲣⲉ ⲅⲁⲣ ⲙⲡⲣⲱⲙⲉ ⲉϥ	this place." For the Son of Man
ϣⲟⲡ ⲙⲡⲉⲧⲛ̄ϩⲟⲩⲛ ⲟⲩⲉϩⲧⲏⲩⲧⲛ̄	exists within you. Follow
ⲛ̄ⲥⲱϥ ⲛⲉⲧϣⲓⲛⲉ ⲛ̄ⲥⲱϥ ⲥⲉⲛⲁ	him. Those who seek him will
ϭ̣ⲛⲧϥ̄ ⲃⲱⲕ ϭⲉ ⲛ̄ⲧⲉⲧⲛ̄ⲧⲁϣⲉⲟⲉⲓϣ	find him. Go then and preach
ⲙⲡⲉⲩⲁⲅⲅⲉⲗⲓⲟⲛ ⲛ̄ⲧⲙⲛⲧⲉⲣⲟ ⲙⲡⲣ̣̄	the gospel of the kingdom. Do not
ⲑ	[9]
ⲕⲁ ⲗⲁⲩ ⲛ̄ϩⲟⲣⲟⲥ ⲉϩⲣⲁⲓ̈ ⲡⲁⲣⲁ ⲡⲉⲛ	lay down any rules beyond what
ⲧⲁⲓ̈ⲧⲟϣϥ̄ ⲛⲏⲧⲛ̄ ⲟⲩⲇⲉ ⲙ̄ⲡⲣ̄ϯ ⲛⲟ	I have appointed for you, nor give
ⲙⲟⲥ ⲛ̄ⲑⲉ ⲙⲡⲛⲟⲙⲟⲑⲉⲧⲏⲥ ⲙⲏⲡⲟ	a law like the Lawgiver
ⲧⲉ ⲛ̄ⲥⲉⲁⲙⲁϩⲧⲉ ⲙ̄ⲙⲱⲧⲛ̄ ⲛϩⲏⲧϥ	in case you be dominated by it.'
ⲛⲧⲁⲣⲉϥϫⲉ ⲛⲁⲓ̈ ⲁϥⲃⲱⲕ	When he had said these things, he departed.

Textual Issues

8,18. ⲛϣⲏⲣⲉ, Wilson/MacRae. MS reads ⲡϣⲏⲣⲉ. | **8,22.** ⲙⲡⲣ̄. Cf. ⲙ[ⲡⲓ], Till. | **9,2.** ⲙⲡⲣ̄ ϯ on MS. Cf. ⲙ̄ⲡⲓϯ, Till.

Translation Issues

8,12–13. ⲁⲥⲡⲁⲍⲉ from ἀσπάζομαι is usually translated as 'greeted' as Wilson/MacRae, Tuckett, Bass. However, it can also be used as to 'say farewell' (e.g. Acts 20.1, 21.6). | **8,15.** ϫⲡⲟ″ 'acquire' as in Crum, 779a. Cf. 'receive', Wilson/MacRae, Tuckett, Bass. The translation 'acquire' stresses the active participation of the disciples.

(3) Mary's Arising (9,5–22)

ⲛⲧⲟⲟⲩ ⲇⲉ	But they
ⲛⲉⲩⲣ̄ⲗⲩⲡⲉⲓ ⲁⲩⲣⲓⲙⲉ ⲙ̄ⲡϣⲁ ⲉⲩ	were grieved, they wept much,
ϫⲱ ⲙⲙⲟⲥ ϫⲉ ⲛⲛⲁϣ ⲛ̄ϩⲉ ⲉⲛⲛⲁⲃⲱⲕ	saying, 'How shall we go
ϣⲁ ⲛϩⲉⲑⲛⲟⲥ ⲛ̄ⲧⲛ̄ⲧⲁϣⲉⲟⲉⲓϣ ⲛ̄	to the nations and preach
ⲡⲉⲩⲁⲅⲅⲉⲗⲓⲟⲛ ⲛⲧⲙⲛ̄ⲧⲉⲣⲟ ⲙⲡϣ`ⲏ'	the gospel of the kingdom of the

ⲣⲉ ⲙⲡⲣⲱⲙⲉ ⲉϣϫⲉ ⲡⲉⲧⲙ̄ⲙⲁⲩ ⲙ̄	Son of Man? If they did not
ⲡⲟⲩϯⲥⲟ ⲉⲣⲟϥ ⲛⲁϣ ⲛ̄ϩⲉ ⲁⲛⲟⲛ ⲉⲩ	spare him, how will they
ⲛⲁϯⲥⲟ ⲉⲣⲟⲛ ⲧⲟⲧⲉ ⲁⲙⲁⲣⲓϩⲁⲙ ⲧⲱ	spare us?' Then Mary
ⲟⲩⲛ ⲁⲥⲁⲥⲡⲁⲍⲉ ⲙⲙⲟⲟⲩ ⲧⲏⲣⲟⲩ	rose, she greeted them all,
ⲡⲉϫⲁⲥ ⲛⲛⲉⲥ`ⲥ´ⲛⲏⲩ ϫⲉ ⲙⲡⲣ̄ⲣⲓⲙⲉ	she said to her brothers, 'Do not weep,
ⲁⲩⲱ ⲙⲡⲣ̄ⲣ̄ⲗⲩⲡⲉⲓ ⲟⲩⲇⲉ ⲙ̄ⲡⲣ̄ⲣ̄ ϩⲏ̣ⲧ	and do not grieve, and do not
ⲥⲛⲁⲩ ⲧⲉϥⲭⲁⲣⲓⲥ ⲅⲁⲣ ⲛⲁϣⲱⲡⲉ	doubt! For his grace will be
ⲛ̄ⲙ̄ⲙⲏⲧⲛ̄ ⲧⲏⲣ<ⲧ>ⲛ̣ ⲁⲩⲱ ⲛⲥ̄ⲣ̄ⲥⲕⲉⲡⲁ	with you all and will protect
ⲍⲉ ⲙⲙⲱⲧⲛ̄ ⲙⲁⲗⲗⲟⲛ ⲇⲉ ⲙⲁⲣⲛ̄	you. Rather let us
ⲥⲙⲟⲩ ⲉⲧⲉϥⲙⲛ̄ⲧⲛⲟϭ ϫⲉ ⲁϥⲥⲃ̄	give thanks for his greatness, for he has prepared
ⲧⲱⲧⲛ̄ ⲁϥⲁⲁⲛ ⲛ̄ⲣⲱⲙⲉ ⲛⲧⲁⲣⲉⲙⲁ	us; he has made us Men.' When
ⲣ̣ⲓϩⲁⲙ ϫⲉ ⲛⲁ̈ⲓ ⲁⲥⲕⲧⲉ ⲡⲉⲩϩⲏⲧ	Mary had said these things, she turned their mind
[ⲉϩ]ⲟⲩⲛ ⲉⲡⲁⲅⲁ̣ⲑⲟⲛ	[t]o the Good.

Textual Issues

9,17. ⲧⲏⲣ<ⲧ>ⲛ̣: Wilson/MacRae write that there is only room for one letter after ⲧⲏⲣ and reconstruct ⲧⲏⲣⲥ̣. This would presumably make the sense: 'For all of his grace will be with you.' The word order makes this doubtful, as ⲭⲁⲣⲓⲥ and ⲧⲏⲣⲥ have three words between them. Till/Schenke write: 'It must mean ⲧⲏⲣⲧⲛ, even though according to the photograph only one letter seems to fit.' Pasquier and Hartenstein follow with ⲧⲏⲣ<ⲧ>ⲛ̣, and King 'with you all'. Cf. Wilson/MacRae and Tuckett use ⲧⲏⲣⲥ and translate 'entirely with you' and 'wholly with you' respectively.

Translation Issues

9,10. ⲣⲱⲙⲉ is gender inclusive and should be translated as 'human'. However, the phrase 'the Son of Man' is so familiar in the study of the New Testament and Early Christianity that I have decided to use it here and later ('Men' 9,20; 'Perfect Man' 18,16). | **9,15–16.** ⲙ̄ⲡⲣ̄ⲣ̄ ϩⲏ̣ⲧⲥⲛⲁⲩ lit. 'do not make heart two'.

(4) Peter's Request to Mary (9,22–10,9)

ⲁⲩⲱ ⲁⲩⲣ̄ⲁⲣⲭⲉ	$22_{\text{cont.}}$	And they beg[an]
[ⲥⲑⲁⲓ] ⲛ̣ⲣ̄ⲅⲩⲙ[ⲛ]ⲁⲍⲉ ϩⲁ ⲡⲣⲁ ⲛ̄ⲛ̄ϣⲁ		to de[b]ate the wor[ds]
[ϫ]ⲉ ⲙⲡ̣[ⲥⲱⲣ]		of the [Saviour].

ⲓ̈	[10]
ⲡⲉϫⲉ ⲡⲉⲧⲣⲟⲥ ⲙⲙⲁⲣⲓϩⲁⲙ ϫⲉ ⲧⲥⲱ	Peter said to Mary, ‘Sister
ⲛⲉ ⲧⲛ̄ⲥⲟⲟⲩⲛ ϫⲉ ⲛⲉⲣⲉⲡⲥ̅ⲱ̅ⲣ̅ ⲟⲩⲁϣⲉ̣	we know that the Saviour loved you
ⲛϩⲟⲩⲟ ⲡⲁⲣⲁ ⲡⲕⲉⲥⲉⲉⲡⲉ ⲛ̄ⲥϩⲓ̈ⲙⲉ	more than the other women.
ϫⲱ ⲛⲁⲛ ⲛ̄ⲛ̄ϣⲁϫⲉ ⲙ̄ⲡⲥ̅ⲱ̅ⲣ̅ ⲉⲧⲉⲉⲓⲣⲉ	Tell us the words of the Saviour that you
ⲙⲡⲉⲩⲙⲉⲉⲩⲉ ⲛⲁⲓ̈ ⲉⲧⲉⲥⲟⲟⲩⲛ ⲙ̄ⲙⲟ	remember, those that you know and
ⲟⲩ ⲛ̄ⲛⲁⲛⲟⲛ ⲁⲛ ⲟⲩⲇⲉ ⲙⲡⲛ̄ⲥⲟⲧⲙ`ⲟ′ⲩ	we do not, nor have we heard them.’
ⲁⲥⲟⲩⲱϣⲃ̄ ⲛϭⲓ ⲙⲁⲣⲓϩⲁⲙ ⲡⲉϫⲁⲥ	Mary answered and said,
ϫⲉ ⲡⲉⲑⲏⲡ ⲉⲣⲱⲧⲛ̄ ϯⲛⲁⲧⲁⲙⲁ ⲧⲏⲩ	‘What is hidden from you, I will proclaim to
ⲧⲛ̄ ⲉⲣⲟϥ	you.’

Textual Issues

9,24. ⲥ̅ⲱ̅ⲣ̅ cannot be read, but it is highly probable.

(5) Mary’s Vision (10,9–23)

ⲁⲩⲱ ⲁⲥⲁⲣⲭⲉⲓ ⲛ̄ϫⲱ ⲛⲁⲩ	And she began to say to them
ⲛ̄ⲛⲉⲓ̈ϣⲁϫⲉ ϫⲉ ⲁ{ⲓ̈}ⲛⲟⲕ ⲡⲉϫⲁⲥ ⲁⲓ	these words: ‘I’, she said, ‘I
ⲛⲁⲩ ⲉⲡϫ̅ⲥ̅ ϩⲛ ⲟⲩϩⲟⲣⲟⲙⲁ ⲁⲩⲱ ⲁⲉⲓ	saw the Lord in a vision and I
ϫⲟⲟⲥ ⲛⲁϥ ϫⲉ ⲡϫ̅ⲥ̅ ⲁⲓ̈ⲛⲁⲩ ⲉⲣⲟⲕ ⲙ̄	said to him, “Lord, I saw you
ⲡⲟⲟⲩ ϩⲛ ⲟⲩϩⲟⲣⲟⲙⲁ ⲁϥⲟⲩⲱϣⲃ ⲡⲉ	today in a vision.” He answered
ϫⲁϥ ⲛⲁⲓ̈ ϫⲉ ⲛⲁⲓ̈ⲁⲧⲉ ϫⲉ ⲛ̄ⲧⲉⲕⲓⲙ ⲁⲛ	and said to me, “Blessed (are) you, for you did
ⲉⲣⲉⲛⲁⲩ ⲉⲣⲟⲉⲓ ⲡⲙⲁ ⲅⲁⲣ ⲉⲧⲉⲣⲉⲡⲛⲟⲩⲥ	not waver as you saw me. For where the mind
ⲙ̄ⲙⲁⲩ ⲉϥⲙⲙⲁⲩ ⲛϭⲓ ⲡⲉϩⲟ ⲡⲉϫⲁⲓ̈	is, there is the treasure.” I said
ⲛⲁϥ ϫⲉ ⲡϫ̅ⲥ̅ ⲧ̣ⲉ̣ⲛⲟⲩ ⲡ̣ⲉⲧⲛⲁⲩ ⲉⲫⲟ	to him, “Lord, now the one who sees the
ⲣⲟⲙⲁ ⲉϥⲛⲁⲩ ⲉⲣⲟϥ <ϩⲛ̄> ⲧⲉⲯⲩⲭⲏ <ⲏ>	vision, does he see it through the soul or
ⲡⲉⲡ̅ⲛ̅ⲁ̅ ⲁϥⲟⲩⲱϣⲃ̄ ⲛ̄ϭⲓ ⲡⲥ̅ⲱ̅ⲣ̅ ⲡⲉ	the spirit?” The Saviour answered and
ϫⲁϥ ϫⲉ ⲉϥⲛⲁⲩ ⲁⲛ ϩⲛ̄ ⲧⲉⲯⲩⲭⲏ ⲟⲩ	said, “He sees not through the soul
ⲇⲉ ϩⲙ ⲡⲉⲡ̅ⲛ̅ⲁ̅ ⲁⲗⲗⲁ ⲡⲛⲟⲩⲥ ⲉⲧϣ̣[ⲟⲡ]	nor through the spirit, but the mind, which is
ϩⲛ ⲧⲉⲩⲙⲏⲧⲉ ⲙⲡⲉⲩⲥ̣ⲛⲁⲩ ⲛ̄ⲧⲟ̣[ϥ ⲡⲉⲧ]	between the two. [It is that which]
ⲛⲁⲩ ⲉⲫⲟⲣⲟⲙⲁ ⲁⲩ[ⲱ] ⲛ̄ⲧⲟϥ ⲡ̣[ⲉⲧ …	sees the vision, an[d] it is that [which …

Textual Issues

10,10. ⲁⲛⲟⲕ, Till, Wilson/MacRae, Tuckett. ‘Or - less probably - ⲁⲓⲛⲕⲟⲧⲕ’, Tuckett. | **10,17.** ⲧ̣ⲉ̣ⲛ̣ⲟⲩ following Till and Wilson/MacRae. Wilson/MacRae write that others have read ⲡ̣ⲛ̣ⲟ̣ⲩⲥ̣ but do not name their source, and I have not found it. | **10,18.** MS reads ⲏ̣ ⲧⲉⲯⲩⲭⲏ ϩⲙ̄ (the soul in the spirit), but the emendation is necessary in view of the ascent of the soul after the lacuna.

Pages 11 to 14 missing.

(6) The Ascent of the Soul (15,1–17,9)

ⲓ̣ⲉ̣	[15]
ⲙⲙⲟϥ ⲁⲩⲱ ⲡⲉϫⲉ ⲧⲉⲡⲓⲑⲩⲙⲓⲁ	‘it. And Desire said,
ϫⲉ ⲙ̄ⲡⲓⲛⲁⲩ ⲉⲣⲟ ⲉⲣⲉⲃⲏⲕ ⲉⲡⲓⲧⲛ̄	“I did not see you descending,
ⲧⲉⲛⲟⲩ ⲇⲉ ϯⲛⲁⲩ ⲉⲣⲟ ⲉⲣⲉⲃⲏⲕ ⲉ	but now I see you ascending.
ⲧⲡⲉ ⲡⲱⲥ ⲇⲉ ⲧⲉϫⲓ ϭⲟⲗ ⲉⲣⲉⲏⲡʼ ⲉ	Why then do you lie (since) you belong
ⲣⲟⲉⲓ ⲁⲥⲟⲩⲱϣⲃ̄ ⲛϭⲓ ⲧⲉⲯⲩⲭⲏ ⲡⲉ	to me?” The soul answered
ϫⲁⲥ ϫⲉ ⲁïⲛⲁⲩ ⲉⲣⲟ ⲙ̄ⲡⲉⲛⲁⲩ ⲉⲣⲟï	and said, “I saw you. You did not see me,
ⲟⲩⲇⲉ ⲙⲡⲉⲉⲓⲙⲉ ⲉⲣⲟⲉⲓ ⲛⲉⲉⲓϣⲟ	nor did you know me. I was
ⲟⲡ ⲛⲉ ⲛ̄ϩⲃ̄ⲥⲱ ⲁⲩⲱ ⲙⲡⲉⲥⲟⲩⲱⲛⲧ	to you garments and you did not recognize me.”
ⲛ̄ⲧⲁⲣⲉⲥϫⲉ ⲛⲁï ⲁⲥⲃⲱⲕ ⲉⲥⲧⲉⲗⲏⲗ	When she had said these things, she departed rejoicing
ⲛ̄ϩⲟⲩⲟ | ⲡⲁⲗⲓⲛ ⲁⲥⲉⲓ ⲉⲧⲛ̄ ⲧⲙⲉϩ	greatly. | Again she came into the hand of the
ϣⲟⲙⲛⲧⲉ ⲛ̄ⲛⲉⲝⲟⲩⲥⲓⲁ ⲧⲉⲧⲟⲩⲙ`ⲟʹⲩ	third of the powers, the one that is called
ⲧⲉ ⲉⲣⲟⲥ ϫⲉ ⲧⲙⲛⲧⲁⲧⲥⲟⲟⲩⲛ [ⲁⲥ]ⲣ̣̄	Ignorance. [She]
ⲉⲝⲉⲧⲁⲍⲉ ⲛ̄ⲧⲉⲯⲩⲭⲏ ⲉⲥϫ[ⲱ ⲙ̄]	questioned the soul, sa[yi]ng,
ⲙⲟⲥ ϫⲉ ⲉⲣⲉⲃⲏⲕ ⲉⲧⲱⲛ ϩⲛ̣ [ⲟ]ⲩⲡ̣ⲟ̣	“Where are you going? In
ⲛ̣ⲏⲣⲓⲁ ⲁⲩⲁⲙⲁϩⲧⲉ ⲙ̄ⲙⲟ ⲁⲩ[ⲁ]ⲙ̣ⲁ̣ϩ̣	[w]ickedness, they bound you. Indeed, they
ⲧⲉ ⲇⲉ ⲙ̄ⲙⲟ ⲙ̄ⲡⲣ̄ⲕⲣⲓⲛⲉ ⲁⲩ[ⲱ] ⲡⲉ	b[o]und you. Do not judge.” An[d] the
ϫⲉ ⲧⲉⲯⲩⲭⲏ ϫⲉ ⲁϩⲣⲟ ⲉⲣⲉⲕⲣ̣ⲓ̣ⲛ̣ⲉ̣	soul said, “Why do you judge
ⲙ̄ⲙⲟï ⲉⲙⲡⲓⲕⲣⲓⲛⲉ ⲁⲩⲉⲙⲁϩⲧⲉ	me? I did not judge. They bound

ⲙ̄ⲙⲟⲓ̈ ⲉⲙⲡⲓⲁⲙⲁϩⲧⲉ ⲙⲡⲟⲩⲥ̣ⲟ̣ⲩ	me; I did not bind. They did not
ⲱⲛⲧ ⲁⲛⲟⲕ ⲇⲉ ⲁⲓ̈ⲥⲟⲩⲱⲛⲟⲩ ⲉⲩ	recognize me, but I recognized them.
ⲃⲱⲗ ⲉⲃⲟⲗ ⲙⲡⲧⲏⲣϥ ⲉⲓⲧⲉ ⲛⲁ ⲡ̣	All things are dissolving, both the things of the
ⲕ̣ⲁ̣ϩ̣	earth
ⲓ̅ⲋ̅	[16]
ⲉⲓⲧⲉ ⲛⲁ ⲧⲡ[ⲉ] ⲛ̣̄ⲧⲉⲣⲉⲧⲉⲯⲩⲭⲏ ⲟⲩ	and the things of the heav[en]." When the
ⲱⲥϥ̄ ⲛ̄ⲧⲙⲉϩϣⲟⲙⲛⲧⲉ ⲛ̄ⲛⲉϫⲟⲩⲥⲓ	soul had destroyed the third of the powers,
ⲁ ⲁⲥⲃⲱⲕ ⲉⲡⲥⲁ ⲛⲧⲡⲉ ⲁⲩⲱ ⲁⲥⲛⲁⲩ	she went upwards and saw
ⲉⲧⲙⲁϩϥⲧⲟⲉ ⲛ̄ⲛⲉϫⲟⲩⲥⲓⲁ ⲁⲥⲣ̄ ⲥⲁ	the fourth of the powers. She made
ϣϥⲉ ⲙ̄ⲙⲟⲣⲫⲏ ⲧϣⲟⲣⲡ ⲙ̄ⲙⲟⲣ	seven forms. The first form
ⲫⲏ ⲡⲉ ⲡⲕⲁⲕⲉ ⲧⲙⲉϩⲥⲛ̄ⲧⲉ ⲧⲉⲡⲓ	is Darkness, the second is
ⲑⲩⲙⲓⲁ ⲧⲙⲉϩϣⲟⲙⲛⲧⲉ ⲧⲙⲛ̄ⲧⲁⲧ	Desire; the third, Ignorance;
ⲥⲟⲟⲩⲛ ⲧⲙⲉϩϥⲧⲟⲉ ⲡⲉ ⲡⲕⲱϩ ⲙ̄ⲡ	the fourth is Zeal for
ⲙⲟⲩ ⲧⲙⲉϩϯⲉ ⲧⲉ ⲧⲙⲛ̄ⲧⲉⲣⲟ ⲛ̄ⲧⲥⲁⲣⲝ	Death; the fifth is Kingdom of Flesh;
ⲧⲙⲉϩⲥⲟⲉ ⲧⲉ ⲧⲙⲛ̄ⲧⲥⲁⲃⲏ ⲛⲥⲉϭⲏ	the sixth is Foolish Wisdom of
ⲛ̄ⲥⲁⲣⲝ ⲧⲙⲉϩⲥⲁϣϥⲉ ⲧⲉ ⲧⲥⲟⲫⲓ	Flesh; the seventh is Wisdom
ⲁ [ⲛ̄]ⲣ̣ⲉϥⲛⲟⲩϭⲥ ⲛⲁⲓ̈ ⲛⲉ ⲧⲥⲁϣϥⲉ ⲛ̄	[of the] Wrathful One. These are the seven
ⲛ̣ⲉ̣[ϫ]ⲟⲩⲥⲓⲁ ⲛⲧⲉ ⲧⲟⲣⲅⲏ ⲉⲩϣⲓⲛⲉ	p[o]wers of Wrath. They ask
ⲛ̄ⲧⲉⲯⲩⲭⲏ ϫⲉ ⲉⲣⲉⲛⲏⲩ ϫⲓⲛ ⲧⲱⲛ	the soul, "Where do you come from
ⲧϩⲁ̣ⲧⲃⲣⲱⲙⲉ ⲏ ⲉⲣⲉⲃⲏⲕ ⲉⲧⲱⲛ	Human-Slayer? Or where do you go
ⲧⲟⲩⲁ̣ⲥϥⲙⲁ ⲁⲥⲟⲩⲱϣⲃ̄ ⲛ̄ϭⲓ ⲧⲉ	Space-Destroyer?" The soul
ⲯⲩⲭⲏ ⲡⲉϫⲁⲥ ϫⲉ ⲡⲉⲧⲉⲙⲁϩⲧⲉ ⲙ̄	answered and said, "That which bound
ⲙⲟⲓ̈ ⲁⲩⲕⲟⲛⲥϥ̄ ⲁⲩⲱ ⲡⲉⲧⲕⲧⲟ ⲙ̄	me has been slain, and that which surrounds
ⲙⲟⲓ̈ ⲁⲩⲟⲩⲟⲥϥ<ϥ> ⲁⲩⲱ ⲧⲁⲉⲡⲓⲑⲩⲙⲓⲁ	me has been destroyed. And my desire
ⲁⲥϫⲱⲕ ⲉⲃⲟⲗ ⲁⲩⲱ ⲧⲙⲛⲧⲁⲧⲥⲟⲟⲩ(ⲛ)	deceased, and ignorance
ⲁⲥⲙⲟⲩ \`ϩ̣ⲛ̄' ⲟ̣ⲩ[ⲕⲟⲥⲙ]ⲟⲥ ⲛ̄ⲧⲁⲩⲃⲟⲗⲧ' ⲉ	died. In a [wor]ld I was dissolved
ⲓ̅ⲍ̅	[17]
ⲃⲟⲗ ϩⲛ̄ⲛ ⲟⲩⲕⲟⲥⲙⲟⲥ [ⲁⲩ]ⲱ ϩⲛ̄ ⲟⲩ	from a world, [an]d in a
ⲧⲩⲡⲟⲥ ⲉⲃⲟⲗ ϩⲛ ⲟⲩⲧⲩⲡⲟⲥ ⲉⲧⲙ̄	type from a type which is
ⲡⲥⲁ ⲛⲧⲡⲉ ⲁⲩⲱ ⲧⲙⲣ̄ⲣⲉ ⲛⲧⲃ̄ϣⲉ ⲉⲧ	above, and the chain of forgetfulness which

ϣⲟⲟⲡ ⲡⲣⲟⲥ ⲟⲩⲟⲓ̈ϣ ϫⲓⲛ ⲙ̄ⲡⲓⲛⲁⲩ	exists only for a while. From this time on,
ⲉⲉⲓⲛⲁϫⲓ ⲛⲧⲁⲛⲁⲡⲁⲩⲥⲓⲥ ⲙⲡⲉ	I will receive rest from the
ⲭⲣⲟⲛⲟⲥ ⲙⲡⲕⲁⲓⲣⲟⲥ ⲙⲡ`ⲁⲓ´ ⲱⲛ ϩⲛ̄	time of the season of the age, in
ⲛⲟⲩⲕⲁⲣⲱϥ ⲛⲧⲉⲣⲉⲙⲁⲣⲓϩⲁⲙ ϫⲉ	silence."' When Mary had said
ⲛⲁⲓ̈ ⲁⲥⲕⲁⲣⲱⲥ ϩⲱⲥⲧⲉ ⲛ̄ⲧⲁⲡⲥ̄ⲱ̄ⲣ̄	these things, she was silent as the Saviour
ϣⲁϫⲉ ⲛⲙ̄ⲙⲁⲥ ϣⲁ ⲡⲉⲉⲓⲙⲁ |	had spoken with her to this point.

Textual Issues

15,17. ⲕⲣⲓⲛⲉ seems a natural fit, particularly due to ⲉⲙⲡⲓⲕⲣⲓⲛⲉ (15,18). | **15,22.** ⲕⲁϩ is read underneath ⲡ. It is the only word on line 22. The reading of ⲕⲁϩ is disputable but fits well in opposition to ⲡⲉ (16,1). | **16,5.** The MS reads ⲛⲙ̄ⲙⲟⲣⲫⲏ with ⲛ and ⲙ̄ joined, which is 'presumably the scribe's attempt to correct a false start', Wilson/MacRae. | **16,13.** ⲛ̣ⲉ̣[ⲝ]ⲟⲩⲥⲓⲁ: Till reads ⲙ̣ⲉ̣[ⲧ]ⲟ̣ⲩⲥⲓⲁ, 'participants'. ⲛⲉⲝⲟⲩⲥⲓⲁ 'seem[s] to fit ... equally well', Wilson/MacRae, 465, and it is also used in 15,11 and 16,4. | **16,19.** MS reads ⲁⲩⲟⲩⲟⲥϥ. It should read ⲁⲩⲟⲩⲟⲥϥϥ. | **16,21.** ϩ̣ⲛ̄ inserted by scribe above the line.

Translation Issues

15,4. 'Since' supplied by Wilson/MacRae, Pasquier and Tuckett. | **15,8.** Tuckett inserts 'simply' as in 'I was to you (simply) a garment', Tuckett. Cf. 'I served you as a garment', Wilson/MacRae. | **15,10.** ⲉⲧⲛ̄ can have the sense of coming into the hand of (ⲧⲱⲣⲉ/ⲧⲟⲟⲧ-), Crum, 61b. This translation shows the powers (false) sense of authority. See also '*tomba aux mains de*', Pasquier. Other translations simply read 'it came to the third power', Wilson/MacRae, Tuckett. | **15,16–20.** These clauses can be translated in an active or passive sense: 'they bound you', or 'you are bound'. Wilson/MacRae, Tuckett and King use the passive. | **15,20–22.** Tuckett and King translate the things being dissolved as the subject of the soul's recognition: 'I have recognized *that* the All is being dissolved'. This does not seem to work grammatically. | **17,5–6.** The syntax of the final sentence is not clear here: 'rest of the time', Wilson/MacRae, cf. 'rest from time', Pasquier. Pasquier's suggestion works well here as temporality can be used as a means of oppression, as in the Apocryphon of John.

(7) Controversy over Mary's Vision (17,10–18,15)

ⲁϥⲟⲩⲱϣⲃ̄ ⲇⲉ ⲛ̄ϭⲓ ⲁⲛⲇⲣⲉⲁⲥ ⲡⲉϫⲁϥ	Then Andrew answered and said
ⲛ̄ⲛⲉⲥⲛⲏⲩ ϫⲉ ⲁϫⲓ ⲡⲉⲧⲉⲧⲛ̄ϫⲱ	to the brothers, 'Say whatever you say
ⲙⲙⲟϥ ϩⲁ ⲡⲣⲁ ⲛ̄ⲛⲉⲛⲧⲁⲥϫ[ⲟ]ⲟⲩ	about what she said.
ⲁⲛⲟⲕ ⲙⲉⲛ ϯⲣ̄ⲡⲓⲥⲧⲉⲩⲉ ⲁⲛ ϫ̣ⲉ	I myself do not believe that
ⲁⲡⲥ̅ⲱ̅ⲣ̅ ϫⲉ ⲛⲁï ⲉϣϫⲉ ⲛⲓⲥⲃⲟⲟⲩ	the Saviour said such things,
ⲉ ⲅⲁⲣ ϩⲛ̄ⲕⲉⲙⲉⲉⲩⲉ ⲛⲉ ⲁϥⲟⲩⲱ	for surely these are alien teachings.'
ϣⲃ̄ ⲛ̄ϭⲓ ⲡⲉⲧⲣⲟⲥ ⲡⲉϫⲁϥ ϩⲁ ⲡⲣⲁ	Peter answered, he spoke about
ⲛⲛⲉⲉⲓϩⲃⲏⲩⲉ ⲛⲧⲉⲉⲓⲙⲓⲛⲉ ⲁϥ	such matters. He
ϫⲛⲟⲩⲟⲩ ⲉⲧⲃⲉ ⲡⲥ̅ⲱ̅ⲣ̅ ϫⲉ ⲙⲏⲧⲓ̣	asked them about the Saviour, 'Did
ⲁϥϣⲁϫⲉ ⲙⲛ̄ ⲟⲩⲥϩⲓ̈ⲙⲉ ⲛϫⲓⲟⲩⲉ	he speak with a woman secretly
ⲉⲣⲟⲛ ϩⲛ <ⲟⲩ>ⲟⲩⲱⲛϩ ⲉⲃⲟⲗ ⲁⲛ ⲉⲛⲛ̣ⲁ̣	(and) not openly to us? Are we all to
ⲕⲧⲟⲛ ϩⲱⲱⲛ ⲛ̄ⲧⲛ̄ⲥⲱⲧⲙ̄ ⲧⲏⲣ̣ⲛ̄	turn and listen
ⲛⲥⲱⲥ ⲛ̄ⲧⲁ̣ϥⲥⲟⲧⲡⲥ ⲛϩⲟⲩⲟ ⲉⲣ̣ⲟⲛ	to her? Did he choose her over us?'
ⲓⲏ	[18]
ⲧⲟⲧⲉ ⲁ̣[ⲙ]ⲁⲣⲓϩⲁⲙ ⲣⲓⲙⲉ ⲡⲉϫⲁⲥ ⲙ̄	Then Mary wept. She said to
ⲡⲉⲧⲣⲟⲥ <ϫⲉ> ⲡⲁⲥⲟⲛ ⲡⲉⲧⲣⲉ ϩïⲉ ⲉⲕ	Peter, 'My brother Peter, what do you
ⲙⲉⲉⲩⲉ ⲉⲟⲩ ⲉⲕⲙⲉⲉⲩⲉ ϫⲉ ⲛ̄ⲧⲁï	think then? Do you think that I
ⲙⲉⲉⲩⲉ ⲉⲣⲟⲟⲩ ⲙⲁⲩⲁⲁⲧ ϩⲙ̄ ⲡⲁ	have thought of these (things) myself in my
ϩⲏⲧ ⲏ ⲉⲉⲓϫⲓ ϭⲟⲗ ⲉⲡⲥ̅ⲱ̅ⲣ̅ ⲁϥⲟⲩ	heart, or that I am lying about the Saviour?' Levi
ⲱϣⲃ̄ ⲛ̄ϭⲓ ⲗⲉⲩⲉⲓ ⲡⲉϫⲁϥ ⲙⲡⲉⲧⲣⲟ`ⲥ´	answered, he said to Peter,
ϫⲉ ⲡⲉⲧⲣⲉ ϫⲓⲛ ⲉⲛⲉϩ ⲕϣⲟⲡ ⲛⲣⲉϥ	'Peter, you are always
ⲛⲟⲩϭⲥ ϯⲛⲁⲩ ⲉⲣⲟⲕ ⲧⲉⲛⲟⲩ ⲉⲕⲣ̄	wrathful! I see you now
ⲅⲩⲙⲛⲁⲍⲉ ⲉϩⲛ ⲧⲉⲥϩⲓ̈ⲙⲉ ⲛ̄ⲑⲉ ⲛ̄	disputing with the woman like
ⲛⲓⲁⲛⲧⲓⲕⲉⲓⲙⲉⲛⲟⲥ ⲉϣϫⲉ ⲁⲡ	the adversaries. If the
ⲥⲱⲧⲏⲣ ⲇⲉ ⲁⲁⲥ ⲛⲁⲝⲓⲟⲥ ⲛ̄ⲧⲕ ⲛⲓⲙ	Saviour made her worthy, who are you
ϫⲉ̣ ϩⲱⲱⲕ ⲉⲛⲟϫⲥ ⲉⲃⲟⲗ ⲡⲁⲛⲧⲱ`ⲥ´	to reject her? Surely
ⲉⲣ̣ⲉⲡⲥⲱⲧⲏⲣ ⲥⲟⲟⲩⲛ ⲙ̄ⲙⲟⲥ ⲁⲥ	the Saviour knew her
ⲫⲁⲗⲱⲥ ⲉⲧⲃⲉ ⲡⲁï ⲁϥⲟⲩⲟϣⲥ̄ ⲛ̄ϩⲟⲩ	infallibly, and therefore he loved her more
ⲟ ⲉⲣⲟⲛ	than us.

Textual Issues

17,20. MS reads ⲟⲩⲱⲛϩ. | **18,2.** <ϫⲉ> inserted by Till, Pasquier. Cf. Wilson/MacRae and Tuckett who do not insert ϫⲉ.

(8) Levi's Final Words and the End (18,15–9,5)

ⲙⲁⲗⲗⲟⲛ ⲙⲁⲣⲛ̄ϣⲓⲡⲉ ⲛ̄ⲧⲛ̄	Rather, let us be ashamed and
ϯ ϩⲓ̈ⲱⲱⲛ ⲙⲡⲣⲱⲙⲉ ⲛⲧⲉⲗⲓⲟⲥ	put on the Perfect Man
ⲛ̣ⲧⲛ̄ϫⲡⲟ̣ϥ ⲛ̣ⲁ̣ⲛ̣ ⲕ̣ⲁ̣ⲧⲁ ⲑ̣ⲉ ⲛ̄ⲧ̣ⲁϥ	and acquire him for ourselves as he
ϩⲱⲛ ⲉⲧⲟⲟⲧⲛ̄ ⲛ̄ⲧⲛ̄ⲧⲁϣⲉⲟⲉⲓϣ	commanded us and preach
ⲙⲡⲉⲩⲁⲅⲅⲉⲗⲓⲟⲛ ⲉⲛⲕⲱ ⲁⲛ ⲉϩⲣⲁⲓ̈	the gospel, not laying down
ⲛⲕⲉϩⲟⲣⲟⲥ ⲟⲩⲇⲉ ⲕⲉⲛⲟⲙⲟⲥ̣ ⲡⲁ	other rules or another la[w] beyond
ⲣⲁ ⲡⲉⲛⲧⲁⲡⲥ̄ⲱ̄ⲣ̄ ϫⲟⲟϥ [ⲛ̄ⲧⲉⲣⲉ]	what the Saviour told us. [When]
[ⲓ]ⲑ̣	[19]
[8±] ⲁ̣ⲓ̈ ⲁⲩⲱ ⲁⲩⲣ̄ⲁⲣⲭⲉⲓ ⲛ̄	[8±] and they began to
ⲃⲱⲕ [ⲉⲧⲣⲉⲩⲧ]ⲁⲙⲟ ⲛ̄ⲥⲉⲧⲁϣⲉⲟⲉⲓ̣ϣ	depart [to tea]ch and to preach.
ⲡ̣[ⲉ]ⲩⲁⲅⲅⲉⲗⲓⲟⲛ	[The Gos]pel
ⲕⲁⲧⲁ	according to
ⲙ̣ⲁⲣⲓϩⲁⲙⲙ	Mary

Textual Issues

18,17. ⲛ̣ⲧⲛ̄ϫⲡⲟ̣ϥ ⲛ̣ⲁ̣ⲛ̣ ⲕ̣ⲁ̣ⲧⲁ from Wilson/MacRae. Cf. ⲛ̣ⲧⲛ̄[.......ⲕⲁⲧ]ⲁ, Till. | **19,1.** Missing eight letters reconstructed: [ⲗⲉⲩⲉⲓ ⲇⲉ ϫⲉ ⲛ], Till. | **19,2.** Reconstruction ⲉⲧⲣⲉⲩⲧ supplied by Till.

(B) Text and Translation of POxy.GM

The following transcription of the Greek text of POxy.GM mainly follows that found in Tuckett's most recent critical edition, with some changes.[6] Other critical editions used include Parsons (1983)[7] and Lührmann (2004).[8] As the MS is so fragmentary, and much of the below is reconstruction, I have put the extant letters in bold font. An image of the Greek fragment can be found online at *Oxyrhynchus Online: Image Database.*

[6] Tuckett, *Mary*, 108.
[7] Parsons, '3525: Gospel of Mary', 12–14.
[8] Lührmann, *Die apokryph gewordenen Evangelien*, 108–9.

ου̣δε νο̣μ̣[*ον*
…………

τ]**αυτα ειπ̣ων {αυ}< ε>ξ**[*ηλθεν οι δε λυπηθησαν*
δακρουντες πολλα και] **λεγοντες· πως π**[*ορευωμεθα προς τα εθνη*
κηρυσσοντες το ευα]**γγελιον τη**[*ς*] **β**[*ασιλειας του υιου του α̅ν̅ο̅υ̅ ει*
γαρ μηδ εκεινου εφεισα]**ν̣το πως ημων φ**[*εισονται τοτε αναστασα Μαρι*
αμμη και ασπαζομενη α]**υτους κατεφιλησε̣** [*αυτους και ειπεν τοις αδελφοις αυτης*
μη δακρυετε μη λυπ]**εισθε μηδε δισταζετε̣ι̣** [*η χαρις γαρ αυτου εσται*
μ]**ε̣θ̣ υ̣μων σ̣κ̣επουσα υμας μαλλον ευ**[[.]]**χαρι̣**[*στωμεν τη μεγαλει*
οτ]**η̣τ̣ι̣ αυ̣τ(ου) οτι συ̣ν̣η̣ρτηκ̣εν ημας και α̅ν̅ο̅**[*υ̅ς̅ πεποιηκεν ουτω λεγουσα*
Μαρια]**μ̣μ̣η μετεστρεψεν τον νουν αυτων ε̣**[*π αγαθον και ηρξαν συν*
ζη]**τ̣**[*ει*]**ν περι των αποφθεγματων του σωτηρ**[*ος λεγει Πετρος*
προ]**ς Μαριαμμην· αδελφη οιδαμεν οτι πολλ**[*α ηγαπημενη ης υπο του*
σωτ]**ηρος ω̣ς ουκ αλλη γυνη ειπον ουν ημειν ο̣**[*σους συ γινωσκεις*
λογο]**υ̣ς του σωτηρος** [*ους*] **η̣μ̣ε̣ι̣ς ουκ ηκουσαμε̣ν̣ υ̣π̣ε̣**[*λαβε Μαριαμμη λεγου*
σα οσα υμ]**α̣ς λανθανει και απομνημονευω α̣ν̣α̣**[*γγελω υμιν και ηρχεν αυ*
τοις του]**τ̣ω̣ν τω̣ν λογ(ων)· εμ**[*οι*] **ποτε εν οροματι ιδ**[.................
........] **κ̣υ̣ρ̣ι̣ε̣ σημερον** **βε**

nor a l[aw
…………

When he had said this, he de[parted. But they were grieved,
weeping much and] **saying, ‘How are we to g**[o to the nations
and preach the go]**spel of the k**[ingdom of the Son of Man? For if
they did not spare him,] **how will they s**[pare us?’ Then Mary, arising
and greeting th]**em, kissed** [them, and said to her brothers,
‘Do not weep, do not grie]**ve, do not doubt!** [For his grace will be
w]**ith you, protecting you. Rather let** [us] **give than**[ks for his great-
ness] **for he has united us and** [has made us M]**en**.’ [When she had said these things,
Mar]**y turned their mind to** [the Good. And they began to
deba]**te the sayings of the Saviou**[r. Peter said
to] **Mary, ‘Sister, we know that you were greatly l**[oved by the
Savi]**our like no other woman. Tell us** [those words that you know
of the Saviour [which] **we have not heard.’** [Mary answered, saying,
‘What is] **unknown to you and I remember, I will pr**[oclaim to you.’
And she began

(saying) to them th]**ese words, 'To m**[e] **once in a vision** [..........
20.....] **"Lord, today ... '**

Textual Issues

3. ουδεν in Parsons and Lührmann. | **5.** α̣.ξ[ηλθεν] in Parsons. Lührmann reads ἐ̣ξ[ηλθεν]. | **16.** Parsons, Lührmann and Tuckett have α̣π̣α̣[γγελω], but the verb αναγγελω is also possible. | **20.** Lührmann reconstructs the line as: [ειπον ·] κ̣υ̣ρ̣ι̣ε̣ σημερον σ[ε ειδον.] υ̣π̣ε̣λ̣α̣β̣ε̣ λ̣ε̣γ̣[ων · μακαρια ει συ ...]

(C) Texts and Translation of PRyl.GM

The following transcription of the Greek text of PRyl.GM mainly follows that found in Tuckett's most recent critical edition, with some changes.[9] Other critical editions include Roberts (1938)[10] and Lührmann (2004).[11] An image of the Greek fragment can be found online at *Manchester Digital Collections.*

Recto (→)

κ̣α	21
το λοιπον δρομου και̣[ρο]υ χρονου	the remainder of (the) course of seas[on], of time,
αι̣ω̣νος αναπαυσιν ε̣[ν] σιγη· ταυ	of age, (in) rest i[n] silence.
τ[α] ε̣ιπουσα η Μαρι̣αμμη εσιωπη	When she had said these thin[gs], Mary was silen[t]
σε[ν] ως του σωτηρος μεχρι ω̣δε	as the Saviour had spoken to this point.
ειρηκοτος Ανδρεας λεγε[ι α]δελ	Andrew says, 'Brothers,
φοι τι υμειν δοκει̣ πε[ρ]ι των {π̣ε̣	what does it seem to you abo[u]t what
ρι των} λαληθεντων [εγω̣ μεν	has been said? For [I] myself
γαρ ου πιστευω ταυτ[[ε]]'α' <τ>[ο]ν σ[ω	do not believe that t[h]e S[a]viour
τηρα ειρηκεναι· εδοκει γ[αρ ετε	said such things, f[or] they seem to [be
ρογνωμονειν τη εκ[ε]ιν[ου εν	di]fferent from h[is i]dea.'

9 Tuckett, *Mary*, 112–15.
10 Roberts, '463: The Gospel of Mary', 18–23.
11 Lührmann, *Die apokryph gewordenen Evangelien*, 112–13.

νοια <πετρος λεγει> περι τοιουτ[ω]ν πρα[γμα	(Peter said), asking about
των εξεταζομενος ο̣ σω[τηρ]	such matters, 'Did the Savi[our]
λαθρα γ̣υ̣ν̣[α]ι̣κι ελαλει και <ου> φ[α	speak secretly with a wo[m]an and not
νερως ινα παντες ακου̣σ[ωμεν	o[p]enly, so that [we] all might listen?
μη α]ξιολογωτερ̣α̣ν̣ η̣[.]ω̣ν̣[…	[Is she m]ore worthy of esteem than us?'
ε̣	

Textual Issues

6–7. περι των: dittography. | **8.** ταυτα corrected on MS. <τ>[ο]ν: MS reads σ[.]ν. | **11.** πετρος λεγει not on MS. | **13.** ου not on MS.

Verso (↓)

κβ	22
του σωτηρος Λευε[ι]ς λεγει Πετρω̣	of the Saviour'. Lev[i] says to Peter,
Πετρε ἀ[ει] σο[ι] το οργιλον̣· παρ̣ακει	'Peter, wrath is always with yo[u],
ται και αρ̣τ̣ι ουτως συνζητει[ς] τ̣η	and so now you are disputing with the
γυναικι ως̣ αντικειμενος̣ α̣υ̣τ̣η	woman like an adversary to her.
ει ο σωτη[ρ] αξιαν αυτην ηγησατο	If the Saviour deemed her worthy,
συ τ̣ις ει ε̣ξουθενων αυτην παν	who are you to reject her?
τως̣ γαρ̣ ε̣κεινος ειδως αυτην α̣σ̣	For surely he, knowing her i[n]fallib[ly],
φ̣[αλ]ω̣[ς] ηγαπησεν μαλλ[ο]ν αι̣σχυ[ν]	loved (her). Rath[e]r l[et] us be as[h]amed
θ̣ω̣[με]ν και ενδυσαμενο̣[ι] τον	and having put on the
τ̣[ελειο]ν α̅ν̅ο̅ν̅ εκεινο το προστα<χ>	P[erfec]t Man; let [u]s do what
θ[εν η]μειν π[ο]ι̣ησωμεν κηρυσ{ε}	was comm[an]ded of us, to pre[ach
σ̣[ειν το] ευαγγ[ε]λ̣ιον μηδεν ο[ρ]ι̣ζον	the] gos[p]el, la[yi]ng down nothing
τ̣[ες μ]ηδε νο̣μοθε̣τ[ο]υντ̣ες ως ει	[n]or law-making, as [the]

π̣[εν ο] σ̣ωτηρ [ταυ]τα ειπ̣ω̣ν ο Λ̣ευ	Saviour sai[d].' When he had said [the]se things
[εις με]ν̣ απ̣[ελθων] η̣ρ̣χεν κη[ρυσ	Levi dep[arted] and he began
σειν το ευαγγελι]ον [κατα Μαριαμ]	to p[reach. The Gosp]el [according to Mary.]

Textual Issues

4. αντικειμενος: αντικειμενοι in Tuckett, but the remains of the letter on the MS suggest ς.

APPENDIX C

The Gospel of Mary: Synopses of the Greek and Coptic MSS

BG 8,22–10,17	**POxy.GM**
'Do not lay down any rules beyond what I have appointed for you, nor give a law like the Lawgiver in case you be dominated by it'.	nor a l[aw
When he had said these things, he departed. But they were grieved, they wept much, saying, 'How shall we go to the nations and preach the gospel of the kingdom of the Son of Man? If they did not spare him, how will they spare us?'	When he had said this, he de[parted. But they were grieved, weeping much and] saying, 'How shall we g[o to the nations and preach the go]spel of the k[ingdom of the Son of Man? **For** if they did not spare him,] how will they s[pare us?'
Then Mary rose, she greeted them **all,** she said to her brothers, 'Do not weep, **and** do not grieve, **and** do not doubt! For his grace will be with you **all** and will protect you. Rather let us give thanks for his greatness, for he has **prepared** us; he has made us Men'.	Then Mary, arising and greeting th]em, **kissed [them** and said to her brothers, 'Do not weep, do not grie]ve, do not doubt! [For his grace will be w]ith you, protecting you. Rather let [us] give than[ks for his greatness,] for he has **united** us **and** [has made us M]en'.
When **Mary** had said these things, she turned their mind to the Good. And they beg[an] to de[b]ate the **wor[ds]** of the [Saviour].	[When she had said these things, **Mar]y** turned their mind to [the Good. And they began to deba]te the **sayings** of the Saviou[r.
Peter said to Mary, 'Sister, we know that **the Saviour loved you more than the other women.** Tell us the words of the Saviour **that you remember**, those that you know **and we do not, nor** have we heard **them'**.	Peter said to] Mary, 'Sister, we know that **you were greatly l[oved by the Savi]our like no other woman**. Tell us [those words that you know] of the Saviour [which] we have not heard'.

Mary answered and said, 'What is **hidden from you,** I will proclaim to you'. And she began to say to them these words: **'I'**, she said, **'saw the Lord** in a vision, and I said to him, "Lord, I saw you today in a vision"'.	[Mary answered, saying, 'What is] **unknown to you and I remember**, I will pr[oclaim to you'. And she began (saying) to them th]ese words, **'To m[e] once** in a vision [................] "Lord, today ..."'

BG 17,5–19,5	**PRyl.GM**
'(From this time on, I will receive) **rest, from the time of the season of the age,** in silence."'	**the remainder of (the) course of season, of time, of age, (in) rest** i[n] silence.
When **Mary** had said these things, **she** was silent, as the Saviour had spoken **with her** to this point.	When **she** had said these thin[gs], **Mary** was silen[t], as the Saviour had spoken to this point.
Then Andrew answered and said **to the brothers**, **'Say whatever you say** about what **she** said. I myself do not believe that the Saviour said such things, for **surely these** **are** alien **teachings.'**	Andrew says, **'Brothers, what does it seem to you** abo[u]t what **has been** said? **For** [I] myself do not believe that t[h]e S[a]viour said such things, f[or] **they seem to** [be di]fferent **from h[is i]dea**.
Peter **answered, he spoke** about such matters. **He asked them about the Saviour**, 'Did **he** speak with a woman secretly (and) not openly **to us**? **Are we** all **to turn and** listen **to her**? **Did he choose her** over us?'	(Peter said), **asking** about such matters, 'Did **the Savi[our]** speak secretly with a wo[m]an and not o[p]enly, so that [we] **all** might listen? **[Is she m]ore worthy of esteem** than us?
Then Mary wept. She said to Peter, 'My brother Peter, what do you think then? Do you think that I have thought of these (things) myself in my heart, or that I am lying about the Saviour?'	-- -- -- -- of the Saviour?'
Levi **answered,** he said to Peter, 'Peter, you are always **wrathful! I see you** now disputing with the woman like **the adversaries**. If the Saviour made her worthy, who are you to reject her? Surely the Saviour knew her infallibly, and therefore he loved her **more than us**. Rather, let us be ashamed and **put on** the Perfect Man **and acquire him for ourselves**	Lev[i] says to Peter, 'Peter, **wrath** is always with yo[u], **and so** now you are disputing with the woman like **an adversary to her**. If the Saviour deemed her worthy, who are you to reject her? **For** surely he, knowing her i[n]fallib[ly], loved (her). Rath[e]r, l[et] us be as[h]amed and **having put on** the P[erfec]t Man;

as he commanded us and preach the gospel, **not** laying down **other rules** or **another** la[w] **beyond what** the Saviour told us.'	**let [u]s do what was** comm[an]ded of us, to pre[ach the] gos[p]el, la[yi]ng down **nothing** [n]or law-**making, as** [the] Saviour sai[d].
[When] [........] and **they** began to **depart [to tea]ch and** to preach.	When he had said [the]se things **Levi dep[arted]** and **he** began to p[reach.
[The Gos]pel according to Mary.	The Gosp]el [according to Mary.]

BIBLIOGRAPHY

Primary Sources

Philosophical Sources

Bury, R. G., trans. *Plato: Timaeus. Critias. Cleitophon. Menexenus. Epistles.* LCL 234. Cambridge, MA: Harvard University Press, 1929.

Fowler, H. N., trans. *Plato: Euthyphro. Apology. Crito. Phaedo. Phaedrus.* LCL 36. Cambridge, MA: Harvard University Press, 1914.

Long, A. A., and D. N. Sedley. *The Hellenistic Philosophers: Translations of the Principal Sources with Philosophical Commentary*. Vol. 1. Cambridge: Cambridge University Press, 1987.

Coptic Nag Hammadi, Berlin Codex, Codex Tchacos, Pistis Sophia

Bibliothèque Copte de Nag Hammadi Section: Textes. 38 vols., Québec and Louvain: Les Presses de l'Université Laval, 1977–2019.

Kasser, Rodolphe, and Gregor Wurst. *The Gospel of Judas, Critical Edition: Together with the Letter of Peter to Philip, James, and a Book of Allogenes from Codex Tchacos.* Washington, DC: National Geographic, 2007.

Robinson, James M. *The Coptic Gnostic Library.* 5 vols., NHS, Leiden: Brill, 2000.

Schmidt, Carl. *Pistis Sophia*. Translated by Violet MacDermot. NHMS 4. Leiden: Brill, 1978.

Apocalypse of Peter

Buchholz, Dennis D. *Your Eyes Will Be Opened: A Study of the Greek (Ethiopic) Apocalypse of Peter*. SBLDS 97. Atlanta, GA: Scholars Press, 1988.

Elliott, J. K. 'The Apocalypse of Peter'. Pages 593–612 in *The Apocryphal New Testament: A Collection of Apocryphal Christian Literature in an English Translation*. Oxford: Clarendon Press, 1993.

Kraus, Thomas J., and Nicklas, Tobias. *Das Petrusevangelium und die Petrusapokalypse: Die griechischen Fragmente mit deutscher und englischer Übersetzung*. Berlin and New York: de Gruyter, 2004.

Epistula Apostolorum

Elliott, J. K. 'The Epistle of the Apostles (Epistula Apostolorum)'. Pages 555–88 in *The Apocryphal New Testament: A Collection of Apocryphal Christian Literature in an English Translation*. Oxford: Clarendon Press, 1993.

Guerrier, Louis (with Sylvain Grébaut). *Le Testament en Galilée de Notre-Seigneur Jésus-Christ*. Patrologia Orientalis. Paris: Firmin-Didot, 1913; repr. Turnhout: Brepols, 1982.

Schmidt, Carl, and Isaak Wajnberg. *Gespräche Jesu mit seinen Jüngern nach der Auferstehung; ein katholisch-apostolisches Sendschreiben des 2. Jahrhunderts*. TU 43. Leipzig: Hinrichs, 1919.

Other Ancient Sources

Bardy, Gustave, ed., Jean Sender, trans., *Théophile d'Antioche: Trois Livres à Autolycus*. SC 20. Paris: Éditions du Cerf, 1948.

Ehrman, Bart D. ed. *The Apostolic Fathers*. LCL 24. Cambridge, MA and London: Harvard University Press, 2003.

Irenaeus. 'Against the Heresies (Detection and Overthrow of Gnosis Falsely So- Called)'. Pages 41–141 in Robert M. Grant. *Irenaeus of Lyons*. The Early Church Fathers. London: Routledge, 1997.

Irenaeus. *Irénée de Lyon, Contre les hérésies, Livre 1*. Edited and translated by Adelin Rousseau and Louis Doutreleau. 2 vols. SC 263–264. Paris: du Cerf, 1979.

Minns, Denis, and Paul Parvis, eds. *Justin, Philosopher and Martyr: Apologies*. OECT. Oxford: Oxford University Press, 2009.

Secondary Literature

Adams, Edward. *Constructing the World: A Study in Paul's Cosmological Language*. Studies of the New Testament and Its World. Edinburgh: T&T Clark, 2000.

The Stars Will Fall from Heaven: Cosmic Catastrophe in the New Testament and Its World. Library of New Testament Studies 347. London and New York: T&T Clark, 2007.

Adams, Sean A. *The Genre of Acts and Collected Biography*. SNTSMS 156. New York: Cambridge University Press, 2013.

Ashton, John. *Understanding the Fourth Gospel*. 2nd ed. Oxford: Oxford University Press, 2007.

'The Transformation of Wisdom: A Study of the Prologue of John's Gospel'. *NTS* 32.2 (1986): 161–86.

Attridge, Harold W. 'Genre Bending in the Fourth Gospel'. *JBL* 121.1 (2002): 3–21.

'"Let Us Strive to Enter That Rest": The Logic of Hebrews 4:1–11'. *HTR* 73.1–2 (1980): 279–88.

Baird, William. 'Visions, Revelation, and Ministry: Reflections on 2 Cor 12:1–5 and Gal 1:11–17'. *JBL* 104.4 (1985): 651–62.

Bass, Ardyth L. '*Composition and Redaction in the Coptic Gospel of Mary*'. Milwaukee, WI: PhD Thesis, Marquette University, 2007.

Bauckham, Richard. 'Pseudo-Apostolic Letters'. *JBL* 107.3 (1988): 469–94.

The Theology of the Book of Revelation. New Testament Theology. Cambridge: Cambridge University Press, 1993.

'The Two Fig Tree Parables in the Apocalypse of Peter'. *JBL* 104.2 (1985): 269–87.

Beasley-Murray, George Raymond. *Jesus and the Kingdom of God*. Grand Rapids, MI: Eerdmans, 1986.

Beavis, Mary Ann. *Mark's Audience: The Literary and Social Setting of Mark 4.11–12*. JSNTSup 33. Sheffield: JSOT Press, 1989.

'The Power of Jesus' Parables: Were They Polemical or Irenic?' *JSNT* 82 (2001): 3–30.

Bernabé, Alberto, and Ana Isabel Jiménez San Cristóbal. *Instructions for the Netherworld: The Orphic Gold Tablets*. Religions in the Graeco-Roman World 162. Leiden and Boston: Brill, 2008.

Bieringer, Reimund. '"I Am Ascending to My Father and Your Father, to My God and Your God" (John 20:17): Resurrection and Ascension in the Gospel of John'. Pages 209–35 in *The Resurrection of Jesus in the Gospel of John*. Edited by Helmut Koester and Reimund Bieringer, WUNT I 222. Tübingen: Mohr Siebeck, 2011.

Bock, Darrell L. *Luke 2: 9:51–24:53*. BECNT. Grand Rapids, MI: Baker, 1996.

Bockmuehl, Markus. *Ancient Apocryphal Gospels*. Interpretation. Louisville, KY: Westminster John Knox Press, 2017.

de Boer, Esther A. 'A Stoic Reading of the Gospel of Mary: The Meaning of "Matter" and "Nature" in the Gospel of Mary 7.1–8.11'. Pages 199–219 in *Stoicism in Early Christianity*. Edited by Tuomas Rasimus, Troels Engberg-Pedersen, and Ismo Dunderberg. Grand Rapids, MI: Baker Academic, 2010.

The Gospel of Mary: Listening to the Beloved Disciple. London and New York: T&T Clark, 2004.

Bousset, Wilhelm. *Kyrios Christos: A History of the Belief in Christ from the Beginnings of Christianity to Irenaeus*. Translated by John E. Steely. 5th ed. Nashville, TN and New York: Abingdon Press, 1970.

Bovon, François. 'Fragment Oxyrhynchus 840, Fragment of a Lost Gospel, Witness of an Early Christian Controversy over Purity'. *JBL* 119.4 (2000): 705–28.

Luke 2: A Commentary on the Gospel of Luke 9:51–19:27. Edited by Helmut Koester. Translated by Donald S. Deer. Hermeneia. Minneapolis, MN: Fortress Press, 2013.

Brakke, David. *The Gnostics: Myth, Ritual, and Diversity in Early Christianity*. Cambridge, MA: Harvard University Press, 2010.

'Parables and Plain Speech in the Fourth Gospel and the Apocryphon of James'. *JECS* 7.2 (1999): 187–218.

Talking Back: A Monastic Handbook for Combating Demons. Cistercian Studies Series 229 (Collegeville, MN: Liturgical Press, 2009), 1–40.

Brayford, Susan. *Genesis*. Septuagint Commentary Series. Leiden and Boston: Brill, 2007.

Bremmer, Jan N. 'Descents to Hell and Ascents to Heaven in Apocalyptic Literature'. Pages 340–57 in *The Oxford Handbook of Apocalyptic Literature*. Edited by John J. Collins. Oxford and New York: Oxford University Press, 2014.

Brock, Ann Graham. *Mary Magdalene, The First Apostle: The Struggle for Authority*. Cambridge, MA: Harvard University Press, 2003.

Brown, Raymond E. *The Gospel According to John, XIII–XXI*. ABRL. New York: Yale University Press, 1970.

The Gospel and Epistles of John: A Concise Commentary. Collegeville, MN: Liturgical Press, 1988.

'The Paraclete in the Fourth Gospel'. *NTS* 13.2 (1967): 113–32.

The Virginal Conception and Bodily Resurrection of Jesus. New York: Paulist Press, 1973.

Burkett, Delbert. *The Son of Man Debate: A History and Evaluation*. Cambridge: Cambridge University Press, 1999.

Burkitt, F. C. 'Pistis Sophia Again'. *JTS* 26.104 (1925): 391–9.

Burridge, Richard A. *What Are the Gospels? A Comparison with Graeco-Roman Biography*. SNTSMS 70. Cambridge: Cambridge University Press, 1992.

'Who Writes, Why, and for Whom?' Pages 99–115 in *The Written Gospel*. Edited by Markus Bockmuehl and D. A. Hagner. Cambridge: Cambridge University Press, 2005.

Cameron, Ron. *The Other Gospels: Non-Canonical Gospel Texts*. Philadelphia, PA: Westminster John Knox Press, 1982.

Chandler, Daniel. 'An Introduction to Genre Theory', 2000 [1997], 1. Available from http://visual-memory.co.uk/daniel/Documents/intgenre/chandler_genre_theory.pdf.

Collins, Adela Yarbro. *Cosmology and Eschatology in Jewish and Christian Apocalypticism*. Supplements to the Journal for the Study of Judaism 50. Edited by John J. Collins. Leiden and New York: Brill, 1996.

Collins, John J. 'Introduction: Towards the Morphology of a Genre'. *Semeia* 14 (1979): 1–20.

Collins, Raymond F. *Second Corinthians*. Paideia. Grand Rapids, MI: Baker Academic, 2013.

Colpe, C. 'Die "Himmelsreise der Seele" ausserhalb und innerhalb der Gnosis'. Pages 429–47 in *Le origini dello gnosticismo, Colloquia di Messina 13–18 aprile 1966*. Edited by U. Bianchi. Leiden: Brill, 1967.

Comfort, Philip. *Encountering the Manuscripts: An Introduction to New Testament Paleography and Textual Criticism*. Nashville: B&H Publishing, 2005.

Concannon, Cavan W. *Assembling Early Christianity: Trade, Networks, and the Letters of Dionysios of Corinth*. Cambridge: Cambridge University Press, 2017.

Copenhaver, Brian P. *Hermetica: The Greek Corpus Hermeticum and the Latin Asclepius in a New English Translation with Notes and Introduction*. Cambridge: Cambridge University Press, 1992.

Corrigan, Kevin, and Tuomas Rasimus, eds. *Gnosticism, Platonism and the Late Ancient World: Essays in Honour of John D. Turner*. NHMS 82. Leiden and Boston: Brill, 2013.

Creech, David. *The Use of Scripture in the Apocryphon of John: A Diachronic Analysis of the Variant Versions*. WUNT II 441. Tübingen: Mohr Siebeck, 2017.

Crum, W. E. *A Coptic Dictionary*. Oxford: The Clarendon Press, 1939.

D'Angelo, Mary Rose. '"I Have Seen the Lord": Mary Magdalen as Visionary, Early Christian Prophecy, and the Context of John 20:14–18'. Pages 95–122 in *Mariam, the Magdalen, and the Mother*. Edited by Deirdre Good. Bloomington, IN: Indiana University Press, 2005.

Davies, J. G. 'The Primary Meaning of Παράκλητος'. *JTS* 4.1 (1953): 35–8.

Davies, Stevan. 'The Christology and Protology of the "Gospel of Thomas"'. *JBL* 111.4 (1992): 663–82.

Davies, W. D., and Dale C. Allison. *Matthew 8–18*. Vol. 2 of International Critical Commentary. London and New York: T&T Clark, 1991.

DeConick, April D. ed. *The Codex Judas Papers: Proceedings of the International Congress on the Tchacos Codex Held at Rice University, Houston, Texas, March 13–16, 2008*. NHMS 71. Leiden and Boston: Brill, 2009.

'The "Dialogue of the Savior" and the Mystical Sayings of Jesus'. *VC* 50.2 (1996): 178–99.

Holy Misogyny: Why the Sex and Gender Conflicts in the Early Church Still Matter. New York and London: Continuum, 2011.

'John Rivals Thomas: From Community Conflict to Gospel Narrative'. Pages 303–12 in *Jesus in Johannine Tradition*. Edited by Robert T. Fortna and Tom Thatcher. Louisville, KY: Westminster John Knox Press, 2001.

The Original Gospel of Thomas in Translation: With a Commentary and New English Translation of the Complete Gospel. LNTS. London: T&T Clark, 2006.

Seek to See Him: Ascent and Vision Mysticism in the Gospel of Thomas. VCSup 33. Leiden: Brill, 1996.

Deleuze, Gilles, and Félix Guattari. *A Thousand Plateaus: Capitalism and Schizophrenia*. Translated by Brian Massumi. Minneapolis: University of Minnesota Press, 1980; repr. London and New York: Continuum, 2004.

Denzey Lewis, Nicola. *Cosmology and Fate in Gnosticism and Graeco-Roman Antiquity: Under Pitiless Skies*. NHMS 81. Leiden and Boston: Brill, 2013.

Introduction to 'Gnosticism': Ancient Voices, Christian Worlds. New York and Oxford: Oxford University Press, 2013.

Derrida, Jacques. 'The Law of Genre'. *Glyph* 7 (1980): 176–232.

Desjardins, Michel Robert. *Sin in Valentinianism*. SBLDS 108. Atlanta: Scholars Press, 1990.

Dettwiler, Andreas. *Die Gegenwart des Erhöhten: eine exegetische Studie zu den johanneischen Abschiedsreden (Joh 13,31-16,33) unter besonderer Berücksichtigung ihres Relecture-Charakters*. Göttingen: Vandenhoeck & Ruprecht, 1995.

Diehl, Judith A. 'What Is a "Gospel"? Recent Studies in the Gospel Genre'. *Currents in Biblical Research* 9.2 (2011): 171–99.

Dillon, John. 'The Descent of the Soul in Middle Platonic and Gnostic Theory'. Pages 357–64 in *The Rediscovery of Gnosticism: Proceedings of the International Conference on Gnosticism at Yale, March 28–31, 1978*. Edited by Bentley Layton. Vol. 1 of Studies in the History of Religion 41. Leiden: Brill, 1980.

The Middle Platonists, 80 B.C. to A.D. 220. Revised. New York: Cornell University Press, 1996.

Dodd, C. H. *The Interpretation of the Fourth Gospel*. Cambridge: Cambridge University Press, 1955.

Donaldson, Terence L. *Jesus on the Mountain: A Study in Matthean Theology*. JSNTSup 8. Sheffield: JSOT, 1985.

Dunderberg, Ismo. *The Beloved Disciple in Conflict? Revisiting the Gospels of John and Thomas*. New York: Oxford University Press, 2006.

Beyond Gnosticism: Myth, Lifestyle, and Society in the School of Valentinus. New York: Columbia University Press, 2008.

'Secrecy in the Gospel of John'. Pages 221–44 in *Mystery and Secrecy in the Nag Hammadi Collection and Other Ancient Literature: Ideas and Practices*. Edited by Christian H. Bull, Liv Ingeborg Leid, and John D. Turner. Leiden: Brill, 2012.

Dunning, Benjamin H. 'What Sort of Thing Is This Luminous Woman? Thinking Sexual Difference in *On the Origin of the World*'. *JECS* 16.1 (2009): 55–84.

Edmonds, Radcliffe G., III. *Myths of the Underworld Journey: Plato, Aristophanes, and the 'Orphic Gold Tablets'*. Cambridge: Cambridge University Press, 2004.

Redefining Ancient Orphism: A Study in Greek Religion. Cambridge: Cambridge University Press, 2013.

Edwards, Robert Michael. 'The Rhetoric of Authority: The Nature of Revelation in the First Apocalypse of James'. Pages 65–79 in *La Littérature des Questions et Réponses dans l'Antiquité profane et chrétienne: De l'enseignement à l'exégèse*. Edited by Marie-Pierre Bussières. Instrumenta Patristica et Mediaevalia 64. Turnhout: Brepols Publishers, 2013.

Ehrman, Bart D. *Peter, Paul, and Mary Magdalene: The Followers of Jesus in History and Legend*. New York: Oxford University Press, 2006.

The Orthodox Corruption of Scripture: The Effect of Early Christological Controversies on the Text of the New Testament. Oxford and New York: Oxford University Press, 1993.

Ehrman, Bart D., and Zlatko Pleše. *The Apocryphal Gospels: Texts and Translations*. Oxford and New York: Oxford University Press, 2011.

Elliott, J. K. *The Apocryphal New Testament: A Collection of Apocryphal Christian Literature in an English Translation*. Oxford: Oxford University Press, 2005.

Emmel, S. L., Helmut Koester, and Elaine Hiesey Pagels. *Nag Hammadi Codex III,5: The Dialogue of the Savior*. Leiden: Brill, 1984.

Epp, Eldon Jay. 'The Multivalence of the Term "Original Text" in New Testament Textual Criticism'. *HTR* 92.3 (1999): 245–81.

Evans, Craig A. 'Jesus in Gnostic Literature'. *Biblica* 62.3 (1981): 406–12.

Evans, Erin. *The Books of Jeu and the Pistis Sophia as Handbooks to Eternity: Exploring the Gnostic Mysteries of the Ineffable*. NHMS 89. Leiden and Boston: Brill, 2015.

Falkenberg, René. 'Matthew 28:16–20 and the Nag Hammadi Library: Reception of the Great Commission in the Sophia of Jesus Christ'. Pages 93–104 in *Mark and Matthew II: Comparative Readings: Reception History, Cultural Hermeneutics, and Theology*. Edited by Eve-Marie Becker and Anders Runesson. WUNT 304. Tübingen: Mohr Siebeck, 2013.

Fallon, Francis T. 'Gnostic Apocalypses'. *Semeia* 14 (1979): 123–58.

'The Law in Philo and Ptolemy: A Note on the Letter to Flora'. *VC* 30.1 (1976): 45–51.

Ferreira, Johan. *Johannine Ecclesiology*. LNTS 160. Sheffield: T&T Clark, 1998.

Fitzmyer, Joseph A. *The Gospel According to Luke X–XXIV*. AB 28A. New York: Doubleday, 1985.

Foster, Paul. 'The Epistles of Ignatius of Antioch and the Writings That Later Formed the New Testament'. Pages 159–86 in *The Reception of the New Testament in the Apostolic Fathers*. Edited by Andrew Gregory and Christopher M. Tuckett. Oxford: Oxford University Press, 2005.

'Polymorphic Christology: Its Origins and Development in Early Christianity'. *JTS* 58.1 (2007): 66–99.

'The Gospel of Philip'. Pages 68–83 in *The Non-Canonical Gospels*. Edited by Paul Foster. London and New York: T&T Clark, 2008.

France, R. T. *The Gospel of Mark: A Commentary on the Greek Text*. NIGTC. Grand Rapids, MI and Cambridge: Eerdmans, 2002.

Frey, Jörg. 'Das Freer-Logion'. Pages 1059–61 in *Antike Christliche Apokryphen in Deutscher Übersetzung: Band in Zwei Teilbänden: Evangelien Und Verwandtes.* Edited by Jens Schröter and Christoph Markschies. Vol. 2. Tübingen: Mohr Siebeck, 2012.

'Zu Text und Sinn des Freer-Logion'. *ZNW* 93.1–2 (2002): 13–34.

Frow, John. *Genre*. London and New York, 2006.

Fuller, Reginald H. *The Formation of the Resurrection Narratives*. Philadelphia, PA: Fortress Press, 1980.

Gathercole, Simon. *The Gospel of Judas: Rewriting Early Christianity*. Oxford and New York: Oxford University Press, 2007.

The Gospel of Thomas: Introduction and Commentary. TENT 11. Leiden and Boston: Brill, 2014.

'"The Heavens and Earth Will Be Rolled Up": The Eschatology of the Gospel of Thomas'. Pages 280–302 in *Eschatologie – Eschatology. The Sixth Durham-Tübingen Research Symposium: Eschatology in Old Testament, Ancient Judaism and Early Christianity (Tübingen, September, 2009)*. Edited by Hans-Joachim Eckstein, Christof Landmesser, and Hermann Lichtenberger. Tübingen: Mohr Siebeck, 2011.

'Quis et Unde? Heavenly Obstacles in Gos. Thom. 50 and Related Literature'. Pages 82–101 in *Paradise in Antiquity: Jewish and Christian Views*. Edited by Markus Bockmuehl and Guy G. Stroumsa. Cambridge: Cambridge University Press, 2010.

Glaser, Timo. 'Liaisons Dangereuses: Epistolary Novels in Antiquity'. Pages 244–56 in *A Companion to the Ancient Novel*. Edited by Edmund P. Cueva and Shannon N. Byrne. Blackwell Companions to the Ancient World. Chichester and Malden, MA: Wiley Blackwell, 2014.

Goodacre, Mark. *Thomas and the Gospels: The Case for Thomas's Familiarity with the Synoptics*. Grand Rapids, MI: Eerdmans, 2012.

Graf, Fritz, and Sarah Iles Johnston. *Ritual Texts for the Afterlife: Orpheus and the Bacchic Gold Tablets*. London and New York: Routledge, 2007.

Gregory, Andrew. 'Non-Canonical Epistles and Related Literature'. Pages 90–114 in *The Oxford Handbook of Early Christian Literature*. Edited by Christopher Tuckett and Andrew Gregory. Oxford: Oxford University Press, 2015.

Gregory, Andrew, and Christopher Tuckett. 'Series Preface'. Pages xii–xiv in *Gospel of Mary*. By Christopher Tuckett. Oxford: Oxford University Press, 2007.

Hahn, Ferdinand. *The Titles of Jesus in Christology: Their History in Early Christianity*. Translated by Harold Knight and George Ogg. Library of Theological Translations. Cambridge: James Clarke Co., 2002.

Haines-Eitzen, Kim. *Guardians of Letters: Literacy, Power, and the Transmitters of Early Christian Literature*. Oxford and New York: Oxford University Press, 2000.

Harnack, Adolf. 'Die Verklärungsgeschichte Jesu, der Bericht des Paulus (I Kor. 15, 3ff) und die beiden Christusvisionen des Petrus'. *Sitzungsberichte der Königlich Preussischen Akademie der Wissenschaften zu Berlin* (1922): 62–80.

Hartenstein, Judith. 'Dialogische Evangelien'. Pages 1051–9 in *Antike christliche Apokryphen in deutscher Übersetzung: Band in zwei Teilbänden: Evangelien und Verwandtes*. Edited by Christoph Markschies and Jens Schröter. Vol. 2. Tübingen: Mohr Siebeck, 2012.

Die zweite Lehre: Erscheinungen des Auferstandenen als Rahmenerzählungen frühchristlicher Dialoge. TU 146. Berlin: de Gruyter, 2000.

'Erscheinungsevangelien (Gespräche mit dem Auferstandenen) im Kontext frühchristlicher Theologie: Anknüpfungspunkte und Besonderheiten der christologischen Vorstellungen'. Pages 305–32 in *The Apocryphal Gospels within the Context of Early Christian Theology*. Edited by Jens Schröter. Leuven: Peeters, 2013.

Haxby, Mikael. '*The First Apocalypse of James: Martyrdom and Sexual Difference*'. Cambridge, MA: PhD Thesis, Harvard University Press, 2013.

Hedrick, Charles W. 'Kingdom Sayings and Parables of Jesus in the Apocryphon of James: Tradition and Redaction'. *NTS* 29.1 (1983): 1–24.

Helmer, Robert C. '*"That We May Know and Understand": Gospel Tradition in the Apocalypse of Peter*'. Milwaukee, WI: PhD Thesis, Marquette University, 1998.

Hennecke, E., and W. Schneemelcher, eds. *Neutestamentliche Apokryphen in deutscher Übersetzung: Evangelien*. 3rd ed. Vol. 1. Tübingen: Mohr Siebeck, 1959.

Hill, Charles E. *The Johannine Corpus in the Early Church*. Oxford: Oxford University Press, 2004.

Hills, Julian V. 'Parables, Pretenders, and Prophecies: Translation and Interpretation in the Apocalypse of Peter 2'. *Revue Biblique* 98.4 (1991): 560–73.

Tradition and Composition in the Epistula Apostolorum. HTS 57. Cambridge, MA: Harvard University Press, 2008.

Himmelfarb, Martha. 'The Experience of the Visionary and Genre in the Ascension of Isaiah 6–11 and the Apocalypse of Paul'. *Semeia* 36 (1986): 97–112.

Hogeterp, Albert L. A. 'The Gospel of Thomas and the Historical Jesus: The Case of Eschatology'. Pages 381–96 in *The Wisdom of Egypt: Jewish, Early Christian and Gnostic Essays in Honour of Gerard P. Luttikhuizen*. Edited by A. Hilhorst and G. H. van Kooten. AGJU/AJEC 59. Leiden: Brill, 2007.

Hornschuh, Manfred. *Studien zur Epistula Apostolorum*. Patristische Texte und Studien 5. Berlin: de Gruyter, 1965.

Hurtado, Larry W. *Lord Jesus Christ: Devotion to Jesus in Earliest Christianity*. Grand Rapids, MI and Cambridge: Eerdmans, 2003.

'The Greek Fragments of "The Gospel of Thomas" as Artefacts: Papyrological Observations on P. Oxy. 1, P.Oxy 654, and P. Oxy 655'. Pages 19–32 in *Das Thomasevangelium: Entstehung – Rezeption – Theologie*. Edited by Jörg Frey, Enno Edzard Popkes, and Jens Schröter. Berlin and New York: de Gruyter, 2008.

Iricinschi, Eduard. '*Scribes and Readers of Nag Hammadi Codex II: Book Production and Monastic Paideia in Fourth-Century Egypt*'. PhD Thesis, Princeton, 2009.

Jakab, A. 'The Reception of the Apocalypse of Peter in Ancient Christianity'. Pages 174–86 in *The Apocalypse of Peter*. Edited by Jan N.

Bremmer and István Czachesz. Studies on Early Christian Apocrypha 7. Leuven: Peeters, 2003.

Janssen, Martina. 'Mystagogus Gnosticus? Zur Gattung der "gnostischen Gespräche des Auferstandenen"'. Pages 21–260 in *Studien zur Gnosis*. Edited by Gerd Lüdemann. Studies in the Religion and History of Early Christianity. Frankfurt am Main: Peter Lang, 1999.

Jenott, Lance. 'Reading Variants in James and the Apocalypse of James: A Perspective from New Philology'. Pages 55–84 in *Snapshots of Evolving Traditions: Jewish and Christian Manuscript Culture, Textual Fluidity, and New Philology*. Edited by Liv Ingeborg Leid and Hugo Lundhaug. Berlin and Boston: de Gruyter, 2017.

The Gospel of Judas: Coptic Text, Translation, and Historical Interpretation of 'the Betrayer's Gospel'. STAC 64. Tübingen: Mohr Siebeck, 2011.

Jenott, Lance, and Elaine Pagels. 'Antony's Letters and Nag Hammadi Codex I: Sources of Religious Conflict in Fourth-Century Egypt'. *JECS* 18.4 (2010): 557–89.

Johnston, George. *The Spirit-Paraclete in the Gospel of John*. SNTSMS 12. Cambridge: Cambridge University Press, 1970.

Kaler, Michael. 'Just How Close Are the Gnostic Revelation Dialogues to Erotapokriseis Literature, Anyway?'. Pages 37–49 in *La Littérature des Questions et Réponses dans l'Antiquité profane et chrétienne: De l'enseignement à l'exégèse*. Edited by Marie-Pierre Bussières. Instrumenta Patristica et Mediaevalia 64. Turnhout: Brepols Publishers, 2013.

Kazen, Thomas. 'Sectarian Gospels for Some Christians? Intention and Mirror Reading in the Light of Extra-Canonical Texts'. *NTS* 51.4 (2005): 561–78.

Keener, Craig S. *The Gospel of John: A Commentary*. Vol. 1. Grand Rapids, MI: Baker Academic, 2003.

Kelhoffer, James A. 'The Witness of Eusebius's Ad Marinum and Other Christian Writings to Text-Critical Debates Concerning the Original Conclusion to Mark's Gospel'. Pages 121–64 in *Conceptions of 'Gospel' and Legitimacy in Early Christianity*. WUNT 324. Tübingen: Mohr Siebeck, 2014.

King, Karen L. 'The Gospel of Mary Magdalene'. Pages 601–34 in *Searching the Scriptures, II: A Feminist Commentary*. Edited by Elisabeth Schüssler Fiorenza. New York: Crossroad, 1994.

The Gospel of Mary of Magdala: Jesus and the First Woman Apostle. Santa Rosa, CA: Polebridge Press, 2003.

'Hearing, Seeing, and Knowing God: Allogenes and the Gospel of Mary'. Pages 319–32 in *Early Christian Voices in Texts, Traditions, and Symbols: Essays in Honor of François Bovon*. Edited by David H. Warren, Ann Graham Brock, and David W. Pao. Leiden and Boston: Brill, 2003.

'Martyrdom and Its Discontents in the Tchacos Codex'. Pages 23–42 in *The Codex Judas Papers: Proceedings of the International Congress on the Tchacos Codex Held at Rice University, Houston, Texas, March 13–16, 2008*. Edited by April D. DeConick. NHMS 71. Leiden and Boston: Brill, 2009.

'Mystery and Secrecy in the Secret Revelation of John'. Pages 61–86 in *Mystery and Secrecy in the Nag Hammadi Collection and Other Ancient Literature: Ideas and Practices*. Edited by Christian H. Bull, Liv Ingeborg Leid, and John D. Turner. NHMS 76. Leiden and Boston: Brill, 2012.

'Prophetic Power and Women's Authority: The Case of the Gospel of Mary (Magdalene)'. Pages 21–41 in *Women Preachers and Prophets Through Two Millennia of Christianity*. Edited by Beverly Mayne Kienzle and Pamela J. Walker. Berkeley and LA: University of California Press, 1998.

'The Place of the Gospel of Philip in the Context of Early Christian Claims about Jesus' Marital Status'. *NTS* 59.4 (2013): 565–87.

The Secret Revelation of John. Cambridge, MA and London: Harvard University Press, 2006.

What Is Gnosticism? Cambridge, MA: Harvard University Press, 2005.

'Why All the Controversy? Mary in the Gospel of Mary'. Pages 53–74 in *Which Mary? The Marys of Early Christian Tradition*. Edited by F. Stanley Jones. SBL Symposium Series 19. Edited by Christopher R. Matthews. Atlanta: Society of Biblical Literature, 2002.

Klauck, Hans-Josef. *The Apocryphal Gospels: An Introduction*. Translated by Brian McNeil. London: T&T Clark, 2003.

Koester, Helmut. *Ancient Christian Gospels: Their History and Development*. London: SCM Press; Philadelphia: Trinity Press International, 1990.

'One Jesus and Four Primitive Gospels'. *HTR* 61.2 (1968): 203–47.

'The Text of the Synoptic Gospels in the Second Century'. Pages 19–37 in *Gospel Traditions in the Second Century: Origins, Recensions, Text, and Transmission*. Edited by William L. Peterson. Christianity and Judaism in Antiquity. Notre Dame, IN: University of Notre Dame Press, 1989.

Koester, Helmut, and Elaine Pagels. 'Introduction'. Pages 1–19 in *Nag Hammadi Codex III, 5: The Dialogue of the Savior*. CGL. Leiden: Brill, 1984.

Koschorke, Klaus. 'Eine gnostische Paraphrase des johanneischen Prologs: zur Interpretation von "Epistula Petri ad Philippum" (NHC VIII, 2) 136,16–137,4'. *VC* 33.4 (1979): 383–92.

Kraus, Thomas J., and Tobias Nicklas. *Das Petrusevangelium und die Petrusapokalypse. Die griechischen Fragmente mit deutscher und englischer Übersetzung*. Berlin and New York: de Gruyter, 2004.

Krause, Martin. 'Die literarischen Gattungen der Apokalypsen von Nag Hammadi'. Pages 621–37 in *Apocalypticism in the Mediterranean World and the Near East: Proceedings of the International Colloquium on Apocalypticism, Uppsala, August 12–17, 1979*. Edited by David Hellholm. Tübingen: Mohr Siebeck, 1983.

Kruger, Michael J. *The Gospel of the Savior: An Analysis of P.Oxy. 840 and Its Place in the Gospel Traditions of Early Christianity*. TENT 1. Leiden: Brill, 2005.

Lampe, G. W. H., ed. *Patristic Greek Lexicon*. London: Oxford University Press, 1961.

Lang, T. J. *Mystery and the Making of a Christian Historical Consciousness: From Paul to the Second Century*. BZNW 219. Berlin: de Gruyter, 2015.

Lapham, F. *Peter: The Myth, the Man and the Writings: A Study of the Early Petrine Text and Tradition*. London and New York: T&T Clark, 2004.

Layton, Bentley. 'Ptolemy's Epistle to Flora'. Pages 306–15 in *The Gnostic Scriptures: A New Translation with Annotations and Introductions*. Garden City: Doubleday, 1987.

Lehtipuu, Outi. *The Afterlife Imagery in Luke's Story of the Rich Man and Lazarus*. NovTSup 123. Leiden and Boston: Brill, 2007.

Debates over the Resurrection of the Dead. Oxford Early Christian Studies. Oxford and New York: Oxford University Press, 2015.

Létourneau, Pierre. *Le Dialogue du Sauveur (NH III,5)*. BCNH:T 29. Louvain: Peeters, 2003.

'The Dialogue of the Savior as a Witness to the Late Valentinian Tradition'. *VC* 65.1 (2011): 74–98.

Lincoln, Andrew T. *Ephesians*. World Bible Commentary 42. Waco, TX: Word, 1990.

Long, A. A., and D. N. Sedley. *The Hellenistic Philosophers: Volume 1, Translations of the Principal Sources with Philosophical Commentary*. Cambridge: Cambridge University Press, 1987.

Lucchesi, E. 'Évangile selon Marie ou Évangile selon Marie-Madeleine?' *Analecta Bollandiana* 103.3–4 (1985): 366.

Lührmann, Dieter. *Die apokryph gewordenen Evangelien: Studien zu Neuen Texten und zu Neuen Fragen*. NovTSup 112. Leiden and Boston: Brill, 2004.

Luijendijk, AnneMarie. 'Sacred Scriptures as Trash: Biblical Papyri from Oxyrhynchus'. *VC* 64.3 (2010): 217–54.

Lundhaug, Hugo. *Images of Rebirth: Cognitive Poetics and Transformational Soteriology in the Gospel of Philip and the Exegesis on the Soul*. NHMS 73. Leiden and Boston: Brill, 2010.

'An Illusion of Textual Stability: Textual Fluidity, New Philology, and the Nag Hammadi Codices'. Pages 20–54 in *Snapshots of Evolving Traditions: Jewish and Christian Manuscript Culture, Textual Fluidity, and New Philology*. Edited by Liv Ingeborg Lied and Hugo Lundhaug, TU 175. Berlin and Boston: de Gruyter, 2017.

Luttikhuizen, Gerard P. *Gnostic Revisions of Genesis Stories and Early Jesus Traditions*. NHMS 58. Leiden and Boston: Brill, 2006.

'The Evaluation of the Teaching of Jesus in Christian Gnostic Revelation Dialogues'. *NovT* 30.2 (1988): 158–68.

'The Suffering Jesus and the Invulnerable Christ in the Gnostic Apocalypse of Peter'. Pages 187–99 in *The Apocalypse of Peter*. Edited by Jan N. Bremmer and István Czachesz. Studies on the Early Christian Apocrypha 7. Leuven: Peeters, 2003.

Marincola, John. 'Genre, Convention, and Innovation in Greco-Roman Historiography'. Pages 281–324 in *The Limits of Historiography: Genre and Narrative in Ancient Historical Texts*. Edited by C. S. Kraus. Mnemosyne, Bibliotheca Classica Batava: Supplementum 191. Leiden: Brill, 1999.

Marjanen, Antti. 'The Mother of Jesus or the Magdalene? The Identity of Mary in the So-Called Gnostic Christian Texts'. Pages 31–42 in *Which Mary? The Marys of Early Christian Tradition*. Edited by F. Stanley Jones. SBL Symposium Series 19. Atlanta: Society of Biblical Literature, 2002.

The Woman Jesus Loved: Mary Magdalene in the Nag Hammadi Library and Related Documents. NHMS 40. Leiden: Brill, 1996.

Markschies, Christoph, and Jens Schröter, eds. *Antike christliche Apokryphen in deutscher Übersetzung: Evangelien und Verwantes*. Vol. 2. Tübingen: Mohr Siebeck, 2012.

Martin, Dale. *The Corinthian Body*. New Haven, CT and London: Yale University Press, 1995.

Martyn, J. Louis. *History and Theology in the Fourth Gospel*. 3rd ed. New Testament Library. Louisville, KY and London: Westminster John Knox Press, 2003.

May, Gerhard. *Creatio ex Nihilo: The Doctrine of 'Creation out of Nothing' in Early Christian Thought*. Translated by A. S. Worrall. London and New York: T&T Clark, 2004.

Metzger, Bruce M. *Manuscripts of the Greek Bible: An Introduction to Greek Palaeography*. Oxford and New York: Oxford University Press, 1981.

The Canon of the New Testament: Its Origin, Development and Significance. Oxford: Clarendon Press, 1989.

Meyer, Marvin W. *The Letter of Peter to Philip*. SBLDS 53. Chico, CA: Scholars Press, 1981.

Meyer, Marvin, and Madeleine Scopello. 'The Secret Book of James'. Pages 19–30 in *The Nag Hammadi Scriptures: The International Edition*. Edited by Marvin Meyer. New York: Harper Collins, 2007.

'The Wisdom of Jesus Christ'. Pages 283–96 in *The Nag Hammadi Scriptures: The International Edition*. Edited by Marvin Meyer. New York: Harper Collins, 2007.

Mohri, Erika. *Maria Magdalena: Frauenbilder in Evangelientexten des 1. bis 3. Jahrhunderts*. Marburger theologische Studien 63. Marburg: Elwert, 2000.

Moore, A. L. *The Parousia in the New Testament*. NovTSup 13. Leiden: Brill, 1966.

Morris, Leon. *Luke: An Introduction and Commentary*. Tyndale New Testament Commentaries. Grand Rapids, MI and Cambridge: Eerdmans, 1988.

Muddiman, John. *A Commentary on the Epistle to the Ephesians*. Black's New Testament Commentaries. London and New York: Continuum, 2001.

Nasrallah, Laura Salah. *An Ecstasy of Folly: Prophecy and Authority in Early Christianity*. HTS 52. Cambridge, MA: Harvard University Press, 2003.

Nicklas, Tobias. 'Gnostic "Eschatologies"'. Pages 601–28 in *Eschatology of the New Testament and Some Related Documents*. Edited by J. van der Watt. WUNT II 315. Tübingen: Mohr Siebeck, 2011.

Niederwimmer, Kurt. *The Didache: A Commentary*. Edited by Harold W. Attridge. Translated by Linda M. Maloney. Hermeneia. Minneapolis, MN: Fortress Press, 1998.

van Os, Bas. 'John's Last Supper and the Resurrection Dialogues'. Pages 271–80 in *John, Jesus, and History: Aspects of Historicity in the Fourth Gospel. Volume 2*. Edited by Paul N. Anderson, Felix Just, and Tom Thatcher. Atlanta, GA: Society of Biblical Literature, 2009.

Osborn, Eric. *Clement of Alexandria*. Cambridge and New York: Cambridge University Press, 2005.

Pagels, Elaine H. *The Gnostic Gospels*. New York: Random House, 1979.

The Gnostic Paul: Gnostic Exegesis of the Pauline Letters. Philadelphia, PA: Fortress Press, 1975.

'"The Mystery of the Resurrection": A Gnostic Reading of 1 Corinthians 15'. *JBL* 93.2 (1974): 276–88.

Parker, David C. *The Living Text of the Gospels*. Cambridge: Cambridge University Press, 1997.

Parkhouse, Sarah. 'Identity, Death and Ascension in the Gospel of John and the First Apocalypse of James'. Forthcoming.

'Matter and the Soul: The Bipartite Eschatology of the Gospel of Mary'. Pages 216–32 in *Connecting Gospels: Beyond the Canonical/Non-Canonical Divide*. Edited by Francis Watson and Sarah Parkhouse. Oxford: Oxford University Press, 2018.

'The Fetishization of Female Exempla: Mary, Thecla, Perpetua and Felicitas'. *NTS* 63.4 (2017): 567–87.

Parrott, D. M. *Nag Hammadi Codices III,3–4 and V,1, with Papyrus Berolinensis 8502,3 and Oxyrhynchus Papyrus 1081: Eugnostos and the Sophia of Jesus Christ*. Leiden and New York: Brill, 1991.

Parsons, P. J. '3525: Gospel of Mary'. Pages 12–14 in *The Oxyrhynchus Papyri*. Graeco-Roman Memoirs 70, Vol. 50. London: Egypt Exploration Society, 1983.

Pasquier, Anne. 'L'eschatologie dans L'Évangile selon Marie: étude des notions de nature et d'image'. Pages 390–404 in *Colloque international sur les textes de Nag Hammadi (Québec, 22–25 août 1978)*. Edited by Bernard Barc. Québec: Les Presses de l'Université Laval, 1981.

L'Évangile Selon Marie. BCNH:T 10. Québec: Les Presses de l'Université Laval, 1983.

Peel, Malcolm L. 'Gnostic Eschatology and the New Testament'. *NovT* 12.2 (1970): 141–65.

Penn, Michael Philip. *Kissing Christians: Ritual and Community in the Late Ancient Church*. Divinations: Rereading Late Ancient Religion. Philadelphia, PA: University of Pennsylvania Press, 2005.

Perkins, Pheme. 'Gnostic Christologies and the New Testament'. *CBQ* 43.4 (1981): 590–607.

The Gnostic Dialogue: The Early Church and the Crisis of Gnosticism. New York: Paulist Press, 1980.

Gnosticism and the New Testament. Minneapolis, MN: Fortress Press, 1993.

'Johannine Traditions in Ap. Jas. (NHC I,2)'. *JBL* 101.3 (1982): 403–14.

Petersen, Silke. *Zerstört die Werke der Weiblichkeit! Maria Magdalena, Salome und andere Jüngerinnen Jesu in christlich-gnostischen Schriften*. NHMS 48. Leiden: Brill, 1999.

Pétrement, Simone. *A Separate God: The Origins and Teachings of Gnosticism*. Translated by Carol Harrison. San Francisco, CA: Harper & Row, 1984.

Piovanelli, Pierluigi. 'Entre oralité et (ré)écriture : Le modèle des erotapokriseis dans les dialogues Apocryphes de Nag Hammadi'. Pages 93–103 in *La Littérature des Questions et Réponses dans l'Antiquité profane et chrétienne: De l'enseignement à l'exégèse*. Edited by Marie-Pierre Bussières. Instrumenta Patristica et Mediaevalia 64. Turnhout: Brepols Publishers, 2013.

Pleše, Zlatko. *Poetics of the Gnostic Universe: Narrative and Cosmology in the Apocryphon of John*. NHMS 52. Leiden and Boston: Brill, 2006.

Popkes, Enno Edzard. 'Von der Eschatologie zur Protologie: Transformationen apokalyptischer Motive im koptischen Thomasevangelium'. Pages 211–34 in *Apokalyptik als Herausforderung neutestamentlicher Theologie*. Edited by Michael Becker and Markus Öhler. WUNT II 214. Tübingen: Mohr Siebeck, 2006.

Puech, Henri-Charles, and Beate Blatz. 'The Gospel of Mary'. Pages 391–5 in *New Testament Apocrypha*. Edited by Wilhelm Schneemelcher. Translated by R. McL. Wilson. 2nd ed. Vol. 1. Louisville, KY and London: Westminster John Knox Press, 2003.

Quispel, G. *Ptolémée. Lettre à Flora: Texte, Traduction et Introduction*. Paris: Les Éditions du Cerf, 1949.

Ramelli, Ilaria. *The Christian Doctrine of Apokatastasis: A Critical Assessment from the New Testament to Eriugena*. VCSup 120. Leiden: Brill, 2013.

Rasimus, Tuomas, Troels Engberg-Pedersen, and Ismo Dunderberg, eds. *Stoicism in Early Christianity*. Grand Rapids, MI: Baker Academic, 2010.

Ridderbos, Herman. *The Gospel of John: A Theological Commentary*. Translated by John Vriend. Grand Rapids, MI and Cambridge: Eerdmans, 1997.

Roberts, C. H. '463: The Gospel of Mary'. Pages 18–23 in *Catalogue of the Greek Papyri in the John Rylands Library*. Vol. 3. Manchester: Manchester University Press, 1938.

Robinson, James M. 'Jesus from Easter to Valentinus (Or to the Apostles' Creed)'. *JBL* 101.1 (1982): 5–37.

Roy, Louise, and Donald Rouleau. *L'Épître apocryphe de Jacques (NH I,2) suivi de l'Acte de Pierre (BG 4)*. BCNH:T 18. Québec: Les Presses de l'Université Laval, 1987.

Rudolph, Kurt. 'Der Gnostische "Dialog" als Literarisches Genus'. Pages 85–107 in *Probleme Der Koptischen Literatur*. Edited by Peter Nagel. Halle: Wissenschaftliche Beiträge der Universität Halle-Wittenberg, 1968.

Salles, Ricardo, ed. *God and Cosmos in Stoicism*. Oxford: Oxford University Press, 2009.

Schaberg, Jane. *The Resurrection of Mary Magdalene: Legends, Apocrypha, and the Christian Testament*. London and New York: Bloomsbury, 2004.

Schenke, Hans-Martin. 'Function and Background of the Beloved Disciple'. Pages 598–613 in *Der Same Seths: Hans-Martin Schenkes kleine Schriften zu Gnosis, Koptologie und Neuem Testament*. Edited by Gesine Schenke Robinson, Gesa Schenke, and Uwe-Karsten Plisch. Leiden and Boston: Brill, 2012.

Schenke Robinson, Gesine. 'The Relationship of the Gospel of Judas to the New Testament and to Sethianism'. *Journal of Coptic Studies* 10 (2008): 63–98.

Schmidt, Carl. *Pistis Sophia*. Translated by Violet MacDermot. CGL: NHMS 4. Leiden: Brill, 1978.

Schnackenburg, Rudolf. *The Gospel According to John: Vol. 3. Commentary on Chapters 13–21*. Translated by David Smith and G. A. Kon. Kent: Burns & Oates, 1988.

Schneemelcher, W. *New Testament Apocrypha: Gospels and Related Writings*. Translated by R. McL. Wilson. 6th ed. Vol. 1. Louisville, KY and London: Westminster John Knox Press, 1991.

Schneider, C. 'Anapausis'. *Reallexikon für Antike Christentum* I (1950): 414–18.

Schröter, Jens. 'Zur Menschensohnvorstellung im Evangelium nach Maria'. Pages 178–88 in *Ägypten und Nubien in spätantiker und christlicher Zeit. Akten des 6. Internationalen Koptologenkongresses Münster, 20.–26. Juli 1996. Band 2 Schrifttum, Sprache und Gedankenwelt*. Edited by Stephen Emmel, Martin Krause, Siegfried G. Richter, and Sofia Schaten. Wiesbaden: Reichert Verlag, 1999.

Shepherd, Thomas R. 'Narrative Analysis as a Text Critical Tool: Mark 16 in Codex W as a Test Case'. *JSNT* 32.1 (2009): 77–98.

Sheridan, Ruth. 'John's Gospel and Modern Genre Theory: The Farewell Discourse (John 13–17) as a Test Case'. *Irish Theological Quarterly* 75.3 (2010): 287–99.

Shisha-Halevy, Ariel. 'Future, Present, Narrative Past: A Triple Note on Oxyrhynchite Tempuslehre'. Pages 249–309 in *Sprache und Geist. Peter Nagel zum 65. Geburtstag*. Edited by Walter Beltz, Ute

Pietruschka, and Jürgen Tubach. Halle: Martin-Luther-Universität Halle-Wittenberg, 2003.

Shoemaker, Stephen J. 'Rethinking the "Gnostic Mary": Mary of Nazareth and Mary of Magdala in Early Christian Tradition'. *JECS* 9.4 (2001): 555–95.

Siker, Jeffrey S. 'The Parousia of Jesus in Second- and Third-Century Christianity'. Pages 147–67 in *The Return of Jesus in Early Christianity*. Edited by John T. Carroll. Peabody, MA: Hendrickson, 2000.

Smith, Daniel Lynwood, and Zachary Lundin Kostopoulos. 'Biography, History and the Genre of Luke-Acts'. *NTS* 63.3 (2017): 390–410.

Stanton, Graham N. *Jesus and Gospel*. Cambridge: Cambridge University Press, 2004.

Strawbridge, Jennifer R. *The Pauline Effect: The Use of the Pauline Epistles by Early Christian Writers*. SBR 5. Berlin: de Gruyter, 2015.

Stroumsa, Guy G. *Hidden Wisdom: Esoteric Traditions and the Roots of Christian Mysticism*. 2nd ed. Leiden and Boston: Brill, 2005.

Talbert, Charles H. *Ephesians and Colossians*. Paideia. Grand Rapids, MI: Baker Academic, 2007.

Tannehill, Robert C. *The Narrative Unity of Luke-Acts: A Literary Interpretation. Volume 1: The Gospel According to Luke*. Philadelphia, PA: Fortress Press, 1986.

Tardieu, Michel. *Écrits Gnostiques: Codex de Berlin*. Paris: Les Éditions du Cerf, 1986.

Tardieu, Michel, and Jean-Daniel Dubois. *Introduction à la littérature gnostique. I: Collections retrouvées avant 1945*. Paris: Les Éditions du Cerf, 1986.

Tervahauta, Ulla. *A Story of the Soul's Journey in the Nag Hammadi Library: A Study of Authentikos Logos (NHC VI,3)*. Novum Testamentum et Orbis Antiquus 107. Göttingen: Vandenhoeck & Ruprecht, 2015.

Thielman, Frank. *Ephesians*. BECNT. Grand Rapids, MI: Baker Academic, 2010.

Thomassen, Einar. 'Gnostics and Orphics'. Pages 463–74 in *Myths, Martyrs, and Modernity: Studies in the History of Religions in Honour of Jan N. Bremmer*. Edited by Jitse Dijkstra, Justin Kroesen, and Yme Kuiper. Studies in the History of Religions 127. Leiden and Boston: Brill, 2010.

The Spiritual Seed. The Church of the Valentinians. NHMS 60. Leiden and Boston: Brill, 2006.

Till, Walter C. *Die gnostischen Schriften des koptischen Papyrus Berolinensis 8502: Zweite, erweiterte Auflage bearbeitet von Hans-Martin Schenke*. TU 60. Berlin: Akademie Verlag, 1972.

Tite, Philip L. *Valentinian Ethics and Paraenetic Discourse: Determining the Social Function of Moral Exhortation in Valentinian Christianity*. NHMS 67. Leiden and Boston: Brill, 2009.

Todorov, Tzvetan. 'The Origin of Genres'. Pages 193–209 in *Modern Genre Theory*. Edited by David Duff. New York: Longman, 2000.

Trevett, Christine. 'Prophets, Economics, and the Rites of Man'. Pages 43–64 in *Revelation, Literature, and Community in Late Antiquity*. Edited by Philippa Townsend and Moulie Vidas. Tübingen: Mohr Siebeck, 2011.

Tuckett, Christopher M. 'Forty Other Gospels'. Pages 238–53 in *The Written Gospel*. Edited by Markus Bockmuehl and Donald A. Hagner. Cambridge: Cambridge University Press, 2005.

The Gospel of Mary. Oxford and New York: Oxford University Press, 2007.

Nag Hammadi and the Gospel Tradition: Synoptic Tradition in the Nag Hammadi Library. Edinburgh: T&T Clark, 1986.

'"Nomina Sacra": Yes and No?'. Pages 431–58 in *The Biblical Canons, Bibliotheca Ephemeridum Theologicarum Lovaniensium*. Edited by J. M. Auwers and H. J. de Jonge. Leuven: Peeters, 2003.

'Synoptic Tradition in Some Nag Hammadi and Related Texts'. *VC* 36.2 (1982): 173–90.

Turner, John D. *The Book of Thomas the Contender from Codex II of the Cairo Gnostic Library from Nag Hammadi (CG II, 7): The Coptic Text with Translation, Introduction and Commentary*. SBLDS 23. Missoula, Montana: Society of Biblical Literature and Scholars Press, 1975.

'The Johannine Legacy: The Gospel and Apocryphon of John'. Pages 105–45 in *The Legacy of John: Second-Century Reception of the Fourth Gospel*. Edited by Tuomas Rasimus. NovTSup 132. Leiden and Boston: Brill, 2010.

Sethian Gnosticism and the Platonic Tradition. BCNH:E 6. Québec: Les Presses de l'Université Laval, 2001.

Van Unnik, W. C. 'The Origin of the Recently Discovered "Apocryphon Jacobi"'. *VC* 10.3 (1956): 149–56.

van der Vliet, Jacques. 'Fate, Magic and Astrology in Pistis Sophia, Chaps 15–21'. Pages 519–36 in *The Wisdom of Egypt: Jewish, Early Christian and Gnostic Essays in Honour of Gerard P. Luttikhuizen*. Edited by A. Hilhorst and G. H. van Kooten. Ancient Judaism and Early Christianity 59. Leiden and Boston: Brill, 2005.

'Spirit and Prophecy in the Epistula Iacobi Apocrypha (NHC I,2)'. *VC* 44.1 (1990): 25–53.

Vander Stichele, Caroline. 'The Head of John and its Reception or How to Conceptualize "Reception History"'. Pages 79–93 in *Reception History and Biblical Studies: Theory and Practice*. Edited by Emma England and William John Lyons. Library of Hebrew Bible/Old Testament Studies 615. London and New York: Bloomsbury T&T Clark, 2015.

Watson, Francis. 'A Gospel of the Eleven: The Epistula Apostolorum and the Johannine Tradition'. Pages 189–215 in *Connecting Gospels: Beyond the Canonical/Non-Canonical Divide*. Edited by Francis Watson and Sarah Parkhouse. Oxford: Oxford University Press, 2018.

Gospel Writing: A Canonical Perspective. Grand Rapids, MI and Cambridge: Eerdmans, 2013.

Welburn, A. J. 'The Identity of the Archons in the "Apocryphon Johannis"'. *VC* 32.4 (1978): 241–54.

Williams, F. E. 'The Apocryphon of James (I, 2)'. Pages 29–31 in *The Nag Hammadi Library in English*. Edited by James M. Robinson. Leiden and New York: Brill, 1996.

Williams, Francis E. 'The Apocryphon of James – 1,2: 1.1 – 16:30'. Pages 13–53 in *Nag Hammadi Codex I (The Jung Codex)*. Edited by Harold W. Attridge. NHMS 22. Leiden: Brill, 1985.

Williams, Michael A. *The Immovable Race: A Gnostic Designation and the Theme of Stability in Late Antiquity*. NHS 29. Leiden: Brill, 1985.

'Secrecy, Revelation, and Late Antique Demiurgical Myths'. Pages 31–58 in *Rending the Veil: Concealment and Secrecy in the History of Religions*. Edited by Elliot R. Wolfson. New York: Seven Bridges Press, 1999.

Rethinking 'Gnosticism': An Argument for Dismantling a Dubious Category. Princeton, NJ: Princeton University Press, 1996.

Wilmet, M. *Concordance du Nouveau Testament sahidique, II. Les mots autochtones, 3*. CSCO 185. Louvain: Secrétariat du CorpusSCO, 1959.

Wilson, R. McL. *The Gospel of Philip: Translated from the Coptic Text, with an Introduction and Commentary*. London: A. R. Mowbray & Co, 1962.

'The New Testament in the Gnostic Gospel of Mary'. *NTS* 3.3 (1957): 236–43.

Wilson, R. McL., and George W. MacRae. 'The Gospel According to Mary: BG, 1:7,1–19,5'. Pages 453–71 in *Nag Hammadi Codices V,2–5 and VI with Papyrus Berlinensis 8502,1 and 4*. Edited by D. M. Parrott. NHS 11. Leiden: Brill, 1979.

Wisse, Frederick. 'The Coptic Versions of the New Testament'. Pages 131–41 in *The Text of the New Testament in Contemporary Research: Essays on the Status Quaestionis*. Edited by Bart D. Ehrman and Michael W. Holmes. Grand Rapids, MI: Eerdmans, 1995.

Woll, D. Bruce. 'The Departure of "The Way": The First Farewell Discourse in the Gospel of John'. *JBL* 99.2 (1980): 225–39.

Wolters, Al. 'Worldview and Textual Criticism in 2 Peter 3:10'. *Westminster Theological Journal* 49 (1987): 405–13.

Zamagni, Claudio. 'Is the Question-and-Answer Literary Genre in Early Christian Literature a Homogeneous Group?'. Pages 241–68 in *La Littérature des Questions et Réponses dans l'Antiquité profane et chrétienne: De l'enseignement à l'exégèse*. Edited by Marie-Pierre Bussières. Instrumenta Patristica et Mediaevalia 64. Turnhout: Brepols Publishers, 2013.

Zelyck, Lorne R. *John among the Other Gospels: The Reception of the Fourth Gospel in the Extra-Canonical Gospels*. WUNT II 347. Tübingen: Mohr Siebeck, 2013.

INDEX

Printed by Printforce, United Kingdom